RAISING
TURKEYS DUCKS GEESE PIGEONS AND GUINEAS

CYNTHIA HAYNES

 TAB BOOKS Inc.
Blue Ridge Summit, PA 17214

This book is dedicated to all poultry handlers who are serious
about raising poultry successfully.

Library of Congress Cataloging in Publication Data

Haynes, Cynthia.
Raising turkeys, ducks, geese, pigeons, and guineas.

Bibliography: p.
Includes index.
1. Poultry. 2. Pigeons. I. Title.
SF487.H414   1987   636.5   87-1908

ISBN 0-8306-0803-6
ISBN 0-8306-2803-7 (pbk.)

Questions regarding the content of this book
should be addressed to:

Reader Inquiry Branch
Editorial Department
TAB BOOKS Inc.
P.O. Box 40
Blue Ridge Summit, PA 17214

Contents

Foreword

It was estimated by the United Nations Food and Agriculture Organization that in the mid-1970s, 22 percent of the population in developing countries were undernourished. And the number of malnourished or those facing outright starvation is believed to be increasing, although the number varies from year to year depending on crop conditions in different parts of the world.

By the year 2000, the world's population may climb to 6.2 billion. Each day there are 300,000 more people to feed than the day before. Finding ways to feed these people is clearly one of the greatest challenges we face today.

An inadequate supply of high-quality protein is one of the principal causes of the malnutrition affecting about one-fifth of the population in developing countries. Protein is essential in human nutrition, and animal proteins generally contain higher proportions of some essential amino acids, such as methionine, than do vegetable proteins. They also contribute iron, calcium, many vitamins, and other micronutrients. Animal proteins are the principal source of an essential vitamin, B_{12}.

Protein from poultry meat and eggs can play a role in reducing malnutrition in developing countries. They are already significant sources of food protein throughout the world, and their use is increasing. This is because of their low cost and wide acceptance—there is no major taboo to poultry consumption as there is with beef or pork among various peoples.

Another great advantage of poultry over other livestock is their superior efficiency in converting feed nutrients into edible products. So, in total intake and output, meat and egg production from poultry are second only to milk production from dairy cattle in their efficiency of conversion of feed to energy, protein, or edible product.

In developing countries, particularly those with pastoral husbandry, the main source of feed for poultry is from scavenging of plants, insects, and small animals. Also, poultry utilize waste from the kitchen, from the harvest of crops, and from the home slaughter of animals. So even under pastoral conditions, poultry make use of "waste" products.

Poultry form a "bank" of protein and other

nutrients that contribute to food reserves in times of short-term food crop crises. Populations of poultry are more readily built up after a disaster than are other livestock because of their shorter reproductive cycle. Poultry have the added advantages of being small enough to be eaten at one meal—an advantage for areas without refrigeration—and a convenient size for barter.

There are factors, such as lack of resources, markets, research, and production technology, that limit poultry output, especially in developing countries: In contrast to rearing poultry under intensive confinement as many developed countries do, most of the developing countries still rear poultry using a pastoral, free-range system. These are often mixed-cropping systems combining a close interaction of animals and plants. However, the technology of large-scale, modern, highly efficient poultry production has proven rather easy to transfer to developing countries.

Poultry production in the more advanced countries, after all, did not undergo any great technological developments until the beginning of this century. The invention of large incubators, lamp-heated brooders, techniques to determine the sex of day-old chicks, improved feeds, and intensive rearing contributed to a revolution in poultry farming in the United States. In 1930, less than 50 percent of the chicks were mechanically incubated and hatched in hatcheries. By 1938, hatchery production had climbed to 66 percent, and it reached 88 percent by the late forties. Integration of poultry breeding, growing, and processing facilities led to substantial improvements in production efficiency as well as genetic improvements in breeds.

What happened in the United States can happen in developing countries. In spite of the factors currently limiting poultry output, it is likely that protein from poultry meat and eggs will figure more in the diets of people of the world than protein from milk or other animals. This makes poultry most important to human health and well-being throughout the remainder of this century.

H. Graham Purchase
Special Scientific Adviser to the Director
Beltsville Agricultural Research Center
(as printed in Agricultural Research, May 1985)

Preface

While operating a small country hatchery and breeder farm for eight years, I found many handlers interested in raising turkeys, guineas, pigeons, ducks and geese. I also realized too many handlers were either terrified by "myths" or had the wrong ideas about what these birds would do for them.

The majority of small-scale poultry raisers begin their poultry experience with chickens. After these handlers have "tested" their poultry raising abilities with chickens, most feel more confident in trying other species of fowl for food, pleasure and profit. Whether they are interested in only a few ducks to decorate their new farm pond or an entire flock of turkeys for extra pocket money, these handlers need accurate, unshadowed, and money-saving tips and information. Inaccurate information and myths can put a halt to what could be an adventure in knowledge or a profitable business.

Turkeys have taken most of the brunt of these exaggerated tales. You would think such a species which has falsely been accused as being dumb, hard to raise, prone to heart attacks because of overhead airplanes, purposely drowning in the rain and suc-

cumbing to every disease germ listed in the *Merck Veterinary Manual* would have become extinct by now. Turkeys would surely be considered a delicacy at the supermarket commanding premium prices because such a competitive industry would not venture to raise these "risky" birds in great numbers.

My aim is to eliminate poultry myths by acquainting handlers with the individual management practices of each species. This information can allow poultry handlers to realize a greater poultry world which awaits them. Handlers need only to apply proper care in combination with knowledge of the habits of these contrasting, yet interesting, birds.

It's not easy for beginners to make a first time success of raising these birds if they aren't sure what is true and what is false. Unfortunately there are far too many experts who are not knowledgeable enough to help small growers because they, too, might be intimidated by myths. They are familiar with poultry raising, but not in the sense all have actually raised the poultry themselves. Placing what is learned into practice is the ultimate in knowledge. Furthermore, their office hours and schedules do not always coincide with the immediate information a handler might need. If you have an extension agent, university poultry specialist, or a veterinarian nearby that caters to small-scale poultry raisers, consider yourself fortunate because many small raisers are on their own.

Another setback for small-scale raisers has been the acquisition of some of these birds at a reasonable price. Turkey prices, in particular, have curtailed the pleasures for many in raising and eating fresh turkey today—a treat our forefathers took for granted. Although more and more hatcheries and feed stores are now making poults available to poultry raisers because of demand, many are also taking advantage of this demand and somewhat low availability by charging outrageous prices to the public.

I've witnessed failures in raising various species of poultry when handlers believe they are all managed exactly like chickens. These birds are doomed from the start. Many beginners assume turkeys are difficult to raise, while ducks and geese are easy. Nothing could be further from the truth. Each species has its own personality, traits, habits and needs. The fact that they are all cared for differently determines their specific care and management.

Information pertaining to raising these distinct species of poultry can be more of an economic priority with these birds because their individual initial cost is usually far more than that of a chick. Therefore, any handler raising these birds should have all the detailed information available at his fingertips.

Most hatcheries and feed stores are swamped with questions from their customers. To avoid these time-consuming questions, some include limited care instructions with their customers' poultry shipments. Hatcheries in particular know repeated business depends on the type service they provide and on the success their customers have with their birds. Because of this, I've had to research and experiment on my own birds over the years in order to supply the most accurate and workable information to my customers. My customers also supplied me with all the questions handlers normally ask. My task has been to find the answers to these questions and place them into a workable form in this book.

Handlers cannot always rely on information received from feed stores and poultry experts. I've been rightly appalled at the misleading information frequently given to poultry handlers. I've seen birds die, cripple, and choke needlessly because of incorrect feed or medication recommended. I've seen handlers advised to purchase every gadget under the sun except the correct equipment for the bird in question. Many have suggested the wrong type of poultry to fit the needs of unwary handlers. I've witnessed some so-called "experts" snickering over a beginner's limited knowledge. All this can lead to failures and frustration—conditions that can singe the ambitions of even the most enthused handler.

Everyone who raises poultry is a handler. To enjoy poultry, they must be handled physically, economically, and above all, wisely. It's up to you, the handler, to make your venture a success. With the groundwork provided in this book, I sincerely hope all handlers achieve this goal.

Acknowledgments

I'd like to express my sincere thanks to all those companies and individuals who thought this project was worthy of their help. I regret not listing the dozens of individuals who contributed to bits and parts of this book, because it is those bits and parts which pulled everything else together. The following individuals spent extra time with my research to both enlighten and inform me: Rainie Bishop, Bob, Anthony Bogucki, Dr. Syed A. Bokhari, Brad Blume, Paul Cooney, Diane Cooper, Gary Cooper, Bob DeLancey, John Gascoyne, Henry Geerling, Glenn Geiger, Kim Hastings, Lorraine and Stan Kellerman, Don and Barb Kratt, Tom Lippi, Edward and Becky Mendes, Mr. and Mrs. Nowak, Mr. and Mrs. Pallieau, Ruth Price, John A. Ruthven, Dr. L. Dwight Schwartz, Bob Shipley, Dr. Fred T. Shultz, Dr. John L. Skinner, Loyl Stromberg, Texas Agricultural Extension agents, Donna Van-Wagoner, Mr. and Mrs. Wilcox, Hugh Woodall, Jean Wysocky, and Leon Zimdars.

Introduction

To be successful, handlers should have all the information they need at their fingertips. They should not have to feel guilty when problems crop up and they are unable to locate information quickly to help themselves. The majority of handlers are extremely serious about their intentions to raise poultry. They want to manage them correctly, economically and on their own. They should not have to comb through a myriad of books to find what they desire to learn. Some needed information just can't wait that long.

This book was designed to fill these needs. Very little, if any, information has been left out. In the following pages are tips to purchase your birds economically. These are important because these five species of poultry usually cost more initially than chickens. The following pages will tell you why they cost more and why some birds are difficult to obtain. Also included are tables and information to help you decide if it's more economical to hatch your own birds or purchase them. And, because good health is so important for the handler as well as the birds, various forms of human health hazards are discussed. Concise information on the problems and diseases for all five species should help eliminate guesswork when managing your birds.

This book will give those who raise poultry as a hobby a new perspective when reviewing the breed descriptions and personalities of these birds. Handlers with marketing and economics in mind can make good use of the present commercial management practices and trends mentioned throughout. It was researched and written with all types of handlers in mind—beginners, experienced, children and adults, those who raise these birds seriously for pleasure, hobby, 4-H projects and show, and those who are interested in the values of these birds when supplying food and eggs for the table.

Part 1

Turkeys

Chapter 1

Choosing Your Poults

ORIGIN AND HISTORY

There are only two species of wild turkeys in the world—the North American (Fig. 1-1) and the Ocellated (Fig. 1-2). The North American Wild turkey is the one from which all domestic breeds of turkeys have originated. The Ocellated turkey, sometimes referred to as the Mexican turkey, is claimed by some historians to be responsible for the color of the Narragansett. This is due to the white penciled markings on the wing feathers, otherwise the Ocellated turkey is colored the same as the Bronze turkey.

The North American turkey originally roamed over the eastern two-thirds of the United States, Ontario, and the eastern part of Mexico. The majority of today's North American Wild turkeys inhabit the southern states. They also extend north to New York and Wyoming and south to Mexico. This is approximately one-third of its original habitat. It's likely the North American turkey's range would have been diminished moreso if it were not for conservation, management, and releasing efforts.

The colorful Ocellated turkey is native to the Yucatan Peninsula in Mexico. It has a gray tail with metallic blue and copper eye spots. It's about 32-39 inches (81-99 cm) in length. Its habits are similar to the North American wild turkey.

The North American turkey is our largest and only type of poultry that has been domesticated from wild stocks native to the United States. All other domesticated poultry originated in other countries, and were later brought to the United States. In 1906 more records were found in Madrid, Spain showing a Spanish adventurer, Pedro Nino, had come across the wild turkey on the Cumana coast north of Venezuela in 1499. This was seven years after the discovery of America. Records also show Christopher Columbus took turkeys back to Europe in 1492. These were most likely the first introductions of turkeys into Europe.

Excavations of prehistoric sites in the Tennessee Valley contained turkey bones showing the turkey to have been a source of food perhaps much earlier than 1000 A.D. Some fossil evidence has been dated to show turkeys have existed in America

Fig. 1-1. Three wild Rio Grande turkey gobblers in the Arkansas National Wildlife Refuge, Texas. (Photo by Luther C. Goldman, courtesy of U.S. Fish and Wildlife Service)

for 10 million years. The actual domestication of turkeys is said to have been initiated by the Aztecs. There is also archeological evidence the Southwestern Indians confined (if not domesticated) turkeys as early as the birth of Christ.

Benjamin Franklin proposed the turkey as the official United States bird, but the bald eagle was chosen over the turkey. In writing to his daughter, Franklin said, "I wish the bald eagle had not been chosen as the representative of our country . . . The turkey is a much more respectable bird . . . and withal a true original native of America."

Around 1910, a man named Jesse Throssell, was approached by a sportsman on his father's farm in England. The hunter, Lord Rothschild, was aware the Throssells raised turkeys on their farm. He asked if Jesse could supply him with large turkeys well over 20 pounds so he could give them to

Fig. 1-2. An Ocellated turkey tom and his mate on left. (Courtesy of San Antonio Zoo, photo by Rainie Bishop)

friends as Christmas gifts. Jesse searched out extra large turkeys from other flocks around the country. After a few years of breeding these turkeys, he created the John Bull and the Sheffield strains that produced toms of over 40 pounds and hens over 20 pounds.

For many years before, the Standardbred Bronze was the most popular variety. The Broad-Breasted was limited to a variety that had breasts at least 3 1/2 inches wide at a point 1 3/4 inches above the keel. Breeders in states along the Pacific Coast continued developing the Broad-Breasted Bronze and by 1943 most hatcheries offered them.

While all this was beginning, George Nicholas started the Nicholas Turkey Breeding Farms (NTBF). This was to be a whole new wave in turkey improvements genetically. The first white-feathered turkeys related to most of those raised commercially today were actually mutants, a type showing up in the Lancaster strain of bronze turkeys. From this white turkey, George Roberts developed the Lancaster White. Nicholas was impressed with this turkey's rapid growth rate to a large size. He then chose the best specimens of this white strain from the San Joaquin Valley and crossed them with his own strain of bronze hens. Later, he mated them among themselves and the result was a 6-percent hatch of white poults which was the start of the Nicholas White in 1956. An extensive pedigree program began and a geneticist, Dr. Fred T. Shultz, was consulted on a regular basis. In 1959 the first sales of commercial quantities of the Nicholas White hatching eggs were made. This was the largest start of the commercial change from broad-breasted bronze to large white turkeys.

The single-tube method of artificial insemination (A.I.) was developed by Bill Scott at one of Nicholas's farms from an idea picked up in Great Britain. Although A.I. had been known about for years, it was infrequently practiced and was done by hand. Al G. Horsting, who previously worked at NTBF, invented a machine to do A.I. Many turkeys produced in the world are hatched from eggs fertilized by his machines. Most of today's commercial turkeys are the result of artificial insemination.

VARIETIES AND STRAINS

The North American Wild turkey is the breed from which all domestic breeds of turkeys have originated. There are eight standard recognized varieties of this breed. Within the eight standard domestic varieties are various strains. Strains occur when certain characteristics in type are bred into a particular variety by various handlers and breeders.

Following are the eight varieties of domestic turkeys recognized and admitted to the American *Standard of Perfection* by the American Poultry Association: The Bronze, White Holland, Narragansett, Black, Slate, Bourbon Red, Beltsville Small White, and the Royal Palm. Compared with other species, turkeys have a small number of recognized varieties; geese have 14, ducks have 29, standard-size chickens have 162, and bantam chickens have 209 varieties.

The North American Wild turkey is not even included in the Standard although it's native to the United States. There are many handlers who raise and enjoy only Wild turkeys. If not fed a fatty ration, they will fly easily. They will become tame and follow people, dogs, goats, horses, and sheep just as any other variety of turkey. Wild turkeys can be raised in small or large flocks and butchered. Their slightly gamey taste is very appealing to many handlers. To raise for meat, they can cost a handler more than commercially raised white or bronze strains unless breeders are kept for reproducing. Even then the feed to meat ratio will not be as good. It takes a Wild turkey hen about two years to get to about eight pounds. Depending upon the strain, a Wild turkey tom will weigh from 12 to 28 pounds. These weights seem to vary with the type feeds available to the birds.

A yearling Wild turkey male is frequently called a jake. Older males are usually called gobblers. A jake and young hen will mate the first year, but the fertility is usually about 50 percent less than normal. In the northern states the breeding season begins about the first or second week of April, or in rare instances at the end of March. A Wild turkey's breeding season is very short. During the two week breeding season, a hen will lay a clutch of from 8 to 17 eggs. As with all turkeys, the eggs are cream colored with brown speckles. Occasionally if this one clutch of eggs is disturbed or wrecked, a Wild turkey hen will lay one more clutch.

Extra precautions are usually necessary when Wild turkeys are ranged. Although they can fly, they won't unless they are startled or scared. They are roamers, however. They've been known to leave for as long as 30 days before coming back home. Most will wander for two to seven days before returning. Perhaps they find a good feeding area, or occasionally some other turkey lover feeds them. They can be indifferent to their homestead yet become homeward-bound. Because of predators, vehicles, and thieves, it's wise to confine them with a large outdoor pen or occasionally let them range while you watch. They can even be trained to come when you call.

Many inexperienced handlers believe and refer to the Bronze turkey (Fig. 1-3) as the Wild turkey. This is incorrect. The Bronze is only a variety of turkey. Upon first observation, the coloring and markings appear similar, but closer inspection reveals that the Wild turkey's tail is tipped in chestnut rather than white as with the Bronze. The Wild turkey also has a much sleeker and more slender body. Toms of both the Wild and Bronze have a beard, but the Wild turkey obtains a much longer beard as he matures (see Fig. 1-1). Where the domestic turkey's beard never grows much beyond 1 1/2 inches, the Wild turkey's beard will grow about 1 inch per year. This is how the Wild turkeys' age can be estimated. The beards from the breast of Wild turkeys is sometimes kept by turkey hunters as a trophy.

In the *Standard of Perfection* reference book, the Bronze is listed as the largest turkey. Beginners should not be influenced by this. The standard Bronze, whether termed Broad-Breasted Bronze, or simply Bronze, is only the largest of those admitted to the Standard. There are many more turkeys of various strains that are larger. The standard weight for a young tom is 25 pounds, a young hen's standard weight is 16 pounds. Young turkeys are yearlings. The standard weights for an old tom is 36 pounds, an old hen is listed at 20 pounds. Because poultry judges and fanciers need some type of standard description from which to judge and compare to, the Standard is a must.

Fig. 1-3. Pair of Bronze turkeys.

6

Fig. 1-4. A pair of White Holland turkeys.

Some handlers prefer to raise the Bronze because they do not care for white-feathered birds; they claim the traditional turkey should always be the copperish-bronze with black and brown feathers and grayish-black shanks. It's the beautiful feathers of the common turkey that took the Bronze out of the commercial markets: when a white turkey was produced that could surpass the Bronze in growth and weight, commercial growers no longer had to bother with dark pinfeathers or black pigment oils in the pores of the skin.

Due to the popularity of the white turkey in the commercial markets, very few farms now commercially produce Bronze hatching eggs. This means the cost of buying Bronze hatching eggs is higher, and handlers must absorb this with the poults they purchase. In comparing the two, the meat is not any different, nor is one easier to raise than the other. As far as the dressed-out appearance goes, a handler that properly feathers out a good strain of Bronze, butchers at the right age and procures good plucking machines to clean the birds, should have dressed-out birds that compare with the dressed-out carcass of the white. Even white birds, if not

properly feathered and butchered, will not appear completely clean.

Varieties of turkeys, other than the commercial white, will cost even more than Bronze because they are raised in smaller numbers. The White Holland (Fig. 1-4) is raised commercially and sometimes referred to as the Broad-Breasted White of the large whites. It attains weights similar to the Bronze and has pinkish-white shanks.

The Narragansett turkey (Fig. 1-5) is a rich metallic black with steel-gray and has salmon-colored shanks. Penciling and banding of tan and white on the tail and wings gives the Narragansett a striking appearance. Young toms are 23 pounds, old toms top 33 pounds. Young hens are 14 pounds and old hens are 18 pounds.

Black turkeys (Fig. 1-6) might acquire a slight tinge of bronze over their metallic black feathers, mainly on the back and tail. They have slaty black shanks when they are young, which gradually turn to buffed pink with age. They attain weights of 23 pounds for young toms, 33 pounds for old toms. Young hens are 14 pounds, old hens are 18 pounds.

Slate turkeys are an overall slaty-ashy-blue

color. The deep pink shanks highlight the seemingly one tone appearance of the feathers. Young toms are 23 pounds, old toms reach 33 pounds. Young hens are 14 pounds and old hens are 18 pounds.

The Bourbon Red turkey (Fig. 1-7) appears to have a rich dark chestnut mahogany body with tail and wings white. Close observation shows there is also black, red, and rust. Shanks are reddish-pink. Many poor specimens appear drab and faded. It might be hard to check out the background of Bourbon Red poults sold at hatcheries to assure good

Fig. 1-7. Bourbon Red turkeys (Courtesy of Watt Publishing Company)

coloring. Weights for them are 23 pounds for young toms, 33 pounds for old toms. Young hens are 14 and old hens are 18 pounds.

The Beltsville Small White turkey was "designed" for households who needed a smaller table bird. Young toms attain 17 pounds, old toms reach 21 pounds. Young hens are 10 pounds, old hens are 12 pounds. Shanks are pinkish-white. At shows, well-fleshed birds under the standard weights are not cut in points, but toms more than three pounds and hens more than two pounds over the standard weights are disqualified because the small weight is a very important characteristic of this turkey variety.

Royal Palm turkeys have a base color of white with metallic black over most of the back with breast and body feathers only tipped in black. The tail is pure white with two bands of metallic black. Shanks are pinkish-white to pink. Young toms are 16 pounds, old toms are 22 pounds. Young hens are 10 pounds, old hens 12 pounds. In the show, specimens over two pounds of these standard weights are cut in points.

Other nonstandard varieties exist, but are more rare. They include the Slate Blue, Nebraskan, Nebraskan Royals, Jersey Buffs, Crimson Dawn, Nittany, and the New turkey.

Some strains are better than others. When compared, some hatcheries consistently hatch white poults that are much larger and heftier than others. This few ounces more on a poult seems to give that extra push that induces fast growing. A few different strains can be tried. Individual poults or boxes of poults can even be compared in weights by weighing and recording the weights of day-olds and one-week-olds. If this information is not recorded, the chances are the following season you won't remember how heavy the poults looked or felt.

Some of the more well-known strains of large and medium commercial whites are Nicholas (Fig. 1-8), Orlopp, Wrolstad, Rose-A-Linda, Kent-Conyer, Hybrid, and White Holland. Practically all of Swift's Butterball brand turkeys are of the Nicholas strain. Nicholas sells stock for only one type of bird. It's a three-way cross—male line toms crossed on the cross hen from two female lines. A few well-known strains of the small commercial whites are Orlopp, Nicholas, and Diamond Hybrid. Small whites require more feed per pound of edible meat produced. Unless one wants a small carcass with a fair amount of fat, they're an expensive way to get meat.

The Small White and Bronze have the least amount of strains. In fact, in the last 10 years, all the strains have whittled down to 50 percent of what was being bred. The Bronze strains have been done away with more than any of the whites during this period. There is currently only a few well-known Bronze strains as compared to 15 strains consistently bred 10 years ago. At this rate, the poultry industry might be down to less than a dozen strains in the next 20 years. This seems to be the trend in the very competitive turkey industry.

Fig. 1-8. Some tom breeders of the Nicholas strain. (Courtesy of Nicholas Turkey Breeding Farms)

WHICH SEX?

Not all hatcheries involved in selling to small-scale handlers provide the service of sexing poults. The main reason is the extra cost to have a sexor come in and vent sex. There is currently no way to feather sex poults by examining day-old wing growth as there is with chicks. The poults must be vent sexed. This, combined with problems of disposing of leftover day-old poults can become unprofitable for hatcheries that don't deal solely with poult sales. Poults are costly to produce. Hatcheries do not want to "dump" leftover poults, or run sales on these leftovers that might create too much of a demand due to the attractive price.

Hatcheries that sell to commercial growers sell sexed poults. One reason is these growers want their toms toe-trimmed and desnooded. They also might be selling for a particular market that demands a smaller or larger bird. Many raise toms and hens separately. They also are aware that the conversion of feed to meat factor is better for toms. This means toms can be grown to only 14 1/2 weeks, producing the same amount of meat as 20-week old hens, and at a lower cost. Growers must pay more for toms if purchased separately. Many growers grow for the cut-up turkey parts trade. In this case it's more economical to produce toms because size doesn't matter. Most spent hens and toms, those who have served their useful life to produce hatching eggs, are used in the turkey products trade.

For small-scale growers the difference of raising one sex over the other will mostly be in the cost of the feed to produce. There is no difference in flavor, texture, or appearance between hen and tom turkeys. Meat quality is affected by the age of the bird. If turkeys are to be marketed locally, there will be individual consumer preferences for small, medium, and large birds. This growers can only accomplish, when raising only one sex, if two broods are started at different times. This can be inconvenient because it can be difficult to introduce the younger brood (if more than two weeks apart) into a flock of older turkeys, and separate pens are uneconomical.

The smallest turkeys made available to consumers are fryer roasters, which range from five to nine pounds. The largest available are toms of up to 30 pounds, usually sold around the Thanksgiving and Christmas holidays. The average ready-to-cook whole turkey weight purchased by consumers are 12-pound hens and 18- to 20-pound toms. This makes the average weight purchased 15 to 16 pounds.

Larger hatcheries which do provide services sometimes do not sell poults as sexed to small-scale handlers but only as desnooded. Because only the toms are desnooded, handlers can then separate and count the sexes when poults are received.

By reviewing Table 1-1 on weights and feed consumption, any handler can figure fairly accurately just what the total feed will cost for either sex of a desired dressed-out weight. For example, if 12-pound (16-week-old) dressed hen turkeys are desired, the table shows 14.52-pound hens will require about 40 pounds of feed. A 19.49-pound dressed-out tom requires 66.70 pounds of feed.

PERSONALITIES

Turkeys must be understood. There are many personalities among the various breeds of dogs that should fit their master's tolerance and expectations; the same is true of poultry. Turkeys have many great attributes, but there might be some traits some handlers just can't live with.

In the first few days after they hatch, poults often appear dopey because they keep their eyes shut much of the time. They also quite frequently and harmlessly peck at each other's eyes and toes the first few weeks. This is not cannibalism.

You'll soon find out how much your voice means to the poults. As soon as they hear you, they'll run out to greet you. At most they can become a pest; it can be troublesome when filling feeders or waterers when they're in the way. This over-aggressiveness does not go on forever. By about three weeks of age most poults will calm down. You might even begin to miss these greetings.

Then there are the few tiny toms who have just barely grown wings but have to show their finery off. Just like a mature tom, they fan their little

(Courtesy of Watt Publishing Co.)

Table 1-1. Dressed Weights of Large-Type Turkeys Compared to Liveweights and Feed Required.

Age, weeks	Ready-to-cook weight, lbs	Feed required/lb of ready-to-cook turkey
Toms		
18	19.49	3.42
19	21.08	3.57
20	22.68	3.69
21	24.29	3.82
22	25.81	3.95
23	27.33	4.08
24	28.73	4.21
Hens		
14	10.13	3.12
15	10.94	3.27
16	11.69	3.40
17	12.38	3.50
18	13.02	3.71
19	13.62	3.86
20	14.15	4.02

1986 Revision

Body weights and feed consumption of large-type toms

	Live Weight, lbs.		Feed Required		Metabolizable Energy Intake
Age, weeks	Average	Gain for period	Cumulative, lbs/turkey	Per lb of turkey	kcal/lb of turkey
1	.30	.25	.32	1.26	1630
2	.73	.43	.88	1.29	1670
3	1.30	.57	1.65	1.32	1750
4	2.07	.77	2.80	1.39	1860
5	2.95	.88	4.23	1.46	1980
6	3.96	1.01	5.98	1.53	2110
7	5.12	1.16	8.26	1.63	2250
8	6.38	1.26	11.01	1.74	2390
9	7.76	1.38	14.19	1.84	2540
10	9.26	1.50	17.96	1.95	2690
11	10.87	1.61	22.18	2.05	2840
12	12.56	1.69	26.90	2.15	2990
13	14.32	1.76	32.25	2.26	3140
14	16.13	1.81	38.11	2.37	3295
15	17.99	1.86	44.67	2.49	3450
16	19.86	1.87	51.51	2.60	3605
17	21.74	1.88	59.00	2.72	3770
18	23.62	1.88	66.70	2.83	3950
19	25.52	1.90	75.17	2.95	4140
20	27.43	1.91	83.78	3.06	4350
21	29.30	1.87	92.72	3.17	4540
22	31.10	1.80	101.84	3.28	4730
23	32.81	1.71	111.38	3.40	4920
24	34.41	1.60	120.95	3.52	5110

1986 Revision

Body weights and feed consumption of large-type hens

	Live Weight, lbs.		Feed Required		Metabolizable Energy Intake
Age, weeks	Average	Gain for period	Cumulative, lbs/turkey	Per lb of turkey	kcal/lb of turkey
1	.28	.23	.29	1.26	1630
2	.65	.42	.77	1.29	1670
3	1.18	.53	1.51	1.34	1780
4	1.78	.60	2.46	1.42	1900
5	2.53	.75	3.74	1.51	2020
6	3.44	.91	5.42	1.60	2150
7	4.44	1.00	7.51	1.71	2290
8	5.55	1.11	10.01	1.82	2470
9	6.73	1.18	12.89	1.93	2630
10	7.98	1.25	16.18	2.04	2800
11	9.26	1.28	19.80	2.15	2980
12	10.43	1.17	23.56	2.27	3160
13	11.58	1.15	27.56	2.39	3350
14	12.65	1.07	31.63	2.51	3540
15	13.63	.98	35.72	2.63	3730
16	14.52	.89	39.79	2.75	3930
17	15.34	.82	43.27	2.88	4150
18	16.10	.76	48.31	3.01	4380
19	16.79	.69	52.56	3.14	4630
20	17.40	.61	56.91	3.28	4890

1986 Revision

wings toward the floor, hold their fanned skimpy tail upwards with their heads pulled in and held high, puff their breasts out and strut. Poults also try out their wings early. Most poults look quite surprised when they miss what they were trying to land on. Wild turkey poults have a bit more agility than the domestic breeds. They easily fly to heights of 6 feet at ten days of age.

Although it is fun watching these babies grow, the fights soon begin. Around eight weeks of age, toms begin to grab each other's bald heads and necks and use their neck strength to bring other toms to their mercy. There's no need to be concerned over these fights; I've never seen anyone get hurt. Even toms who have not been beak-trimmed do not draw blood, so you don't have to break them up or watch them closely. Adult (fully grown) toms will fight, however. This can be hazardous and should be prevented.

Toward market age, from about 16 weeks and up, all turkeys will take a liking to your jewelry, and the rivets on your jeans. The first time one of them grabs at the rivet on your back pocket can be quite a shock. It doesn't really hurt even if they aim at your ring and grab your finger instead. Small children, however, can be bothered by this. Children as tall as a grown turkey can be injured, especially if their eyes are at a low enough level to be grabbed at by a turkey. I have not heard of this happening, but the possibility exists. It would be wise to keep small children from market-age turkeys.

Occasionally toms will attack people, but this is rare. However, toms that are mistreated by being kicked at or chased can become frequent attackers. Others who occasionally attack tend to aim their attacks at people who appear frightened of them. Toms can be quite gutsy at times. They will usually take on other animals at least their size, but some also pick fights with dogs, goats, sheep, horses and the like. They get along well with most other poultry, even geese. Brave roosters will take on toms, but usually not for long. Some turkeys have even been known to chase cars.

Turkeys can become your shadow, following you wherever you go and annoying you by being under your feet constantly. They'll call your bluff when they play a game of chicken, which goes something like this: First, the tom fans his wings and tail out. Then he struts up to you as if to dare. This is the same type of courtship display he'll use with a hen except he'll stomp his feet around her as if doing a Mexican Hat dance. Now, it's your turn—walk stiffly and purposely towards him and he'll back away. Take your original position and tom will again dare you. This game can be played for hours. As many as four can play. The only problem with this game is nobody seems to win.

Kickball is another favorite game of some toms. With the ball in front of him, tom will quickly jump, stomping the ground inbetween as he tries to kick the ball. Usually it takes three or four jumps and a few stomps before the foot makes contact with the ball, but the kick can send the ball quite a distance. Kick the ball back to tom and he'll do it again. Toms play these games because of their pretentious aggressiveness, which can be a bit overdone. This is why precautions should be taken when more than one tom is kept over for breeding the following season.

Toms can be utilized as watch birds to some degree. Only toms actually gobble, and they will gobble up a storm when strangers appear. Hens make a low clicking sound. Hens are not quite so active as toms, and they do enjoy being fussed over.

Heavy turkeys can fly short distances. Some of the lighter-weight turkeys are claimed to out pace a race horse. Wild turkeys prefer to run because they do this much better than flying. They usually don't fly unless startled or frightened.

As for those myths that keep popping up—are turkeys dumb? Do they drown themselves in the rain? Will they have a heart attack if a plane flies overhead? Are they really so dumb they don't know how to drink? Will most of them die because they're hard to raise?

First, if turkeys are dumb, they would not have survived in the wild or throughout the many years of domestication. Fossil evidence shows turkeys have roamed America for ten million years. Early writers describe the domesticated turkey as early as 1524. For a species to survive this length of time,

it must be cunning, alert, and hardy. Compared to wild turkeys, today's domestic varieties and strains seem less cunning, a bit higher strung, and more docile. This is what domestication does to most animals and fowl. The natural cunning needed to elude predators is lost in the domestication process. The actions a turkey exhibits can be misconstrued by the average observer. Their normal curiosity, friendliness, aggressiveness, and bravery can seem to be stupidity to people who think all animals should be wary and, thus, wise.

Drowning? No. I've never seen or heard of any case of turkeys drowning in the rain. If you've ever tried to drown a young cull turkey, you'd know what I mean; they don't drown easily. What can happen to any young domestic upland fowl, including chicks, is that they become wet to the skin and immediately chill. With turkeys, unless they're taken up by the handler and quickly dried, they'll succumb to death faster than young chickens. Mature turkeys that chill might come down with a respiratory disease and die if not treated promptly.

Mature turkeys can die rather suddenly from extreme heat, and this can resemble a heart attack. Blackhead also can cause a healthy looking bird to suddenly fall over dead. They do not die from planes, jets, or saucers flying overhead. If they did, I'm sure many commercial growers would think twice about raising 5-10,000 turkeys on range. Turkeys are known to trample each other if scared, which usually results in scratches over the back. Chickens react in the same way when they're being rounded up for market.

Poults are often thought of as dumb because they must have their beaks dipped into drinking water to get them started. After all, it's a big decision for a day-old to decide if he wants to be warm or quench his thirst. Because poults love warmth, they naturally choose the heat first. But they're not immune to suggestions; just showing them how the water quenches thirst gets them drinking. A few might have to be reminded. Turkey or chicken hens show their offspring how to eat and drink and the babies simply imitate. How is a day-old poult to know what a waterer looks like and where it is unless shown? (*Note*: Poults hatched at home will not be thirsty the first day.)

Under proper management, turkeys are very hardy. It only takes a watchful eye and knowledge of their needs to raise practically the whole brood successfully. Some handlers permit their Wild turkeys complete freedom even during severe winters. The adults usually fair very well roosting in dense brush. In fact, we once had a large white turkey hen called Martha, who roosted outdoors throughout the entire year, braving below-zero winter storms. She didn't seem to mind so we didn't force her to take shelter.

Again, if turkeys were as difficult to raise as some believe, growers would not attempt to raise them commercially. Furthermore, they'd be charging a premium price for them at the supermarket. If a handler claims to have had problems raising turkeys, the chances are good that they were not managed according to their needs.

HOW MANY?

Figuring the flock size is not quite as complicated for turkeys as it is for egg-laying chickens. Turkey eggs are wholesome and can be eaten just as well as any chicken egg, but economically it's not feasible to keep them solely for eating eggs. Handlers need only to figure on the amount of turkey meat their family can consume in a year's time. If turkeys are to be grown for small-scale marketing, plus for family eating, then those to be sold are added to those you plan to keep in the freezer.

If you plan to keep breeders in addition to freezer turkeys, first read the information under "Purchase or Hatch" in this chapter. This will help you decide on the amounts to keep for breeding— or if you can profitably keep breeders.

When turkeys are to be purchased for show or as a hobby, and fancy varieties are to be raised, the poults will command a higher price. This higher cost can become the deciding factor in the amount to be purchased. Wild turkeys can cost as much as $6-$8 each for day-olds.

Usually 15-20 poults must be shipped in a box to maintain the required body heat for safe shipment. Occasionally some hatcheries will ship as few as two poults in a mixed order containing chicks.

These few poults will usually be very expensive. In larger lots, usually 80 poults will be shipped together in a 100-chick size box. There are a few hatcheries who ship 100 poults to a box. Personally, I've found 100-poult shipments to contain smaller poults, although I have not seen every hatchery's poults. The 80-poult shipments frequently have all ventilation holes open. The amount of poults in relation to environmental temperatures determines the temperature in the box. This temperature must be 90-95 degrees Fahrenheit (32-35 degrees Celsius) for poults to be shipped safely. A handler can save money by being able to purchase in larger lots. Even the postage will be less expensive when broken down into the cost per poult.

If a handler cannot use or raise larger lots, he should co-op with others who want to purchase turkeys. Thus, the first handler becomes the middleman and the retailer. Here's how it can be done: After finding your poult source, figure exactly how much a certain large lot of poults will cost. Add postage, insurance, cost to run a few classified ads, gasoline for vehicle if poults must be picked up at the post office, and a specific amount to cover phone calls made to a hatchery and other handlers for pick-up when poults are received. Divide the amount of poults into this total figure for a per poult cost. It's risky to figure on more than 100 poults if you only want a few yourself unless you're sure of the demand for poults in your area. You'll have to time poult availability with the other handlers' time of demand. This means you must know that if the orders you take from handlers in March will still enable you to order turkeys for mid-May or the end of May. Of course, you can chance ordering the poults in December or January if you're not afraid of the possibility of being stuck with more poults than you need.

To roughly figure how many other handlers might be needed to co-op with you, the following averages can be used as a guide for handlers purchasing poults at a reasonable price: The average amount of white poults purchased by small-scale raisers is 18. The average amount of Bronze poults purchased by small-scale raisers is 11. These figures are actual hatchery figures for poults picked

Fig. 1-9. Candling out infertile turkey eggs during incubation is a yearly job at large commercial hatcheries. (Courtesy of Cooper Hatchery, Inc.)

up at the hatchery by the customer. Averages for shipped poults would be higher because of body heat requirements causing some handlers to unwillingly purchase more poults than actually wanted. If you order 100 white poults and you only want 10, this means about five handlers (customers) are needed to co-op with. Their per poult cost will also include the expenses previously figured in.

Get your order into the hatchery as early as possible so poults will not be sold out for the time you'd like them to be shipped. It's good to figure on the middle to the end of May because this is when most handlers want poults. This will make your co-oping easier. Purchasing straight-run large whites will also make sales easier.

At about the end of March to the first week in April, place a classified ad in a local farm-type newspaper. When handlers call, tell them the ex-

pected date of delivery to your residence. Explain poults must be picked up the day they arrive. If they choose to order, require that a deposit of at least half their ordered poult cost be sent to you. Tell them this deposit is not refundable should they change their mind for any reason or fail to pick up poults when they arrive. This prevents most of any cancellations or "no-shows" that might occur at the last minute to leave you in a bind. You might even want to request money orders or certified checks be sent only. It's entirely up to you. Give them a pick-up date ahead of time.

The morning before poults are to arrive, call the hatchery one more time to confirm the delivery date. This way you can be ready for them and ready to make a few quick calls to the other handlers. It's a good idea to phone the other handlers the night before poults are expected so they don't

15

make plans that would prevent them from picking up their poults on time. Tell them to expect them the next day or two and you will call them for immediate pick-up; also explain they will be at fault if you cannot get through to them by phone. If some do not come for their poults promptly you'll have to take the responsibility of getting the poults watered and under heat until they arrive.

Occasionally you might get a handler who will take advantage by showing up three or more days late. He'll still want to pay the same price and receive the same amount of poults, but figures he can avoid any of those early poult losses. There's a few ways to handle this type. If you haven't already sold the poults to someone else, charge him twenty-five cents or more per poult for each day he's late. Some are more than happy to pay, just as long as the poults have been started for them. If poult losses occurred between yours and his, divide the losses between both of you. Incidentally, keep any extra poults (there's usually 2-4 per every 80 or 100 poults shipped) the hatchery includes in the shipment to cover losses. These extras need not go to the others since you've done all the leg work. Of course if one handler is purchasing 90 poults and you are purchasing only 10, it's more than fair to give him most of the extras. This co-oping is the most economical way for a handler to purchase his poults.

It's becoming tougher every year for small-scale handlers to purchase poults at a reasonable price. Larger commercial turkey hatcheries, which previously sold small lots, are closing their doors yearly to the small-scale raiser because of economics (and perhaps because commercial production increases yearly and they just don't need to bother with the small sales). With North Carolina leading the states by producing over 32.650 million turkeys a year and consumers purchasing over 71 million whole ready-to-cook (RTC) turkeys throughout the year, these increasing figures are bound to push the small-scale raiser around some. (The holiday estimates for purchased RTC turkeys breaks down to 45 million turkeys for Thanksgiving, 13 million turkeys for Christmas, and 9 million turkeys for Easter.) Postal rates have also skyrocketed, along with utilities, supplies, equipment, and man-

ual labor. These commercial buyers do not want to share the extra inflationary cost a multitude of small buyers might create. After all, they want to purchase poults at a reasonable price too.

WHEN TO START

In the commercial world, poults are available every month of the year for growers. In this way, each typical 40- × -500-foot turkey barn can grow out three full flocks of hens or two flocks of toms within a year. This is possible because fowl are photo sensitive. Lights combined with a controlled environment induce turkey hens to lay eggs throughout the entire year, including the winter months. This means poults can be hatched and raised anytime of the year (Fig. 1-9).

Most hatcheries catering to the small raiser will supply poults only from March to July. If your goal is to raise turkeys strictly for Thanksgiving, poults do not need to be started until the middle of July. Keep in mind, however, that this growing period is during the hottest months of the year. You'll save tremendously on brooding costs because heating elements won't operate as long, but unless the poults can be kept from becoming overheated during those hot days, their growth will be set back. High temperatures cause poor feather growth and the birds will consume less feed. When they consume less feed, they don't grow at their normal rate. Poults grow the fastest during the first eight weeks of their life. Anything that interferes with their growth during this period, including disease, parasites, nutritionally unbalanced rations, lack of rations, lack of water, stress, chilling, and overheating, will stunt them.

By looking over Table 1-1 a handler can figure how long he must grow a turkey of each sex to reach a particular weight. Most commercial turkey hens are grown to an average of 16 weeks of age to produce a 12-pound dressed-out (eviscerated and gutted) bird. Toms are commercially grown to an average of 19 weeks to produce a 21-pound bird for consumers. In Table 1-1 the dressed-out weights of the turkeys can be estimated.

Starting poults from the middle of May to the end of May for Thanksgiving allows 26-28 weeks

Fig. 1-10. The hen poult is shown on the left, tom on the right.

of growing. Because the feed to meat ratio begins to decline from the age of eight weeks, the longer the turkeys are kept past the market age, the more their meat will cost per pound. (Market age refers to the age in which most commercial turkeys are slaughtered. With toms, this age ranges between 19-25 weeks. With hens, the age is between 16-17 weeks.)

At commercial turkey hatcheries, poults are higher priced from June through August, and lower priced from September through May. This won't help most small-scale growers because the majority of these hatcheries do not retail small lots of turkeys. The hatcheries small-scale growers must deal with will charge the same price throughout their selling season. A handler can occasionally purchase leftover mixed poults to save money, but most times these are unavailable at the peak period of demand.

Supplemental ranging of turkeys might save some feed costs and the grow-out period will be about the same because birds eat to satisfy energy requirements anyway. Confinement rearing will only reduce the grow-out time if perfect environmental conditions are provided—correct humidity,

temperature, etc. Likewise, if turkeys are stressed on range from high temperatures, the grow-out time will be longer because birds eat less in higher temperatures.

If a handler can provide the correct nutritional rations combined with a comfortable environment, this will cut down on the total grow-out time and poults can be purchased later in the season.

PURCHASE OR HATCH?

Many handlers wonder if hatching their own poults is worthwhile. This depends on the following factors: The cost of purchased poults; the total cost to rear and keep breeders throughout the year; if you're willing to place breeders on a holding-breeder diet; how much must be paid per pound for feed; the cost of utilities in your area; the amount your labor hours are worth; whether you have the proper facilities for raising poults and breeders; if money must be invested for equipment; if you're expecting the hens to hatch and raise the poults; and how much time and patience you allow yourself. If breeders are not kept, can disease-free and very fertile hatching eggs be secured, and at what

17

cost? How experienced and adept are you at hatching? Are you able to absorb lost profits if egg production or hatching does not go well? How many poults do you need to raise yearly, and will hatching your own poults from your own eggs complement these needs? Are the breeders to be raised from poults?

Handlers deciding between hatching their own poults or purchasing poults should seriously think about these factors. A pair of heavy-breed turkeys purchased as poults and kept for breeding can cost about $84 to purchase and feed throughout the first 60 weeks, even when a holding-breeder ration is fed. If the breeders were allowed normal feed intake prior to and during the breeding season, the total costs would be much more. The following year, the same breeders would cost even more to feed because you are feeding only adult birds. This feed cost is based on 569 pounds of feed fed to one male and one female from the age of day old up through and to the age of 60 weeks. The total cost of the feed has been figured at the average cost per pound of 14 cents.

The holding and breeding diet is not meant to save money by restricting feed intake (although it does), but is designed to stabilize development and weight gains after a mature body weight is attained. If breeders are kept by small-scale raisers and a breeder ration is not fed, the profits that might have been realized in producing your own poults will be near zero.

Because the ultimate cost is what you'll be paying per pound for the resulting turkey meat, Table 1-2 will help you decide whether it's worthwhile to keep breeders for hatching eggs or to buy poults outright. The following examples of a breeding pair of turkeys will show how to use Table 1-2. Assume these first year breeders will produce 58 hatching eggs to incubate in an incubator. Also assume they will produce 40 poults at a 70 percent hatch, which is average if you are not completely experienced in hatching eggs. Table 1-2 also bases the total feed consumption on using a holding and breeding diet before and during the breeding season since it's unprofitable to figure otherwise unless you're raising rare and expensive poults. The main thing to

remember is you will not be ahead by keeping meat-type breeders if you feed a regular diet. They will also become fat and the egg production will drop drastically. A more detailed system of breeding is explained in Chapter 3 under "Securing Good Fertility." To purchase breeders and raise their offspring for meat:

1. Choose number of hens to raise with 1 tom in far right column in Table 1-2. Write down their initial poult cost. Example: One pair day olds = $4
2. Take corresponding feed needed to feed them the first season (60 weeks) from column four and multiply by the average price you'll pay per pound for feed. Example: 569 pounds × 14¢ = $79.66. This is your total feed cost for the breeders.
3. From the first column, choose amount of poults you expect to hatch from the eggs collected from the breeders. Go to next column for amount of feed required to grow these poults. Then multiply the pounds of feed by the average price you'll pay per pound of feed. Example: 40 hatched poults requiring 3,303 pounds of feed at 14¢ per pound = $462.42. This is the total feed cost for the poults raised up to 22 weeks of age.
4. Add the total feed cost figured from Step 2 and Step 3 and the initial breeder poult cost figured in Step 1. Example: $79.66 + $462.42 + $4 = $546.08. This is your total investment.
5. Divide this total investment by total pounds of meat expected as shown in column three. Example: $546.08 ÷ 1,006 pounds total meat = 54¢. The answer is your total cost per pound of meat.

Cost to purchase all poults outright and raise for meat:

1. Choose number of poults purchased to raise for meat from left column.
2. Take corresponding feed needed in second column and multiply by average price

Table 1-2. Breed or Hatch Chart.

Column 1	Column 2	Column 3	Column 4	Column 5
Poults— no. purchased or hatched	Feed— lbs. to grow to 22 weeks	Meat—total lbs. from grown poults	Feed—required lbs. through breeding season*	No. breeder hens plus one tom
2	165	50	569	1 (pair)
8	660	201	770	2 (trio)
16	1321	402	970	3
24	1982	603	1171	4
32	2642	804	1371	5
40	3303	1006	1571	6
48	3964	1207	1772	7
56	4625	1408	1972	8
64	5285	1609	2173	9
72	5946	1810	2373	10
80	6607	2012	2574	11

* Based on the first season of feeding for 60 weeks and feeding a holding and breeding diet before and during breeding.

you'll pay per pound of feed. Example: 40 poults purchased require 3,303 pounds feed at 14¢ per pound = $462.42. This is your total feed cost to raise the poults to 22 weeks of age.

3. Take this total feed cost and add the total initial poult cost. Example: $462.42 feed costs + $80 poult cost = $542.42. This is your total investment.

4. Divide your total investment by the total average market weight (column 3) of the purchased poults at 22 weeks of age. Example: $542.42 total investment ÷ 1,006 pounds total meat = 54¢. The answer is your total cost per pound of meat.

The costs of energy or utilities used to brood, light, water and incubate can be added to investment costs if desired. If you can use a large amount of poults, extra breeding hens can be figured and the total per pound meat cost compared. The costs tend to be reduced the more breeders you keep.

FINDING POULT SOURCES

This can be more difficult than finding sources to supply chicks, because of the lower availability. It becomes more difficult if you try to shop for the best poults at the lowest cost. It's been a slow evolution but more hatcheries are beginning to have poults available for small-scale handlers.

Besides asking other handlers for known sources for poults, poultry slaughter houses, feed stores, livestock classified ads, state and county agricultural extension agents, local hatcheries, farm magazines, poultry publications, poultry supply houses, and farm catalog stores can lead you to sources. The National Poultry Improvement Plan (NPIP) publications that are printed yearly, can be a big help in locating hatcheries which sell poults.

Even with the NPIP publications, quite a lot of letter writing and phone calls will need to be made to locate hatcheries that sell on a retail scale in smaller lots. Small lots of poults can be anything less than 1,000 poults purchased at one time. Also, some of the hatcheries listed are corporation hatcheries which hatch poults only for their contracted growers. This might sound a bit selfish, but companies in the poultry industry can keep cost down by producing their own poults for their growers. Many also have their own feed mills to keep costs down.

It's a good idea to inquire about sources for poults well in advance of when you desire to have

Fig. 1-11. Note the more docile look about the six-week old hen turkey on top compared to the tough and snooty tom with a deeper forehead on bottom.

them. Four months before you order them is not too far in advance. To ensure poults can be supplied when you want them, they should be ordered by February, so begin checking for hatcheries in October or November the previous year. Don't be disappointed because you waited too long to check the sources out. Be sure poults are "U.S. Pullorum-Typhoid Clean" as classified by the USDA. Poults should also be classified as "U.S. Mycoplasma Gallisepticum Clean" (MG). An additional classification of "U.S. Mycoplasma Meleagridis Clean" (MM) can also be looked for but is not necessary.

SIGHT SEXING

All commercial poults are vent-sexed at the hatchery by persons called sexors. There is presently no way to breed and enable commercially produced poults to be sex-linked. This is when breeder turkeys are genetically selected and when bred produce offspring whose sex can be determined the day of hatching by the color or rate of feathering. Feathering sexing genes are not known to exist in the turkey as they do in the chicken. Colored turkeys can be color-sexed using the sex-linked genes for brown (auburn) with or without Narraganset.

With chickens, mainly broilers, a method of selection termed the "criss-cross inheritance" is employed to produce females that show a rapid feathering in the length of the primary feathers of the wings. The parent stock must possess certain chromosomes for this to occur. This type of sexing in chicks is 99.99 percent accurate on day-olds and 90 percent accurate on three-day-old chicks. By three days of age, 10 percent of the cockerels will begin to feather faster.

Small-scale handlers can attempt vent-sexing at home or use the following method of sight-sexing their poults. Even this method requires that poults be only one or two days old. First hold up a poult in each hand with the side of their heads facing you (Fig. 1-10). Be sure their eyes stay open by gently shaking them. Look for a very slight difference in the length of the forehead. A tom will have a slightly longer forehead, making the top of the head appear longer, and will be an oval shape. A hen will have a shorter forehead, making the whole head appear smaller and round. Then, by looking at the eye, the tom can be seen to have a "mean" or wicked look about him. Hens will have a much sweeter look to their face. If you can't tell the difference, hold up another poult because you might be holding two of the same sex. This is a fairly accurate method for home sexing once you get the hang of it. To see how good you are, mark the poults and compare the sexes later. If sexed or desnooded poults are purchased, it's good practice to test your sexing skill on them. Bronze poults are somewhat harder to sex in this fashion because the stripe markings on the head can throw you off. Differences will be even more noticeable as the poults get older. See Fig. 1-11, which shows a six-week-old tom and hen.

Chapter 2

Poult Management

WATERING ON ARRIVAL

When your day-old poults are first brought home, do not expect to simply place them in or under their brooder. They must first be taught to drink. Failure to do this when quite a few poults are brooded together will result in many deaths a few days later because of dehydration. Raising only 6 or 12 poults does not usually necessitate teaching them to drink. The problem lies in the fact that poults will not venture through the crowd of other poults in search of feed and water.

Begin by using water that is warm or at least room temperature so the poults' systems aren't shocked. You can add 1 teaspoon of sugar to each quart jar of water for extra energy, if desired. Small founts are best for day-old poults because once they find out how to quench their thirst, they will push and shove their way to get to the water. This is especially noticeable when poults have been shipped long distances. This pushing and shoving causes poults to trip into their water founts, and a wet poult will surely die if not dried immediately. Another reason for small founts is that poults will walk right into the water.

All founts but the quail size and the new plastic 1 1/2-quart guard waterers are too large for day old turkey poults during their first few days home. Quail founts are okay to use but their smallness does not attract a poult's attention and they are difficult to clean.

The 5-inch plastic or glass fount bottoms that are fitted with a mason jar top, work well if the fount section is filled with small rocks or marbles. This is important: it keeps the poults from drowning or getting wet and draws their attention to the water. Poults are attracted to anything shiny. Fill the fount bottom with the shiny marbles to the level of the fount edge. The poults need only to be able to dip their beaks into the water. As they peck away at the marbles they will inadvertently peck at the water too. Use the marbles for one week. After that time the poults will just play with the marbles, knocking them out of the waterers. Any poults that accidentally do get wet must be quickly dried with a blow dryer. Dry the poult thoroughly right down to the skin.

After founts are ready and evenly spaced, take one poult at a time from the shipping box. By using your thumb and index finger to steady the poult's head and your other fingers in position underneath the breast in front of the legs, tip the poult's head toward the water and dip his beak *fully* into the water (Fig. 2-1). Hold his beak in the water until he opens his mouth. Immediately raise him from the water. While still holding the body only, pay attention to the poult's throat and mouth. Watch for signs he is swallowing. If not, repeat the procedure because he has not taken any water into his mouth. Probably 95 percent swallow the first time. Taking extra time here to be sure water is swallowed will reward you with fewer or no dead poults due to dehydration.

Throughout the remainder of the first day, shove the poults from the heat source out to the founts to remind them to drink. Do this every few hours and without talking. If the poults hear your voice they will not pay attention to the waterers but will run to greet you instead. If plenty of waterers are placed under and around the curtain edge of a canopy brooder, the poults do not usually need this extra prodding. If this is not the case, use a yardstick to shove the poults gently out from beneath canopy brooders.

If battery brooders are filled to their capacity with the recommended number of poults, there will be no extra room to place waterers under the heat. These poults should be shoved out to where waterers are. Battery brooders need only your arm and hand to corral the poults out to the water. If you must enter your battery brooder from the sides or back, you will need to be quiet and quick in shoving the poults to the waterers or they will all quickly pile out through the same opening your arm is through and land on the floor. Poults can be injured from falling even short heights. Battery water troughs should not be used for day-old poults because it's difficult to keep the poults from getting wet.

Poults that look stressed from shipping (if they're not too perky, sit with heads drawn in and closed eyes) need immediate heat. You still must dip their beaks but some waterers must be placed under the heat source also. Stressed poults should have their beaks dipped at least two more times spaced throughout the first day. Place all the poults back into the shipping box and proceed to dip the beaks as originally done. Add sugar to the water for energy and try to use warm water.

Fig. 2-1. Be sure you see the throat move, showing the poult has actually swallowed some water.

If the poults were stressed enough they will not be eager to drink and you might lose some. It's a good idea to contact the hatchery immediately upon receiving very stressed poults. Tell them you are not sure if they will drink enough to pull through—you will not be able to tell until the fifth day at least. This is when most deaths from dehydration take place. A reliable company should replace all the poults if your loss is great.

Remember: Watering poults correctly and providing the correct brooding temperature are the keys to getting them started successfully. The few extra minutes taken to water poults will save a handler many dollars and headaches.

BROODING TEMPERATURES

Baby turkeys—more than any other poultry—love heat. They might even prefer heat over food and water in the beginning. The initial brooding temperature should be 95 degrees F. (35 degrees C.) when poults are day-olds. Poults raised in a box in your home can first be brooded with a 50-100-watt light bulb. The wattage and amount of bulbs used will depend upon the temperature of the room they're in and the number of poults being brooded.

Heat for baby turkeys should be dispersed evenly. If not, the poults will clamber on top of each other under the warmest part of the brooder in an effort to be warmer still. Two spaced 150-watt light bulbs are usually better than one 250-watt brooder bulb for larger amounts of poults unless cannibalism proves to be a problem when bright lights are used. Then the red 250-watt brooder bulbs should be used. If raised in a building outdoors, two or more 250-watt brooder bulbs might be needed to keep the temperature at 95 degrees F. The trick is to have the heat the same temperature in the entire area the poults take up while sleeping (Fig. 2-2).

After the brooding area is set up, the following procedure to adjust heat should be followed. An oral thermometer from your medicine chest will be much more accurate than the brooder thermometers sold for the purpose. Beginners should use a thermometer for best results. Remember to shake the mercury down past 90 degrees F. first. Then take a reading in various sections under the immedi-

ate brooder area. This will be the total area the poults are expected to occupy while sleeping side by side under the heat.

Make allowances for the poults' fast growth by including enough space under brooders for the time they will be brooded. See "Space Requirements for Poults" in this chapter. When lamp brooding, extra lamps can be added and more floor space allowed later as the poults grow. The heated area should consist of about 1 square foot for every 14 poults during the first two weeks. This is not the total floor area, only the heated portion. From two to four weeks of age this area will need to be doubled by spacing brooder lamps further apart or transferring half the poults into another battery brooder if one has been used. Hanging and floor-type radiant brooders will only need to have the temperature lowered 5 degrees weekly if the total space under the canopy accommodates the total amount of poults at any given age. If it doesn't, a large enough canopy brooder was not used in the beginning.

Set up the brooder at least one day ahead of poult arrival so the temperature can be checked during cooler night hours also. Take a number of readings. Take the temperature reading at the level of the poults' heads. This would be 3 1/2 inches. Do this by placing the thermometer on top of something 3 1/2 inches tall, such as a coffee mug. Be sure to shake the mercury down each time a new reading is taken. Then let it rise again for an accurate reading each time.

Do not try to conserve energy by placing brooder lamps and light bulbs too close to the litter material. This can result in hot spots below the lamp and can cause a fire. Using the right amount of lamps at the correct height and wattage will produce a more evenly dispersed heat when lamps are used. A good rule is to place your hand over the litter directly below the brooder heat. If it feels uncomfortably hot on the backside of your hand, there is a good chance of a fire starting in the litter material. Either raise the lamps, use a smaller wattage, or adjust the control knob to lower heat. Also, do not try to conserve heat by completely covering containers housing poults with anything that will

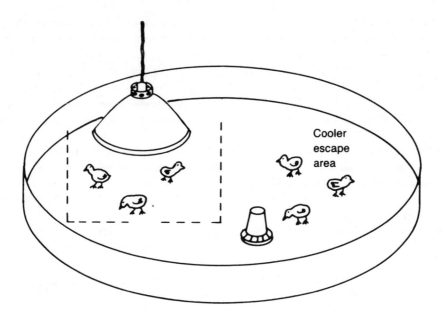

Fig. 2-2. Heat should cover all poults evenly in the sleep area and provide for a cooler area to escape excessive heat build-up.

not allow excess heat to escape. Built-up heat can cause a fire and/or kill the poults.

Lower the temperature 5 degrees weekly the same way: gradually turn the control knob down or slightly raise the lamps a few inches. Take a number of readings throughout the day to assure the temperature is correct. Lowering the temperature gradually like this is not very noticeable to the poults; their bodies soon adjust. Later, when brooding is discontinued, they will have been hardened off enough to accept the much lower temperature without realizing it's 20 degrees cooler than when they were day-olds.

Because poults are more attuned to temperature fluctuations more so than other poultry, do not assume the temperature is correct. Many poults are stressed and therefore lost needlessly each year because of this. Keep regular tabs on the temperature by periodically using a thermometer. Also, do not take heat away from poults any sooner than necessary or they will become stressed. Turkey poults cannot be revitalized as easy as chicks that are chilled.

Poults can become overheated. When they are in their container or brooder you might find them sleeping out away from the lamp or brooder heater. This indicates it's too warm directly under the heat. During the cooler part of the evening either raise the heat lamp, replace it with a lower watt bulb, or turn the brooder temperature control knob to lower temperature. Then wait about 10 minutes and go back and watch where the poults now sleep. Adjusting temperatures during the day when it's warmer will require doing it all over again when the brooder does not have a thermostat.

If poults are in an outdoor building, do not be too quick to lower temperatures. Because outdoor temperatures can vary widely from day to day, affecting the temperatures in uninsulated and unheated buildings, you might be constantly adjusting the temperature. In this case, only adjust brooder temperature if it gets colder than it should be under the heat source. To avoid this, use brooder lamps that contain a thermostat. All canopy-type brooders are made for outbuildings and have thermostats.

Poults will give off body heat. This heat naturally increases as the poults grow. To allow for excess heat that might build up, either from the poults or warmer weather, provide extra space around their area so the poults can move and get away from the heat section if it gets too warm. In this way the poults will make themselves comfortable during the times you cannot watch over them. When poults cannot escape an overly heated area, they will pant and droop their wings to try to cool themselves. Too much heat can dehydrate poults and cause poor feathering.

Unlike chicks, poults will not peep constantly when cold. They are fairly quiet about their doom. Their only indication of feeling cold will be their huddling on top of one another in an effort to get as close as possible to the heat source. Shipped poults peep a lot the first day. This is no indication they are cold. It only means they were excited about their travel.

If there is enough space under heaters, feeders and waterers can be placed there. If not, you will need to shove the poults out near the water and feed every few hours the first two days. They'll find their way back to the heat. The main trouble with keeping waterers and feeders under the heat is the poults might sleep on top of them. This contaminates the feed and water more readily with droppings. It's also more bothersome to replace

feed and water. The alternative is to place feeders and waterers partially under brooder curtains so poults can easily see them (Fig. 2-3). When using lamps, place waterers within a comfortable temperature range around the heat area.

When the temperature is just right, poults will spread out evenly side by side with an occasional poult laying on top of another and some walking on top of others. After you've gained experience you can use the poults as your guide in maintaining the correct temperature by noting the way they situate themselves under the heat. This can pose a problem in itself because you must peek in on them quietly or you'll have them immediately up and scampering to see you because of their curious and friendly nature.

SPACE REQUIREMENTS

Brooding space and growing space are two different things. Figuring brooder accommodations for poults would seem simple if a handler could totally rely on the estimates given by brooder manufacturers, but some are overrated as to the amount of birds the brooders will accommodate and most do not have ratings pertaining to turkey poults.

Fig. 2-3. These day-old poults can easily see their food and drinking water.

By knowing the dimensions of a floor brooder or the heating diameter of a hanging brooder, a handler can estimate the area available beneath the brooder. For instance, a 4-×-4-foot floor brooder will have 16 square feet (or, 144 square inches × 16 feet = 2,304 square inches) of heated area. A hanging brooder that radiates heat to within a 12-foot circle will cover about 108 square feet (or, 144 square inches × 108 feet = 15,552 square inches). Day-old turkey poults take up about 6 square inches each. Because the poults will be under the brooder for at least six weeks, use the size needed for that age. A six-week-old poult takes up about a 1/2-square foot of space (36 square inches). If a 4-foot square floor brooder contains 16 square feet (2,304 square inches) it will accommodate 384 day-old poults (2,304 ÷ 6 square inches) but only 64 poults which are six weeks old. The hanging brooder with a heating radius of a 12-foot circle (15,552 square inches) will accommodate 2,592 day olds (15,552 ÷ 6 square inches = 2,592), but only 432 poults which are six weeks old.

For single-lamp brooders figure the needed brooder space for all poults and hang the lamps 2-3 feet apart to cover the area needed for brooding. Because of insulation variables of a building and temperature differences, the heat from the lamps should be checked with a thermometer. The lamps are sometimes hung closer in the beginning and spaced further apart later, but this can cause more work. Occasionally an extra lamp is added later as the poults grow into the brooding area. A rule of thumb is one lamp for every 50 day-olds and one for every 10 six-week-olds, unless the brooding area is partially closed.

The four-lamp brooders with thermostats will accommodate about 30-35 six-week-old poults in a heated 5-×-6 foot area. Again, because brooding conditions vary, the lamp capacity can vary also. Battery brooders are figured slightly different. See "Battery Brooder Raising" in this chapter.

Remember to figure space needs before your poults are ordered to be sure you can rightly suit them. Because of their rapid growth the poults grow out of an area faster than you might realize. Aside from the brooding area, the growing area should be an extra 1 square foot per poult at six weeks of age. This brings the total brooding and growing space required for poults up to six weeks of age to 1 1/2 square feet per poult.

For easy reference the following guide can be used to figure the *total* required floor space in a building for both brooding and growing each bird:

- Day-old to 2 weeks—3/4 square foot
- 3, 4, 5 weeks—1 square foot
- 6 weeks—1 1/2 square feet
- 7 weeks—1 3/4 square feet
- 8 weeks—2 square feet
- 9 weeks—2 1/2 square feet
- 10 weeks—3 square feet
- 11 weeks—3 1/2 square feet
- 12 weeks-and over—6 to 8 square feet each.

These figures are for the floor space of totally confined turkeys without access to an outdoor pen or yard. This is because there will be days when the birds must remain indoors because of bad weather. Young poults will remain indoors much more than adults.

BOX RAISING

The main concern for any type brooding is that it should be draft-free, cleaned often, and protected from household and neighboring pets, livestock, wild animals and unsupervised curious young children. Although many handlers faithfully follow the first two requirements, many fail to follow the last. Baby poultry are just too tempting a creature not to touch for many small children and pets. I've heard many a horror story from parents who never would have believed Junior would ever flush poults down a toilet to see them swim in a circle. They also never would have believed trusty old Pal or Rover would break down a door while they were gone to gain access to the poults. It's much better to fully protect the poults no matter how trusting you are.

Also keep in mind that, just because you've never had problems with wild animals or a neighbor's dog or cat, doesn't mean you won't now. Neighbors sometimes come and go, and with new neighbors come strange pets you might not be aware of.

Teach inexperienced children to handle the poults properly. Holding does not harm the poults if they're not away from the heat and water too long, and if inquisitive children hold the poults when you're not nearby they are less likely to harm them. Have the child sit on the floor to practice holding a poult. Some children squeeze them too hard because they're afraid of dropping a wiggly poult, while others are afraid to grasp the poult tight enough. You might want to lay a towel across the child's lap in case of accidental droppings. By assuring a child a poult can be held anytime but only in your presence can alleviate problems.

Eliminating drafts also means brooding in an area protected from outside doors that have to be opened. If a brooder must be placed near a door it should be enclosed to form a box-like structure with a partial lid. Do not *fully* enclose poults, however, or they will lose oxygen. As they grow they can become overheated if enough space is not allowed for access to cooler areas. Poults grow extremely quick and soon outgrow their space.

Because poults grow so fast, many handlers will not want to have poults in a box remain in their own homes longer than two weeks because of the offensive smell. But box brooding for those first two weeks does have advantages. A handler can keep a more watchful eye over the poults and can become more attuned to their needs, which will help you realize how to care for them as they get older. And being able to watch the funny behavior of poults can be an adventure in itself.

The container for brooding (box, crate, discarded drawer, cage) should be at least four times the space the poults take up when they're standing side by side. This will usually be four times the size of the shipping container (or the section of the shipping container) the poults took up. The height of the container should be 2-3 feet to keep drafts out and the poults in. For box brooding, place a brooder lamp of sufficient size and wattage to generate 95 degrees F. in one end of the box. This is the sleeping area. At the other end place the feed and water. This will also serve as a cooler area

where the poults can escape if it becomes too warm under the lamp. The cooler area also helps harden the poults off and creates faster feathering so they can go outdoors more quickly.

The floor of the container must be lined with material that is not slippery for at least five days to prevent spraddle legs. Clean, coarse-textured, bunched-up rags or towels work well for a few poults. They can be tossed out when soiled or washed if not caked with manure. To wash, first shake clean. If chlorine bleach is used, you must be sure to rinse the rags thoroughly: bleach can become reactivated when it comes in contact with the droppings. This causes fumes that can kill the poults and harm you as well. Folded newsprint can be slippery. Place shredded newsprint over the top of folded papers. Do not use colored papers because they can be toxic.

Straw litter can be used if it is clean and rough. Other litter materials that have been used successfully for poults include wood chips, shavings, crushed corn cobs, potting soil (peat), and even sand and gravel. The main thing is to be sure the material is not bite-size because baby poultry have been known to choke upon trying to swallow litter material. Wood shavings should not be too fine. Sawdust can cause choking problems. Wood chips are acceptable if you know they haven't been treated with chemicals. Remove any small pieces of bark or twigs from bags of peat being used as litter.

The type of litter used should be changed with the poults' age. A recommended schedule and litter type can be as follows:

- 1 to 7 days old—coarse, clean rags for box-raised poults and coarse, clean straw for hover-type brooders.
- 1 to 4 weeks old—shredded newspapers, wood shavings, and short strands of straw used alone or mixed together.
- 4 weeks and over—a good bed of any type of clean straw.

Setting up the brooder area safely and with the proper temperature and litter during the first week will do a lot to ensure success with your poults.

BATTERY BROODER RAISING

Despite the disadvantages, many handlers use battery brooders for poults. Perhaps there are some handlers who have no other brooding facilities, or there might be the danger of predators. A handler might want his poults nearby where he can really get to know them, but find box-brooding 12 or more poults in a basement or garage an annoying mess. When purchasing large lots of poults for resale, a battery display can be an asset to sales. Handlers do not like to purchase day-old poultry with manure stuck to their feet from box-brooding. The following information applies specifically to battery brooders.

If poults are being shipped in, have the brooder set up beforehand in an area which definitely does not go below 50 degrees F. (10 degrees C.). Depending upon the time of year, some unheated basements are fine. Some might be a bit too cool in early April, and it's not really advisable to cover the brooder to conserve heat. Stacks of newspapers, although good insulation, can get hot enough to possibly cause a fire. Covering with blankets will not do much good and you cannot control the poults' light and air requirements. Although many newer model batteries have an insulation board in the top cover plus a curtain inside to contain the heat, the heat produced dissipates quickly through the metal sides. There are no heat-holding materials in the battery as there is with floor brooding. The litter, wood, and dirt floors under a canopy-type brooder absorbs the heat radiated from the heating element. This absorbed litter heat contributes to the warmth of the poults.

Basements can be an ideal place for a battery simply because the temperature does not usually fluctuate as much as it does in many outdoor buildings. A fairly stable room temperature of 60 to 70 degrees F. (15-21 degrees C.) will assure the brooder of reaching and maintaining the needed 95 degrees F. (35 degrees C.) for day-old poults even if only a few are brooded. The amount of poults under the heating element will affect the amount of time the heating element must operate to maintain the set temperature. It's unwise to brood only a few

poults because the heater will remain on almost constantly.

The standard 2- x -3-foot battery has a heated floor area of only about 2 square feet. This will take care of 48 day-old poults for one week. If all poults will remain in the same brooder for four weeks, plan on initially raising only 12-15 poults. Another alternative is to brood 48 in one brooder the first week, then place half into another brooder the second week. For the next two weeks, use a third brooder and divide all poults into thirds. Place 16 poults into each brooder. The poults should not be raised longer than four weeks in a battery because of the limited space; their heads will rub the ceiling and become scalped. Newer brooders have headroom of only about 9 inches, older models usually have a bit more.

Test the brooder for the correct temperature once its placement is established. If it reaches and maintains 95 degrees F. without poults inside, it will definitely keep the heat once poults are placed into it because of their body heat.

With batteries that have wafers exposed inside, tightly wire a guard around it so poults do not knock the wafer off the screw which would cause the heater to run constantly. Before trying to replace the wafer, the unit should be turned off and allowed to cool to remove the risk of burning yourself. However, this will take quite awhile, and the poults will become cold. After partial cooling, a towel can be laid over the element to protect hands.

Poults can also partially turn a wafer on the screw, which results in a cold brooder because the wafer is allowed to touch the micro-switch. Cut quarter-inch welded wire fabric, and bend and wire it in place tightly to protect the wafer from being disturbed by the poults. Punch or drill a few small holes in which to wire through. Be sure to cleanly trim all points of the fabric off on all sides so poults do not catch themselves. Have the bottom of the bent fabric as close to the floor as possible so poults do not squeeze under and become trapped. Also have the fabric as close to the ceiling as possible so they cannot jump over and become trapped.

In older tier-type brooders that have the individual plugs to each brooder unit on the inside near the element, you must prevent the plugs from being pulled loose by the poults. Tightly tape the plug in place with electrical tape.

Begin heating the brooder by plugging it in and turning the set-screw until the pilot light comes on. When the pilot light goes off, check the temperature. If it's not 95 degrees F., turn the set-screw again just until the pilot light comes on. It's a good idea to make arrows around the set-screw with a permanent marker to indicate high and low directions for turning. The set-screw can easily be turned in the wrong direction. Each time the pilot light goes off after the screw is turned for more heat, check the temperature with an accurate thermometer. Continue to do so until the temperature is 95 degrees F. To keep the screw from moving accidentally, tighten the attached wing nut.

About one hour before poults arrive or are expected, get the brooder floor ready. Line the entire floor area with a fairly thick padding of folded newspapers. Begin laying the paper in the area to be heated. Lay the papers slightly out past the curtain only. This will allow the papers in the unheated portion to be changed without disturbing the papers and poults under the heat. Then finish covering the floor of the unheated portion.

Sprinkle sand over the floor or occasionally dampen very lightly with a hand mist sprayer so the exposed folded newspapers are not slippery. This is the method I've used for years. The dampening procedure need only be done a few times when new paper is laid down because the birds' own droppings will take care of any slipperiness later. Lay down clean, thick, rough towels or rags evenly under the heat over the papers. Be sure the curtain is in place.

Fill all feeders heaping full and close up the water troughs by placing the grill behind them. Adjust the grills over the feeders to the widest setting.

Fill recommended water founts with warm water. About two quarts of drinking water are needed for 48 day-old poults. Place waterers into the cool area of the brooder, with one near an entry grill by a feeder if you are using stacked brooders. You should not attempt to use the attached water troughs until poults are seven days old. When you do, leave at least one fount waterer the first day and be sure the grill over the water trough is on the lowest setting at first in case the poults still want to wallow in them.

When removing the poults from a shipping box, bend up only one corner of the lid to grab a poult so others don't escape. Place the box at a convenient height so poults don't fall from brooder while you bend down to grab another. At this point you'll be teaching the poults to drink (refer to "Watering on Arrival" in this chapter).

If poults must go in from a side entrance in stack brooders, use the grill to block the poults as others are dipped and placed into the brooder. If this is not done, poults will clamber to the entry and pile out onto the floor. Be especially quiet until all poults are dipped and closed in or they'll crowd toward you upon hearing your voice. Poults should all begin to eagerly drink unless they are stressed, as reviewed earlier.

Keep a light on constantly in the room, preferably so it shines on the feeders. Throughout the first day, check how much and how often poults are drinking. The water level should be noticeably lower. Poults will usually be pecking at the feed too, but this is less important.

Don't be too concerned about small areas of the newspaper that become wet because a few poults stepped into the waterers. At this point, if areas are soaked, simply lay a folded newspaper over the top of the wet spot. It's too difficult to remove all the papers from under the poults unless your brooder has a guard over the curtain that can be lowered to confine the turkeys under the heat. Always be sure this guard is securely in place when not being used. These guards have a tendency to fall down, preventing poults from getting to the heat or trapping them under the constant heat of the heating element.

After five days, it's safe to remove the newspapers in the cool area. The poults are now large enough so their legs don't get caught in the wires when they sit down. (Small breed turkeys should have the papers left another few days.) Leave the towel and newspapers in the heated section for another week, changing when needed. Because all poults sit back there constantly, sometimes legs still get caught. Besides, the paper and towel help confine the heat.

Line the dropping pan with newspapers for easy dropping removal and to absorb moisture. Cedar shavings, dried moss, or sand can be used instead and scraped off when soiled. Powdered limestone can be sprinkled on the newspapers of litter to sweeten the ammonia odor. A wide drywall patching or taping knife scrapes trays very well.

On the fourth or fifth day (no later) begin to add cod-liver oil to the surface of the poults' water to prevent rickets. Battery birds are slightly more prone to rickets than floor-raised birds. Four ounces of a good fresh poultry grade of cod-liver oil is usually enough for 25 poults until four weeks of age. Continue the oil until poults have good access to *direct* unscreened sunlight.

Check interior of brooder daily for dead poults. Pay particular attention to dark corners. The wet, soiled newspapers and dead poults should be quickly incinerated or buried to keep animals and flies away. The papers take too long to decompose in a compost heap to make it a good litter retrieval. If flies are a problem around batteries, hang flystrips. Flies can lay eggs in the dropping pans between clean-ups. Do not use insecticide sprays anywhere near baby poultry because it can kill them. Even small drafts will carry the spray. Some brands of disinfectant and fragrance sprays will also kill baby poultry.

If powdered limestone sprinkled over the dropping trays doesn't help, you can place moth crystals in bowls out of the reach of children and pets. If the odor still annoys you and trays are cleaned regularly, you might wish to set up a different system of brooding.

A few times weekly scrub and disinfect waterers. Feeders do not need to be changed and washed if poults are not allowed to walk over the top of feed after they are a week old. Washing feeders can cause more problems if seams are not thoroughly dried out. To dry seams out completely takes a few hours, although it's not wise to leave poults without feed this long. Perhaps one feeder can be washed and dried at a time so feed is always available.

Occasionally throughout the brooding period, run your fingers through the feed in the troughs clear down to the bottom to check for hardened feed which would indicate that moisture has gotten into it. This will mold and can kill the poults if eaten.

Further brooding management consists of lowering the temperature 5 degrees weekly by loosening the wing nut and turning the set-screw back slightly. Use a good thermometer to check the temperature. Experience will later enable a handler to use the poults themselves as the guide to their comfort—watching where they sleep and whether they huddle or pant.

OUTDOOR RAISING

Poults can be totally brooded in small enclosures outdoors. Most of these enclosures have an attached sun porch to help harden the poults for when the artificial heat will be taken away. The rays of the sun will also help to avoid the problem of rickets.

The dimensions of the boxed brooder area should allow 1/2 square foot for each poult that will be brooded until six weeks of age. Then about 3 square feet should be added for a feeder and waterer. A 3-×-3-foot enclosure will house 12 poults comfortably for six to seven weeks, and will allow space for a feeder and a waterer inside. The height of the brooder box should be at least 24 inches in the highest end and no lower than 20 inches in the short end that is created by a shed roof. Even this height will provide enough head space for roosting poults. Short roosts should be installed early during brooding so poults learn to roost.

The heat for the brooder is supplied by ordinary light bulbs. The size wattage to use will depend mainly upon outdoor temperatures and the size and amount of poults being brooded. Smaller watt bulbs can replace the higher watt bulbs when poults grow larger and give off more body heat. A thermostat is a must for poults because they are more affected by temperature changes than chicks. Figure 2-4 gives construction information for the brooder.

The sun deck should allow at least 15 inches of headroom for six-week-olds. Use 1/2-inch galvanized mesh hardware cloth for the deck floor, but do not allow poults out onto sun deck until two weeks of age—and then only if the weather is warm and sunny. An outside temperature of 75 degrees F. is ideal for two-week poults. Construct a slip door that will prevent the poults from going outdoors before two weeks or in bad weather. Avoid manure build-up under deck; it will attract flies. Frequent rotation of the entire unit will permit collected droppings to air dry. Keep the unit on ground where water does not set. Use the driest ground area available.

Sides and top of sun deck are covered with 1-inch chicken wire or 1/2-inch galvanized mesh hardware cloth. The 1/2-inch mesh is more expensive but does not allow rats and least weasels to enter as the chicken wire freely does. If plaster lath wood strips are used on the top and sides, attach them with 1/2-inch spaces between laths to help keep predators out and to prevent poults from getting their heads stuck.

When poults are allowed outdoors, you must check if they are all back in the brooder box before darkness. If not, poults might sleep on the deck and become chilled or pile and smother.

A very large version of this entire unit has been successfully used to keep a few grown turkeys confined especially when communicable diseases on surrounding grounds were a problem. It's not wise to use the same large unit as a brooder, although it can be done by using heat lamps, a thermostat, and careful judgement.

POULT SHELTER

Poults of any age should have shelter from the elements and predators or they will not last long. They can occasionally range, preferably in a penned area, if it's safe. At night and during inclement weather even older poults should be confined to a building of some sort.

Most of today's commercial turkey growers confine poults in a controlled environment until they are marketed (Fig. 2-5). Lighting, feeding, watering, and ventilation are automatically controlled to allow for maximum growth and comfort of the birds. It's mainly in the western part of the United States that adult turkeys might be ranged with the addition of a range shelter to protect them from inclement weather.

A small separate house can be used only for brooding, and the poults then placed in a larger building to finish growing (Fig. 2-6). When separate brooding quarters are not available, an alternative is to section a small part of a larger building off for brooding. When brooding is completed, the sections are taken down so poults have more room.

Some commercial growers use plastic curtains to confine the heat to the smaller area where the poults are brooded. This conservation of accumulated heat also helps keep drafts away and keeps poults from straying. Two or even three curtains can be used to give growing poults gradual freedom. The curtain system saves a great amount of labor, and poults will not become upset due to moving. Sometimes upsetting the poults can cause an instance of cannibalism that might have never occurred before.

The criteria for any building that houses poultry is the same: It must be predator-proof, dry, draft-free, ventilated, and built on high ground. These are especially important for poults. A handler will usually have more invested into turkeys than other fowl and just the loss of a few poults will eat up his profit.

I've known handlers who have practically thrown $50 worth of day-old poults into the stall of an unheated barn only to wonder the next morning if they should have provided some type of heat. I assume these have been spur-of-the-moment shoppers who didn't really know they wanted poults until they saw them. Being too ashamed to ask for advice cost them money, plus they missed out on experiencing the failures or accomplishments of this new endeavor. It was over before it began.

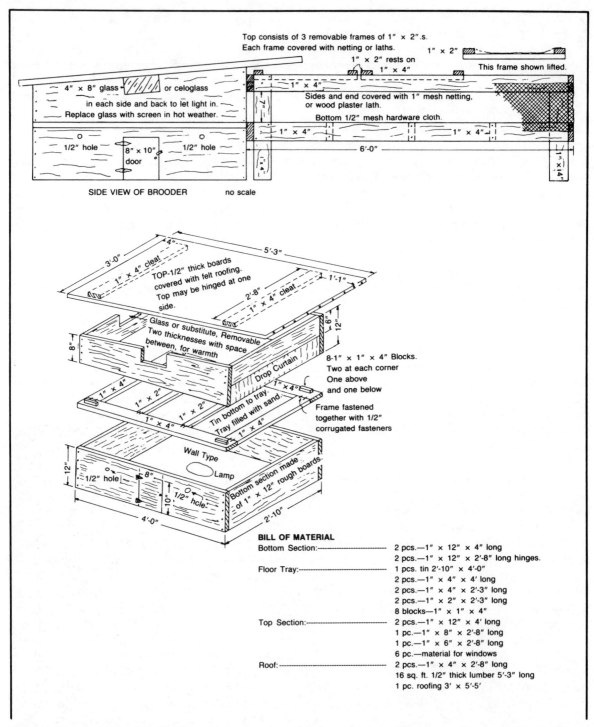

Fig. 2-4. Although designed for 60 chicks, this homemade outdoor brooder is great for 16 poults. (Courtesy of Texas Agricultural Extension Service)

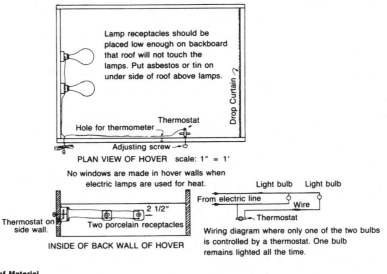

Lamp receptacles should be placed low enough on backboard that roof will not touch the lamps. Put asbestos or tin on under side of roof above lamps.

Drop Curtain

Thermostat

Hole for thermometer

Adjusting screw

PLAN VIEW OF HOVER   scale: 1″ = 1′

No windows are made in hover walls when electric lamps are used for heat.

Thermostat on side wall.

2 1/2″

Two porcelain receptacles

INSIDE OF BACK WALL OF HOVER

Light bulb   Light bulb

From electric line

Wire

Thermostat

Wiring diagram where only one of the two bulbs is controlled by a thermostat. One bulb remains lighted all the time.

List of Material

12 feet of No. 14 weatherproof electric wire, plus an additional length to reach from brooder to an electric outlet.
1—electric plug.
2—porcelain light sockets (covered terminal type)
1 thermostat (brooder type). Optional, since heat may be controlled manually.
2—50 watt, 2-100 watt, and 2-200 watt light bulbs.
Use only two of the bulbs at any one time. Use the size to give the required temperature.

Fig. 2-5. This confined flock of turkey hens in a controlled environment will be used to produce hatching eggs. (Courtesy of Nicholas Turkey Breeding Farms)

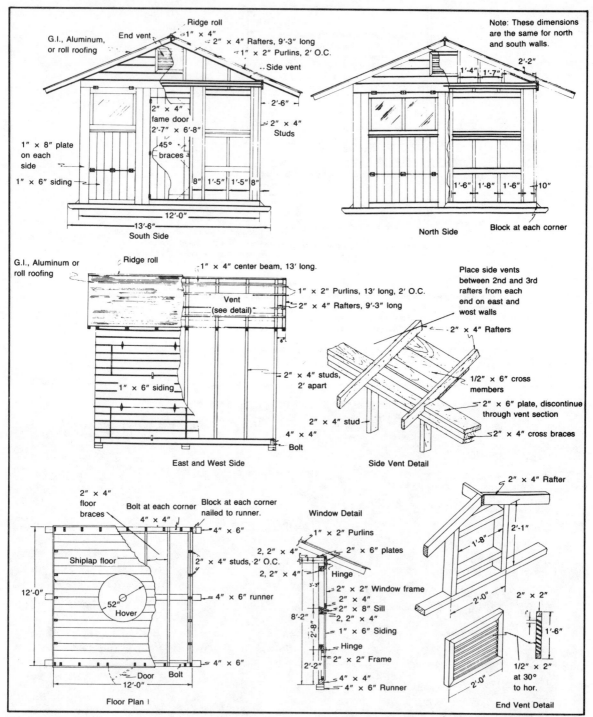

Fig. 2-6. This brooder house will accommodate 72 poults up to eight weeks of age. (Courtesy of Texas Agricultural Extension Service)

Most of the building requirements are simple to understand and comply with. A predator-proof building means there are no entries from which even a rat can enter. If rats are a problem, get rid of them before they get rid of your poults. This means exterminating them, tightly closing the perimeter of the building, and possibly placing sheet metal under exposed floors or installing rat wall foundations.

A dry building can only be obtained with adequate ventilation, high ground, and perhaps insulation. Tiny poults do not require much ventilation. A few open eaves is usually sufficient or enough is drawn in through cracks and crevices. But poults grow fast and soon the ventilation must be increased to dilute carbon monoxide and moisture and to replenish oxygen.

If a building is fairly tight, drafts are not usually a problem. Checking for drafts is simple. With doors closed, hold a length of thread and slowly move it over and around poults. Look for obvious thread movement, which would indicate a draft. By following the draft with the thread, a handler can find the source of the draft and remedy it.

A wooden enclosure for brooding can also be built into the corner of a building or set up right in the middle. Construct a lid from plywood or large scrap drywall to help conserve heat. The lid must always be on loosely and not completely cover the container, or the poults can become overheated and suffocate. This set-up is used with brooder heat lamps. Its success depends upon maintaining a good hot area and a good cool area so poults can get away from too much heat. A good hot area will assure that poults never get cold even when outdoor temperatures drop substantially at night.

Shelter for poults will need an electrical hook-up to provide lighting. Many handlers use heavy-duty outdoor extension cords for the building. Cords should not lay over the ground because they could become accidentally disconnected. Furthermore, power can be drawn from a cord into the ground and run up your electrical power bill—even if it's not being used but only plugged into the power source in the home.

If you want poults outdoors occasionally, an outdoor pen can be built off to the side of the brooder area. It's dangerous to allow poults to come and go as they please, so be sure a door is included on their entry. Before dusk, check that all poults are indoors and not huddled somewhere out in the pen or they'll quickly chill, pile, and smother.

Poults cannot be trusted to stay near their building if left loose. Some might stray if given long periods of freedom. It will be difficult to find them once they settle down in a thicket of weeds at nightfall. If predators don't get them, the cool morning dew or a night rain usually will. Poults aren't as homebodied as chicks. They wander and barely ever look back. Many do not get scared when home is not in sight and might not cry for help. If you can stand guard, the poults can be set free awhile and later herded back into the building.

CULLING

Poults that are to be used for breeding should be culled (pulled from) the flock early by leg or wing banding or color marking. The use of an anti-infective spray containing methyl violet or gentian violet stains the feathers for about six weeks. Dark feathered birds do not show the dark purple spray easily unless sprayed heavily on a single area.

There is usually not much culling done with young poults because there is a more limited amount of strains, and they are high priced in comparison to chicks.

A handler should choose those birds which feather fast and well because this is a hereditary factor. Poults that might grow faster than others in a brood can also be marked. These marked birds can then be culled again at the market age of 22 weeks. Remember, keeping very large and heavy toms will prevent normal breeding. Choose a tom for overall conformation and one which is smaller than the others marked. Restricted feeding will help keep toms and hens in a better condition for breeding. You do not want them to acquire too much fat. Breeder toms should not have wings clipped or it will be difficult for them to breed normally. Toe and beak trimming also should not be done to breeder toms because their claws and beaks are used to steady the hen during penetration. If a handler

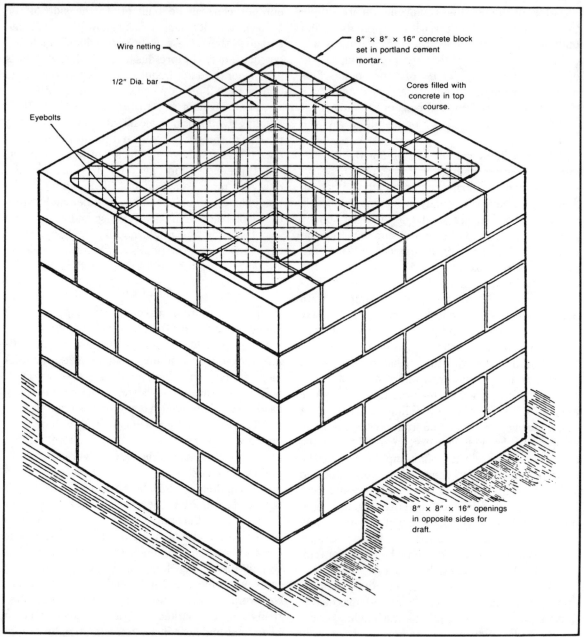

Wire netting

1/2" Dia. bar

Eyebolts

8" × 8" × 16" concrete block set in portland cement mortar.

Cores filled with concrete in top course.

8" × 8" × 16" openings in opposite sides for draft.

Fig. 2-7. This simple incinerator can be used to heat water for scalding when butchering. (Courtesy of Michigan State University Agricultural Engineering Dept.)

wants to prevent the hens' backs from becoming scratched from a tom's claws, hens can wear turkey saddles.

Further culling of poults is called for when in-

dividual birds develop signs of abnormalities—retarded growth, crossed beaks, rickets, one eye missing, or a crooked breast bone. These abnormalities will not affect the eating qualities of the bird,

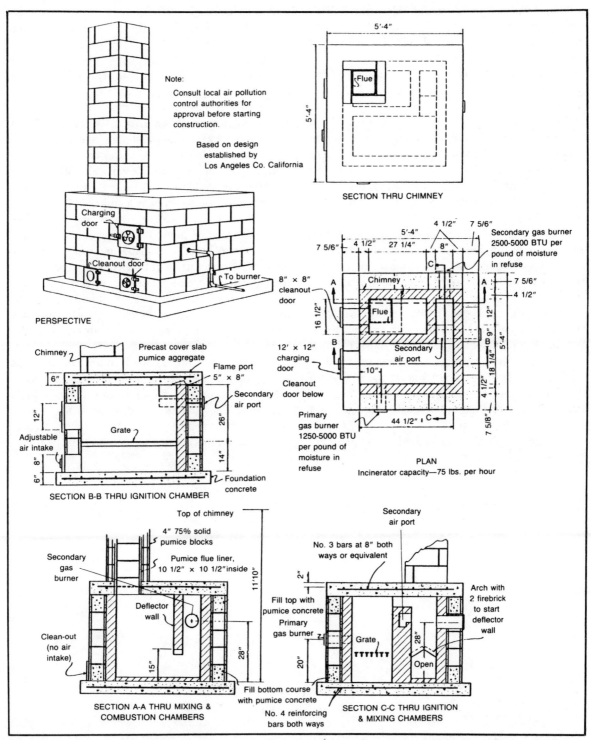

Fig. 2-8. An incinerator that will burn more thoroughly. (Courtesy Michigan State University Agricultural Engineering Dept.)

but some will not grow correctly depending upon what type of abnormality it is. If the abnormality causes the bird to suffer it should be disposed of humanely as soon as noticed.

If a handler prefers a bloodless method of disposal, drowning is the answer. The poult is hand held or weighted under in a bucket full of water until the body stretches out, tremors, and relaxes in that order. Day-old poults take about one minute to cease bodily functions. The larger poults take much longer. You might want to simply cut off their heads (as if they were being butchered) if you feel too squeamish to wait around while doing the dastardly deed.

Small four to five-week old poults of two pounds can be butchered and eaten, unless the bird was disposed of because of a disease. If the bird has been recently medicated, it's also unwise to eat the meat.

Proper disposal of the carcass is another point of consideration. Incineration can be an economical, quick, and effective way to dispose of dead birds on the farm. You might, however, need to comply with local requirements on the use of incinerators. In Air Pollution Control areas, incinerators must be certified before using (Figs. 2-7 and 2-8).

A disposal pit on well-drained soil with an access hole and tight-fitting cover is used by some large-scale raisers. It's considered uneconomical for small-scale raisers.

Burying the carcass is probably the most widely used system of disposal by small-scale raisers. Even this must be done correctly to keep animals from digging the carcass up and to avoid attracting flies. Dig a shallow pit on an area of well-drained soil which is not used. The pit should be the thickness of the carcass plus 6 inches. Cover completely with 6 inches of soil and tamp down well. After a few days it's advisable to cover the area again with another foot of soil to prevent a sinkhole from forming after the carcass deteriorates and as further insurance against animals digging it up.

A "burn barrel" is also sometimes used. A 55-gallon drum with vent holes near the bottom on the sides can become an effective way to dispose of dead birds. The fire must remain long enough to completely destroy *all* remains so other animals cannot get at them. Use a heavy grate on top of the burner.

Commercial raisers with many dead birds sometimes have the birds picked up by a rendering plant to be ground into livestock by-products and feed. They can also end up as fancy bars of scented soap on store shelves. Proper disposal prevents contamination of the soil, air, and water.

Chapter 3

Mature Turkey Management

PURCHASING

There might be some handlers who decide to purchase grown turkeys either for butchering or to be used as breeders. This section is to help those handlers purchase healthy, good-looking turkeys at a reasonable price.

Most adult turkeys are offered for sale just prior to Thanksgiving. This can be because they were raised by other small-scale raisers like yourself, for extra pocket money, or because handlers simply do not want to feed the turkeys during the winter. Butchering services might be performed by some of these seller/growers.

Your best price on adult turkeys can come in the summer when handlers want to get rid of some of these big eaters. Turkeys sold for butchering will usually command a higher price. They can be sold per pound of live weight or dressed weight. Sometimes they're sold in pairs or trios as exhibition-type birds. Occasionally a handler might come across an excellent pair of adult turkeys for as low as $25 for the pair. This is less than it would cost to purchase

and raise them from poults.

Exceptionally large toms—those over 40 pounds—or hens over 24 pounds, are usually last year's birds or older unless they've been on a restricted diet. Breeder toms should be this year's birds, otherwise they can be too heavy to successfully breed naturally. For butchering purchases, you should try to select young turkeys six months or younger, although we've butchered our own three-year-olds and have found the meat to still be tender and moist. When purchasing turkeys from another handler, you might not be aware of the feeding practices, which affects meat quality.

Sick turkeys will usually look sick. Look out for turkeys that sit idle and do not look perky or energetic. Ragged feathers can mean disease or parasites, but many times turkeys will have ragged feathers because they are kept closely confined. When a turkey sits idle with its eyes closed, head hanging down and/or feathers fluffed out, the turkey is not healthy and should not be purchased.

If a turkey appears healthy, continue by checking the eyes, nostrils and area below the eyes. Bubbles in the eyes or crust formations indicate a respiratory disease. Nostrils should be clean and dry. They should contain no watery discharge, crusts, or dirt. If swelling is noticed below the eye in the cheek area, the turkey has coryza, a very infectious upper respiratory disease. Turkeys that have had coryza and have recovered can become carriers—another reason for purchasing first-year turkeys. Listen to the turkeys: mouths open with noisy labored breathing indicates disease.

The hindend of the turkey should be clear of any watery fecal material over the feathers, which would indicate infection or parasites. Watch that the turkey walks normally. In adult turkeys, limping is usually caused by a sprain. Disorders such as perosis or rickets would show at a young age—the turkey would not be able to reach adulthood because it could not support the added growth weight and would be unable to walk.

Do not be afraid of purchasing good healthy turkeys whose only fault is a few crooked toes. They'll still fare well and breed (as long as toms are not older, heavy birds). Crooked toes is more common in any heavy-type bird.

Check legs, especially on older turkeys, for leg mites. This will be indicated by legs that have lost their coloring and have a thickened look with raised, rough-looking scales, white dust, and crust. Treatment can be very successful if the turkey is not yet lame from the infestation, but it's difficult to manage a strong turkey during treatment. Older turkeys will have pale-looking, thick legs, but the scales should not be raised.

Always pen up new birds and keep them away from other poultry you have for at least two weeks. Many diseases will advance within this period and symptoms can be more readily observed. Be aware of transmission of possible diseases during the two weeks the turkeys are penned up. All equipment used for the new birds should be restricted to their use only. Take care of the home flock before tending to the new birds. Wear boots that you change before entering and upon leaving the building that houses the new birds to help prevent spreading diseases that might exist.

Lastly—as a courtesy to other handlers, to yourself, and to your birds, never walk into another handler's pens. If the handler insists it's fine with him, it should make you think before purchasing birds from such a flock. This is how many diseases are spread.

TRANSPORTING AND HANDLING

Rounding up turkeys for butchering can be a chore if not planned in advance. Because of the labor involved in handling turkeys, commercially raised turkeys are corralled into chutes and then into trucks to be hauled away. Most are raised in large buildings. Some are kept confined while other growers have small sectioned pens out to the sides of the building. Large sliding doors allow the turkeys out into the pens or keep them confined during inclement weather. A chute can be constructed to "drive" turkeys up into a vehicle (Fig. 3-1).

Some small-scale raisers might wish to raise a large flock on range using turkey shelters. In this way, a large building does not have to be built. The turkeys are ranged only until they are to be butchered.

Ranged turkeys must either be corralled into a small area so they don't scatter (Fig. 3-2) or, they have to be removed from their roosts during the night. When corralled, they can then be driven through a chute. In some situations it's simpler to take turkeys from the roosts during the night and place into holding pens, cages, or a vehicle. It depends upon how many turkeys are to be caught.

Corralling consists of using plywood sheets, hog panels, or something similar that will form a temporary chute or wall. The turkeys are grouped near a corner of a fenced area or to the side of a building after erecting a pen. Panels should be no lower than 3 feet, and preferably 4 feet high. A small, permanent three-sided pen should be built in advance. If not, arrange some panels up near the building or fence to form three sides. Other panels are used to form barriers to each side of the open front. This prevents the turkeys from walking around the sides rather than into the corral. Feeding turkeys near the area to be corralled a few days prior to loading or corralling will assist in getting

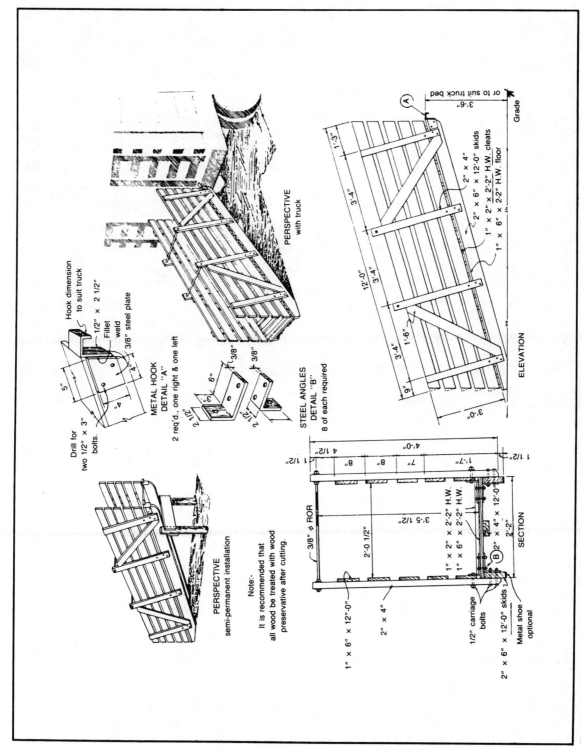

Fig. 3-1. A chute such as this is almost a must when large flocks of turkeys are to be marketed. (Courtesy of USDA)

41

Fig. 3-2. Crates standing on their sides and cages can be used to help corral turkeys into a building.

the turkeys to the desired location.

Depending upon how many turkeys are to be corralled, use a long cut length of chicken wire to round up the birds if they're out on range. With someone on each end of the chicken wire netting, get behind a group of the turkeys and slowly drive them up toward the pen. Don't worry about a few stragglers, they can be rounded up later. As the turkeys are rounded into the temporary pen, bring the netting up to the pen to close it off and confine them. Commercial growers use a corral and chute method most often.

The individual handling of turkeys can be a lot of work and a struggle unless it's done properly. Turkeys are not caught by their legs and held upside down and flapping. This will only work against you and turkeys will become bruised. Even a 12-year-old child (Fig. 3-3) can handle a fully grown turkey by using the correct method: Grab one wing

only over the wing joint near the body and walk the turkey. If both wings are grabbed, there will be a lot of wing flapping and struggling by both of you. If you're of tall stature, you do not necessarily have to bend down to walk the turkey. Most will come willingly even if they must tiptoe. For lifting a turkey up into a vehicle, keep holding the one wing and with the other hand, bend down and grab one leg.

When you must secure a grown turkey alone in order to vaccinate, wing clip, etc., stand the turkey on the ground between your legs with the wings folded down (Fig. 3-4). Small turkeys are held between the legs but not allowed to touch the ground.

When transporting loose turkeys in the back of a pickup truck, you must of course have a cover of chicken wire and a stock rack of some sort, unless you use a van. Don't be conservative with the straw. Place plenty of fluffed-up straw 2-3 feet deep

Fig. 3-3. Turkeys must sometimes be dragged, but it's much easier than carrying one.

under their feet. This will help the turkeys obtain their footing and result in less bruises.

If turkeys are going to shows or fairs, and only a few need to be transported, crates and cages can be used in the back of a pickup truck bed. If feather quality is important, as it is for shows, or if the birds must travel a long distance, be sure the length and width of the container is large enough to prevent broken feathers. Small cages or crates can be tough on feathers. If feathers are broken near the skin and bleeding develops, birds traveling long distances will begin to peck at the wound. Under these circumstances, it's not unusual to have dead birds at the end of the destination.

One of the most important things for a handler to remember is to keep the height of the container low to prevent the turkeys from standing. When turkeys are allowed to stand in a moving vehicle, they get bounced to and fro and become injured.

Fig. 3-4. An eye drop type of vaccine being given to a tom almost single-handedly.

43

Simply being allowed to walk and turn around will cause feathers to become caught in cages and broken off.

Any cage or crate used in an open truck bed should be hauled up close to the cab window. This prevents a terrific draft while the vehicle moves. Furthermore, cover the entire container loosely with a tarp that breathes, or birds can become overheated and suffocate. It must be a porous cloth-type tarp or heavy commercial cloth dropcloth. A large loose-weave blanket can suffice.

Use baling twine to encircle the tarp once it's placed over the cage to prevent the wind from blowing it up and off while the vehicle moves down the highway. A draft on a hot day can become strong and cool enough while moving at a high rate of speed to cause turkeys to acquire a respiratory problem.

Never transport birds in a closed car trunk for any length of time. I've seen many birds suffocate because of this. Heat builds up and oxygen becomes depleted quickly. More ventilation is needed when temperatures are higher, but be careful not to create drafts.

In an emergency when a few birds must quickly be transported, it's safer to tie both legs together around the hock joints and lay the birds on the inside of the vehicle floor. Place something up to the bird so he cannot roll around. A burlap or feed bag can be used for a few turkeys, but cut out a hole in which to bring the turkey's head and neck through. Then tie the open end of the bag together with twine. Don't keep the turkey's head in an enclosed feed bag or it can suffocate.

If turkeys are allowed to drink freely before their travel and are loaded quickly and correctly—that is, there's plenty of no-draft ventilation and turkeys are not crowded into containers, they can easily travel for a few hours without food and water. If the trip is longer than two hours, stop and allow turkeys to refresh and replenish their moisture loss by drinking water.

SPACE REQUIREMENTS

Although housing for mature turkeys need not be fancy, it's most important that they have enough space, particularly inside buildings. Not crowding mature turkeys will mean litter stays cleaner longer, birds will not become ragged and dirty-looking, feed and water will stay cleaner, turkeys won't become as easily overheated during hot months, chances of disease and parasites will be lessened because of cleaner and drier litter, roosting space will be plentiful, and you won't have to push your way through a crowd of turkeys just to fill feeders and waterers.

The following square footage should be allowed for each large variety turkey in a combined flock of sexes who are confined without attached outdoor pens or range:

- 9 weeks—2 1/2 square feet
- 10 weeks—3 square feet
- 11 weeks—3 1/2 square feet
- 12 weeks and over—6 to 8 square feet

Mature turkeys with pens or range will sometimes have to be confined because of stormy weather. If at all possible, give mature turkeys this amount of space even if pens and ranges are utilized too. Turkeys always look better when reared in spacious quarters. Feed consumption and continued growth can be better too because birds have more ventilation between them to keep their bodies at a more comfortable temperature. If they become overheated, turkeys will eat less and grow slower. Research done with chickens has shown for every increase of 2 degrees above 45 degrees F. (on up to 75 degrees) chickens will consume about one and a half percent less feed.

When turkeys are ranged with range shelters being used, just enough space is allowed in the shelter for them all to roost comfortably. Floor area in this type of shelter is not used for feeding and watering, but even these allow about 5 square feet for each mature turkey.

A typical commercial turkey barn is 40 × 500 feet. This is 20,000 square feet. In this size building, 7,000 toms or 10,000 hens can be housed. This is only 2.85 square feet for each tom and only 2 square feet for each hen. This is barely the amount of space a laying chicken should have. The differ-

Fig. 3-5. Because of an automatically controlled environment, these closely confined breeders look very good. (Courtesy of Cooper Hatchery, Inc.)

ence is in the controlled environment, the grower's practice of beak trimming, toe trimming, and desnooding of toms. Toms and hens are housed separately (Fig. 3-5). If a handler wants to try raising more turkeys in this fashion he should be experienced with the turkeys' needs and be able to supply these needs to the ultimate.

SHELTER REQUIREMENTS

Even if turkeys will only be around until 20 weeks when they can be butchered, it's still important to provide the six following requirements for shelter:

- Proper living space.
- Ventilation.
- Draft-free environment.
- High and dry grounds.
- Easy access to building by vehicles.
- Protection from predators.

Living Space. When maturing turkeys have enough space within their housing, they are apt to be healthier, have cleaner looking feathers, space will be more readily available for roosting, litter will stay cleaner longer, mating is more easily accomplished, overheating can be avoided, and caring for them will be less of a chore.

Turkeys kept over through cold months are fairly hardy, but for their comfort and to avoid unnecessary rations from being consumed, it's best to reduce the total cubic footage of their living space. This smaller area can become more easily heated by using the turkeys' own body heat. Reduce the ceiling height rather than the floor area, unless grown turkeys already have more than 8 square feet per bird. Then another temporary wall can be put up. A large sheet of heavy plastic stapled in place will serve as a temporary winter wall or ceiling. If nails are to be used, place a thin strip of lath or furring lumber over the entire edge of the plastic before nailing to prevent the plastic from ripping. Ventilation will have to be increased when the cubic footage is reduced.

Ventilation. The main purpose of ventilation is to keep the interior of the building drier. Ventilation also removes carbon dioxide and ammonia

fumes and odors. Ventilation can seem to be complicated and proper ventilation is not always provided by handlers. Refer to Chapter 18 for ventilation principles that are the same for any livestock or poultry.

Drafts. Preventing drafts adds to the birds' comfort and helps guard against stress and respiratory infections. If turkeys must roost nightly with constant cold air blowing over them, they become uncomfortably stressed, which can lower their resistance to fight off infectious bacteria. Turkeys are less susceptible to drafts than chickens, possibly because of their habit of sleeping with their heads tucked under their wings.

When ventilating with fans, vent boards, eaves, or windows, drafts must not be created over the roosting area while exchanging outside air with inside air. Open-sided range shelters sometimes need burlap draped around the sides during very windy nights.

Location. Many diseases of poultry get their start from dampness, because bacteria and parasites need dampness to multiply. Turkey houses and range areas should be on high and dry grounds to prevent diseases and parasite infestation. Metal buildings begin to rust and wood buildings begin to decay. Litter on dirt floors inside buildings will absorb ground moisture and become damp, requiring frequent litter removal. Wet mud will not be tracked into buildings if it sets on high and dry ground. Outdoor pens can be made more dry and sanitary by laying down 6-12 inches of sand and gravel. An even layer of pea gravel or stones can also be used so water filters down into the ground. Pens of this type using stones can have disinfectants poured or sprayed over the surface. High and dry housing permits better air circulation (Fig. 3-6).

If a building on low ground must be used, bring in extra dirt and gravel to bank up around the perimeter of the building. Slope the gravel so rain water is diverted away from the building. Install gutters to carry roof water away from building. Dirt floors can be built up with one or two feet of heavy sand or sand and gravel.

Access. Feed, water, and straw can become heavy. Twelve mature toms will consume almost

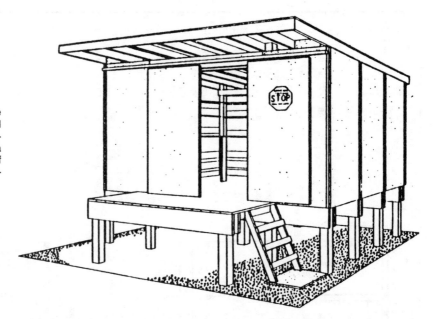

Fig. 3-6. This pesticide storage shed would be excellent high-level housing for turkeys—with the addition of windows, a ramp, and a sun porch (if desired). (Courtesy of Michigan State University Agricultural Engineering Dept.)

100 pounds of feed per week. It's very convenient if this feed does not have to be carried or carted long distances; store it where it is to be used (Fig. 3-7). Vehicles should be able to get to this area easily without becoming stuck in mud or having to drive between obstacles. It's best to install a driveway that leads to the building. Hauling manure away from the building and loading heavy turkeys into vehicles will be much easier too. If the building is used in the winter, a snowplow can be used to clear this drive. Be sure the finished drive is capped with a crown so rain water will run off.

Predators. All poultry buildings should be built or redone to keep out predators, thieves, and wild birds. Most predators of turkeys are larger animals, but the tiny least weasel or even rats can cause losses. All small openings should be repaired and eaves should be screened. Predators and wild birds can be carriers of disease and parasites.

There seems to be more thievery on farms and ranches where turkeys are raised. Perhaps this is because of their economic value. A lot of chickens would have to be taken to make up for the taking of just a few turkeys, and larger livestock are difficult to handle even if the thieves kill them out in the field. Turkeys are taken any time of the year, but most often prior to the Thanksgiving holiday.

I've known of thieves taking 6-week-old poults out of brooder houses after placing them haphazardly into potato sacks. See the section "Protection Against Predators" in Chapter 18.

After gaining knowledge on the shelter requirements for turkeys, the construction or renovation of a building can then be undertaken. Many types of buildings, even very primitive existing buildings, can be redone and still include the basic requirements for sheltering turkeys.

Where plenty of good range area is available, a range shelter on skids will provide nightly roosting quarters and protection from sun, rain, and nighttime predators. A safe range shelter should have screening on all sides with a door that can be locked. Range shelters can be convenient because turkeys will not have to be urged up to a more distant building for shelter. Nearby quarters will allow them to take to shelter more quickly. If turkeys must continually walk long distances to get out of the sun, they will not stay as long on range. A range shelter is meant to keep them on range for longer periods.

A few breeder hens allowed to range can use a doghouse or 55-gallon drum near shade for nesting purposes only. In emergencies, one pair of adult turkeys can be housed in a very large doghouse but

47

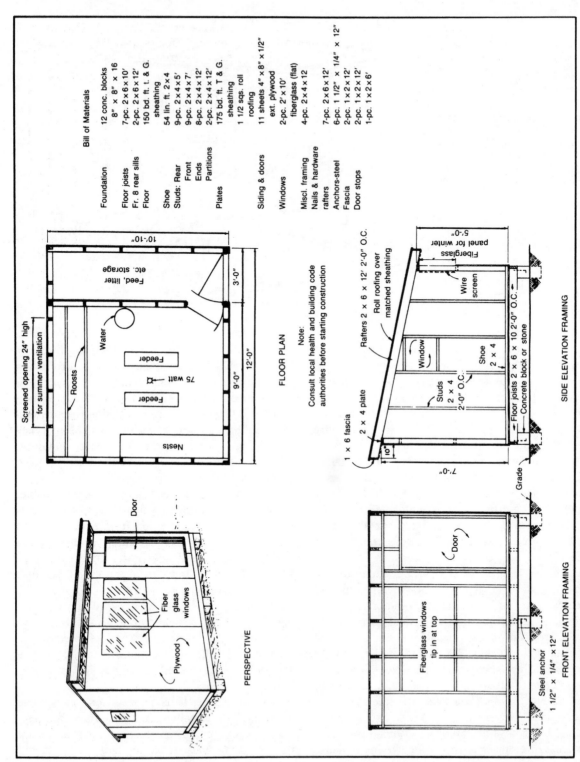

Bill of Materials

Foundation	12 conc. blocks 8" × 8" × 16
Floor joists	7-pc. 2 × 6 × 10'
Fr. 8 rear sills	2-pc. 2 × 6 × 12'
Floor	150 bd. ft. t. & G. sheathing
Shoe	54 lin. ft. 2 × 4
Studs: Rear	9-pc. 2 × 4 × 5'
Front	9-pc. 2 × 4 × 7'
Ends	8-pc. 2 × 4 × 12'
Partitions	2-pc. 2 × 4 × 12'
Plates	175 bd. ft. T & G. sheathing
	1 1/2 sqs. roll roofing
Siding & doors	11 sheets 4" × 8" × 1/2" ext. plywood
Windows	2-pc. 2' × 10' fiberglass (flat)
Miscl. framing	4-pc. 2 × 4 × 12
Nails & hardware	
rafters	7-pc. 2 × 6 × 12'
Anchors-steel	6-pc. 1 1/2" × 1/4" × 12"
Fascia	2-pc. 1 × 2 × 12'
Door stops	2-pc. 1 × 2 × 12'
	1-pc. 1 × 2 × 6'

FLOOR PLAN

10'-10"

Feed, litter etc. storage

3'-0"

Water

Roosts

Feeder

75 watt

Feeder

Nests

9'-0"

12'-0"

Screened opening 24" high for summer ventilation

Note:
Consult local health and building code authorities before starting construction

PERSPECTIVE

Door

Fiber glass windows

Plywood

SIDE ELEVATION FRAMING

Fiberglass panel for winter

5'-0"

Wire screen

Rafters 2 × 6 × 12' 2'-0" O.C.

Roll roofing over matched sheathing

Window

Studs 2 × 4 2'-0" O.C.

Shoe 2 × 4

Floor joists 2 × 6 × 10 2'-0" O.C.

Concrete block or stone

2 × 4 plate

1 × 6 fascia

10"

7'-0"

Grade

FRONT ELEVATION FRAMING

Door

Fiberglass windows tip in at top

Steel anchor 1 1/2" × 1/4" × 12"

Fig. 3-7. A house for about 15 grown turkeys with a convenient feed room. (Courtesy of Texas Agricultural Extension Service)

48

feathers will become ragged-looking. Even this must be ventilated and should be insulated and out of the direct sun. Provide a sturdy door so turkeys can be locked up tightly at night. Storms and winter weather can become a problem when using such small housing. To provide for when turkeys must be kept locked inside during inclement weather, cut a rectangular hole near the bottom of one side of the house with a hinged cover to permit the turkeys' heads to go through for feeding. Construct a small shed roof over this opening to keep out rain and snow. After feeding, it's best to close up the opening. Small pens can also be used next to this type of small housing for a feed area (Fig. 3-8).

Buildings with full lofts can be used for insulating during the cold months. Layers of loose straw or bales of straw in the loft will work as insulation over the ceiling. This is frequently called a "straw loft."

RANGING TURKEYS

Handlers can utilize fields by ranging turkeys, and at the same time the turkeys can devour many insect pests.

Many people refer to a ranged turkey's meat as organically grown. Some feel the meat of these turkeys takes on a more gamey taste, similar to the wild turkey. Some commercial growers still range turkeys in the summer, although most are raised in confinement. Much commercial ranging takes place in the western part of the United States (Fig. 3-9).

Ranged turkeys can be subject to health problems because their environment is less controlled. Turkeys should never be ranged during the black fly (buffalo gnats or turkey gnats) season in infested areas. This is usually June and July, but it depends upon the area. These members of the Simuliidae family are bloodsuckers and transmit Leucocytozoon disease to turkeys. These tiny 6mm-long flies breed readily in fast flowing, well-oxygenated streams of water. They often attack in swarms and can cause anemia or even kill the birds. Black flies are most common in the northern temperate zones but have occurred in the South.

During this fly season, turkeys should be taken off range and placed into buildings that have all openings tightly screened with fine mesh. Black flies are tough to control, so it's easiest to just confine the turkeys. Young turkeys are most susceptible. If they are to be grown on range, dispose of adult turkeys that might carry the parasite before the insect season and before the young turkeys are placed on range. This will prevent the fly from transferring the parasite from the adult turkeys to the young turkeys. Ranges for turkeys should always be on dry ground. Low-lying, damp grounds will breed disease germs and are unhealthy for turkeys.

Although turkeys will greedily eat grasshoppers and other insects while on range, a weatherproof feeder (Fig. 3-10) and nearby drinking water should be provided. Depending upon how many turkeys are on range, the feeder should be large enough to hold at least one to two weeks of feed. Manufactured range feeders have skids so the feeder can be moved more easily. Most have a rain shield around the perimeter. Driving rains will get feed wet—which isn't a problem if turkeys will soon eat the damp feed. The morning after a hard rain, handlers should run their hand down and around the feed pan to check for damp and hardened feed that can quickly mold in warm weather. This can kill or sicken turkeys. Do not unconsciously throw moldy feed out on the ground where the turkeys or other livestock and pets can get at it. Figure 3-11 gives construction details for the range feeder in Fig. 3-10.

The aflatoxin is the most frequently found toxic compound in moldy feed. Aflatoxin reduces growth rate, hatchability, and egg production. It's known to increase a turkey or chicken's susceptibility to disease by interfering with the immune response. This toxin also prevents nutrient and fat absorption. It's been associated with hemorrhagic disease in young turkeys. Spoiled feed can also contain botulin toxin which causes paralysis a few hours after the poisoned feed is eaten. Preservatives such as the following antimycotic drugs can be used or obtained in feeds susceptible to dampness and spoiling: Calcium propionate, gentian violet, mycostatin, proprionic acid, and sodium proprionate.

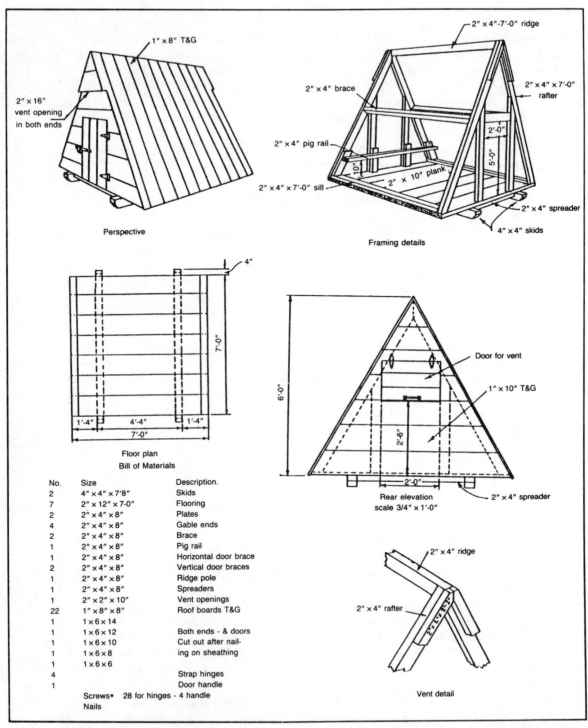

Perspective

1″ × 8″ T&G

2″ × 16″ vent opening in both ends

Framing details

2″ × 4″-7′-0″ ridge

2″ × 4″ brace

2″ × 4″ × 7′-0″ rafter

2″ × 4″ pig rail

2′-0″

5′-0″

10″

2″ × 10″ plank

2″ × 4″ × 7′-0″ sill

2″ × 4″ spreader

4″ × 4″ skids

Floor plan

4″

7′-0″

1′-4″ 4′-4″ 1′-4″

7′-0″

Rear elevation
scale 3/4″ × 1′-0″

6′-0″

Door for vent

1″ × 10″ T&G

2′-6″

2′-0″

2″ × 4″ spreader

Vent detail

2″ × 4″ ridge

2″ × 4″ rafter

Bill of Materials

No.	Size	Description.
2	4″ × 4″ × 7′8″	Skids
7	2″ × 12″ × 7-0″	Flooring
2	2″ × 4″ × 8″	Plates
4	2″ × 4″ × 8″	Gable ends
2	2″ × 4″ × 8″	Brace
1	2″ × 4″ × 8″	Pig rail
1	2″ × 4″ × 8″	Horizontal door brace
2	2″ × 4″ × 8″	Vertical door braces
1	2″ × 4″ × 8″	Ridge pole
1	2″ × 4″ × 8″	Spreaders
1	2″ × 2″ × 10″	Vent openings
22	1″ × 8″ × 8″	Roof boards T&G
1	1 × 6 × 14	
1	1 × 6 × 12	Both ends - & doors
1	1 × 6 × 10	Cut out after nail-
1	1 × 6 × 8	ing on sheathing
1	1 × 6 × 6	
4		Strap hinges
1		Door handle
	Screws•	28 for hinges - 4 handle
	Nails	

Fig. 3-8. A well-constructed hog hut on skids which can be used for a half dozen adult turkeys. (Courtesy of Michigan State University Agricultural Engineering Dept.)

50

Fig. 3-9. A large flock of ranged turkeys in Sand Pete County, Utah. Note range shelter in background does not provide roosts. (Courtesy of Norbest, Inc.)

Hot, bare, dry, rough ranges can initiate hemorrhagic enteritis in young turkeys between 4 and 13 weeks of age. This viral intestinal disorder has been termed ''bankruptcy gut'' because it's been observed in most of the major turkey producing areas such as Arkansas, Minnesota, North Carolina, Texas, and Virginia. Bare, rough ranges can also cause injuries to the footpads of turkeys. The injury then becomes infected and is called Bumblefoot.

Ranges should be areas not used by chickens within the last 18-24 months to avoid cecal worm infection which can transmit Blackhead disease. Turkeys on range should be periodically wormed also.

Turkeys do not have to stay on range. Most can be allowed on range during the day and taught to come back to the building for roosting if no other tempting outdoor roost sites are available. Coming back to the building continually before dusk is a matter of habit for turkeys. Wild turkeys are a bit more rangy. They've been known to go off to greener pastures and return one whole month later.

Turkeys can also be ranged in order to clean

Fig. 3-10. A 30-bushel capacity range feeder on skids for adult turkeys. (Courtesy of University of Missouri Extension Division, Columbia, MO)

51

Construction Notes

A. Detail of 1 in. angle iron which is used to support roof in open position and hold roof in closed position. The support is permanently fastened on the fixed half of the roof and is hooked behind a screw or nail on the hinged half. To lower roof the brace is merely slipped off to the nail, the roof is lowered and the brace is slipped back on the same nail.

B. 1 in. x 4 in. x 7 in. boards which are placed on middle and two end 2 x 4's to support 1 x 3 around edge of roof. These braces are only used on fixed half of roof.

C. Space for feed to flow should be 3 1/2-4 in. high.

D. Construction shown is for fixed half of roof. Construction for half which raises is identical except additional 1 x 4's are placed under the three 1 in. x 4 in. x 15 in. braces. On the fixed half these braces are nailed directly to the 2 x 4's which support the roof. The added 1 x 4's are 22 in. long and extend down to the 1 x 3 around the edge of the roof. For additional strength two more 1 in. x 4 in. x 22 in. boards are fastened midway between the original 1 x 4's. Place outer edge of corrugated roofing down. Treat runners with wood preservative.

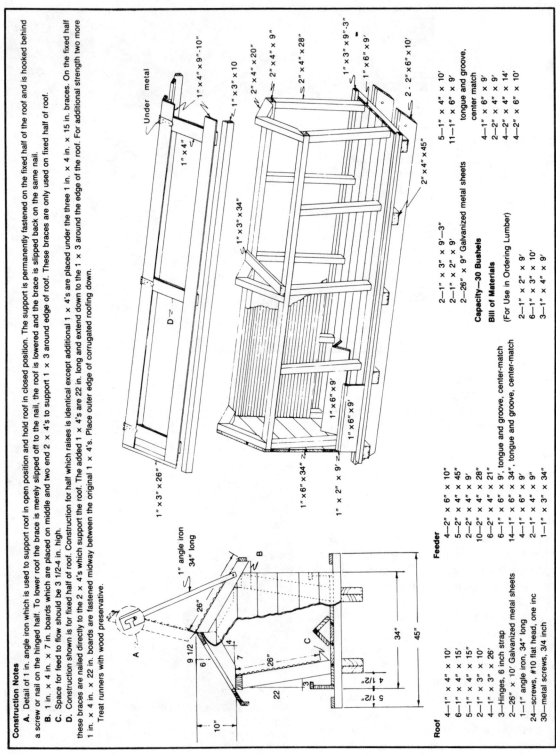

Roof

4—1" x 4" x 10'	
6—1" x 4" x 15'	
5—1" x 4" x 15"	
2—1" x 3" x 10'	
4—1" x 3" x 26'	
3—Hinges, 6 inch strap	
2—26" x 10' Galvanized metal sheets	
1—1" angle iron, 34" long	
24—screws, #10 flat head, one inc	
30—metal screws, 3/4 inch	

Feeder

4—2" x 6" x 10"	
5—2" x 4" x 45"	
2—2" x 4" x 9'	
10—2" x 4" x 28"	
6—1" x 4" x 21"	
6—1" x 6" x 9', tongue and groove, center-match	
14—1" x 6" x 34", tongue and groove, center-match	
4—1" x 6" x 9'	
2—1" x 4" x 9'	
1—1" x 3" x 34"	

2—1" x 3" x 9'—3"	
2—1" x 2" x 9'	
2—26" x 9" Galvanized metal sheets	

Capacity—30 Bushels

Bill of Materials
(For Use in Ordering Lumber)

2—1" x 2" x 9'	
6—1" x 3" x 10'	
3—1" x 4" x 9'	

5—1" x 4" x 10'	
11—1" x 6" x 9'	
	tongue and groove, center match
4—1" x 6" x 9'	
2—2" x 4" x 9'	
4—2" x 4" x 14'	
4—2" x 6" x 10'	

Fig. 3-11. Construction details for turkey range feeder shown in Fig. 3-10. (Harold Biellier, Walter Russell, Dept. of Poultry Husbandry and Ralph Ricketts, Dept. of Agricultural Engineering. Courtesy of University of Missouri Extension Division, Columbia, MO)

52

up ground fruit in orchards. Turkeys are especially fond of apples.

Turkeys on range need shade from the sun. Corn or sunflowers can provide this shade if planted early enough. A range shelter can also be provided (Fig. 3-12). Range shelters should preferably be screened on all sides and have a door. A door can make confining the birds a simple matter when they are to be rounded up, as for marketing and butchering.

If clean range cannot be provided, but you'd like your turkeys outdoors, consider constructing a sun porch (Fig. 3-13).

ROOSTS

Adult turkeys will sleep on floors, but allowing them to roost will enable them to better control the air circulation around their bodies at night for comfort. As turkeys roost, they fluff up their feathers around their body, which permits the air to circulate over and around their entire body. In hot weather, this helps to cool the bird. In cold weather the body heat can freely flow through the feathers and circle the entire body without being obstructed. Roosting also keeps the birds' feet warm.

Roosts for turkeys should not be too high off the ground. High roost can cause injury to the foot pad and bumblefoot. Heavy birds such as turkeys are more susceptible to this type of injury—constant jumping from high roost brings their weight forcefully down onto their feet. Their wings are not much help in making their landing any lighter. A one-foot-high roost will work well.

To prevent crowding on the roost boards allow at least 2 lineal feet for each turkey. Turkeys will fight for roost space if not enough is available. An 8-foot length of roost will very often be supporting 65 to 100 pounds of birds. It's important to construct heavy-duty roosts. Roosting material made from 2- × -4s turned with the narrow edge up will support many pounds of turkeys even if in 12-foot lengths. The main thing is to be sure it is securely attached to walls on the ends. This sometimes necessitates cross sections of lumber on the walls at both ends if a stud does not intersect for attaching.

If dropping boards (where manure collects for cleaning) are used under roosts, the roosts can be higher, but steps made from boards, bleacher-style, should be provided just in front of or to the side of the boards and roosts. Dropping pits can be used for turkeys, with or without roosts above (Fig. 3-14). This is a wooden box-type construction that is placed under roosts. The top is covered with a wire mesh to allow droppings to fall through. The droppings are later cleaned out, sometimes from outdoors through a long rectangle cut out of the wall that has a hinged flap. If heavy wire mesh is sturdily supported to prevent sagging on the top of a pit, the structure itself can be used for roosting.

LITTER

Various types of litter material can be used for adult turkeys. Many times the type of litter used depends upon what is available in your immediate area. The best type of litter material would be one that doesn't pack down, is lightweight, quickly absorbs moisture, is not dusty, has no signs of mold, is economical and readily available. Numerous by-products of farm crops and industry are used for litter. These include crushed corn cobs, wood shavings, sawdust, sugarcane, and straw.

Litter material is used to absorb the moisture from droppings and spilled water whose wetness could initiate disease and parasites. When litter is of a type which doesn't pack down easily, it has a chance to dry. Removal of old litter or additions of new litter will keep the area under the turkeys' feet dry.

There are two systems of using litter with pros and cons for both. One is the built-up system where new fresh litter is added to the top of the old. The first layer for adult turkeys might be 6-12 inches, depending upon the type used. Each additional layer periodically placed over the soiled litter might be 6 inches. After a few months time, the original litter gets packed down and might begin to decay underneath. The floor can easily become two feet taller in a short time. This system calls for total litter removal only two or three times a year. Some say this breeds disease, germs, and parasites. Others say complete and frequent litter removal

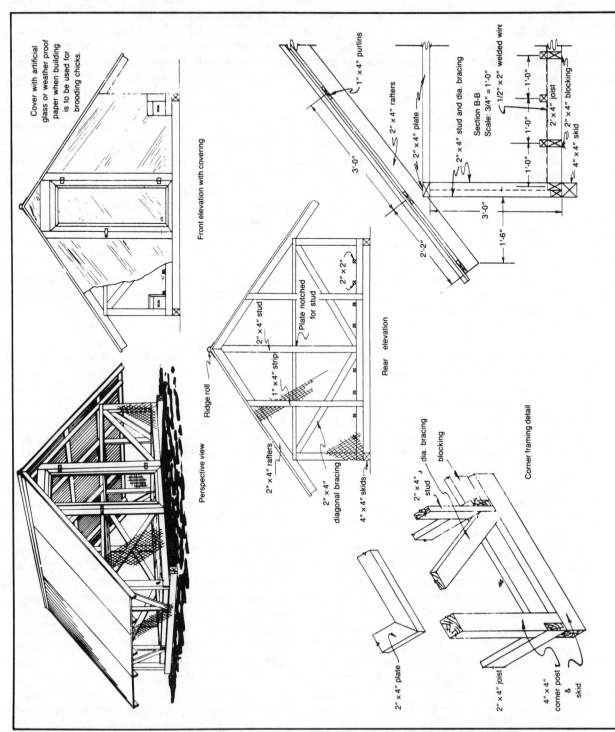

Cover with artificial glass or weather proof paper when building is to be used for brooding chicks.

Front elevation with covering

1" x 4" purlins

2" x 4" rafters

2" x 4" plate

2" x 4" stud and dia. bracing

Section B-B
Scale: 3/4" = 1'-0"

1/2" x 2" welded wire

2" x 4" joist

2" x 4" blocking

4" x 4" skid

3'-0"

3'-0"

1'-6"

2'-2"

1'-0"

1'-0"

1'-0"

1'-0"

Ridge roll

2" x 2"

Plate notched for stud

2" x 4" stud

1" x 4" strip

Rear elevation

2" x 4" rafters

2" x 4" diagonal bracing

4" x 4" skids

Perspective view

2" x 4" dia. bracing

blocking

2" x 4" stud

Corner framing detail

2" x 4" plate

2" x 4" joist

4" x 4" corner post & skid

Fig. 3-12. If roosts are built into this range shelter it should accommodate 18 adult-size turkeys. (Courtesy of Texas Agricultural Extension Service)

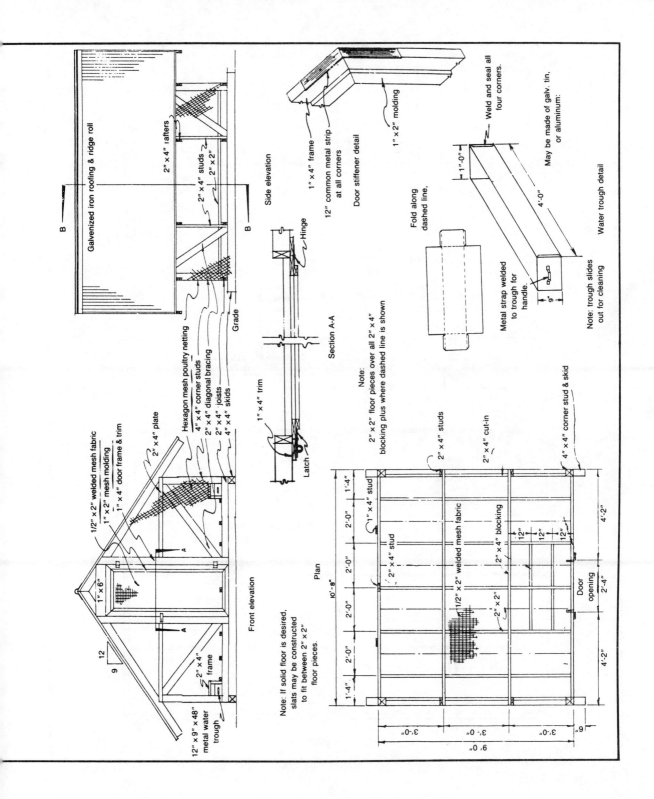

Galvanized iron roofing & ridge roll

2" x 4" rafters

2" x 4" studs

2" x 2"

Side elevation

B

B

Grade

1" x 4" frame

12" common metal strip at all corners

1" x 2" molding

Door stiffener detail

Weld and seal all four corners.

1" - 0"

4' - 0"

9"

May be made of galv. tin, or aluminum.

Fold along dashed line.

Metal strap welded to trough for handle.

Water trough detail

Note: trough slides out for cleaning

1/2" x 2" welded mesh fabric
1" x 2" mesh molding
1" x 4" door frame & trim
2" x 4" plate

Hexagon mesh poultry netting
4" x 4" corner studs
2" x 4" diagonal bracing
2" x 4" joists
4" x 4" skids

Hinge

1" x 4" trim

Section A-A

Latch

Note:
2" x 2" floor pieces over all 2" x 4"
blocking plus where dashed line is shown

1" x 6"

A

A

Front elevation

12

9

2" x 4" frame

12" x 9" x 48"
metal water trough

Note: If solid floor is desired,
slats may be constructed
to fit between 2" x 2"
floor pieces.

Plan

10' - 8"

1' - 4"   2' - 0"   2' - 0"   2' - 0"   2' - 0"   1' - 4"

2" x 4" studs

1" x 4" stud

2" x 4" stud

2" x 4" cut-in

1/2" x 2" welded mesh fabric

2" x 2"

2" x 4" blocking

12"   12"   12"

4" x 4" corner stud & skid

4' - 2"

Door opening

2' - 4"

4' - 2"

6"

3' - 0"   3' - 0"   3' - 0"

9' - 0"

55

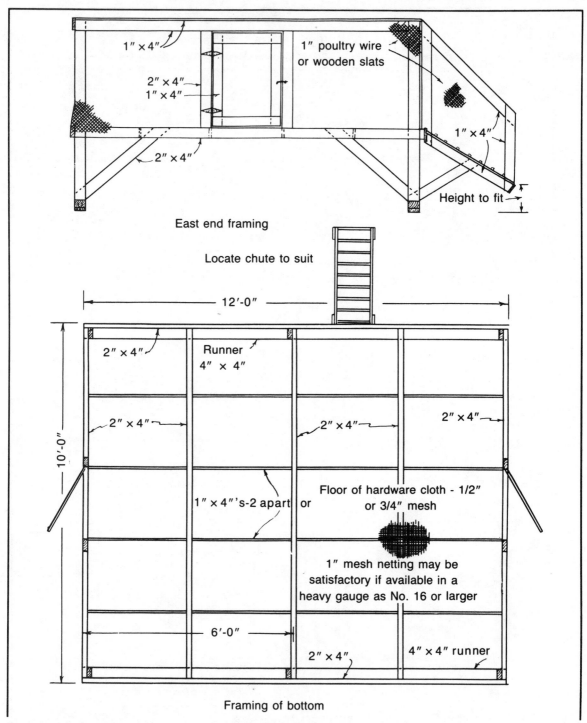

East end framing

Locate chute to suit

Framing of bottom

Fig. 3-13. This sun porch could also be used as a range shelter because of attached skids. (Courtesy of Texas Agricultural Extension Service)

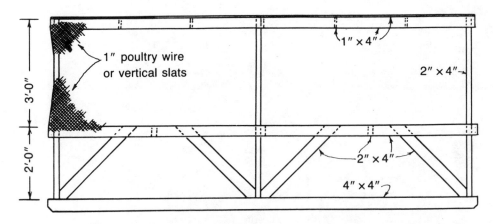

3'-0"

2'-0"

1" poultry wire
or vertical slats

1" × 4"

2" × 4"

2" × 4"

4" × 4"

Side framing

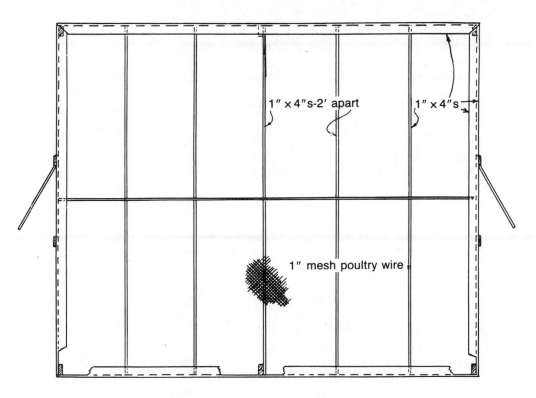

1" × 4"s-2' apart

1" × 4"s

1" mesh poultry wire

Framing of cover

57

Fig. 3-14. Years ago many turkey houses contained dropping pits below roosts, but it's still a good idea to put to use today. (Courtesy of USDA)

stirs up disease germs and parasites.

If disease becomes evident or parasites are a problem, it always helps to completely remove all litter, disinfect and/or apply insecticides. Remember, infectious soiled litter is contagious to other poultry and sometimes other animals and man. Burn diseased litter if at all possible. Otherwise bury deeply.

Always check for mold in the litter. Mold contains toxic substances that can cause respiratory and organ related diseases. It is not only a health hazard for turkeys, but the mold contains specific antigens that can cause a handler to contract Farmer's Lung Disease. Moldy litter will have a musty, moldy odor and is usually gray or black in color. Even bales of straw that look fairly golden can have mold spores in the center of the bale. Often the bales are rained on in the field and winds quickly dry the outside but not the inside.

Straw is usually available at a reasonable price. It should be bright golden, clean, fresh-smelling, and not dusty. Do not use dusty straw for turkey litter; turkeys are more sensitive to high dust environments than chickens.

Never use hay as bedding material even if it does not appear green. Hay quickly decomposes and heats up when added to potent poultry manure. The ammonia fumes will become stronger, and heated hay has even been known to start fires. Money is only wasted when hay is purchased for litter. It has very poor absorption qualities besides.

Proper ventilation is a must to help keep litter dry. This will cut down on more constant litter renewal and costs. If litter always seems damp, ventilation must be upgraded.

Ammonia fumes created from droppings can be cut down by "sweetening" the litter. Occasionally sprinkle powdered agricultural limestone over the soiled litter to neutralize it. The powdered limestone is inexpensive and can be purchased at any feed, grain, and seed dealer.

DUST BATHS

A dust bath serves a valuable purpose for turkeys and other fowl. They lay over dirt and sand and use their wings to vigorously flap the dirt into their feathers. The sand and dust settles onto their skin after filtering through their feathers and becomes a soothing substance. A very good and vigorous dust bath can smother lice, but should not be relied on for complete control of lice. After this dusting, the turkey will stand up and shake the dust and sand from the feathers. Turkeys do not dust as often as chickens, but when they do it can mean a large amount of lice or other parasites are present. Toms rarely dust themselves.

Dirt floors can be utilized for dusting. One foot of sand can be spread over existing floors. If floors are clay, 2 feet of sand can be used. Besides becoming a better floor for dusting purposes, sand is a more sanitary base for litter and it absorbs and drys faster than clay soil. If a dirt floor is not available for confined turkeys, a dust box will work. It should be at least 2 feet square and 8 inches deep. Place 4 inches of dry sand into the box. Wood ashes and/or lice powder can occasionally be sprinkled over the sand and mixed in to help control lice between regular lice treatments. Keep the dusting box in an open area to prevent hens from nesting in it. Never place it directly under roost or droppings will foul the sand and the turkeys will not want to use it.

Along with dust bathing, turkeys further groom their feathers by extracting oil from the gland at the base of the tail (uropygial gland) and run the oil through the feathers with their beak. This is called preening.

GROOMING FOR SHOW

Turkeys entered into shows will be judged for the standard accepted qualities of the particular variety. This includes the standard accepted weight for young toms, old toms, young hens, and old hens for specific varieties. The Royal Palm and Beltsville Small White turkeys are the only two varieties cut in points for being overweight. Royal Palms must not be more than 2 pounds overweight. Beltsville Small Whites are disqualified if toms are more than 3 pounds overweight and hens are more than 2 pounds overweight. If there is a tie of two or more Beltsvilles with equal points, the smallest is claimed the winner because smallness is desired in this variety. General disqualifications for any turkey are deformed wings, a crooked breastbone, or a pendulous crop.

Turkeys entered in meat pens at fairs are usually of a strain of the commercial varieties and usually white. Conformation to standards is just as important in a meat bird as a fancy or breeder pen bird. The only differences may be the weight and age allowed. Good meat and market qualities depend upon these factors. Some fairs judge meat birds on butchered carcass appearance. In this way the entire carcass, including bone formation, fleshing, and skin, is clearly visible. Fleshing can be determined on a live market-age turkey by pinching the breast area between your thumb and index finger. This fleshing is the small amount of fat lying over well-rounded, filled-out, firm meat.

Select your specimens from among the flock at least six weeks before the show. Because the shape, conformation, and vitality is given more consideration at a show than any other factor, the ideal body should be chosen first. Look for general appearance first. Check eyes for clearness and rare blindness of one eye. Eyes should appear oval and full. Check the beak for crookedness. It should be curved and of medium length. Run your hand down over the neck to check for smoothness. Neck should curve gracefully. Toms should be heavily carunculated over the neck. Run your hand down over the back to detect any abnormal bone growths or crookedness. Back should be broad and slope from neck and slightly curve near tail. Each area to the sides of the backbone should be of equal widths and extend towards tail. Examine the thighs for strength, firmness, and fleshing right down to the hocks. Make sure the shanks are straight and clean. Shanks should be of good thickness and about the same length as the keel. Be sure scaly leg mites are not present if scales stand out or crusts appear. The four toes should be checked for straightness and be well spread.

Next, examine the breast carefully; this is important especially in a meat bird. Feel the size and straightness of the keel bone. The very front should appear full and well-rounded and carried slightly upwards (Fig. 3-15). The very face of the keel should appear flat and wide. Check for possible breast blisters on the breast and on the body near the base of the neck. Wings should be folded

Fig. 3-15. A good-looking tom with a full, well-rounded breast. (Courtesy of Watt Publishing Co.)

smoothly and set well up on the sides. Feel the crop for any abnormalities. The tail should extend low in a continued line with the back and be reasonably long. Skin should be fine-textured. Check for lice around the vent and under the wings. Treat for parasites if found.

The turkeys selected should be separated from all other poultry until show time. This allows more time to be devoted to them and helps feathers and skin stay better groomed and cleaner. Keep the selected turkeys in a separated pen with plenty of clean straw to keep feathers and feet looking good. The litter will serve as a grooming aid. Continue feeding a well-balanced ration. In addition, feed small amounts of crumble feed moistened with warm water, powdered milk, and a half teaspoon of cod-liver oil. Remove any of this mixture not eaten so it does not spoil. Feed this conditioner once a day for up to three weeks before the show. Continued feeding of cod-liver oil can produce a fishy taste in the butchered meat, and white feathers might take on a yellow cast from the oil. Feed this conditioner sparingly to Royal Palms and Beltsville Small Whites because it can cause them to gain too much.

If grounds are clean, free of disease, and green, the selected turkeys can range. This does produce very healthy-looking birds. You must be sure the turkeys can be watched constantly while outdoors. I know of many handlers losing prize specimens to thieves and dogs just a few days before fair time. It might be impossible to replace just one bird if a pen of three is required.

White feathered turkeys should be allowed in the sunlight as often as they can be watched the last four weeks. This helps bleach the feathers to snow white. The red, white, and blue head, wattle, and neck carnucles of a tom take on an even more impressive look against snow-white feathers. Color-feathered varieties should be kept out of direct sunlight to prevent dark colors from fading or turning red. An iron supplement will help enrich the feather colors in these varieties.

Final grooming should be done the day before the birds are shown. Never completely bath the turkeys because this could cause respiratory problems. Do not use any type of soap on their head or especially near the eyes and nostrils. This has been known to cause a sniffling condition and the turkey might be sent home disqualified. Complete bathing will also cause the natural shine of the feathers to be lost because feather oils will be removed. Feathers can be easily ruined from wetting. Very dirty areas can be spot shampooed. Use ordinary shampoo, not harsh oil-cutting detergents. Gently rub shampoo in one direction only—with the feather grain—so the feather webs stay intact.

At the bottom of each feather is the quill. This is what attaches the feather to the skin. Above this is the fluff (or undercolor, depending upon whether feathers are colored). Above this fluff is the web of the feather. This web is actually formed by numerous pairs of barbs on each side of the feather shaft. Each individual barb has its own hairlike barbs called barbules. These barbules have even tinier hairlike hooks called barbicels. The barbicels attach themselves to the barbules of the next barb above in succession—this is what forms the web. When the barbicels are forced apart, the web is no longer a continuous united series of barbs. The whole feather then looks ragged, torn, or rough. This is why the feathers should never be rubbed in the wrong direction.

After spot shampooing, rinse thoroughly, partially blow dry with a hair dryer, and finish by air drying. Complete blow drying can separate the web and dry up the feather oils.

White feathered turkeys can be cleaned by dusting the entire body with cornmeal or cornstarch. Cornmeal tends to absorb oils, so it should be used only if the feathers appear too oily or greasy. Usually just a powdering of cornstarch will be enough. Powder all the way down to skin by lightly patting the feathers. The turkey will later work the cornstarch out of the feathers by shaking them.

White birds are sometimes submersed in diluted laundry bluing to remove yellowing of the feathers. Though done quite frequently, this practice can be regarded as faking depending upon the judge—check first. The other methods to whiten feathers should be tried first to avoid having to wet the turkey. The use of dyes and bleaches is strictly forbidden.

It's sometimes suggested that vent feathers be trimmed. This gives a cleaner appearance and is frequently done to breeder turkeys to facilitate breeding. Trim sparingly, however, because feather cutting can be claimed faking and the bird can become disqualified—sometimes judges have varying viewpoints on this.

Clean the shanks, feet, toes, and nails with a small amount of liquid dishwashing detergent mixed with a capful of peroxide to about 4 cups of warm water. The peroxide is not used for bleaching but only to soften dead skin for easier removal. This is the same procedure done when manicuring. Use a soft nail brush to gently scrub dirt from the top of shanks down over the direction the scales grow so they don't become broken. Finish scrubbing the bottom of feet and the underside of the toenails. Thoroughly rinse with clear water.

Use a water-dampened cloth to remove dirt from face, head, wattles, and carnacles. Use the soft nail brush and clear water to clean over and under beak. The finishing touch is oiling these areas so they take on a rich gleaming appearance. After drying, rub a small amount of mineral oil, cod-liver oil, vegetable oil, or petroleum jelly into these skin areas. A nail buffer can be used to buff the beak and toenails.

When transporting, be sure to use a roomy but shallow container which prevents the turkeys from standing and breaking feathers. Handle your birds often before showing so they show well. Hens are the most well-behaved for posing. Use a table or bale of straw so turkey does not walk away. To become familiar with the parts of a turkey, study Fig. 3-16.

SECURING GOOD FERTILITY

Good fertility begins with well-fed but not overfed

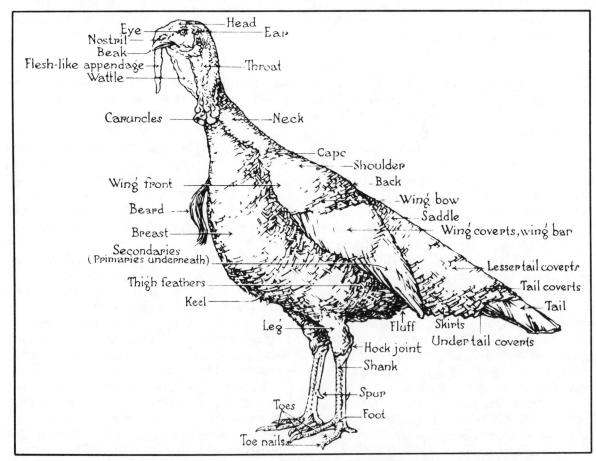

Fig. 3-16. An outline chart of a tom turkey (by Hashime Murayama, © 1930, National Geographic Society)

toms and hens. Overweight toms and hens are the main cause of infertile eggs when natural breeding is attempted. Overweight, top-heavy toms become unbalanced and awkward when mating. Overweight hens become fat and lazy and do not lay well.

Feed the turkeys a balanced ration but in a limited amount beginning at 16 or 20 weeks of age. In the commercial trade this is called a prebreeding or holding diet. If toms and hens are to be mated naturally by handlers, both should be placed on the holding diet. If hens are to be artificially inseminated, only hens need to be on this diet.

A holding diet consists of reducing the feed intake, usually at 20 weeks of age, to 63 percent of what is usually consumed. The feed intake is then gradually increased up to the age when lights are to be used to stimulate production in the hens. Light stimulation for toms preferably begins four weeks before light stimulation for the hens. The gradual increase in feed continues until the hens begin laying. Hens can lay at 35 weeks. A breeder's age of sexual maturity is 30 weeks of age. Turkeys are photo sensitive and lay according to the amount of light they're subjected to. Longer periods of lighting convince their bodies that the longer daylight hours of spring have arrived. Spring is the natural time breeding and laying begin.

Commercial breeders begin light stimulation for hens at 30 weeks of age. Toms are given lighting at 26 weeks of age. A breeder ration is fed at 30 weeks of age. Artificial insemination is begun shortly after hens are 30 weeks of age. At 35 weeks, the hens begin laying. From this point on, the feed intake is gradually decreased along with the normal decrease in egg production. Hens continue to lay for the next 25 weeks on up to 60 weeks of age. During this period, the hens produce 88-93 total eggs. Turkey hatching eggs are expensive to produce even commercially. The trade pays 50 cents for each purchased egg.

At the end of this laying cycle, the hen is usually considered "spent" and is sent for market slaughter. Occasionally hens may be molted for 90 days and then resume another 25 week period of laying. This second laying cycle will produce about 75-80 eggs and they might be somewhat less fertile.

Small-scale handlers can manage their breeders in much the same way. The only difference might be the age of the turkeys. If the turkeys were started earlier than July or August, they could be stimulated with lights to begin laying in the winter months—35 weeks later—if desired. Most handlers, however, will not want to be bothered with such early eggs. They will also not want to hatch and raise such early poults from these eggs.

Many small-scale handlers choose breeders from among a flock of turkeys that are to be butchered for Thanksgiving. This can be a big mistake if the breeders are allowed to continually gain weight past 16 or 20 weeks of age right along with the rest of the flock. Some handlers begin poults in May and grow the flock up to Thanksgiving. By then the birds are 24 or 26 weeks old. Breeders fed normal amounts of rations up to this age will have already become overweight for good spring breeding. Actually, poults to be used strictly for spring breeding do not have to be started until July or August to produce eggs the following spring for May or June hatched poults.

Usually by the time most handlers want to begin collecting turkey eggs for hatching, it is springtime and the required 14 hours of total light has become a reality. Most handlers will not use extra lighting unless very early eggs are desired.

What handlers should endeavor to do is place the breeders on the holding diet at 20 weeks of age, feeding 63 to 70 percent of the normal consumption. Then, 15 weeks before the hens are expected to begin laying (about January) the feed is gradually increased every five weeks up until laying begins. From that point on, the feed is again gradually decreased every five weeks. Five weeks prior to expected laying, a breeder ration should be fed. (Refer to Table 5-6.)

Good fertility will be obtained by keeping the breeder's weights down and feeding the nutrient enriched breeder ration. Artificial insemination is not really a necessity when breeding on a small-scale. Those handlers interested in experimenting with the procedure can use the following described method. Commercial inseminators use various types of sophisticated equipment to make the job more sanitary, faster, and more productive.

The first job is collecting the semen. This procedure is called "milking the tom (or stag)." To ensure that good-quality semen is successfully collected, a handler must have a thorough knowledge of the process. There must also be a clean, well-lit work area. The tom must be relaxed for milking. Avoid chasing toms or rough-handling them. Have him penned beforehand right in the corner next to the table or where you'll be sitting to do the milking.

Quickly grab the tom and swing him onto the table, taking your right hand and grabbing the left leg without resistance. Use the left hand to simultaneously grab the tom's right wing near the body and quickly bring him onto the table on his back. This position for milking will require one person to hold the tom's legs and body and one to do the actual milking. Another method for two people is for one to sit and hold the tom in the lap with the tail end towards another who will be milking. Milking can sometimes be accomplished easier by one person because there is no need to coordinate movements. If milking will be done by one person only, the tom's legs must be held together by a rope or something similar to prevent movement and resistance. To further prevent movement the handler's leg can be placed over the neck of the turkey. The tom lays on his breast with his side towards the handler, the vent area slanted upwards and the head down. Commercial inseminators use a tom milking bench (Fig. 3-17). A special milking bench is also made for guineas.

After the tom is secured, the next step is the actual milking or stimulation process. This technique has been called the massage technique. Before beginning, remove any dirt or feces from the vent area to prevent collecting contaminated semen. The abdominal area is massaged to cause a protrusion of the papila (copulatory organ). The papila is then squeezed to release the semen. Excessive massaging can result in droppings being excreted while milking, which results in dirty semen. Feed can be withheld a half day before collection to help avoid dirty semen.

With one hand holding the tail back, massage the abdominal region until the papila enlarges and partially protrudes from the vent. Move the hand from the abdomen up to the papila to squeeze the semen out with a short, sliding downward movement (Fig. 3-18). A collection device such as a glass beaker or a stoppered funnel should be instantly ready to collect the semen. Commercial inseminators use a collecting device (semen collecting jacket), which is combined with the milking bench. The device forms a vacuum to gently suck the semen into a vial (Fig. 3-18).

Semen collected should be clean, thick, and white. The average tom releases 2/10 to 1/2 cc of semen per milking. Some commercial inseminators use a diluant or semen extender to aid the mobility of the sperm. The collected semen should not be shaken or handled roughly or sperm mobility may be impaired. The sperm will move from the site of introduction up to a primary storage site in the hen. After an egg is laid, the oviduct is then empty for 30-45 minutes. During this time the sperm move further up to a second storage site in the infundibulum (Fig. 3-19). This is where fertilization takes place when an egg is released into the infundibulum (funnel).

To avoid the death of the sperm, it should be introduced into the hen within 30 minutes from the time the first drop was collected. Introducing the good healthy sperm into the correct place in the oviduct of the hen will provide an optimum fertile period of 20 days. This period will give a 90-percent fertility rate. The percentage rate gradually declines until the fertility is zero percent at the end of 40 days. In comparison, a chicken has an optimum fertile period of only 10 days, which drops to zero percent at the end of 20 days. The period of highest fertility occurs a day or two after the hen is inseminated. This fertility period from 90 percent to zero is called the fertility curve.

Although the fertility from one insemination (A.I.) will last a good 20 days, more frequent A.I. should be done at the time the hen begins laying. For example, after the first A.I., wait three days and give a second A.I. Then wait seven days and give the third A.I. From there on, give the A.I. at 14-day intervals the next four times. After the sev-

Fig. 3-17. A tom milking bench in use to restrain a tom when collecting semen at a turkey stud farm. (Courtesy of USDA)

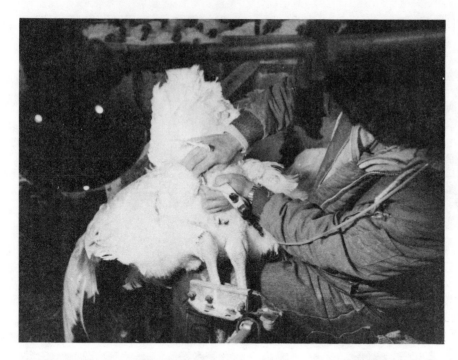

Fig. 3-18. When the semen appears, a collecting device is used to contain it. (Courtesy of International A.I. Inc.)

enth A.I., inseminate at seven-day intervals until egg laying comes to a halt about 15 weeks later.

The actual insemination is done with the handler sitting with the hen's breast in his lap and her head down between the handler's legs with the vent pointing up towards the handler. To insert the semen, a 3/8-inch-wide, 4- or 6-inch long syringe (without a needle) can be used to release the sperm into the oviduct. Use a sterile syringe for each hen to prevent spreading infertility. It's important to keep hens calm before and during the A.I. procedure. Hens should not be roughed-up, scared, and stressed. A relaxed hen is easier to work with, the A.I. will take better, and her egg-laying pattern will not be upset.

With the hen penned next to the handler, grasp both her legs at the same time with the right hand. Simultaneously grab the right wing with the left hand. Immediately straighten the hen's legs and gently place her between your knees to eliminate struggling and resistance. Then place your left hand over the vent with the side of the hand resting firmly against the tail. By firmly moving the hand back and slightly to the left, toward the tail, the edge of the vent opening is pulled back to expose the oviduct.

Lay the tip of the syringe in the center of the everted oviduct and slowly remove the left hand's pressure off the tail. As this is done, slowly move the syringe 3 inches down into the vaginal canal (Refer to Fig. 3-19). No obstructing tissue should be felt. Do not force the syringe or the vagina can become punctured. If the syringe goes smoothly inward 3 inches without obstructions encountered, the syringe is positioned correctly. Release the sperm from the syringe and then withdraw. The left hand holds the tail tightly and the hen is let loose from the knees so the hen quickly and safely gets to her feet. The tail is then let go. Commercial inseminators use a semen dispenser which releases a specific amount of semen into the hen (Fig. 3-20). Even lightweight turkey varieties can benefit from A.I.—obtaining more highly fertile eggs and better hatching.

Ordinarily turkey semen cannot be stored long, but a discovery was made in 1980 which will serve to revolutionize and save the industry millions of dollars in labor and feed costs. The discovery was made by Thomas Sexton and colleagues at the Agricultural Research Service-Avian Physiology

Laboratory at Beltsville, Maryland. They found, by using an automatic stirring device while semen was refrigerated, that after being mixed with a chemical medium, the sperm were prevented from settling and therefore losing mobility and dying. The medium used for mixing is called the Beltsville Poultry Semen Extender, which consists of various salts and sugars of a balanced pH that Sexton has modified several times for semen from chickens, Aleutian Canada geese, ducks, whooping cranes, and seaside sparrows.

This discovery means that Turkey Stud Farms can now exist. These are centralized farms that can now keep only the very best toms and service other breeding farms as well because the semen can be transported for a longer period of time. Before these stud farms became feasible, every breeder had to keep a certain amount of toms for each hen flock. Breeders had little chance to select and use the best toms. Now workers can artificially inseminate the same number of hens in 8 hours which use to take 10 hours. Eliminating toms from the flocks also creates space and feed rations for more hens. This will greatly benefit the sophisticated companies that al-

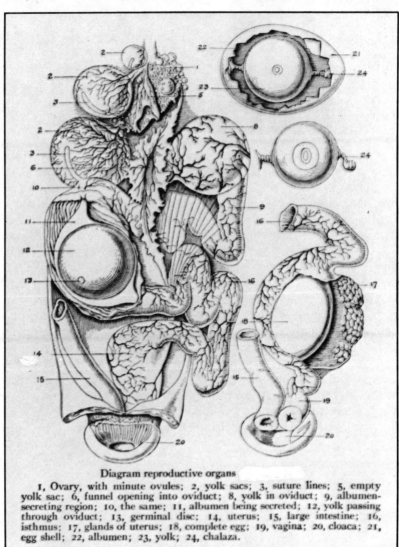

Fig. 3-19. Diagram of hen's reproductive organs and parts of an egg. Site of sperm introduction would be through no. 20 and into no. 19. (From *Commercial Poultry Raising* by H. Armstrong Roberts, 1918)

Diagram reproductive organs

1, Ovary, with minute ovules; 2, yolk sacs; 3, suture lines; 5, empty yolk sac; 6, funnel opening into oviduct; 8, yolk in oviduct; 9, albumen-secreting region; 10, the same; 11, albumen being secreted; 12, yolk passing through oviduct; 13, germinal disc; 14, uterus; 15, large intestine; 16, isthmus; 17, glands of uterus; 18, complete egg; 19, vagina; 20, cloaca; 21, egg shell; 22, albumen; 23, yolk; 24, chalaza.

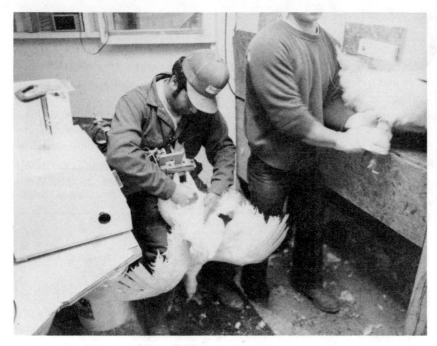

Fig. 3-20. A machine being used which dispenses a specific amount of semen into a hen. (Courtesy of International A.I. Inc.)

ready raise their own grains, breed their own stock, process the turkey products, produce vaccines and diagnose disease in their laboratories, have their own hatcheries and computerized feed mills, and conduct taste panels for meat quality and feed testing programs for their stock.

Obtaining fertile eggs is only part of gaining good hatches. Collecting frequently prevents eggs from becoming broken or overheated. Cool quickly by collecting eggs in open wire baskets. A hen's body temperature is about 105 degrees F. (40 degrees C.). From this temperature, the egg must cool as quickly as possible to 60 degrees F. (15.55 degrees C.) to keep the fertility viable and prevent slow premature incubation which can kill the immature embryo. An egg temperature of 68 degrees F. (20 degrees C.) held for a few hours will deteriorate an egg's quality and hatchability. A freshly laid egg will take over one hour to cool to below 60 degrees F. (15 degrees C.) in a 50-degree F. (10-degree C.) room.

Store hatching eggs at 55 degrees F. (13 degrees C.) in a partially damp area such as a basement. A humidity level between 75 and 85 percent is good. Above 85 percent and molds will begin to grow within the egg. (Turkey eggs used for eating and cooking should be stored at 45 degrees F. between 75 and 85 percent humidity.) Humidity levels can be checked with the same type hygrometer used for incubating. Store hatching eggs no longer than two weeks before placing in incubator or under broody hens for incubation. The longer the eggs are stored, the more the percentage of hatchability is lowered. The incubation time for hatching is 28 days.

Chapter 4

Turkey Equipment

The type of equipment a handler will need and use for his turkeys will depend upon how many turkeys are being raised, the method of raising, whether they are to be confined or ranged, how much time and labor a handler wants to exert in feeding and watering, and the amount of finances to be personally expended. It's good to keep in mind that better, more costly equipment can be less expensive than paying for constant replacements.

Consider the amount of time the equipment will actually be used, based on how many years you plan to raise poultry and how often certain equipment will be used. Much of the same type equipment used for chicks can be utilized for poults, and in this case there will be more wear and tear on it. The important thing is to purchase good-quality equipment that can easily be maintained. The following is intended to help handlers choose basic and nonessential equipment more wisely, because equipment catalogs do not list all the advantages and disadvantages of the products.

New plasticware has been made available only recently; really good innovations and ideas have been slow in coming about for small-scale raisers. There has always been a problem in watering poults successfully without them getting themselves wet from drinking as they push and shove or walk into their water containers. Waterers are now available that keep poults dry. These are explained fully in this chapter under "Waterers." Also available are new plastic feeders, both a trough and a hanging tube type. I'm sure most companies will follow suit in introducing similar plasticware as the public demand increases.

BANDS

These are used mainly to mark poults for purposes of culling when breeding is to be attempted. Made of aluminum or plastic, bands are attached around the leg or pierced into the webbed part of the wing (Fig. 4-1) Bands are applied with a special pliers and wing banding is used for lifetime identification.

First the wing band is pushed through the webbed portion of the wing (similar to human ear piercing). The pliers are then brought into position

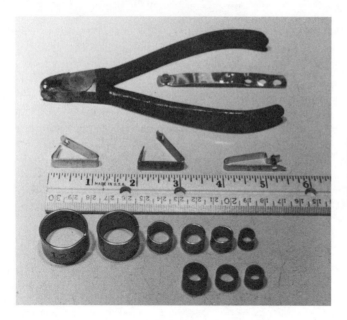

Fig. 4-1. Various bands and applicator, from top left to right: legband clincher with aluminum legband, aluminum poult wing-tag, steel poult wing-tag, lightweight "Zip" wing band, duckling butt-end legbands, and three large to small pigeon bandettes. (Bands courtesy of National Band and Tag Co.)

to finish the application (Fig. 4-2). One type, called the tab-end zip wing band by National Band and Tag Co., uses no tool to apply. The wing bands for turkeys are available in two sizes in the aluminum type. The 1 1/8 inch is for poults, and the 1 3/4 inch is for larger turkeys. When the small sizes are placed on poults, they usually become more difficult to easily see when the turkey gets larger. Some handlers place the larger tag on the birds when they grow older. There is also a large size of steel construction. The tool-applied bands are considered tamperproof. These stay in place better than most leg bands and don't seem to bother the bird as much.

As turkeys grow large it's sometimes difficult to read leg bands unless you're checking for color only. Wing bands can be inspected easily on a large turkey by grabbing both wings, pushing the bird to the ground and spreading the wing outward. The same wing, either left or right, should be banded on all poults so inspection is easier. If your purpose of identification is for proof of ownership should your turkeys stray or become stolen, wing bands leave noticeable marks if removed. Wing bands are available in colors but are usually difficult to see on a large bird.

Colored plastic spiral and bandette leg bands are used for very small poults. As the bird grows, a larger size must replace the smaller size. There are plastic spirals up to 1-inch diameter to fit the legs of large tom turkeys. Spirals come in single fold and double fold. A single is only one and one-half of a wound rod. A double is somewhat safer and is two full turns of plastic rod. Spirals can be a nuisance to replace as the bird grows but they do have the advantage of being available in a variety of colors that can be spotted easily as the bird walks around. They are inexpensive and do not require tools to apply and remove, although for proof of ownership they can be removed easily, leaving no marks. Otherwise, spirals stay put very well.

Adjustable aluminum tongue and slot bands that can be applied to either a leg or wing are available, but if used on turkeys will not adjust to the width of a large tom's leg. If used on the wing, it is not large enough to be seen easily on grown birds and is not tamperproof.

Aluminum rivet seal leg bands that are sealed with special pliers have some drawbacks. Unless using only color for identification, numbers and letters can be hard to read. It seems the bands must always be wiped of stuck on mud and dirt before they can be read. I've found they eventually come off even when carefully applied—butt-end bands are better.

BEAK AND TOE TRIMMING DEVICES

Electric beak trimmers shorten the upper beak by cutting and heat cauterizing the cut (Fig. 4-3). Nail clippers can be used carefully but clotting the end of the beak must be done. Electrically trimmed beaks last longer than those trimmed with nail clippers. If done at one day of age the very tip of the beak remains for 10-15 days, allowing poults to eat and drink properly. The beak grows out again and the operation must be repeated if you want the beaks to stay trimmed.

Electric beak trimming devices can be an unprofitable expenditure for some small-scale raisers, especially if the poults will be marketed later. But for handlers who insist their poults are beak-trimmed, the accuracy provided by the use of these devices cannot be beat because the right amount is removed each time quickly and with very little bleeding. The same device can be used to toe-trim using a different attachment. (Also see Chapter 7.)

Nail clippers can be used for both beak and toe-trimming day-olds. Desnooding is done with small nail clippers or a strawberry huller at one day of age. Time must be taken to assure accuracy, but with experience, 100 poults can be taken care of safely and quickly in 15 minutes.

To beak trim safely, cut only the upper portion of the beak where the egg tooth ends. If bleeding does occur, quickly dip the beak into fine powdered mash until the blood clots. The toes are trimmed

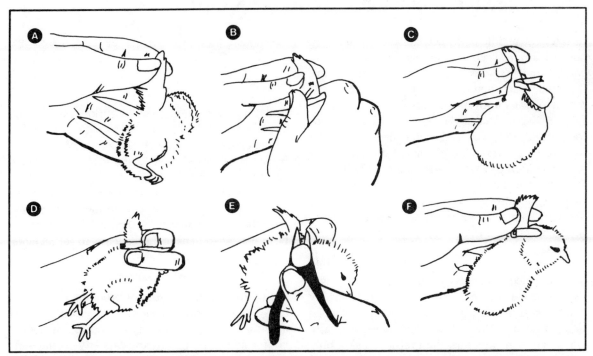

Fig. 4-2. (A) Hold chick in left hand with tip of right wing between thumb and forefinger. Hold chick's head between second and third finger. (B) With band between thumb and forefinger of right hand, push band through web of wing directly at the elbow joint. Be careful not to puncture the flesh or tear the tendon at the leading edge of the wing. (C) Band as applied before clinching. (D) With thumb and forefinger of the left hand, close the band until the rivet is inserted into the hole of the band. (E) While holding band closed, clinch the rivet with band pliers. (F) Turn band with rivet under wing. This will not allow the band to turn over end of wing. The chick is now banded for life. (Photographs simulated with permission of Hy-Line International)

Fig. 4-3. Beak trimming machine showing turkey beak placement over beak support. (Courtesy of Lyon Electric Co.)

through the middle of the second scale. Usually all toes are trimmed. For use as a marking system any combination of toes can be trimmed. When toes are trimmed, place poults in a box with clean, soft towels or rags until blood clots.

Personally, I've never found a need to beak or toe-trim day-olds. Later, if cannibalism occurs, the few troublemakers can be singled out and beak-trimmed. Rather than toe-trimming, I've tried to keep the older poults quiet and managed well so they don't pile on top of one another. As for breeders, toms can be rough with their claws on the backs of hens. In this case, turkey saddles can be used.

Desnooding of toms kept for breeding is highly recommended. When toms fight over right to reign, they grab one another's snood, which considerably lengthens as they become upset. This snood can be pulled loose and the turkeys could bleed to death. No snood, and the toms will grab neck skin only with no serious harm. Desnooding has even been done by some handlers by using the thumb and forefinger nails and pinching it off. No serious bleeding is caused when desnooding but slight pressure with a cotton ball can be applied for a few seconds. In a straight-run box of poults all can be

desnooded rather than sorting them and doing toms only.

BELLS

Bells were sometimes used by turkey raisers long ago to keep track of their turkeys out on range. It's a type of legband with a few large round bells. The legbands were made of leather and strapped around the bottom of the shank of one leg. It's fairly difficult to find these odd contraptions unless a "back-to-the land" type catalog can be found. The band could be made from leather shoe strings. These can be of use when hens on range leave to set on eggs.

BROODERS

There are four main types of brooding equipment today that operate using gas or electric. Most manufacturers give capacity ratings for chicks but not for poults. Some rate the capacity for day-olds only, but since the brooders are usually used for up to six weeks of age, a handler should purchase a brooder that will accommodate them to this age. Allow 6 square inches of heated area for day-olds and 1/2 square foot of heated area for each six-week-old poult.

The least expensive brooding system is the single-lamp reflectors which are hung over the poults' brooding area—for use when only a few are to be brooded. Although these might be more difficult to operate properly by beginners, practice and perseverance will make you a pro. The temperature is controlled by raising, lowering, and adding lamps. The metal reflector serves to reflect bulb heat toward the poults and helps to prevent moisture from dripping onto the bulb from above. Four-lamp brooders are available with flat-formed guards attached to allow the lamp to be hung or set on the floor. The four-lamp brooder contains a thermostat that controls one bulb in order to regulate the total heat output (Fig. 4-4).

The infrared glass bulbs for these lamp brooders are usually purchased separately using 250-watt red or white glass. The red glass infrared bulbs usually cost twice as much as the white frosted, but will prevent cannibalism to a much greater degree. Cannibalism often starts because bright lights show up every speck of feed and de-

Fig. 4-4. A four-lamp reflector brooder with wafer thermostat. (Courtesy of Brower Equipment Company)

bris on the backs of poults. The red bulb lessens the attraction of these small specks by making everything appear one color—red.

Lamp brooders are more effective when used in a partially closed-off brooder area so heat does not readily escape. Fewer single-lamp brooders are needed in a partially enclosed box-like structure. If these are used in an open pen in a building, the temperature is harder to control, more lamps will be needed, or the four-lamp brooder with the thermostat might run constantly trying to keep a set temperature in a cold room.

For single-lamp brooders, allow 6 square inches of brooder space for each day-old poult and hang lamps 2-3 feet apart to cover the brooding area. Additional lamps are hung as the poults outgrow the area. A rule of thumb is one lamp for every 50 day-olds and one for every 10 six-week-olds. If an enclosure is used, the lamps will maintain the heat better and are simply raised to lower the temperature as the poults grow. The four-lamp brooders throw off heat in a 5- × -6-foot area. Although this unit will brood hundreds of day-old poults, the unit is quickly outgrown and will brood only 120 six-week-old poults unless in an enclosure. Be sure lamps are not near enough to surfaces to cause a fire. If placed in an enclosure, test the heat by placing your hand on the sidewalls and ceiling. If it's hot to touch, a fire can be started. Install and use lamps with common sense.

Four-lamp brooders naturally cost more than a single lamp, but four single lamps with bulbs will cost about the same as one four-lamp brooder with bulbs, but do not have a thermostat.

Another type brooder is the floor brooder. It sets on legs and is raised as the poults grow. The shape varies from round, square, or gable-roofed, to octagon with raised or flat tops. Most floor brooders manufactured today are the square, flat-roofed, electric variety. The others are usually found second-hand. These electric brooders are rated at 110- to 120-volt and 250- to 1,000-watt. All contain a thermostat to control the temperature, which can be set. Four-foot-square models are usually rated for 400 chicks. Although these floor brooders contain the heat better around the poults

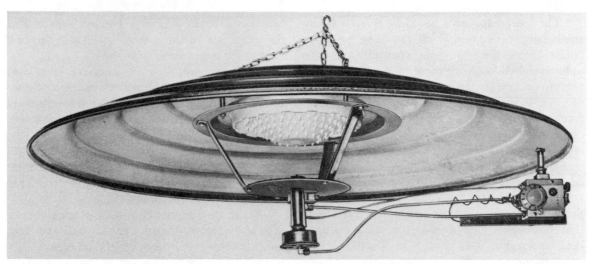

Fig. 4-5. Hanging radiant brooders such as this produce infrared rays from the center ceramic cone. (Courtesy of Shenandoah Manufacturing Co., Inc.)

by use of a curtain, the heating area is only what's directly under the brooder. A 4-foot-square floor brooder would contain only 16 square feet (2,304 square inches). This is enough space for about 384 day-old poults, but only enough for 64 six-week-old poults. Two-foot square models are also available. These would take care of 16 poults up to six weeks of age.

Electric floor brooders are not as energy efficient as the hanging radiant brooders. Because the legs are almost always in contact with damp litter they become corroded. The adjustment slots for raising the legs become corroded too, eventually preventing any adjustment for height to be made at all. The legs can be replaced with angle iron when completely worn, however, and the brooder height can be raised by setting bricks under each leg when adjustments are badly corroded. Prices for the small floor brooders begin at about $40.

For brooding very large amounts of poults, the hanging radiant-type brooders take care of the largest amount of birds (Fig. 4-5). Most are shaped like an upside-down, 4-foot saucer. They operate mainly on natural and bottle gas, although electric ones are available. The principle advantage behind these gas models is that the radiant heated ceramic cones in the center of the dome which produce infrared rays continue to heat the area even after the

thermostat shuts the element off. These rays only heat poults and objects, they do not warm the air.

Most gas models heat a 12-foot-diameter area and will take care of 2,592 day-old poults or 432 six-week old poults. Electric hanging models will heat only the area directly under the canopy. This will accommodate 360 day-olds or 60 six-week-old poults.

Also available are small, box-shaped models—using natural or bottle gas—that do not have a canopy and are hung from the ceiling. These are positioned so the infrared rays are directed toward the birds. All gas-operated infrared brooders can be utilized for other baby farm animals such as lambs and baby pigs. Gas models cost more than electric because more is involved in manufacturing the fittings. Prices are just over $100.

Battery stack brooders are becoming very popular with small-scale raisers (Fig. 4-6). Commercial growers cannot economically afford to use batteries to their advantage because of the high cost in purchasing and using. These are for the small-scale raisers who want to brood small amounts of birds, be able to water and feed them quickly, and keep them nearby to watch—as in a basement. The trays below the racks allow for cleaning the droppings without moving the birds and feeders as would be necessary with a cardboard box.

Battery brooders of today are designed to be stacked on top of each other or placed into racks that will hold five brooders. The older types can still be used. Many of these styles were heavy and contained several stationary compartments in one frame, making a very heavy and awkward piece of equipment. Not many single units were made years ago. For the small-scale raiser, however, lower secondhand costs may outweigh the disadvantages of an older model.

Most new single-compartment battery brooders are approximately 2 × 3 feet in diameter (not counting attached feed and water pans). They will brood 48 day-old poults for about one week and 12-15 four-week-old poults. Because of their limited height, poults should not remain in them for more than four weeks or the tops of their heads will rub the brooder ceiling and scalp the birds. Most new batteries are only 9 inches high inside. One single unit costs about $100. A five-unit with rack is about $600.

The basic features of all battery starting brooders are the same: They have removable dropping pans with wire floors above; all are operated by electricity; temperature is controlled by a thermostat and regulated with a setscrew. Most newer single-compartment models contain the heating element in the back portion with a curtain to help hold the heat in the rear.

Batteries are not without disadvantages. Many assume batteries will prevent the disease coccidi-osis, but these brooders can, in fact, make the problem worse. Birds on litter build up an immunity to the disease, so the severity of the outbreaks is not realized. The disease is spread by contact with the droppings. The brooder racks in batteries do collect small amounts of droppings in the crevices unless they are laboriously scrubbed daily. If a coccidiostat in the feed is fed to battery birds, the disease it brings on at about four weeks of age to provide immunity, will be a more severe form. On the other hand, if no coccidiostat is fed and racks are always scrubbed, the birds cannot build up an immunity. Then, when placed out on litter, they are suddenly attacked by the infectious organisms.

Batteries will not operate properly in rooms of less than 50 degrees F. (10 degrees C.) This means many handlers in colder areas who want to start their birds early, cannot do so in an outdoor building. They might not be able to do so in an unheated basement or garage either. They'll only find the heating element running constantly trying to keep the set temperature. This can be devastating to poults because they must have the correct temperature to survive. Even temperatures 5 degrees below required can stress poults to a point of death.

Poults have a bad habit of going near the inside plugs of older model battery brooders and near the wafer thermostats of newer batteries. They are able to remove the plug from the outlet or turn the wafer so the brooder becomes cold. Sometimes they'll knock the wafer completely off the set-

Fig. 4-6. Battery stack brooder showing cutaway view of insulation board and wafer thermostat. (Courtesy of Brower Equipment Company)

screw, in which case the brooder gets extremely hot. You can easily burn your hands by trying to replace it unless the entire brooder is turned off and allowed to cool. Wafers must have a guard constructed around them to prevent poults from touching them. Quarter-inch stiff cage wire fabric can be bent to form a box around the wafer unit. Be sure to trim all short wire ends that protrude near the bottom and bring the shaped guard down as far as possible so poults do not get feet or heads caught. The inside plugs of older models must be taped or wired in place to keep poults from pulling them from the socket.

The 1/2-inch spaced wire rack floors of batteries will cripple poults if a handler does not use precautions. The longer length of a poult's leg causes the hock joint to get caught down in the wire when young poults sit and try to get up. Any poult seen sitting for any length of time over bare wire should be inspected. If you notice it before the joint swells, hold the two sections of the leg—the shank and lower thigh (drumstick)—together and carefully remove the leg with the widest width of the hock joint pointing toward the corners of the spacing for easier removal. If swelling of the joint is considerable, the leg cannot easily be removed. The wire can be cut (and later repaired) but poults in this condition usually become crippled. This problem can be prevented by thickly lining the entire rack floor with folded newspapers or old towels for the first five days. After this time, the legs grow enough so they do not easily get caught.

I've seen many feed stores use these brooders or wire cages for day-old poults. Because of lack of experience or the store's interest only in the promotional aspects of selling their feed, the dealers place the poults on the bare wire. Many poults can work their leg loose from the wire, but usually not without damage. The damage does not show until the unlucky customer's poults get some weight on them at about four weeks of age. The previously injured poult begins to show obvious signs of crippling. The best thing a handler can do if these "feed promotion poults" must be purchased at a feed store, is to check the hock joints of each poult purchased for signs of any red or dark-colored bruises or swelling.

Another disadvantage is that the water troughs supplied with batteries allow day-old poults to get wet. The troughs must be closed up for the first few days and small founts used on the wire floor. If the battery can be opened from the top, placing the filled founts into the brooder poses no problem. If the fount must go in from the side, however, it takes a lot of patience and experience to keep the overly aggressive, inquisitive poults from running and piling out of the opening as the fount is being replaced or removed. Poults can become injured as they fall to the floor.

Dropping pans in batteries used for poults must be cleaned frequently. If not, as the filled trays are slid out for cleaning, manure is knocked onto the floor or into waterers below, fouling drinking water. As with any brooding system, handlers should check daily for dead poults. With batteries, dark corners are sometimes difficult to inspect. Any dead poults that are overlooked can be difficult and annoying to remove later as they are trampled and embedded into the wire.

Poults in batteries usually acquire rickets easier than floor-raised poults. Extra Vitamin D must be given until they are allowed outdoors under the direct rays of the sun.

For display purposes, I've used batteries for poults for many years, but they can be difficult for those handlers not accustomed to their use.

CAGES

When a handler first receives his day-old poults, cages are usually one of the last things on his mind. A beginner without cages might not realize he should have rounded some up until he needs them. Perhaps the poults must be moved from a brooder to a brooder house or grow-out building. If poults are being vaccinated, wing-clipped, or beak-trimmed, small cages can help keep poults sorted during the procedure. The poults can be taken from the cage, worked on, then placed back under the brooder without mix-ups over who was or wasn't worked on.

Boxes work fine for very young poults, but a few small 1- × -2-foot cages with handles are very handy in the building. For ease of handling, boxes can have handles cut on sides. Boxes are not always obtainable and are more awkward to carry than these small-handled cages. There can be a problem with disposal of boxes too. Just six poults who are six weeks old can weigh 24 pounds, so cages should be small and lightweight.

Medium-sized cages aren't used much when raising turkeys. Very small cages and extra-large cages always come in handy for turkeys. Grown turkeys are sometimes transported to a butchering facility or to a show. Boxes don't fit the bill for a dozen or more birds weighing 300 pounds or more. Cages for grown turkeys are used mainly for transporting long distances. They are not usually used for carrying these heavy birds. Plastic oversized (34 × 24 × 13 inches high) poultry coops (crates) are available for grown turkeys, but even these will allow only a maximum of three adult hens or two large toms to be safely transported. If a handler transports his turkeys to shows, the plastic coops can be an advantage because the 13-inch height keeps turkeys from standing and moving around.

If turkeys are to ride in an open bed of a truck, the coops should still be covered lightly with a porous (breathing) tarp to prevent drafts on the birds. These coops do have small enough holes in the sidewalls to contain even four-week-old poults. For most purposes though, the coops can be an unprofitable expenditure for many small-scale turkey raisers.

A more economical and useful cage for small-scale raisers is one made of lightweight galvanized rabbit hutch wire. The height need only be 13-15 inches. The dimensions of the cages are entirely up to a handler. The cages are usually placed into the bed of a truck and the turkeys then placed into them. Cages sized to fit the bed of a truck can easily be planned for. If turkeys are to be butchered on the farm, these same cages can be used as a holding crate to empty the turkeys' crops. Raised up off the ground on blocks, the caged turkeys are prevented from eating litter so dressing out the birds is more sanitary and less troublesome.

Even though large turkeys are not usually carried around in cages, be sure cages are lightweight; wooden boxes and crates are bothersome to move and store. They also do not last long if exposed to the weather and become extremely heavy if rained on.

CHUTES

If large lots of turkeys are raised, chutes can be used to direct turkeys up into vehicles or from vehicles to buildings. A lightweight chute can be built from wire hog panels. A heavy chute that need not be moved much can be built from wood. (Refer to Fig. 3-1.)

FEEDERS

Unless using feeder trays on a battery brooder, feeders must be provided for poults. Clean, discarded egg cartons do not work well with poults although they do with chicks. Most cartons are usually tipped over easily as poults step on the edges. If egg cartons must be used in a pinch the first day or two, be sure the styrofoam cartons are free of lice by dipping them into bleach water, rinsing, then thoroughly drying. Lice can be unintentionally transmitted from homegrown eggs to poults from the cartons used for storing eggs, and lice can kill baby poults. If cartons are used too long, poults might pick off styrofoam pieces and choke. Use a heavy platter the first few days instead.

A good poult feeder keeps poults from walking on the feed, can be refilled easily, will hold at least one day's supply of feed, and can be washed quickly and easily. For very small poults, its sides should be no taller than 2 inches to allow poults easy access to feed. A wooden reel trough feeder can be constructed (Fig. 4-7). For a few box-raised poults, the very small, 6-inch-diameter, round, nine-hole feeders can be used, but will only suffice for about two weeks. These only hold about 1 cup of feed.

For very large amounts of poults brooded under hanging or floor brooders, many commercial growers use "feeder lids." These are made of molded, high-impact polypropylene plastic and

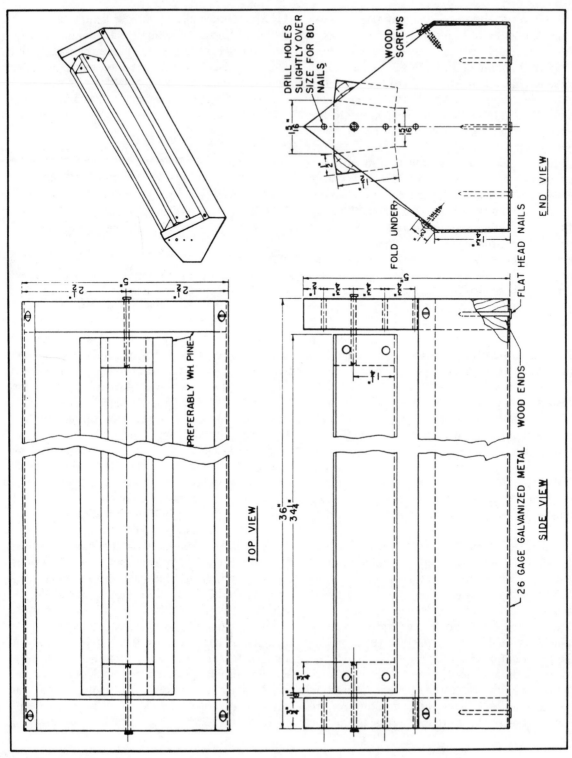

Fig. 4-7. A good homemade feeder to start poults at about one week of age. (Courtesy of Michigan State University Agricultural Engineering Dept.)

measure about 22 × 14 × 2 inches high with dimpled bottoms for foot traction. The trays are very inexpensive and can be washed, stacked, and reused. The poults are able to see the feed and eat more freely. These are used for about one week. In large areas they should be spaced around the brooder with a portion of the lid slid under the edge of floor brooders.

The newest advance in poultry feeders are the various styles of plasticware. These units can last longer than galvanized ware, are easier to clean, do not have sharp cutting edges, will not rust, and are lower priced than metal products. Their bright colors can also help to attract poults to feed. Following is a background on some of them, with advantages and possible disadvantages for use with poults.

The plastic reel feeders measure about 20 inches from outside edge to outside edge. The four-sided reel spins freely to keep poults from roosting over the feed. One particular model has a snap end so two feeders can be attached to one another (See Fig. 2-3). It holds 4 cups of feed. These are excellent for poults on up to three weeks of age. Older poults can easily tip the feeders when they place their feet on the edges of a partially filled feeder. Attaching two feeders together helps prevent this. Heavier metal reel-top troughs are available in 12-, 18-, 24- and 36-inch lengths.

Another model 18 inches long contains two compartments separated by a divider (Fig. 4-8, left). It does not tip as easily, but poults are able to walk over the top of feed and soil it with droppings. Although one side can be used for drinking water, this is not recommended for poults because they can get into the water too easy.

The 26-hole feeder/waterer keeps poults off of their feed and out of their water (Fig. 4-8, right). The center divider allows feed in one side and water in the other. Because the water can be spilled easily while being carried, it must be filled at the place the poults drink. This can be a problem with curious poults who constantly get in the way. As a feeder only, the unit works well if a handler does not mind the small extra chore of snapping the lid in place. Metal slide-top feeders are also available in 12-, 18- and 24-inch lengths. These can easily cut fingers as they are being cleaned.

Wire-top galvanized chick troughs help prevent poults from walking over feed. These can also be used for water but must be filled in place to prevent spilling. They are available in 24- and 36-inch lengths (Fig. 4-9). Older poults can use the metal reel feeders with adjustable legs (Fig. 4-10). The 2 1/4-inch-deep troughs can be raised from 1/4 inch to 2 inches from the floor. They're manufactured

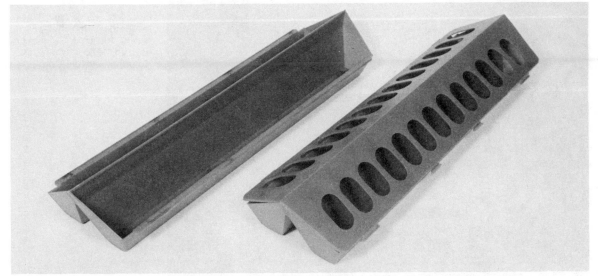

Fig. 4-8. Divided plastic feeder on left, 26-hole divided feeder-waterer on right. (Courtesy of Kuhl Corp.)

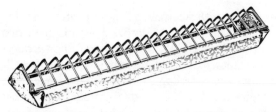

Fig. 4-9. Wire-top galvanized chick troughs such as this will help poults from walking over feed. (Courtesy of New Delphos Manufacturing Co.)

Fig. 4-10. Adjustable metal reel-type feeder that can be used for day-old poults and older when adjusted up to the 4 1/4-inch height. (Courtesy of New Delphos Manufacturing Co.)

in 36- and 48-inch lengths. Larger types are available with a 2-inch spaced wire grill top and adjustable wire legs. Pans on these are wider, come 40 and 60 inches long and 3 inches deep. Larger metal reel tops with adjustable wire legs are also available for larger poults. The trough is 60 inches long,

7 1/4 inches wide, and 3 1/2 inches deep.

A better type of feeder for poults might be the new plastic unit that can be placed on the floor or hung from the ceiling and raised as poults grow (Fig. 4-11). The feeder is filled from the top and includes a lid and rope for hanging. Also included

Fig. 4-11. A plastic chick feeder that can be hung from ceiling for older poults or used on the floor for day-olds. (Courtesy of Kuhl Corp.)

is a feed saver grill that helps prevent poults from shoving feed out with their beaks. The unit holds 22 pounds (10 kg.) of feed. One can be used for each set of 50 day-old poults. Provide one for every 15 poults that are four weeks old. Eight-week-olds will require one for every eight poults. At six weeks of age, poults can graduate to the hen-size hanging feeders that hold 55 pounds (25 kg.) of feed. These are available in plastic and metal.

Metal hanging chick feeders are also available for day-old and older poults. These are 1 3/4-3 inches deep on the base and hold 16-50 pounds of feed. Base pan diameters are about 12-15 inches. Lids are available to protect feed and prevent poults from becoming trapped inside.

When feeding older turkeys, a trough, hanging tube, or hoppers are used indoors. Ordinary round feed pans do not work well with turkeys because they constantly overturn them.

Trough-type feeders are not specifically manufactured for turkeys. These will usually have to be constructed from wood. Types manufactured for chickens will not work well for adult turkeys because the larger types are set on legs and contain a small roost along the side. Turkeys are lia-ble to knock these over and might even try out the roost. Also, most have wire grills over the feed area that must be at least 2 3/4 inches apart or turkeys cannot fit their head down through.

Hanging tube and pan feeders work great with turkeys (Fig. 4-12). These are gravity feeders that are hung from the ceiling. Most are made of galvanized metal. Kuhl has recently made available a 55-pound capacity plastic tube feeder with lid. Because of the heavy weight of feed, these metal feeders usually hold 25 to 40 pounds of feed only. Larger turkey flocks will require additional hanging feeders. One hanging feeder holding 40 pounds of feed being refilled weekly would suffice for a half dozen mature turkeys.

Tube feeders have adjustable tubes, bottoms, or grills to restrict the amount of feed flowing down into the pan. This helps prevent waste when the turkeys beak the feed sideways from the pan. This type of adjustment can only be done with gravity-type feeders. Fine mash can occasionally get caught up in the tube even if adjustment is opened for full-feed flow. This is quickly remedied by manually rocking the tube back and forth a few times until the feed is shaken down.

Fig. 4-12. Turkeys can begin to use hanging tube feeders at an early age to save a handler labor, as with these six-week-olds.

Some tube feeders come with a 3- or 4-inch-deep pan. Some pans are sold separately from the tube. A 3-inch-deep pan is acceptable, but a 4-inch-deep pan is better. Another accessory from one company is a round grill that slides down over the tube and lays over the exposed feed. This can also prevent beaking (bridging) the feed out of the pan.

Most adult turkeys will attempt to roost on the tube's upper edge. They soon discover there's not enough room and fall backwards. Covers can be purchased separately for some tube feeders but are usually unnecessary with large grown turkeys.

Because tube feeders are hung from the ceiling with chains or heavy wire, they can be adjusted to the exact height of a turkey's shoulders. They will also last longer because they are not in direct contact with corrosive manure and damp litter.

The main drawback with most tube feeders is the narrow width of the tube top. If they were built somewhat wider on the top, it would be much easier to fill them with feed. Also, it's rough trying to steady these feeders as feed is being poured into them—the swaying can cause a handler to spill feed all over. Shenandoah has a wide-lip tube feeder specially designed for turkeys. It contains three chains to help keep the feeder more evenly balanced (Fig. 4-13).

Hoppers are the largest type feeders manufactured for small-scale growers. They are also called range or tank feeders. They can be used on range with a lid and rain shield or indoors. Made of galvanized metal, the smallest can be purchased in a 150-pound capacity with lid and optional reversible stand and rain shield or as a complete unit. It's approximately 36 inches tall. The next size is a 700-pound capacity complete with lid and rain shield, and skids for easier moving. This unit has a pre-set, 3-inch feed flow with an optional adjustment band for restricting feed opening to 2 inches. A 750-pound capacity unit is also available with lid, rain shield, and skids. Warner has the largest turkey feeders. These are available in 1,000- and 1,400-pound capacities and stand 41 and 45 inches tall. They come complete with lid, either a built-in or skirted rain shield, skids, and have an outside lever to easily control feed flow (Fig. 4-14). Others

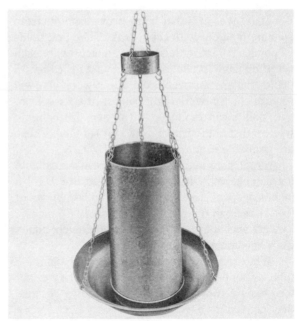

Fig. 4-13. An evenly balanced hanging tube feeder such as this will be much easier to fill. (Courtesy of Shenandoah Manufacturing Co., Inc.)

are adjusted by snap lug hooks, an outside hook and wire, or the entire band must be rotated manually.

FEED SCOOPS

Feed scoops are not usually given much notice, but a poorly designed scoop can cause aching muscles if a lot of feed has to be scooped up. Many handlers use bowls, pans, and pails to scoop small amounts of feed. If not done carefully, feed can be wasted and accidentally spilled when filling small feeders.

Purchase scoops made to last so replacements are not necessary. Excellent stainless steel scoops can be purchased at restaurant supply stores. Plastic scoops tend to break too easily—there's a lot of weight and pressure the scoop must endure. Test your scoop before purchase to be sure it fits your individual hand and will not cause strain in your forearm. While holding the scoop's handle, apply pressure on the scoop end. If you feel a pull in the forearm, try a shorter scoop. Long scoops can require two hands to dig into and lift feed up. A short, fat rounded, stainless steel scoop is ideal. Remem-

No. T-928

Fig. 4-14. With a feed capacity of 1,400 pounds, this 235-pound range feeder is the largest manufactured today. (Courtesy of the Warner Corp.)

ber, a lot of feed will be scooped to young poults. By three weeks of age, each poult will be consuming almost 1 pound (.45 kg.) of feed weekly. Scoops can be used for all poultry, from day-old to adult.

FEED STORAGE CONTAINERS

Feed that is not being used should be stored in an insect- and rodent-proof container, and within easy access to where it is used. Rats can chew through thin metal and thick wood containers. Good containers for storing feed are 55-gallon metal drums (barrels), heavy metal trash cans, and 50-pound lard tins. All should have tight-fitting lids. Lard tins can be purchased at a butcher supply store. Drums can sometimes be obtained for free and will hold 300 pounds of feed. Feed can be poured into these containers or bags of feed simply set into them. Be sure all containers are perfectly dry—especially in the bottom—or mold can form, hardening and spoiling the feed for further use. If stored outdoors, prop the bottom of the container under one side so rain

will quickly run off the lid. Sometimes a rock or other weight is needed to keep the lid snug and prevent the wind from blowing it off. In buildings, it's best to keep the container up off damp litter or ground to prevent rusting and condensation on the interior which can mold the feed. Heavy metal-lined boxes are sometimes used to store feed, but are more cumbersome to move about than a drum or barrel even when empty.

FENCING

If a fenced pen must be built to confine poults within a building, it must have 1-inch spacings to prevent day-olds from slipping through. Using treated wood around the bottom first with the chick size fencing above will help prevent the bottom edges of the fencing from rusting. Damp litter and floors can cause fence bottoms to rust out within two years. A good grade of chick fencing positioned over a 2-foot height of plywood, treated boards, or railroad ties will be usable for about five years.

83

The wood barriers will also help keep out drafts from across the floor. When constructing the barrier, keep in mind the amount of litter build-up that might affect the initial constructed height later. If poults will remain in the same pen throughout brooding and you practice the built-up litter system rather than complete litter removal, litter can easily build up to a 2-foot height within that time. It's always the bottoms of indoor pens that will rust first. Outdoors, it's still a good practice to build fencing over wood first so that it will last.

Fencing other than chicken wire or cage wire is available, but because of the larger spacings it can only be used for larger poults. Welded wire is fairly inexpensive but cannot be used until poults are about six weeks old. Welded wire should be used indoors only because it rusts quickly near the welds when exposed to the weather. This causes the welds to break loose and the fence is soon useless. Indoors, off damp litter and ground, welded wire fencing can last a number of years.

Woven wire is best used for larger turkeys. If woven wire poultry fence is found, the bottom will have 1- to 4-inch graduated spacings. With the smaller spacings near the bottom, poults of four to six weeks can be confined. Regular woven wire livestock fencing can only be used for grown turkeys because poults can slip through the bottom. Woven wire can be used indoors or out, but it's more economical to use a cheaper wire indoors and the more expensive woven wire outdoors. For a multi-purpose pen, a 2-3-foot strip of chicken wire can be placed around the bottom diameter of a woven or welded wire fencing.

In planning the pen size, remember the larger the pen, the less likely turkeys are to fly over if it is not covered. If you have problems with turkeys flying over fencing, you can clip their wings. A pen at least 60 inches in height is recommended; 72 inches is better for all size turkeys when not covered. When purchasing any fencing, the smaller the gauge number, the thicker and stronger the wire. Stronger wire naturally will last longer.

FOUNT HEATERS

Fount heaters are used mainly for handlers who keep breeders throughout cold months. Birds can go longer without feed than water. A water warmer will keep water from freezing so the turkeys have more water available to them. There are three main types of water heaters: The base heater, rod heater, and the heat cable.

Base heaters are run by electricity and are used under a fount. One type has a 100-watt element and a thermostat that keeps drinking water at 50 to 55 degrees F. (10-13 degrees C.). It operates only when water temperature begins to go below 50 degrees F. The 16-inch base has a 6-foot long cord and operates on 110-120-volt, ac. Another base heater is 14 3/4 inches wide, 250-watt and 115-volt ac. The thermostat has a bimetal switch to keep water temperature between 90 and 130 degrees F. (32-54 degrees C.) (Fig. 4-15).

Because drinking water only needs to be just above freezing, a base heater that keeps water temperature above 32 degrees F. (0 degrees C.) is sufficient. Any warmer and the unit will cost more to operate. These heaters should be kept off damp litter or they will rust quickly.

Rod heaters must be used with caution. If the turkeys trip over the cord and knock the heater out onto the litter, some can become hot enough to start the litter on fire. These are simply 8-inch or longer rods heated by electricity and controlled by a thermostat. They are used directly in the open pan of water. They should not be used in plastic pans—if the pan should become dry, the cold air will cause the thermostat to keep the heating unit on.

The last type of fount heater is the heat cable made specifically for the narrow water troughs.

Fig. 4-15. This electric base heater can be used with 3-, 5- and 8-gallon founts. (Courtesy of New Delphos Manufacturing Co.)

They plug into any 110- or 120-volt ac outlet and operate only when surface temperatures approach freezing. These thin cables are available in 10- and 15-foot lengths and have a hermetically sealed thermostat.

GUARDS

Guards are a continuous barrier to keep poults confined near their source of brooder heat. Brooder guards such as this are used for about two weeks. Guards made specifically for this purpose are usually difficult to find. A folding guard can be made with 1-×-8s and hinges. Thick plywood or 1-×-8-inch boards can also be set into 2-×-2-inch stands, hurdle-style. Keep lengths of each section short, perhaps 1 foot, to prevent obvious corners from being formed when set in place around poults. Poults might crowd into these corners to sleep away from the heat. A four-section guard can be made, but the four corners must be rounded out with sheet metal or 1/4-inch fencing. The height of the brooder guards should be at least 8 inches for poults. An 8-inch strip of ribbed galvanized sheet metal can be used to form a circle around poults. The ribbing helps keep the strip from falling over. A brooder guard can also be made with welded galvanized cage wire with 1/4-inch or 1/2-inch spacings. Purchased in a 32-inch width, the wire can be cut into 8-inch strips and fastened securely between strips with wire or clips to form a circle (Fig. 4-16).

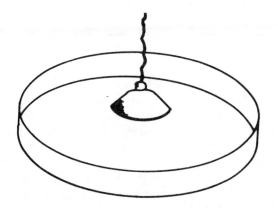

Fig. 4-16. A 32-×-36-inch piece of 1/4-inch or 1/2-inch welded wire will make a round brooder guard of about 3 feet wide.

Another type of guard is the corner guard used to keep poults from piling into dangerous open corners. Poults are attracted to open corners. They will crowd into them to sleep, but finding it's too cold there, they'll climb on top of one another to try and keep warm. Poults can get chilled and smothered if this happens. Corner guards should be used throughout the brooding period and sometimes afterward (to be safe) until all poults are consistently roosting. Use galvanized sheet metal or 1/4-inch welded wire at least 2 feet tall by 18 inches wide. Secure into all open corners to round them out. Pack straw behind guards to keep poults from falling down behind them and becoming trapped.

NESTS AND NEST TRAPS

Special manufactured nests are hard to find for turkeys and their cost might not warrant purchase by small-scale handlers. Most handlers will need to construct one or improvise. Some commercial turkey breeding farms keep hen turkeys in small box-like wooden enclosures for laying and keeping track of the hen's production. Others use a free nest system similar to the system most small-scale growers use. An adaption of this system uses a turkey nest trap (Fig. 4-17). New traps close automatically when the hen enters the nest and automatically resets when the hen leaves. This prevents expensive hatching eggs from becoming broken when hens fight over one nest. The only company I've found that supplies these is Shenandoah Manufacturing Company.

Turkey hens will lay eggs on the floor, but the eggs can become dirty or broken and possibly eaten. Turkeys are not immune from the egg-eating vice. Turkeys on range definitely need a small sheltered nesting area. A full-size 55-gallon drum or one cut down in height makes a good turkey nest when laid on it's side. Otherwise, a wooden box can be constructed measuring 24 inches wide, 20 inches tall, and 24 inches deep. Nail an 8-inch board along the bottom edge of the open front to help keep nesting material in and eggs from rolling out.

PILOT BULBS

This is a miscellaneous item but its functions should

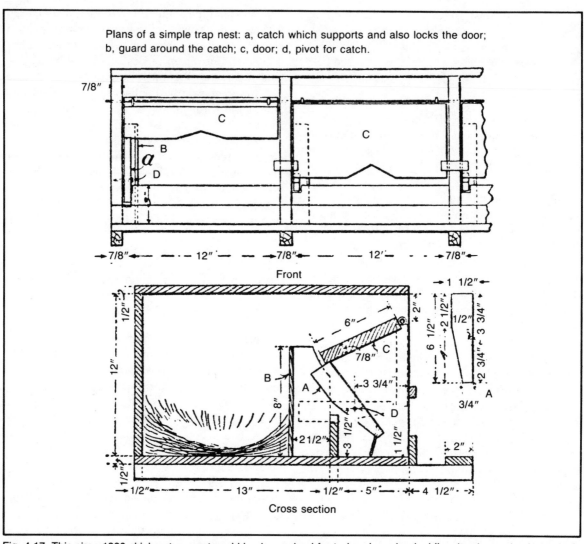

Plans of a simple trap nest: a, catch which supports and also locks the door; b, guard around the catch; c, door; d, pivot for catch.

Front

Cross section

Fig. 4-17. This circa 1930 chicken trap-nest could be improvised for turkey hens by doubling its size and using today's dimension size lumber. (Courtesy of USDA)

be explained. Some beginners believe the pilot bulbs on brooders help to heat them. Pilot bulbs only light up when the thermostat has turned the heating element on. When the set temperature is reached, both the heating element and the pilot bulb will turn off. A brooder will heat even if the pilot bulb burns out. Always check the brooder's temperature if the pilot bulb is not seen on because the power might be disconnected or the bulb simply burned out.

Do not depend upon a pilot bulb attached to a brooder as a source of light for eating and drinking purposes. They are not always lit long enough to allow poults time to eat and drink. Provide another light for this purpose—one that will stay lit constantly or come on at two-hour intervals by using a timer.

The color of the pilot bulb can make a difference. White can encourage cannibalism even through the short time it can remain on. A red bulb is preferred to prevent cannibalism, but green or blue can be used too. Keep a few pilot bulbs handy in case of burn-outs.

SADDLES

Before artificial insemination became widely used, many commercial turkey breeders used saddles on breeding hens (Fig. 4-18). This was to protect the backs of hens from tears and scratches a tom unintentionally inflicts while mating. Turkey mating is a lot different than most chicken matings. The hen stays down while the tom treads the back of the hen with his feet. This treading causes the claws to scratch into the back of the hen. The hen then loses feathers and her back becomes injured.

Small-scale handlers who will be breeding their hens and want to protect their backs can still purchase these inexpensive heavy canvas saddles. Two

Fig. 4-18. Because of the loose, yet secure fit, turkey hens don't mind wearing saddles. ("Jockey" Easy On Turkey Saddle courtesy of Mason City Tent and Awning Co.)

nylon stirrups are sewn onto the saddle. The hen's wings are slid through these stirrups to keep the saddle in place. The hens can wear these throughout the entire breeding season. Commercial breeders used to routinely mark the back of the saddle with turkey I.D. numbers so they could be easily identified at a distance or their eggs marked as to the particular layer. Hens do not seem to mind wearing the saddles.

THERMOMETERS

This is a very important part of poult brooding, especially for beginners. A thermometer's accuracy can literally mean the difference between success or failure. Individual thermometers can vary widely in their readings. I've seen some the same type and make vary as much as 20 degrees! A 5-degree difference can mean a lot when brooding poults. The most accurate thermometers seem to be the tested oral thermometers sold at drug stores. This is the only type I've ever relied upon. Their only drawback is the slow reading and that the mercury must be shaken down before each reading.

There are small dial-type meat thermometers sold at butcher and restaurant supply stores. Used mainly for testing smoked meats, they are fairly accurate and read quickly without having to shake the mercury down. They cost around $15 but can be utilized for baking, cooking, smoking meats, checking room temperatures, incubator temperatures, and water temperatures for perfect scalding during butchering. When purchasing thermometers, it's wise to check a number of them in the display to see if their temperatures vary and by how much.

TOE PUNCH

As with other fowl, a toe punch can be used on poults as a marking system when a handler wants to keep track of his birds. A toe punch quickly pierces a small hole in the webbed part of the foot between the toes. Various combinations of marks can be made to identify individual birds.

WAFERS

These are used routinely in most brooders and

small incubators. Most wafers are constructed of two 3-inch double disks made of tempered brass and attached in the center. The disks are filled with ether, which expands when heated and contracts when cool. The equipment's set-screw is screwed into the nut provided in the center of the wafer. By turning the set-screw, the wafer is adjusted closer or further from a micro-switch which turns the heater on and off (Fig. 4-19). When the wafer disk is heated by the equipment's heating element, the ether expands the wafer. As the wafer enlarges further, it eventually touches the micro-switch which then turns the heating element off in order to maintain a certain set temperature. As the ether cools down and contracts, the wafer comes away from the micro-switch. This causes the micro-switch to turn the heating element on again, and so on.

Only a few companies in the United States manufacture wafers. Many are sold singly without packaging so the brand is unknown. Brower wafers are usually sold in a marked box and contain numbers for various uses of the wafers. Brower wafers should be purchased by wafer numbers because some are made slightly thicker or thinner and contain more or less ether for various degrees of heat. A Brower incubator wafer used in a brooder can cause the temperature to remain too high. One of their brooder wafers, if used in an incubator, can prevent the desired temperature from being reached and maintained. I've come across many handlers who have had troubles getting their incubators to reach and maintain the needed 102 degrees F. in a still-air incubator. The problem was

always found to be an inappropriate wafer. The following wafer numbers are standard Brower wafers:

- 31-W—for temperatures from 70 to 100 degrees F. (21-37 degrees C). They are for most electric, gas, coal, and oil brooders. They are also considered by many to be "universal," although the company says this is untrue and they should only be used for the specified type brooders.
- 1-WB—for temperatures from 80 to 110 degrees F. (26-43 degrees C). They are for electric and gas floor and battery brooders.
- 4-W—similar to the 31-W's but the adaptor is slightly larger for use with four-lamp type brooders. Temperature range is 70 to 100 degrees F.
- 2-W—for temperatures from 100 to 120 degrees F. (38-48 degrees C). They are made specifically for incubators.

Other wafers manufactured by companies such as Beacon, can be used in both incubators and brooders. These wafers are called "universal" because they have a temperature range of 70 to 110 degrees Fahrenheit (21-43.33 degrees C). Dealers sometimes carry these because they only need to keep one type wafer in their stock. The narrowed-down temperature range, however, can be more accurate than these.

Because using an inappropriate wafer can cause problems and sometimes economic loss, all handlers should learn about them. If purchasing a Brower brand wafer, the correct wafer number should be used for the equipment in mind. Some dealers do not know the brand of the wafers they stock, but only that it is claimed to be a universal type. In this case, it's usually safe to assume the brand of wafer can be used for both incubators and brooders.

When a wafer goes bad, a handler will usually notice this by the obvious swelled appearance of a wafer not in use. If a wafer sounds full when being shaken, it's usually safe to use. And if the wafer expands when set in a bowl of warm water it's probably still good. A wafer that doesn't expand is bad and should be replaced. Wafers can leak and

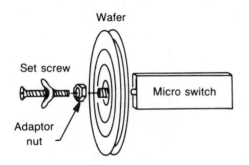

Wafer

Set screw

Micro switch

Adaptor nut

Fig. 4-19. An adaptor nut is usually provided with wafers for screws.

become inaccurate: replace yearly. Always keep at least one new wafer handy for replacements.

WATERERS

A good waterer for turkeys is one that can be cleaned and disinfected easily, constructed to help prevent litter and droppings from fouling the drinking water, heavy enough or designed so turkeys will not tip it, large enough to supply ample fresh water for the amount of turkeys it will serve, and be made to keep water from freezing. (Refer to Table 5-8 for water needs.)

Using the correct waterer in the correct way is extremely important with poults. Using the wrong type waterer can be disastrous. Many years have passed without a good poult waterer being made available for small-scale raisers; it's been a make-do situation. Sometimes small quail-sized founts were employed, but these are difficult to clean. Then there's the mason jar fount trick of placing marbles or stones into the fount to restrict water access (Fig. 4-20). It's as though manufacturers haven't been aware of the problems encountered when watering poults—until now.

Today's poult raisers have plasticware waterers that surpass any previously available. The outstanding feature of the Brower model is the rim guard that keeps poults from falling into the water. Holding 1 1/2 quarts of water, the 7-inch-high waterer is short enough to be used in most battery brooders where access is from the top (See Fig. 2-3).

Ordinary galvanized pans with grills can be used for adult turkeys. The grill prevents turkeys from walking into their water. Most hold 3 gallons of water. These should be set onto a platform so corrosive droppings and damp litter do not quickly rust the bottom out. A float valve can be purchased for galvanized pans that creates an automatic waterer when attached to a hose (Fig. 4-21). Valves will not work when water freezes.

Lightweight plastic pans with plastic grills are now available, but because of their light weight and design, they are easily flipped over by large turkeys. Special plastic pans with wire grills are designed especially for turkeys by the Shenandoah

Company. The pan is larger, measuring 18 inches wide and 4 inches deep. These will not rust and are purchased with either a full action valve, a float valve, or a suspension valve to maintain a constant supply of water at a definite level. If used with the valves, the valves must not be allowed to freeze or they will not work. Some, such as the full action valve, can be used without a water line hookup, although the valve must still be purchased with the pan. If used this way, a little over 3 gallons can be held in the pan. Plastic pans are much easier to clean than metal.

All these pans can be used with base-type water warmers to keep water from freezing. Rod water heaters should not be used inside plastic. If the water runs dry, the heater will get hot and the plastic can melt.

Double-wall vacuum fountains are available to hold 2, 3, 5, or 8 gallons of water (Fig. 4-22). These are all made of galvanized metal. The bottom is filled with water and then the top is placed down over, forming a "double wall." The vacuum created inside controls the water level in the attached pan. If you do not want to carry 8 gallons of water, the larger unit must be filled where it will stay. This requires carrying buckets of water to the waterer or using a hose. To keep the bottoms from rusting and to prevent litter material from being shoved into the water base, a wooden stand should be constructed to set this waterer onto. Algae quickly accumulates inside double-wall fountains in warm weather, so frequent cleaning and disinfecting will

Fig. 4-20. This is an excellent way to water day-old poults if safe waterers are unavailable.

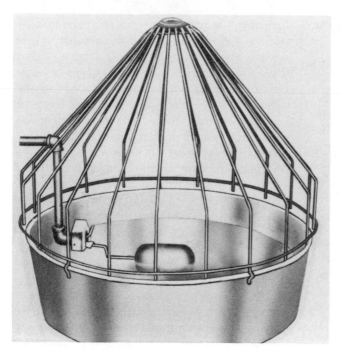

Fig. 4-21. The float valve shown makes this ordinary water pan with grill into an automatic, labor-saving waterer. (Courtesy of Brower Equipment Co.)

Fig. 4-22. A 5-gallon double-wall vacuum fount. (Courtesy of Warner Corp.)

Fig. 4-23. A hanging water trough like this helps keep litter from being scratched into drinking water. (Courtesy of Shenandoah Manufacturing Co., Inc.)

be required. Electric base heaters can be used under these. Both should be kept off the damp litter.

Many commercial growers use bowl-type fountains. Most are made of plastic and hang from the ceiling and are attached to a water line from above. The units operate on water pressures of up to 5 pounds and provide a constant supply of water. When large flocks of turkeys are raised, the units are economical because only about one is needed for every 50 turkeys.

The last types of waterers consist of hanging and standing troughs (Fig. 4-23). A valve is used to control the water level. This is hooked up to a water supply line—either a pressure supply, gravity tank, or drum of water. Some are made of galvanized steel which can corrode more easily. Most are narrow stainless steel troughs. Some contain porcelain coatings. These types last longer because harsh water and medicines will not corrode them.

Range troughs are designed especially for turkeys with a 4 1/2-inch trough width which is 3 1/2 inches deep and 8 feet long. This particular 8-foot unit is hung in a cradle, hammock-style. Other types

are available in 6- and 8-foot lengths to be hung or set on T-shaped stands. Most troughs are V-shaped and 1 1/2-3 1/2 inches wide, but will work for large turkeys. When hung a foot or so off the floor, the litter material is not easily thrown into the drinking water. These troughs can provide cleaner water. Special V-shaped brushes are sold to help clean algae accumulations. One of the 8-foot troughs will take care of as many as 250 adult turkeys. All have roost guards to prevent birds from roosting. Stands that have nut and bolt adjustments will quickly rust tight. Purchase those which slide and lock. The very narrow trough can be used with day-old poults also.

A smaller version of an automatic trough waterer is only 36 inches long. It's made of plastic and contains a float valve to regulate incoming water. It can be attached to a standard garden hose. For floor use, it should be mounted to a block of wood to prevent tipping. Predrilled holes allow this unit to be hung from the ceiling. It's wider (about 6 inches) than the longer automatic troughs, but it does contain a plastic roost guard down the center.

Chapter 5

Turkey Feeding

FEED CONSUMPTION AND ENERGY

Domestic turkeys almost lead the way as the fastest-growing domestic fowl. The Mammoth White Pekin duck wins by just a pinch. The slight difference in growth rate means it takes a turkey one-half a week longer to reach the same 8 pounds as the Pekin. The Pekins require 8 weeks to reach 8 pounds. Turkeys require 8 1/2 weeks to reach 8 pounds. This is close indeed. Cornish Rock Cross broiler chickens are third down the line of fast growers. They require 10 1/2 weeks to reach 8 pounds.

The tremendous difference lies in the feed to meat ratio—the amount of feed it takes to make 1 pound of meat on the bird. This is where turkeys have all fowls up to 15 weeks of age beat. Afterwards the ratio tapers to that of other fowls and keeps tapering. To get 8 pounds of meat on a turkey in 8 1/2 weeks it will take only 13 pounds of feed. To get the same 8 pounds of meat on a Pekin duck will require 22 pounds of feed. A Cornish Rock Cross broiler needs about 19 1/2 pounds of feed to reach 8 pounds.

The first 8 weeks is the fastest growing period of all poultry. This is also the time higher protein rations are fed. From day-old on, this ratio of feed to meat begins to taper down with all fowl. This tapering down makes the overall cost of growing and finishing the bird higher. This is especially true with turkeys—the longer they are kept growing out, the less meat a handler will net per pound of feed eaten by the turkey. This makes it economically important to market and butcher turkeys just as soon as they are finished growing.

In this respect, turkeys cost more per pound to grow out than a Pekin duck or a Cornish Rock Cross broiler. Add this cost to the initial higher price of a turkey poult and the total cost per pound of live weight turkey meat will be approximately 44 cents per pound—not counting brooding and watering costs. The cost of a Pekin duckling and feed will bring the total cost per pound of live weight duckling meat at about 42 cents per pound excluding brooding and watering costs. The cost of a Cornish Rock Cross broiler chick and it's total feed will bring the live weight costs of chicken meat to approximately 35 cents per pound, excluding brooding and watering costs. These costs are for fully confined birds without ranging. This does not include any beak or toe trimming or any other extras.

Depending upon the breed of geese, their initial costs and some ranging will make the live weight goose meat costs about 40-50 cents per pound. Of course there are variables everywhere to affect the total costs per pound of any poultry meat.

By glancing at Table 5-1 a handler can see the conversion of feed to actual meat is better with tom turkeys. This is why many commercial growers prefer toms. They know they will get more for their money even if the toms are butchered early to avoid too large a market bird. Tom poults cost more to purchase than a straight run lot of poults. But if you were to purchase equal numbers of hens and toms, the cost would approximate straight run poults of the same number.

If you want to cut down grow-out time by five or six weeks, you can purchase all toms and raise them just until they reach about 18 pounds. You will definitely save on feed costs this way because of the feed conversion factor. A tom up to 18 pounds has required 42 pounds of feed. A hen of 18 pounds will require 57 pounds of feed to reach this goal. A handler can judge for himself whether the lower feed costs will compensate for the higher priced tom poults by checking poult prices with a few hatcheries and reviewing Table 5-2.

Unlike chickens, where a few hundred strains abound to confuse the handler, turkeys that are made available to small-scale raisers consist of only a few strains. There is no need to worry over which meat strain is better or faster growing because the chances are the next hatchery down the line has the same strain anyhow. For instance, there are about two dozen main strains of the large and medium white turkeys that are usually grown. There are six well-known hatcheries that sell to small-scale raisers, however, and purchase all their turkey hatching eggs from the same company in Texas.

I can't say all the strains available grow equally well, because they don't. Then again, it's not only heredity that will give you a large bird, the hatching egg, too, has a lot to do with growth. Small eggs produce small poults. Although most would not notice this unless various hatches of poults were on hand to compare side by side, there can be a big difference in the initial size of the poults. This may have nothing to do with the original strain. Perhaps they are from hens just beginning to lay. Being particular about the strain or size of the poults is usually beyond your control. Small-scale raisers must pretty much take what's available. Most all turkeys will grow well with proper feed and care.

There are certain things that will influence a turkey's growth rate besides heredity. Some inexperienced handlers believe protein is the *only* factor that causes birds to grow fast and large, when actually the genetic make-up of the bird is what determines just how much protein the body will utilize. Many of these handlers will overfeed protein in trying to grow the bird faster than it's genetic make-up will allow. (If certain amino acids are lacking or are present in too great a quantity, feed consumption can decline.)

Fats and carbohydrates are used by poultry to produce energy. They can also allow the correct amount of nutrients from a balanced ration to be consumed. The main purpose of introducing fats into poultry feeds is to regulate the amount of feed, and therefore, the amount of nutrients the birds consume. The larger the bird, the more energy required to maintain the body and help produce eggs. Poults require less of the energy-producing feeds than grown turkeys. If an excess of energy-producing fats are consumed, they are not able to be utilized and they must end up somewhere. This "somewhere" becomes fatty deposits over the carcass of the bird. Carbohydrates are found in plants and grains in the kernel or framework of the plant. This fibrous substance is mostly indigestible and is called crude fiber. The digestible portions of the carbohydrates are called nitrogen-free extract. The crude fiber has no food value, is indigestible and is passed in the droppings. Thus, it is wasteful to feed very high-fiber feeds.

Energy is measured in calories. A calorie is the amount of heat required to raise the temperature of one gram (28.35 ounces) of water from 16.5 degrees C. (329 degrees F.) to 17.5 degrees C. (347 degrees F.). A kilocalorie (kcal) is 1,000 small calories or one large Calorie (C). This is the nutritional unit term used most often. Calories are commonly used to denote human food, but by scientific measurements, kilocalorie (kcal) is the precise term of measurement as used by the North American poultry feed industry. Scientists can measure the energy that will be available to poultry from various feeds by burning the feeds and measuring the heat produced during the process.

A little over one-fourth of the energy produced by feeds is lost through the droppings. Not all energy is used to maintain and warm the body or produce eggs. The usable energy is called the metabolizable energy (ME) value of a feed. This is how the values of energy in feed are measured. Mature hens become overweight when their estrogen hormone level increases. Fat naturally deposits on the hen's body when estrogen hormones are produced at the start of reproduction. Poultry do not eat in order to feel full. They eat mainly to obtain energy their brain tells their body it should have. Energy is converted from the fats contained in the ration. If enough fat does not exist in the ration the turkey will eat more to try to acquire it. Likewise, if a ration is fat- and calorie-laden, the converted energy requirements will be met more quickly and the turkey consumes less feed.

The environmental temperature has a dramatic effect on the amount of fat the birds require. The colder the temperature, the more fat their bodies require, and the more food they will consume. Birds in colder temperatures are usually consuming more nutrients than those held at warmer temperatures, and they may be healthier—although more expensive to raise. Generally, moderate temperatures of 61-75 degrees F. (16-24 degrees C.) are best for adequate feed intake and adequate nutrient intake. Each rise of 1 degree in the temperature will cause birds to eat 1 1/2 percent less feed. It is therefore economically important to house birds in a moderate temperature.

Commercially prepared feeds are not mixed for extremely low or high temperatures, but rather for moderate environments. Most energy-producing fats and carbohydrates in poultry feeds come from animal and poultry by-products acquired from rendering plants, restaurant greases, and vegetable and plant oils. Fats are also useful in feeds because they improve the consistency.

One area a handler has a lot of control over in producing fast growers is the environment. Because more feed is eaten in cooler temperatures, a handler can make sure the birds are never overheated. He can be sure a cooler area near or in a brooder is provided to promote faster feathering and better growth. He can supply ventilation during warm months to reduce the temperature, especially with older birds. He can and should provide extra artificial lighting during the brooding period to encourage more feed consumption. Also remember that when birds eat less, less nutrients are consumed. This lack of nutrients will cause stunting of growth. When birds are sick or stressed, they utilize less fat to convert into energy and this causes a decrease in feed consumption.

It's suggested that adjustments in the nutrients be made to correspond with colder or warmer temperatures, although for small-scale growers this is not easy or practical. For instance, if the temperature turns hot for one or two days, the turkeys should ideally have a lower fat ration that contains the same nutrients. This will not be possible because a certain amount of fat (usually 3 percent) is always contained in commercially prepared feeds. In cold environments, when feed consumption goes up dramatically, the housing temperature should preferably be raised or extra fat can be fed in the form of fat scraps or lard balls made from scratch feed.

A well-balanced ration will supply the correct amount of fat needed according to the specific age and type of bird in relation to how much energy their body requires. This is correlated to the amount of other nutrients that are required and must be consumed in a total amount of feed. Table 5-1 shows the weekly feed consumption of large variety turkey poults up to eight weeks of age. Table 5-2 shows the weekly feed consumption of large variety turkeys over eight weeks of age. Table 5-3

Table 5-1. Growth Rate, Feed, and Energy Consumption of Large-Type Turkeys Up to 8 Weeks of Age.*

Age (weeks)	Body weight		Feed consumption per week		Cumulative feed consumption		ME* Consumption per week	
	lbs. (kg) M	lbs. (kg) F	lbs. (kg) M	lbs. (kg) F	lbs. (kg) M	lbs. (kg) F	Calories (Mcal) M	Cal. (Mcal) F
1	.24 (0.11)	.24 (0.11)	.22 (0.10)	.22 (0.10)	.22 (0.10)	.22 (0.10)	300 (0.30)	300 (0.30)
2	.59 (0.27)	.52 (0.24)	.44 (0.20)	.37 (0.17)	.66 (0.30)	.59 (0.27)	600 (0.60)	500 (0.50)
3	1.27 (0.58)	1.03 (0.47)	.99 (0.45)	.85 (0.39)	1.65 (0.75)	1.45 (0.66)	1,100 (1.1)	800 (0.80)
4	2.20 (1.0)	1.54 (0.70)	1.34 (0.61)	1.01 (0.46)	2.99 (1.36)	2.46 (1.12)	1,700 (1.7)	1,200 (1.2)
5	3.30 (1.5)	2.42 (1.1)	1.54 (0.70)	1.32 (0.60)	4.54 (2.06)	3.79 (1.72)	2,300 (2.3)	1,600 (1.6)
6	4.41 (2.0)	3.52 (1.6)	1.89 (0.86)	1.67 (0.76)	6.43 (2.92)	5.46 (2.48)	2,900 (2.9)	2,100 (2.1)
7	5.73 (2.6)	4.63 (2.1)	2.37 (1.08)	1.95 (0.89)	8.82 (4.00)	7.43 (3.37)	3,500 (3.5)	2,600 (2.6)
8	7.27 (3.3)	5.73 (2.6)	2.86 (1.30)	2.28 (1.04)	11.68 (5.30)	9.72 (4.41)	4,100 (4.1)	3,100 (3.1)

*Author Note: ME (Apparent Metabolizable Energy) for poultry is the gross energy of the feed consumed minus the gross energy of the droppings.

(Adapted from *Nutrient Requirements of Poultry, 8th Revised Edition*, copyright 1984, National Academy of Sciences.)

Table 5-2. Growth Rate, Feed, and Energy Consumption of Large-Type Turkeys Over 8 Weeks of Age.*

Age (weeks)	Body weight		Feed consumption per week		Cumulative feed consumption		ME* Consumption per week	
	lbs. (kg) M	lbs. (kg) F	lbs. (kg) M	lbs. (kg) F	lbs. (kg) M	lbs. (kg) F	Calories (Mcal) M	Cal. (Mcal) F
9	8.82 (4.0)	6.83 (3.1)	3.32 (1.51)	2.59 (1.18)	15.01 (6.81)	12.32 (5.59)	4,800 (4.8)	3,600 (3.6)
10	10.36 (4.7)	8.15 (3.7)	3.91 (1.78)	2.94 (1.34)	18.94 (8.59)	15.28 (6.93)	5,200 (5.2)	4,100 (4.1)
11	12.12 (5.5)	9.48 (4.3)	4.37 (1.99)	3.23 (1.47)	23.32 (10.58)	18.52 (8.40)	5,700 (5.7)	4,600 (4.6)
12	13.89 (6.3)	10.58 (4.8)	4.95 (2.25)	3.49 (1.59)	28.29 (12.83)	22.02 (9.99)	6,300 (6.3)	5,100 (5.1)
13	15.65 (7.1)	11.68 (5.3)	5.53 (2.51)	3.74 (1.70)	33.82 (15.34)	25.77 (11.69)	7,100 (7.1)	5,500 (5.5)
14	17.64 (8.0)	12.78 (5.8)	5.86 (2.66)	3.85 (1.75)	39.69 (18.00)	29.63 (13.44)	7,800 (7.8)	5,800 (5.8)
15	19.40 (8.8)	13.89 (6.3)	6.37 (2.89)	4.01 (1.82)	46.06 (20.89)	33.64 (15.26)	8,400 (8.4)	6,100 (6.1)
16	21.38 (9.7)	14.77 (6.7)	6.72 (3.05)	4.23 (1.92)	52.78 (23.94)	37.88 (17.18)	8,800 (8.8)	6,400 (6.4)
17	23.15 (10.5)	15.65 (7.1)	6.90 (3.13)	4.47 (2.03)	59.60 (27.03)	42.35 (19.21)	9,600 (9.6)	6,700 (6.7)
18	24.91 (11.3)	16.53 (7.5)	7.21 (3.27)	4.56 (2.07)	66.89 (30.34)	46.92 (21.28)	10,200 (10.2)	6,900 (6.9)
19	26.68 (12.1)	17.19 (7.8)	7.56 (3.43)	4.74 (2.15)	74.46 (33.77)	51.66 (23.43)	10,900 (10.9)	7,100 (7.1)
20	28.22 (12.8)	17.86 (8.1)	7.93 (3.60)	4.91 (2.23)	82.40 (37.37)	56.58 (25.66)	11,600 (11.6)	7,300 (7.3)
21	29.76 (13.5)	-	8.18 (3.71)	-	90.58 (41.08)	-	12,500 (12.5)	-
22	31.31 (14.2)	-	8.42 (3.82)	-	97.19 (44.90)	-	12,900 (12.9)	-
23	32.63 (14.8)	-	8.68 (3.94)	-	107.69 (48.84)	-	13,200 (13.2)	-
24	33.95 (15.4)	-	8.93 (4.05)	-	116.62 (52.89)	-	13,500 (13.5)	-

*Author Note: ME (Apparent Metabolizable Energy) for poultry is the gross energy of the feed consumed minus the gross energy of the droppings.

(Adapted from *Nutrient Requirements of Poultry, 8th Revised Edition*, copyright 1984, National Academy of Sciences.)

Table 5-3. Body Weights and Feed Consumption of Large-Type Turkeys During Holding and Breeding Periods. *

Age (weeks)	Hens Weight lbs. (kg)	(%) Egg production	Feed per day lbs. (g)	Toms Weight lbs. (kg)	Feed per day lbs. (g)
20	15.43 (7.0)		.44 (200)	26.46 (12.0)	.88 (400)
25	17.64 (8.0)		.47 (215)	29.76 (13.5)	.92 (420)
30	19.84 (9.0)	Start light stimulation	.50 (230)	35.28 (16.0)	.97 (440)
35	20.94 (9.5)	66	.57 (260)	37.48 (17.0)	.99 (450)
40	20.50 (9.3)	63	.56 (255)	39.69 (18.0)	1.01 (460)
45	20.06 (9.1)	60	.55 (250)	40.13 (18.2)	1.05 (480)
50	19.84 (9.0)	50	.52 (240)	40.79 (18.5)	1.10 (500)
55	19.84 (9.0)	40	.50 (230)	41.45 (18.8)	1.12 (510)
60	19.84 (9.0)	35	.48 (220)	41.89 (19.0)	1.14 (520)

*These values are based on experimental data involving "in season" egg production (i.e., November through July) of commercial stock. It is estimated that summer breeders would produce 70-90 percent as many eggs and consume 60-80 percent as much feed, respectively, as "in season" breeders.

(Adapted from *Nutrient Requirements of Poultry, 8th Revised Edition,* copyright 1984, National Academy of Sciences.)

shows the amounts of feed breeder turkeys are allowed when on a limited intake ration prior to and during breeding and egg production. Note the energy base for these breeders as compared to 8-24-week-old turkeys in Table 5-6. Table 5-4 shows feed consumption for small breed turkeys

Table 5-4. Weekly Cumulative Feed Consumption of Small Breeds of Turkeys.

| | (SI units) SMALL BREED | | | | (English units) SMALL BREED | | | |
| | Male | | Female | | Male | | Female | |
Age, wks	Avg. mass kg	Feed, kg/bird	Avg. mass kg	Feed, kg/bird	Avg. wt, lb	Feed, lb/bird	Avg. wt, lb	Feed, lb/bird
0	0.05		0.05		0.115		0.115	
1	0.11	0.09	0.11	0.09	0.25	0.2	0.25	0.2
2	0.23	0.27	0.20	0.27	0.50	0.6	0.45	0.6
3	0.45	0.64	0.41	0.59	1.00	1.4	0.90	1.3
4	0.68	1.00	0.64	1.00	1.50	2.2	1.40	2.2
5	0.95	1.41	0.91	1.45	2.10	3.1	2.00	3.2
10	3.13	6.08	2.59	4.99	6.90	13.4	5.70	11.0
16	6.45	15.66	4.54	12.71	14.2	34.5	10.00	28.0
20	8.40	23.52			18.5	51.8		
24								
28								

(Reprinted by permission from ASHRAE Handbook: 1981 Fundamentals.)

such as the Beltsville Small Whites.

NUTRITION REQUIREMENTS
AND FEED COMPOSITION

Feed is composed of various ingredients all working together to provide the needs of the turkeys. A feed that supplies all the needs is considered a "balanced ration." Some nutrients in feed work alone, others, such as Vitamin D_3, are important because they help the body assimilate nutrients. Other examples of the latter are Niacin and Selenium. Niacin assists in the release of energy from other nutrients. Selenium works with Vitamin E to produce good muscle fibers.

The nutritional requirements for turkeys has changed over the years to keep in step with the growth rate and size of today's birds. Because today's turkeys are able to convert more feed to meat and in less time than their ancestors, they have higher nutrient requirements. Nutrients cost money—the more nutrients in a feed, the higher it's cost. The increased growth rate means handlers are freed of extra labor and the birds can be marketed sooner.

The nutrient requirements of turkeys continue to change throughout the growing period according to bodily needs and what the body is able to utilize for health and growth. These requirements vary with environmental variations. This is especially true of turkeys who are ranged outdoors. In an environmentally controlled atmosphere, growers do not have to worry about such variations. The nutrient requirements for poults up to eight weeks of age can be found in Table 5-5.

After brooding, the nutritional requirements of turkeys will change approximately every three to four weeks. Some requirements might be more than the previous three to four weeks while others might be less, depending upon what the body is doing during this period. A specific age and sex of turkey might need more nutrients for consistent growth. Another may require more or less of some nutrients for breeding and egg production (Table 5-6). Five requirements noticeably increase when hens begin to lay eggs. They are: Calcium, Vitamin E, Pantothenic Acid, Niacin, and Chlorine. Poultry as a whole require the following nutrients at all times: protein, amino acids, fats, vitamins, minerals, and water. These are discussed in the following sections of this chapter.

Large feed companies conduct their own research concerning nutrient requirements for poultry. The U.S. Department of Agriculture does similar research and experiments. Many universities research poultry needs. These are also many associations and departments that financially support such research. For instance, the Center for Veterinary Medicine, the Food and Drug Administration of the U.S. Department of Health and Human Services, the Agricultural Research Service of the U.S. Department of Agriculture, the Agricultural Canada, and the American Feed Manufacturers Association supported the most recent study on the nutrient requirements for poultry that was conducted by the National Academy of Sciences.

Good feed companies keep abreast of this research and incorporate the results into their feeds. This they must do because of competition from other feed companies. The best thing a handler can do to feed correctly is to purchase a commercially prepared feed, or have feed ground and mixed with his own grains and vitamin-mineral premixes according to formulas supplied by feed and grain elevators.

Most handlers are never aware of the amount of nutrients their birds are getting because the majority of feed manufacturers will not list amounts on feed tags for fear of giving away their trade formula for mixing. Feed companies are not required to list amounts or the actual origin of the ingredients, only the name of the ingredients.

Both plant and animal proteins are used in poultry feed because one type can provide the nutrients the other is lacking to produce a balanced ration. The bulk of poultry rations consists mainly of cereal-type grains. Soybeans are high in protein and used extensively in poultry feed. These are plant protein.

Feed is often composed largely of animal and plant waste. Some believe recycling has gone a bit too far. We now have many farmers feeding poultry manure and soiled litter to cattle because they

Table 5-5. Nutrient Requirements of Poults Up to 8 Weeks of Age.

Energy Base kcal ME/kg Diet[a] →		Age (weeks)	
		M: 0-4 F: 0-4 2,800	4-8 4-8 2,900
Protein	%	28	26
Arginine	%	1.6	1.5
Glycine + serine	%	1.0	0.9
Histidine	%	0.58	0.54
Isoleucine	%	1.1	1.0
Leucine	%	1.9	1.75
Lysine	%	1.6	1.5
Methionine + cystine	%	1.05	0.9
Methionine	%	0.53	0.45
Phenylalanine + tyrosine	%	1.8	1.65
Phenylalanine	%	1.0	0.9
Threonine	%	1.0	0.93
Tryptophan	%	0.26	0.24
Valine	%	1.2	1.1
Linoleic acid	%	1.0	1.0
Calcium	%	1.2	1.0
Phosphorus, available	%	0.6	0.5
Potassium	%	0.7	0.6
Sodium	%	0.17	0.15
Chlorine	%	0.15	0.14
Magnesium	mg	600	600
Manganese	mg	60	60
Zinc	mg	75	65
Iron	mg	80	60
Copper	mg	8	8
Iodine	mg	0.4	0.4
Selenium	mg	0.2	0.2
Vitamin A	IU	4,000	4,000
Vitamin D[b]	ICU	900	900
Vitamin E	IU	12	12
Vitamin K	mg	1.0	1.0
Riboflavin	mg	3.6	3.6
Pantothenic acid	mg	11.0	11.0
Niacin	mg	70.0	70.0
Vitamin B_{12}	mg	0.003	0.003
Choline	mg	1,900	1,600
Biotin	mg	0.2	0.2
Folacin	mg	1.0	1.0
Thiamin	mg	2.0	2.0
Pyridoxine	mg	4.5	4.5

[a]These are typical ME concentrations for corn-soya diets. Different ME values may be appropriate if other ingredients predominate.

[b]These concentrations of vitamin D are satisfactory when the dietary concentrations of calcium and available phosphorus conform with those in this table.

(Adapted from *Nutrient Requirements of Poultry, 8th Revised Edition,* copyright 1984, National Academy of Sciences.)

Table 5-6. Nutrient Requirements of Turkeys Over 8 Weeks of Age and Breeders.

Energy Base kcal ME/kg Diet[a] →		M: 8-12 F: 8-11 3,000	12-16 11-14 3,100	16-20 14-17 3,200	20-24 17-20 3,300	Holding 2,900	Breeding hens 2,900
Age (weeks)							
Protein	%	22	19	16.5	14	12	14
Arginine	%	1.25	1.1	0.95	0.8	0.6	0.6
Glycine + serine	%	0.8	0.7	0.6	0.5	0.4	0.5
Histidine	%	0.46	0.39	0.35	0.29	0.25	0.3
Isoleucine	%	0.85	0.75	0.65	0.55	0.45	0.5
Leucine	%	1.5	1.3	1.1	0.95	0.5	0.5
Lysine	%	1.3	1.0	0.8	0.65	0.5	0.6
Methionine + cystine	%	0.75	0.65	0.55	0.45	0.4	0.4
Methionine	%	0.38	0.33	0.28	0.23	0.2	0.2
Phenylalanine + tyrosine	%	1.4	1.2	1.05	0.9	0.8	1.0
Phenylalanine	%	0.8	0.7	0.6	0.5	0.4	0.55
Threonine	%	0.79	0.68	0.59	0.5	0.4	0.45
Tryptophan	%	0.2	0.18	0.15	0.13	0.1	0.13
Valine	%	0.94	0.8	0.7	0.6	0.5	0.58
Linoleic acid	%	0.8	0.8	0.8	0.8	0.8	1.0
Calcium	%	0.85	0.75	0.65	0.55	0.5	2.25
Phosphorus, available	%	0.42	0.38	0.32	0.28	0.25	0.35
Potassium	%	0.5	0.5	0.4	0.4	0.4	0.6
Sodium	%	0.12	0.12	0.12	0.12	0.12	0.15
Chlorine	%	0.14	0.12	0.12	0.12	0.12	0.12
Magnesium	mg	600	600	600	600	600	600
Manganese	mg	60	60	60	60	60	60
Zinc	mg	50	40	40	40	40	65
Iron	mg	60	60	50	50	50	60
Copper	mg	6	6	6	6	6	8
Iodine	mg	0.4	0.4	0.4	0.4	0.4	0.4
Selenium	mg	0.2	0.2	0.2	0.2	0.2	0.2
Vitamin A	IU	4,000	4,000	4,000	4,000	4,000	4,000
Vitamin D[b]	ICU	900	900	900	900	900	900
Vitamin E	IU	10	10	10	10	10	25
Vitamin K	mg	0.8	0.8	0.8	0.8	0.8	1.0
Riboflavin	mg	3.0	3.0	2.5	2.5	2.5	4.0
Pantothenic acid	mg	9.0	9.0	9.0	9.0	9.0	16.0
Niacin	mg	50.0	50.0	40.0	40.0	40.0	30.0
Vitamin B_{12}	mg	0.003	0.003	0.003	0.003	0.003	0.003
Choline	mg	1,300	1,100	950	800	800	1,000
Biotin	mg	0.15	0.125	0.100	0.100	0.100	0.15
Folacin	mg	0.8	0.8	0.7	0.7	0.7	1.0
Thiamin	mg	2.0	2.00	2.0	2.0	2.0	2.0
Pyridoxine	mg	3.5	3.5	3.0	3.0	3.0	4.0

[a]These are typical ME concentrations for corn-soya diets. Different ME values may be appropriate if other ingredients predominate.

[b]These concentrations of vitamin D are satisfactory when the dietary concentrations of calcium and available phosphorus conform with those in this table.

(Adapted from *Nutrient Requirements of Poultry, 8th Revised Edition,* copyright 1984, National Academy of Sciences.)

do well on it. No livestock is immune from such feeding practices unless it is grown strictly on grains and grass. These by-products have gone into feeds for many years. A very long time ago when processing was difficult, handlers fed livestock mainly grains and allowed the livestock to range. Here they acquired their own balanced diet with the plant proteins from the grains and grasses and the animal protein from insects or an occasional mouse or snake. The fast growth of poultry today does not allow enough time for such foraging.

Feed manufacturers do have to list the guaranteed amounts of crude protein, fat, and fiber as these pertain to the energy level of the feed. And any added medication must be listed with the percentage contained in the feed. Warning labels pertaining to medications should also be included on the tag.

We might feel we are at the mercy of these companies by having to rely on their judgement to feed our birds, but it's probably safe to say that competition keeps them honest. If the companies didn't keep up with the requirements of today's poultry, poor results would probably be noticed and the company would lose customers. Producing livestock feed commercially is a big business; most of the well-known companies cannot risk dissatisfied customers.

PROTEIN AND AMINO ACIDS

Poults grow at a faster rate than adult turkeys the first few weeks. Because the main function of protein is to stimulate growth, poults will require more protein. The faster a bird's body genetically is able to grow, the more protein is needed. Protein is also used by the body to repair worn tissues, fatten the carcass, and promote good feathering. Adult toms have less of a need for protein than hen turkeys laying eggs, but these hens have less of a need for protein than young poults. Protein makes productive use of consumed energy (fats), so a protein deficiency can cause fat deposits. Fat hens do not breed or lay well. Excess fat deposits in the fat tissues of the bird; this is especially true when they are fed saturated fats (such as animal fats). Unsaturated

fats, such as sunflower oils, do not deposit fat in the tissues.

Protein contains amino acids that allow the protein to be absorbed from the intestine. Their composition depends upon the ingredient from which they came. Some feed ingredients contain a higher percentage of certain amino acids than others. Amino acids end up in the area of the brain by way of the blood and in the liver where they influence the amount of feed a bird eats. Both a deficiency or excess of certain amino acids can cause deficiencies of other needed nutrients.

Rations are frequently and conveniently described by the protein content of particular feeds. It forms the basis upon which feed prices are determined. Protein concentrates are always used and mixed with other feed products such as grains. They should never be fed alone. They are evenly ground with the other feed products to produce a mash or are molded and broken down to form pellets or crumbles. Protein concentrates should never be mixed with whole or cracked grains for feeding. The sand-type consistency of the concentrate will cause it to sift down to the bottom of the feeder and it will be eaten in it's concentrated form.

Most sources of protein come from animal by-products and soybean concentrates. Soybeans must be heat-treated before being incorporated into poultry feeds. Whole fresh soybeans are toxic and inhibit the activity of trypsin, a digestive enzyme in the juice of the pancreas that changes proteins into peptones for ease in digestion. Untreated soybeans induce pancreas enlargement. Many varieties of rapeseed meals contain compounds that reduce growth rate and egg production. Canadian plant geneticists have developed a rapeseed that contains only minute quantities of the toxic compounds. Cottonseed meal contains gossypol pigments in varying amounts according to the strain of the seed. These pigments cause olive-colored egg yolks. Certain fatty acids in cottonseed meal can also cause egg whites to appear pink.

Companies that produce concentrates determine formulas for mixing them with various grains and supplements for use as poultry feed. Most feed dealers, co-ops, feed and grain stores and elevators have formulas for mixing the concentrates to produce starter, grower, finisher, and breeder mash rations. Ration formulas for chickens will not provide the requirements needed by turkeys.

Protein is the most expensive ingredient in any poultry ration. It's a waste of money to feed more than the required amount of protein because a bird can only utilize a certain amount. Excessive protein is passed in the droppings. Some handlers believe protein is the most important ingredient in a poultry ration. With large, fast-growing birds such as turkeys, they might even think protein is what makes good fertile eggs. Protein is probably the most overfed of all nutrients—a very expensive mistake, indeed. There are many more nutrients as important to turkeys.

VITAMINS

There are 13 essential vitamins turkeys must receive to perform and grow normally. If certain amounts of each type vitamin is not received, the bird is then deficient in this vitamin and will not grow normally, feather properly, or utilize other vitamins properly. Diseases and various abnormalities can result. Modern research has revealed just how these various vitamins work in the bodies of poultry.

As previously mentioned, some vitamins are required because they make other substances available for use in the body. Vitamin D_3 is needed to allow calcium to be absorbed, without it the poult will acquire rickets. The deficiency is then both a calcium and a vitamin D deficiency. Most nutrients work *with* the other nutrients and their individual deficiency would not cause other nutrients to be totally unusable in the body.

It seems too many commercially prepared feeds are lacking the total required amount of vitamin D_3. Many handlers have problems with turkeys going down on their legs as they reach four weeks of age. Many are told their poults need more protein, some are told they should feed less protein, others are just baffled. This has added to the myth that turkeys are difficult to grow. Four ounces of fresh cod-liver oil administered in the drinking water is enough for 20 poults during their first four weeks. Don't think a good thing is better by overusing it. Vitamin D_3 is toxic to many birds at over 100 times the requirement.

More information is available concerning the compatability of vitamins, the toxic effects of some, the correlation between vitamins and disease, the performance of antibiotics in feed, and what nutrients are required for top production from today's type of turkey. Following is a list of the 13 vitamins and their known functions:

- Biotin—promotes growth and prevents perosis. A deficiency of biotin can cause fatty liver disease and kidney syndrome. Sources are dried brewer's yeast, liver, molasses, and green leafy plants.
- Choline—prevents perosis.
- Folacin (folic acid)—prevents loss of egg production, anemia, loss of feather pigment, and poor feathering. Sources are soybean meal, wheat bran and middlings, fish meal, liver meal, etc.
- Niacin—a deficiency of niacin can cause hock disorders and poor feather qualities.
- Pantothenic acid—a severe deficiency can cause skin lesions, liver damage, and reduced hatchability. The source for pantothenic acid is calcium pantothenate.
- Pyridoxine (B_6)—deficiencies are rare, but if they occur it can cause a lack of appetite, convulsions and hyperexcitability.
- Riboflavin—promotes growth and hatchability. There are few sources.
- Thiamin (B_1)—maintains the appetite and obtains energy from carbohydrates and protein. Sources include cereal grains and their by-products.
- Vitamin A—used to grow and maintain glands and the mucous membranes in body cavities. A deficiency will cause lesions around eyes. Sources are yellow corn, legumes, grasses, fish oils and supplements.
- Vitamin B_{12}—promotes growth and hatch-

ability. A deficiency causes perosis and a fatty heart, liver, kidneys. Sources are animal origin feeds and poultry droppings.

- Vitamin D_3—needed for calcium absorption to prevent rickets. A good source is cod-liver oil.
- Vitamin E—the antisterility vitamin for good fertility and hatchability. Alfalfa meal is rich in vitamin E.
- Vitamin K—prevents excessive bleeding and shortens the time for blood to clot. A deficiency can cause death from loss of blood during a minor injury. This vitamin is synthesized by bacteria in the intestine.

Vitamins are deficient in many feed ingredients, so they are added in the form of a supplement. These supplements are prepackaged vitamin mixes. Feeding a balanced ration to poults is the best way to ward off vitamin deficiencies that will cause problems later. Commercially prepared feeds contain the prepacked supplemental vitamins, and these vitamin premixes, along with protein concentrates, salt, and minerals, can also be purchased at feed stores to be added to your own grains that are to be ground and mixed. Various formulas for mixing these ingredients are available at feed and grain stores who grind and mix agricultural grains for area farmers.

MINERALS

Minerals help utilize energy and protein and are important for good bones and blood. Oyster shells should be fed free-choice to breeding and laying hens to assure a good supply of calcium for the eggs they'll produce. This mineral is fed free-choice because if too much calcium is mixed into the feed ration, the turkeys are forced to consume too much of it. Too much calcium can actually cause rickets, deposits in the kidney ducts, and bad shells.

Twelve minerals are required by turkeys. A well-balanced ration will include these minerals and usually some trace minerals in the correct proportions. These minerals are made available in poultry feeds by adding many of the following in the form of a premixed supplement: Bonemeal, calcium carbonate, calcite grit, calcium phosphate, calcium sulphate, limestone, magnesium oxide, oyster shells, phosphate rock, potassium chloride, potassium sulphate, sodium bicarbonate, sodium carbonate, sodium chloride (salt), sodium phosphate, sodium sulphate, and phosphoric acid. Trace minerals are required in very small amounts and are usually contained in prepared feeds.

Some mineral requirements decrease as the poult grows but will increase again for turkey hens kept for egg production. The minerals known to be needed by turkeys are:

- Calcium—used for bone formation, normal blood clotting and feed utilization. Too much or too little calcium will cause rickets to develop and eggshells to be thin. Vitamin D_3 is required to allow calcium to be absorbed.
- Chlorine—used with other minerals to develop bones.
- Copper—prevents anemia because it builds blood cells. Also prevents depigmentation of red feathers.
- Iodine—prevents poor growth and produces thyroid hormones.
- Iron—builds blood cells and prevents depigmentation of red feathers. Deficiencies are rare.
- Magnesium—used in the bones with other minerals. Deficiencies rare.
- Manganese—used in combination with calcium and phosphorus within the bones. It prevents perosis (slipped tendon), a serious disorder of turkeys.
- Phosphorus—works with calcium and prevents rickets. It should be fed with calcium at a ratio of two parts calcium to one part phosphorus. Lack of calcium, phosphorus and/or vitamin D will cause rickets.
- Potassium-needed in small quantities. Most feeds contain more than actually needed. Deficiencies are rare.
- Selenium—works with vitamin E for good muscle fibers. It helps to prevent poor growth and bruising.

- Sodium (salt)—promotes thirst, which ensures an adequate water intake so other nutrients can be distributed throughout the body. Large doses are toxic to poultry.
- Zinc—works with other minerals. A deficiency will cause retarded growth, hock joint enlargement, and skeleton abnormalties in young poults.

GRIT

Wild or ranged birds find grit on their own from sand, gravel, and dirt. If turkeys are confined for any length of time, even if only in the early morning hours and at night, supplemental grit must be provided. Many handlers forget to include grit when feeding their poults.

Commercially prepared grit consists of ground minerals and stones. It looks like fine aquarium gravel and is sold in three sizes—starter, grower, and layer. Starter grit is the size used for poults up to two weeks of age. Very small poults need to distinguish grit from feed or too much can be eaten and feed intake is reduced.

Poultry do not have teeth to break down their feed so it must be broken down for them to allow nutrients to be released and then absorbed and utilized in the body. Turkeys have a tongue shaped like a thin arrow or heart. The tongue is used to manipulate the feed for swallowing. After swallowing, the feed goes to the crop. The crop is a temporary storage area that helps soften the feed. From there, the feed goes to the gizzard. The gizzard is really a large muscle and it's function is considered the most important in starting the digestion process. The gizzard muscle contracts and crushes the grit against feed, breaking it into smaller, more digestible pieces. Naturally, large grains and pellets need to be broken down more than mash, so grit is even more important with these feeds. After leaving the gizzard, the feed goes to the pancreas and small intestine directly behind the gizzard where further digestion takes place. Most grit particles are indigestible and pass in the droppings after leaving the digestive tract.

Begin feeding the grit at about three days of age. This is not the period of time from which they were shipped, but rather the days from hatching. Many poults shipped will be almost two days old when received. Sprinkle a small amount (a spoonful or so to get them started) of fine grit lightly over the top of their feed daily. Older poults will usually eat only the amount of grit needed, so grit can be placed in separate containers for free-choice grit feeding. After two weeks of age, a grower-size grit should be fed. The size of grit in relation to the poults' body size is important. Grit that is too small will pass too quickly through the digestive system.

Coarse granite grit is sold in 50-pound bags for about $3. Some feed and grain dealers may sell it by the pound for small-scale growers. If a handler has only a few poults to feed, he can either give the coarse, clean sand in it's place or store the excess grit. The preferred method for storing grit is loose in a covered container. A 50-pound lard tin works well. If stored in the bag, dampness can cause the outer wrapping to tear off (although dampness does not affect grit) or rodents can chew into bags.

A confined flock of 50 large turkeys will consume about 25 pounds of grit per month. Turkeys housed with dirt floors will find a fair amount of stones for use as grit, but turkeys do not scratch around as much as chickens and their supply might be short. Provide grit in a separate feeder so turkeys can eat it free-choice.

MASH, PELLET, AND GRAIN FEEDING

All feeds are originally ground into a powder-type mash. Pellet feeds resemble small bullets. They are manufactured by keeping the ground feed at a higher-than-normal moisture level so it can be pressed through various die molds while being dried and heat-treated. When the final product cools, it's bagged for shipping. Crumbles are similar to pellets, but are broken down into a smaller form to be used mainly for poults. The extra processing of these feeds cause them to be more expensive.

Pellets take longer to fully digest than mash. This allows for better utilization and assimilation of the nutrients they contain. Pelleting a bulky ration also binds the nutrients and enables more nutrients to be consumed.

Mash feeds are considered wasteful because once it gets pushed out of the feeder, it sifts down into the litter never to be seen again. Pellet feeds don't get pushed out of the feeder as easily and when they do, they usually remain on top of litter to be seen and eaten.

Turkeys prefer the palatability of the chunkier feeds. If watched for any length of time, turkeys have a hard time swallowing fine mash. It does not slide down their gullet very easy. Crop binding can occur when mash is not moistened enough in the crop and it impacts into a thick lump instead of continuing on for digestion.

Scratch feeds are various whole and cracked grains mixed together to be fed as a supplemental ration, usually to add variety to the diet. With turkeys, it's mainly fed as a finisher to add fat and fleshing before butchering. Turkeys will eat scratch feed but they are a bit fussier than chickens. Most turkeys do not care for whole or cracked grains until the weather begins to cool down. Perhaps they know extra fattening isn't needed until cold weather sets in. Many handlers like to supplement with cracked grains one month before butchering. It seems to add more fleshing and that slight bit of fat to the carcass that makes it more appealing.

If scratch feed is fed, large grains such as corn should be cracked to aid in digestibility. Whole grains, especially corn, will cause diarrhea. Equal parts of cracked corn, oats, and wheat make a nice scratch feed. Whole oats can become stringy and fibrous if not ground properly. I've seen fine, dusty mashes containing fibrous portions of oats cause respiratory problems in turkeys. If the oats cannot be fully ground, it's best to omit them when having grains and supplements ground and mixed into turkey feed.

If scratch feed is fed as a supplement, you must increase the nutrient content of the grower or finisher feed to compensate for the reduced amount of protein. The protein content of the grains used in the scratch mixture can be figured by referring to Table 5-7. An example for equally mixed grains would be: Cracked corn at 8.8 percent protein + oats at 11.4 percent protein + wheat at 10.2 percent protein = 29.14. Then, the total 29.14 ÷ 3 grains = 9.71 percent total protein. If 100 pounds of each grain were used, this would be 9.71 percent protein in the 300 pounds of grains.

If a 16.5-percent protein grower feed is being fed, this protein percentage would need to be added to the scratch feed protein percentage. Example: Grower feed containing 16.5 percent protein + scratch feed at 9.71 percent protein = 26.21. The total is then divided by 2 feeds; 26.21 percent protein ÷ 2 feeds = 13.10 percent. Because a 16.5-percent ration is needed, the grower would need to be 19.9 percent because the total of the two original feeds would be 3.4 percent short. In our example: 16.5 percent − 13.10 percent = 3.4. Then 16.5 percent + 3.4 (percent short) = 19.9 percent. All this relies on the turkeys consuming equal parts of each feed (one-half of the 13.10-percent scratch = 6.55, and one-half of the 19.9 percent grower = 9.95); 6.55 + 9.95 = 16.5 percent.

It's usually more economical to mix your own scratch feed, and a home-mixed scratch feed often contains a better mixture. Most commercially mixed scratch feeds contain about three-quarters corn and very little oats and wheat. The proportions should be listed on the feed tag label. Pellets containing the correct protein percentage can be mixed with the scratch feed. Scratch should not be mixed with mash because the birds will throw out (bill out) the mash while picking through the scratch grains.

The addition of scratch feed to the diet of breeder turkey hens creates variety, which will usually cause them to produce eggs better. Breeder hens should also have a separate pan full of oyster shells so eggshells are good and firm when laid. Scratch feeds can be mixed by dumping the grains into a 55-gallon drum a little at a time, and mixing with a shovel.

DRINKING WATER REQUIREMENTS

Baby turkeys are voracious drinkers the first two weeks. Although water provides some trace minerals, it's function is primarily to help maintain the body temperature. A lack of drinking water causes the body tissues to dry out. This is dehydration.

Poults that have not learned to drink can be

Table 5-7. Composition of Some Feeds Commonly Used for Poultry.

Entry Number	Feed Name Description	International Feed Number[a]	Dry Matter (%)	ME$_n$ (kcal/kg)		Protein (%)	Ether Extract (%)	Linoleic Acid (%)	Crude Fiber (%)	Calcium (%)	Total Phosphorus (%)	Nonphytate Phosphorus (%)	Potassium (%)	Chlorine (%)
	ALFALFA *Medicago sativa*													
01	meal dehydrated, 17% protein	1-00-023	92	1370	(623)	17.5	2.0	0.47	24.1	1.44	0.22	0.22	2.17	0.47
02	meal dehydrated, 20% protein	1-00-024	92	1630	(741)	20.0	3.6	0.58	20.2	1.67	0.28	—	2.21	0.47
	BAKERY													
03	waste, dehydrated (dried bakery product)	4-00-466	92	3862	(1755)	9.8	11.7	—	1.2	0.13	0.24	—	0.49	1.48
	BARLEY *Hordeum vulgare*													
04	grain	4-00-549	89	2640	(1200)	11.6	1.8	0.83	5.1	0.03	0.36	0.16	0.48	0.15
05	grain, pacific coast	4-07-939	89	2620	(1191)	9.0	2.0	0.85	6.4	0.05	0.32	—	0.53	0.15
	BROADBEAN *Vicia faba*													
06	seeds	5-09-262	87	2431	(1105)	23.6	1.4		6.7	0.11	—	—	—	—
	BLOOD													
07	meal, vat dried	5-00-380	94	2830	(1286)	81.1	1.6	--	0.5	0.55	0.42	—	0.09	0.27
08	meal, spray or ring dried	5-00-381	93	3420	(1555)	88.9	1.0	0.10	0.6	0.06	0.09	—	0.41	0.27
	BREWERS GRAINS													
09	dehydrated	5-02-141	92	2080	(945)	25.3	6.2	2.94	15.3	0.29	0.52	—	0.09	0.12
	BUCKWHEAT, COMMON *Fagopyrum sagittatum*													
10	grain	4-00-994	88	2660	(1209)	10.8	2.5	—	10.5	0.09	0.32	0.12	0.40	0.04
	CANE MOLASSES—SEE MOLASSES													
	CANOLA *Brassica napus-Brassica campestris*													
11	seeds, meal prepressed extracted, low erucic acid, low glucosinolates	5-06-145	93	2000	(909)	38.0	3.8	—	11.1	0.68	1.17	0.30	1.29	—
	CASEIN													
12	dehydrated	5-01-162	93	4130	(1877)	87.2	0.8	—	0.2	0.61	1.00	—	0.01	—
13	precipitated dehydrated	3-20-837	92	4118	(1872)	85.0	0.6	—	0.2	0.68	0.82	—	0.01	—
	CORN, DENT YELLOW *Zea mays indentata*													
14	distillers grains, dehydrated	5-28-235	94	1972	(896)	27.8	9.2	—	11.3	0.10	0.40	—	0.17	0.07
15	distillers grains with solubles, dehydrated	5-28-236	93	2480	(1127)	27.4	9.0	4.55	9.1	0.17	0.72	0.41	0.65	0.17
16	distillers solubles, dehydrated	5-28-237	92	2930	(1332)	28.5	9.0	4.55	4.0	0.35	1.33	1.24	1.75	0.26
17	gluten, meal, 60% protein	5-28-242	90	3720	(1691)	62.0	2.5	—	1.3	—	0.50	0.19	0.35	0.05
18	gluten with bran (corn gluten feed)	5-28-243	90	1750	(795)	22.0	2.5	—	8.0	0.40	0.80	—	0.57	0.22
19	grain	4-02-935	89	3350	(1523)	8.8	3.8	2.20	2.2	0.02	0.28	0.10	0.30	0.04
20	grits by-product (hominy feed)	4-03-011	90	2896	(1316)	10.4	6.9	3.28	6.0	0.05	0.52	—	0.59	0.05
	COTTON *Gossypium spp*													
21	seeds, meal mechanically extracted, 41% protein (expeller)	5-01-617	93	2320	(1055)	40.9	3.9	2.47	10.8	0.20	1.05	—	1.19	0.04
22	seeds, meal prepressed solvent extracted, 41% protein	5-07-872	90	2400	(1091)	41.4	0.5	—	13.6	0.15	0.97	0.29	1.22	0.03
23	seeds, meal prepressed solvent extracted, 44% protein	5-07-873	91	1857	(845)	44.7	1.6	—	11.1	0.15	0.91	—	—	—
	FEATHERS—SEE POULTRY													
	FISH													
24	solubles, condensed	5-01-969	51	1460	(664)	31.5	7.8	—	0.2	0.30	0.76	—	1.74	2.65
25	solubles, dehydrated	5-01-971	92	2830	(1286)	63.6	9.3	0.12	0.5	1.23	1.63	—	0.37	—
	FISH, ANCHOVY *Engraulis ringen*													
26	meal mechanically extracted	5-01-985	92	2580	(1173)	64.2	5.0	0.20	1.0	3.73	2.43	—	0.69	0.29
	FISH, HERRING *Clupea harengus*													
27	meal mechanically extracted	5-02-000	93	3190	(1450)	72.3	10.0	0.15	0.7	2.29	1.70	—	1.09	0.90
	FISH, MENHADEN *Brevoortia tyrannus*													
28	meal mechanically extracted	5-02-009	92	2820	(1282)	60.5	9.4	0.12	0.7	5.11	2.88	—	0.77	0.60
	FISH, WHITE *Gadidae (family)·Lophiidae (family)-Rajidae (family)*													
29	meal mechanically extracted	5-02-025	91	2593	(1179)	62.6	4.6	0.08	0.7	7.31	3.81	—	0.83	0.50
	GELATIN													
30	process residue (gelatin by-products)	5-14-503	91	2360	(1073)	88.0	0.0	—	—	0.50	Trace	—	—	—
	HOMINY FEED—SEE CORN													
	LIVERS													
31	meal	5-00-389	92	2860	(1300)	65.6	15.0	—	1.4	0.56	1.25	—	—	—
	MEAT													
32	meal rendered	5-00-385	92	2000	(909)	54.4	7.1	0.28	8.7	8.27	4.10	—	0.60	0.91
33	with bone, meal rendered	5-00-388	93	1960	(891)	50.4	8.6	0.36	2.8	10.30	5.10	—	1.02	0.74
	MILLET, PEARL *Pennisetum glaucum*													
34	grain	4-03-118	91	2554	(1161)	13.1	4.3	0.84	4.3	0.05	0.32	—	0.43	0.14
	MILLET, PROSO *Panicum miliaceum*													

105

Entry Number	Iron (mg/kg)	Magnesium (%)	Manganese (mg/kg)	Sodium (%)	Sulfur (%)	Copper (mg/kg)	Selenium (mg/kg)	Zinc (mg/kg)	Biotin (mg/kg)	Choline (mg/kg)	Folic Acid (Folacin) (mg/kg)	Niacin (mg/kg)	Pantothenic Acid (mg/kg)	Vitamin B6 (Pyridoxine) (mg/kg)	Riboflavin (mg/kg)	Thiamin (mg/kg)	Vitamin B12 (μg/kg)	Vitamin E (mg/kg)
01	480	0.36	30	0.12	0.17	10	0.34	24	0.30	1401	4.2	38	25.0	6.5	13.6	3.4	4	125
02	390	0.36	42	0.13	0.43	11	0.29	25	0.33	1419	3.3	40	34.0	8.0	15.2	5.8	4	144
03	28	0.24	65	1.14	0.02	5	—	15	0.07	923	0.2	26	8.3	4.3	1.4	2.9	—	41
04	50	0.14	16	0.01	0.15	16	0.10	17	0.15	1960	0.7	55	8.0	3.0	1.8	1.9	—	20
05	110	0.12	16	0.02	0.15	8	0.10	15	0.15	1034	0.5	48	7.0	2.9	1.6	4.0	—	20
06	—	—	—	—	—	—	—	—	—	—	—	—	—	—	—	—	—	—
07	2020	0.16	5	0.32	0.32	10	0.01	4	0.08	695	0.1	29	3.0	4.4	2.6	0.4	44	—
08	3000	0.40	6	0.33	0.32	8	—	306	0.20	280	0.4	13	5.0	4.4	1.3	0.5	44	—
09	250	0.16	38	0.15	0.31	21	0.70	98	0.96	1723	7.1	29	8.0	0.7	1.4	0.5	—	25
10	44	0.09	34	0.05	0.14	10	—	9	—	440	—	19	12.0	—	5.5	4.0	—	—
11	159	0.64	54	—	—	10	1.00	71	0.90	6700	2.3	160	9.5	—	3.7	5.2	—	—
12	18	0.01	4	0.01	—	4	—	33	0.05	205	0.5	1	3.0	0.4	1.5	0.5	—	—
13	17	0.01	4	0.01	—	4	—	32	0.04	206	0.5	1	2.7	0.4	1.5	0.4	—	—
14	209	0.07	22	0.09	0.43	45	0.45	33	0.49	1180	0.9	37	11.7	4.4	5.2	1.7	—	—
15	280	0.19	24	0.48	0.30	57	0.39	80	0.78	2637	0.9	71	11.0	2.2	8.6	2.9	—	40
16	560	0.64	74	0.26	0.37	83	0.33	85	1.10	4842	1.1	116	21.0	10.0	17.0	6.9	3	55
17	400	0.15	4	0.02	0.43	26	1.00	33	0.15	330	0.2	55	3.0	6.2	2.2	0.3	—	24
18	460	0.29	24	0.95	0.22	48	0.10	7	0.33	1518	0.3	66	17.0	15.0	2.4	2.0	—	15
19	350	0.12	5	0.02	0.08	3	0.03	10	0.06	620	0.4	24	4.0	7.0	1.0	3.5	—	22
20	67	0.24	15	0.08	0.03	14	0.10	3	0.13	1155	0.3	47	8.2	11.0	2.1	8.1	—	—
21	160	0.52	23	0.04	0.40	19	0.06	64	0.60	2753	1.0	38	10.0	5.3	5.1	6.4	—	39
22	110	0.40	20	0.04	0.31	18	—	82	0.55	2933	2.7	40	7.0	3.0	4.0	3.3	—	—
23	—	—	—	—	—	—	—	—	—	2685	0.9	46	14.5	—	4.7	—	—	—
24	160	0.02	14	2.62	0.12	45	2.00	38	0.18	3519	0.2	169	35.0	12.2	14.6	5.5	347	—
25	300	0.30	50	0.37	0.40	—	—	76	0.26	5507	0.6	271	55.0	23.8	7.7	7.4	401	6
26	220	0.24	10	0.88	0.54	9	1.36	103	0.23	4408	0.2	100	15.0	4.0	7.1	0.1	352	4
27	140	0.15	5	0.61	0.69	6	1.93	132	0.31	5306	0.8	93	17.0	4.0	9.9	0.1	403	22
28	440	0.16	33	0.41	0.45	11	2.10	147	0.20	3056	0.6	55	9.0	4.0	4.9	0.5	104	7
29	181	0.18	12	0.78	0.48	6	1.62	90	0.08	3099	0.3	59	9.9	5.9	9.1	1.7	90	9
30	—	0.05	—	—	—	—	—	—	—	—	—	—	—	—	—	—	—	—
31	630	—	9	—	—	89	—	—	0.02	11311	5.5	204	29.0	—	46.3	0.2	498	—
32	440	0.58	10	1.15	0.49	10	0.42	103	0.17	2077	0.3	57	5.0	3.0	5.5	0.2	68	1
33	490	1.12	14	0.72	0.50	2	0.25	93	0.64	1996	0.3	46	4.1	12.8	4.4	0.8	70	1
34	25	0.14	31	0.04	0.13	22	—	13	—	793	—	53	7.8	—	1.6	6.7	—	—

Entry Number	Feed Name Description	International Feed Number[a]	Dry Matter (%)	ME_n (kcal/kg)		Protein (%)	Ether Extract (%)	Linoleic Acid (%)	Crude Fiber (%)	Calcium (%)	Total Phosphorus (%)	phytate Phosphorus (%)	Potassium (%)	Chlorine (%)
35	grain	4-03-120	90	2898	(1317)	11.6	3.5	—	6.1	0.03	0.30	0.14	0.43	—
	OATS *Avena sativa*													
36	grain	4-03-309	89	2550	(1159)	11.4	4.2	1.47	10.8	0.06	0.27	0.12	0.45	0.11
37	grain, pacific coast	4-07-999	91	2610	(1186)	9.0	5.0	—	11.0	0.08	0.30	—	0.37	0.12
38	hulls	1-03-281	92	400	(182)	4.6	1.4	—	28.7	0.13	0.10	—	0.53	0.10
	PEA *Pisum* spp													
39	seeds	5-03-600	90	2570	(1168)	23.8	1.3	—	5.5	0.11	0.42	—	1.02	0.06
	PEANUT *Arachis hypogaea*													
40	kernels, meal mechanically extracted (peanut meal) (expeller)	5-03-649	90	2500	(1136)	39.8	7.3	1.43	13.0	0.16	0.56	—	1.13	0.03
41	kernels, meal solvent extracted (peanut meal)	5-03-650	92	2200	(1000)	50.7	1.2	0.24	11.9	0.20	0.63	0.36	1.19	0.03
	POULTRY													
42	by-product, meal rendered (viscera with feet and heads)	5-03-798	93	2670	(1214)	58.0	13.0	2.54	2.0	3.00	1.70	—	0.30	0.54
43	feathers, meal hydrolyzed	5-03-795	93	2360	(1073)	86.4	3.3	—	1.0	0.33	0.55	—	0.31	0.28
	RICE *Oryza sativa*													
44	bran with germ (rice bran)	4-03-928	91	2100	(955)	12.9	13.0	3.57	11.4	0.07	1.50	0.21	1.73	0.07
45	grain, polished and broken (Brewers rice)	4-03-932	89	2990	(1359)	8.7	0.7	—	9.8	0.08	—	—	0.00	0.08
46	polishings	4-03-943	90	3090	(1405)	12.2	11.0	3.58	4.1	0.05	1.31	0.14	1.06	0.11
	RYE *Secale cereale*													
47	grain	4-04-047	88	2626	(1194)	12.1	1.5	—	2.2	0.06	0.32	0.08	0.46	0.03
	SAFFLOWER *Carthamus tinctorius*													
48	seeds, meal solvent extracted	5-04-110	92	1193	(542)	23.4	1.4	—	30.0	0.34	0.75	—	0.76	—
49	seeds without hulls, meal solvent extracted	5-07-959	92	1921	(873)	43.0	1.3	—	13.5	0.35	1.29	0.40	1.10	0.16
	SESAME *Sesamum indicum*													
50	seeds, meal mechanically extracted (expeller)	5-04-220	93	2210	(1005)	43.8	8.6	1.90	9.7	1.99	1.37	0.26	1.20	0.06
	SORGHUM *Sorghum bicolor*													
51	grain, 8-10% protein	4-20-893	87	3288	(1495)	8.8	2.9	1.13	2.3	0.04	0.30	—	0.35	—
52	grain, more than 10% protein	4-20-894	88	3212	(1460)	11.0	2.1	0.82	2.3	0.04	0.32	—	0.33	—
	SOYBEAN *Glycine max*													
53	flour by-product (soybean mill feed)	4-04-594	89	720	(327)	13.3	1.6	—	33.0	0.37	0.19	—	1.50	—
54	protein concentrate, more than 70% protein	5-08-038	93	3500	(1591)	84.1	0.4	—	0.2	0.02	0.80	0.32	0.18	0.02
55	seeds, heat processed	5-04-597	90	3300	(1500)	37.0	18.0	8.46	5.5	0.25	0.58	—	1.61	0.03
56	seeds, meal solvent extracted	5-04-604	89	2230	(1014)	44.0	0.8	0.40	7.3	0.29	0.65	0.27	2.00	0.05
57	seeds without hulls, meal solvent extracted	5-04-612	90	2440	(1109)	48.5	1.0	0.40	3.9	0.27	0.62	0.24	2.02	0.05
	SUNFLOWER, COMMON *Helianthus annuus*													
58	seeds, meal solvent extracted	5-09-340	90	1543	(701)	23.3	1.1	0.60	31.6	0.21	0.93	0.14	0.96	—
59	seeds without hulls, meal solvent extracted	5-04-739	93	2320	(1055)	45.4	2.9	1.59	12.2	0.37	1.00	—	1.00	0.10
	TRITICALE *Triticale hexaploide*													
60	grain	4-20-362	90	3163	(1438)	15.8	1.5	—	4.0	0.05	0.30	0.11	0.36	—
	WHEAT *Triticum aestivum*													
61	bran	4-05-190	89	1300	(591)	15.7	3.0	1.70	11.0	0.14	1.15	0.34	1.19	0.06
62	flour by-product, less than 4% fiber (wheat red dog)	4-05-203	88	2568	(1167)	15.3	3.3	—	2.6	0.04	0.49	—	0.51	0.14
63	flour by-product, less than 9.5% fiber (wheat middlings)	4-05-205	88	1800	(818)	16.0	3.0	1.87	7.5	0.12	0.90	0.23	0.99	0.03
64	flour by-product, less than 7% fiber (wheat shorts)	4-05-201	88	2162	(983)	16.5	4.6	—	6.8	0.09	0.81	—	0.93	0.07
65	grain, hard red winter	4-05-268	87	2800	(1273)	14.1	1.9	0.59	2.4	0.05	0.37	0.11	0.45	0.05
66	grain, soft white winter	4-05-337	89	3120	(1418)	10.2	1.8	—	2.4	0.05	0.31	—	0.40	0.08
	WHEY *Bos taurus*													
67	dehydrated	4-01-182	93	1900	(864)	12.0	0.8	0.01	0.2	0.97	0.76	—	1.05	0.07
68	low lactose, dehydrated (dried whey product)	4-01-186	91	2090	(950)	15.5	1.0	0.01	0.3	1.95	0.98	—	3.00	2.10
	YEAST, BREWERS *Saccharomyces cerevisiae*													
69	dehydrated	7-05-527	93	1990	(905)	44.4	1.0	—	2.7	0.12	1.40	—	1.70	0.12
	YEAST, TORULA *Torulopsis utilis*													
70	dehydrated	7-05-534	93	2160	(982)	47.2	2.5	0.05	2.4	0.58	1.67	—	1.88	0.02

[a] First digit is class of feed: 1, dry forages and roughages; 2, pasture, range plants, and forages fed green; 3, silages; 4, energy feeds; 5, protein supplements; 6, minerals; 7, vitamins; 8, additives; the other five digits are the International Feed Number.

Entry Number	Iron (mg/kg)	Magnesium (%)	Manganese (mg/kg)	Sodium (%)	Sulfur (%)	Copper (mg/kg)	Selenium (mg/kg)	Zinc (mg/kg)	Biotin (mg/kg)	Choline (mg/kg)	Folic Acid (Folacin) (mg/kg)	Niacin (mg/kg)	Pantothenic Acid (mg/kg)	Vitamin B6 (Pyridoxine) (mg/kg)	Riboflavin (mg/kg)	Thiamin (mg/kg)	Vitamin B12 (µg/kg)	Vitamin E (mg/kg)
35	71	0.16	—	—	—	—	—	—	—	440	—	23	11.0	—	3.8	7.3	—	—
36	70	0.16	43	0.08	0.21	8	0.30	17	0.11	946	0.3	12	7.8	1.0	1.1	6.0	—	20
37	73	0.17	38	0.06	0.20	—	0.07	—	0.11	959	0.3	14	13.0	1.3	1.1	—	—	20
38	100	0.08	14	0.04	0.14	3	—	0.1	—	284	1.0	7	3.0	2.2	1.5	0.6	—	—
39	50	0.13	—	0.04	—	—	—	30	0.18	642	0.4	34	10.0	1.0	2.3	7.5	—	3
40	156	0.33	25	0.07	0.29	15	0.28	20	0.76	1655	0.4	166	47.0	10.0	5.2	7.1	—	3
41	142	0.04	29	0.07	0.30	15	—	20	0.39	2396	0.4	170	53.0	10.0	11.0	5.7	—	3
42	440	0.22	11	0.40	0.51	14	0.75	120	0.30	5952	1.0	40	12.3	4.4	11.0	1.0	310	2
43	76	0.20	21	0.71	1.50	7	0.84	54	0.44	891	0.2	27	10.0	3.0	2.1	0.1	78	—
44	190	0.95	324	0.07	0.18	13	0.40	30	0.42	1135	2.2	293	23.0	14.0	2.5	22.5	—	60
45	—	0.11	18	0.07	0.06	—	0.27	17	0.08	800	0.2	46	8.0	—	0.7	1.4	—	14
46	160	0.65	12	0.10	0.17	3	—	28	0.61	1237	0.2	520	47.0	—	1.8	19.8	—	90
47	60	0.12	58	0.02	0.15	7	0.38	31	0.06	419	0.6	19	8.0	2.6	1.6	3.6	—	15
48	495	0.35	18	0.05	0.13	10	—	41	1.43	820	0.5	11	33.9	—	2.3	—	—	1
49	484	1.02	39	0.04	0.20	9	—	33	1.67	3248	1.6	22	39.1	11.3	2.4	4.5	—	1
50	93	0.77	48	0.04	0.43	—	—	100	0.34	1536	—	30	6.0	12.5	3.6	2.8	—	—
51	—	0.15	15	0.01	0.08	—	—	—	0.26	668	0.2	41	12.4	5.2	1.3	3.9	—	7
52	—	0.12	—	0.01	0.11	—	—	—	—	—	—	—	—	—	1.1	—	—	—
53	—	0.12	29	0.25	0.06	—	—	—	0.22	640	0.3	24	13.0	2.2	3.5	2.2	—	—
54	130	0.01	1	0.07	0.71	7	0.10	23	0.3	2	2.5	6	4.2	5.4	1.2	0.2	—	—
55	80	0.28	30	0.03	0.22	16	0.11	16	0.27	2860	4.2	22	11.0	10.8	2.6	11.0	—	40
56	120	0.27	29	0.04	0.43	22	0.10	27	0.32	2794	1.3	29	16.0	6.0	2.9	4.5	—	2
57	—	—	43	0.03	—	15	0.10	45	0.32	2731	3.6	22	15.0	5.0	2.9	3.2	—	3
58	—	0.68	—	—	0.30	—	—	—	—	3791	—	264	29.9	11.1	3.0	3.0	—	—
59	30	0.75	23	2.00	—	4	—	—	1.45	2894	—	220	24.0	16.0	4.7	3.1	—	11
60	44	—	43	—	0.15	8	—	32	—	462	—	—	—	—	0.4	—	—	—
61	170	0.52	113	0.05	0.22	14	0.85	133	0.48	1880	1.2	186	31.0	7.0	4.6	8.0	—	14
62	46	0.16	55	0.04	0.24	6	0.30	65	0.11	1534	0.8	42	13.3	4.6	2.2	22.8	—	33
63	40	0.16	118	0.12	0.26	18	0.80	150	0.37	1439	0.8	98	13.0	9.0	2.2	16.5	—	40
64	73	0.25	117	0.02	0.20	12	0.43	109	—	1813	1.7	107	22.3	7.2	4.2	19.1	—	54
65	50	0.17	32	0.04	0.12	6	0.20	31	0.11	1090	0.4	48	9.9	3.4	1.4	4.5	—	13
66	40	0.10	24	0.04	0.12	7	0.06	28	0.11	1002	0.4	57	11.0	4.0	1.2	4.3	—	13
67	130	0.13	6	0.48	1.04	46	0.08	3	0.34	1369	0.8	10	44.0	4.0	27.1	4.1	23	0.2
68	238	0.25	8	1.50	1.05	7	0.10	7	0.64	4392	1.4	19	69.0	4.0	45.8	5.7	23	—
69	120	0.23	5	0.07	0.38	33	1.00	39	1.05	3984	9.9	448	109.0	42.8	37.0	91.8	1	2
70	90	0.13	13	0.01	0.34	14	1.00	99	1.39	2881	22.4	500	73.0	36.3	47.7	6.2	4	—

★Author's note: ME is metabolizable energy. The "n" means 0-nitrogen (there is no more nitrogen being accumulated than is being lost). For simplification, the calories listed in parenthesis can be considered the same as those for human food although kilocalories is the precise scientific term for measurement. Calories are per 1.1 lbs. of feed, whereas kilocalories are per 2.2 lbs. of feed.

Nutrient Requirements of Poultry, 8th revised edition, copyright 1984, National Academy of Sciences.

picked out at about three to four days of age by their shanks. A dehydrating poult will have legs that appear slightly darkened, shriveled, and dry. A well-watered poult's legs will be slightly plumped out and of good coloring. Once a poult is dehydrated, he is stressed from lack of nourishment because of moisture loss. The poult gradually becomes weaker and does not even try to venture out to eat and drink. Usually no amount of coaxing can get him to begin drinking at this stage. Most dehydrated poults die within five days. Dehydration is the most common cause of mortality during the first week. This is why it's so important to spend those few extra minutes the first day or two in getting poults to drink.

To be sure poults are drinking, there should be a noticeable amount of water gone from the waterers within the first 24 hours. Each poult will consume about one ounce of water the first 24 hours after shipping, or by the third day if home-hatched. Even if only a pint jar is used when raising eight day-old poults, the jar would appear over half empty. For the first few days, you can mark the water level right on the waterer. Poults just shipped should be eagerly drinking the first day, the third day for home-hatched poults. By the end of this first (or third) day, if poults do not seem to be drinking, use the watering method described under "Watering on Arrival" in Chapter 2.

It's more important and naturally more of a chore to get large broods of poults drinking. They seem to get lost in the shuffle. They do not know to push their way through a crowd to search for water, so have plenty of waterers available around them. Once they get a good taste of the water their instincts will bring them to it. Never let waterers run dry. There is usually no problem when only a few (6-12) poults are being brooded. With only a few, the waterers are usually always in sight. Be sure waterers are highly visible by allowing the additional artificial lighting provided to continuously shine on founts.

Drinking water acts as a softening agent of the food eaten. It assists in the digestion of the food and in the assimilation of the nutrients from the food.

Poults should never be given ice-cold water, especially when first watered (or when they've been without water for any length of time). This will chill their insides and they will want to go under the heating element to warm rather than drink more water. Ice-cold water can upset the digestive tract. Even tap water is about 50 degrees F. (10 degrees C.)—a big difference from the poults' body temperature of 105.5 degrees F. (40.83 degrees C.). So give warmed water. After the first few days when poults are drinking freely, water at room temperature is fine.

Excessive heat and humidity will cause the poults to drink more than usual. The composition of the diet will also vary the water intake. Digestive disorders such as coccidiosis can cause an increase in water intake as the poults try to relieve the distress, so observe water intake. Drinking water requirements for turkeys can be estimated by referring to Table 5-8.

Table 5-8. Daily Water Consumption of Turkeys

Per 100 mixed sex turkeys*		
Age (weeks)	Gallons (U.S.)	(Liters)
1	1	3.8
2	2	7.6
3	3	11.4
4	4	15.2
5	5	19.0
6	6	22.8
7	7.5	28.5
8	9.5	36.1
9	11.5	43.7
10	12.5	47.5
12	15.0	57.0
15	16.0	60.8
20	20.0	76.0
35**	M 24.0	91.2
	F 13.0	49.4

**Laying or breeding season at 35 weeks—water consumption separated for each sex.
*Will vary considerably depending on temperature and diet composition.

(Adapted from *Nutrient Requirements of Poultry, 8th Revised Edition,* copyright 1984, National Academy of Sciences.)

FOOD AND WATER ADDITIVES

It is a popular belief that poults cannot be raised without highly medicating their feed and water. Many handlers are led to believe the poults will die if not medicated. This fear causes some handlers to medicate needlessly and sometimes excessively. I've seen handlers lose baby poultry because of this.

Antibiotics have been used in poultry feeds since 1950. Commercially prepared turkey feeds are available to dealers in nonmedicated mixes, although most will stock the medicated types. If a nonmedicated commercially prepared feed is desired, it might be considered a special order, requiring at least a half-ton lot be purchased.

One of the medications used in turkey feeds is Amprollium, a coccidiostat for the prevention of coccidiosis. There are more than 15 types of coccidiostats placed in feeds. It is important that feeds containing Amprollium are not fed to treat outbreaks or fed while medicating water with coccidiostats. The way the coccidiostat in feeds works is that it actually gives the poult the disease in order to build up an immunity within the poult's body. A handler not warned might wonder why his poults have become infected when they've been receiving a preventative in the feed and then try to treat the outbreak by medicating the water while still giving the same medicated feed—a dangerous mistake. One feed company suggests handlers ride out this outbreak of coccidiosis brought on by the medicated feed. If the birds are extremely uncomfortable, then it's recommended a sulfa drug be given to counteract the effects.

Gross overuse of Amprollium can cause nonreversible lameness because it interferes with the normal functioning of vitamin B_1. A vitamin B_1 deficiency results in symptoms such as excitability, flightiness, reduced appetite. If the deficiency continues because of overuse of Amprollium, the lameness and muscle paralysis sets in. If lameness has not set in, the addition of vitamin B_1 will correct the mild symptoms. If found toxic, stop Amprollium feeding and give vitamin B_1. Amprollium can be toxic to guineas and waterfowl, so do not feed to these birds.

Warnings exist on feed tags of medicated bags of feed as to using the feed as the only source of Amprollium. This warning, however, is often placed on the backsides of feed tags where it can easily go unnoticed. There are are least 24 coccidiostats cleared by the Food and Drug Administration (FDA) for use in poultry. Some can be purchased for medicating drinking water.

Histomonastats are medications used to help prevent blackhead (histomoniasis) disease in turkeys. It can be purchased already mixed in turkey grower feed or it can be placed in the drinking water. Again, this type feed might have to be special-ordered. The medication is sometimes difficult to locate and purchase if water medicating and prevention is desired. Some types can be ordered through poultry supply houses. A product called Emtryl (dimetridazole) is the most commonly available type for water medicating. Ipronidazole is used in commercially prepared feeds to aid in the prevention of blackhead. This feed is usually given after the starter feed, at eight weeks when turkeys might be ranged and become more exposed to the organism.

Be sure to observe all warnings and cautions when using any medications. Observe withdrawal times. This is the time from which the bird consumed the medication to the time when the bird or it's eggs are to be eaten. Some medications, such as Ipronidazole, should not be fed to turkeys whose eggs will be eaten by humans. Use medications only if you feel the need. Do not let salesmen or fellow handlers intimidate you by telling you your poults will die if you don't use medications. You should not be afraid of using nonmedicated products if you've never tried to before. You might even find you have better success with your birds if you don't constantly and habitually medicate. If you experience problems one year, first scrutinize the management of your turkeys. Perhaps the problem could have been avoided by better or different management methods. If some turkeys die because of the blackhead parasite transmitted by cecal worms, a handler might either try worming his poultry brood and/or, feed a histomonastat as a preventative measure. Whatever you decide, be sure the decision is yours and that medications are not used as a substitute for good management.

FINISHING OUT

With a continual well-balanced ration available, most turkey hens will be finished out by 16 weeks of age and most toms by 20 weeks of age. A finished bird has sufficient fleshing and fat covering.

Fleshing refers to the amount of well-rounded meat on carcass. The drumsticks, thighs, and breast contain the bulk of the meat. If these are well-fleshed, the back should have a good distribution of flesh. The drumstick should be moderately thick and wide at the hock joint and continue upward to make the drumstick appear plump and well-rounded. The thigh should be well to moderately fleshed. The breast should be moderately long and deep and have enough flesh to give it a rounded appearance. The fleshing should extend the entire length of the breastbone right up to the tip. Even wings should have moderate fleshing.

The fleshing on the breast of a market-age bird can be tested by finding the feather tract to one side of the breast. A feather tract is the noticeably raised portion of skin running from the top to the bottom which contains series of feather follicles. Fat naturally collects under these feather tracts. Take both hands and grab a fold of skin with both thumbs and index fingers; the fold of skin should appear thick, white, or cream-colored. If thin, the skin will look semitransparent and reddish, and the bird should be fattened further. (This test can't be done on breeder toms.)

A well-balanced ration will assure good fleshing in a reasonable amount of time. Fat distribution can be enhanced by feeding a fattening ration supplement of scratch feed containing cracked corn for the last month. The corn will help put a slight bit of fat and coloring over the carcass to make it more appealing. If turkeys do not favor the cracked corn, try mixing it with grower or finisher pellets. Many turkeys will not eat cracked corn by itself unless the weather has become cool.

Many plant products contain Xanthophyll. These are groups of pigments that can impart color in the fat and skin of poultry. Not all plants have enough of these pigments to noticeably change the color. The plants usually contained in poultry feed that have sufficient pigments to color are alfalfa meal, yellow corn, and corn gluten meal. Alfalfa meal imparts a yellow color, corn and corn gluten meal imparts an orange-red color.

HOME-MIXED RATIONS

To mix your own rations less expensively than purchasing commercially prepared feeds, you must be able to obtain the basic grains at a very reasonable cost. Also, the feed should preferably be consumed within a month's time. Even if antioxidation compounds are used in the feed to help preserve its freshness, nutrients will be lost during prolonged storage. Consult Tables 5-1 and 5-2 to figure how long it would take your particular age of turkeys to consume larger lots of feed. This will tell you if purchasing large lots is worthwhile.

Most feed mills that do custom grinding and mixing will not bother with amounts less than a half ton. Some will grind only 1 ton. Many also have a minimum set charge for grinding half-ton lots, which—when added to the cost of the grains, supplements, and concentrates—can cost more per 50- or 100-pound bags than prepared feed. A handler must do some comparison shopping.

First, find out the formula for the type of feed to be mixed. Figure out what proportions and what types of grains are needed to mix a 22-, 19-, 16 1/2-, 14- or 12- percent protein ration—whatever the turkeys' age requirements are. The feed mill who does grinding and mixing will have the formula. They can tell you how much corn, oats, wheat, etc., is needed to mix with a certain amount of protein concentrate, vitamin supplement, mineral supplement, and salt. Check the prices on the mill's grains, their protein concentrate, and supplements to make a completely balanced ration. Check prior with a number of mills in the area. Then check grain prices with farmers who might be selling grains outright to customers. Also find out the hours the grains can be ground at the mill. Grinding and mixing takes

Table 5-9. Bushel Weights for Various Grains. *

Grain	lb/bushel	kg/hectoliter
Barley	36-48	46-62
Corn	46-56	59-72
Oats	22-40	28-52
Rye	49-56	63-72
Sorghum (milo)	51-57	66-74
Wheat	45-63	58-81

*At standard moisture levels, increased weight means more meaty kernel with oats and barley. Non-matured corn, sorghum, and wheat reduces usable energy content and bushel weight.

time. Sometimes an informal appointment must be made in advance to prevent customers from having to wait their turn.

To prevent ground feed from molding later, the grains should have been dried in a grain dryer. Field-dried grains contain enough moisture to later turn moldy. These grains appear dry, but are not dry enough for closed storage. Ask the farmer if the particular grain in question has been dried in a grain dryer. If feed is ground with high-moisture grains, it will become unusable when it molds. It will then have to be buried or dumped onto a compost pile where the poultry and other animals cannot touch it. Moldy feed is quite toxic.

Table 5-9 shows the weights per bushel for various grains that can be used for poultry feeds. Weights will vary depending upon the maturity and dryness of the grains you use.

Corn will constitute the major portion of the mash to be mixed. The next largest portion is the protein concentrates. Even if you have your own homegrown grains, figure the total cost of mixing these into a feed. In this way, you'll know how much your turkeys have cost you to raise. Be sure to add the sometimes forgotten costs, such as gasoline costs to pick up grains from a farmer, feed bags that will be needed, your time and labor to pick up the grains, etc. After everything is totaled, then figure the cost for each 50 or 100 pounds and compare with prepared rations. Your home-mixed grain should consist of a half ton (1,000 pounds) or 1 ton (2,000 pounds). There would be 20 feed bags full of feed from one ton—each bag containing 100 pounds. With 1 ton, simply compare what twenty 100-pound bags already prepared would normally cost, or what forty 50-pound bags would cost. Also ask the feed mill the price of the particular feed if purchased in 1-ton lots. Some have lower prices on 1-ton and half-ton lots.

A word on feed bags: you will have to bring your own or purchase bags to take the feed home. Bring a few extra because not all bags are the same size, and unsettled, freshly ground feed might take up more space in bags. Plastic-type feed bags last the longest. If bags must be purchased from the mill, make sure they are not paper bags that can't be reused. Some mills charge the same amount for these as they do the plastic or burlap bags. Burlap bags are quickly being replaced by the woven plastic bags. Burlap, being a natural fiber, tends to rot and tear easily and does not dry out as quickly if it becomes wet. Although rodents will chew through the plastic bags, they are more attracted to the burlap. Empty plastic feed bags are usually not bothered when stored, but be sure every trace of feed is shaken out from the seams or rodents will go after this small bit of feed.

Chapter 6

Turkey Meat

BUTCHERING STEPS

In the industry, hens are usually butchered at 16 weeks and toms at about 20 weeks. Older turkeys are slaughtered for use in products such as soup. It's not economical to overfeed meat birds because the feed to meat ratio reduces with age. The longer the turkeys are kept, the more the meat will cost per pound.

Lightweight varieties of turkeys are commonly called fryer-roasters. These are marketed at 5 to 9 pounds. Originally, these turkeys were popular because they filled the gap between large turkeys and small chickens. Fryer-roaster turkeys are sold frozen. Fryer-roaster chickens are sold fresh (not frozen). This reduced the popularity of the small fryer-roaster turkeys, which are usually sold at a higher price than the fresh chickens.

Figure 6-1 illustrates a butchered turkey at its prime—well-fattened and free of pinfeathers. Check the fat covering by taking a fold of skin between the thumb and index finger of each hand along one side of the breast where a natural line of fat extends over the raised heavy feather tract. The fat in poultry is judged entirely by accumulations under the skin. Accumulations occur first around the feather follicles in the heavy feather tracts. Poorly fattened turkeys can have some accumulation of fat in the skin along the heavy feather tracts on the sides of the breast. As the fattening progresses to a good finish, the accumulations will be at the junction of the wishbone and keel and also where the thigh skin joins the breast skin. Included will be accumulations around the feather follicles between the heavy feather tracts and over the back and hips. Well-finished older birds contain enough fat in these areas and over the drumsticks so the flesh is difficult to see. Older hens have excessive fat in the abdominal area. A well-finished young turkey will have less fat under the skin between the heavy feather tracts over the breast, drumsticks, and thighs than an older bird.

When holding the fold of skin, an under-fattened turkey will have semi-transparent thin skin

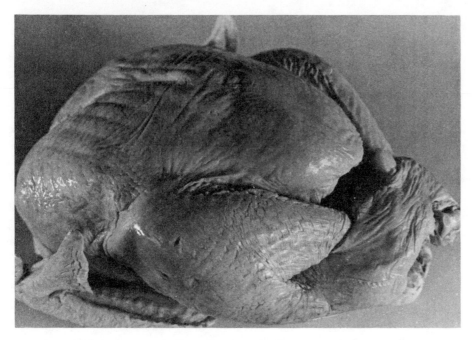

Fig. 6-1. A well-fattened turkey carcass.

that appears reddish. On a prime turkey, the skin will be thick and white to yellowish-white; well-fattened birds will have thick cream-colored skin. This skin-fold test cannot be done on toms during the breeding season because of the curious growth on the breast at this time. It's a thick mass of tissue that swells, serving as a reserve of oil and fat from which the tom draws energy to compensate for lost energy during the breeding season. It's impossible to grab and pinch this skin together. The test is meant for market-age toms and hens.

Pinfeathers are either protruding or non-protruding short stubs of immature feathers. Non-protruding pinfeathers are evident but have not pushed through the outer layer of skin. This is fine. Pinfeathers already through the skin can be difficult to remove unless there is sufficient brush on them to facilitate picking. Delaying butchering until the short stubs being to form a brush on the ends will make picking easier.

If possible, plan outdoor home butchering for cool weather when the fly season is over. Cooler weather also helps to chill the butchered carcasses. The building or area to be used should be reasonably clean and sanitary to prevent bacteria from contaminating the freshly butchered meat. Some

handlers do the entire killing, scalding, and eviscerating outdoors. Some do only the killing, scalding, and picking outdoors and finish the eviscerating indoors, away from insects (and warmer outdoor temperatures).

Gather and pen the birds near the butchering area to save time in handling. Keep them in a raised cage without litter. Give the birds drinking water only—do not feed them for 6 hours or more before butchering. This prevents the crop and the intestines from being filled which means cleaner and more sanitary butchering.

Begin by getting the scalding pot ready. The pot should be large enough so turkeys can be completely submerged. Also plan on whether the turkeys will be hung for bleeding and feather-picking or held into a 55-gallon drum. (The drum is used for bleeding and the feathers can be removed while the turkey is laid on a board across the drum or a work table.)

For just a few birds, the pot of water can be heated to almost boiling on a range in the kitchen and carted to the large pot outdoors. When large amounts (over three large turkeys) are to be scalded, a constant supply of heated water will be needed to maintain the correct water temperature.

Hot coals in an incinerator or ground pit can be used to keep the water hot outdoors, or a drum with a heating element and thermostat (similar to those used in electric hot water heating tanks) can be constructed. The element is inserted with washers into a hole cut near the bottom of the side of the drum and is finished by caulking. Never operate the heater when the drum is empty or the element can burn out.

A portable camp stove can also be used to keep extra smaller pots of water boiling to add to the large scalding pot. It's best to always keep the scalding pot over a fire because smaller pots might not become hot enough by the time they are needed to add to the large pot.

Automatically heated small scalding tanks that maintain the water at the correct temperature. Because keeping the scalding pot hot enough can be a chore, I find this automatic scalder (or the one that can be constructed) a better investment than a picking machine. Feather removal will be tough if the scalding is not done at the correct temperature. Processing plants use a scalder that rotates the birds while they are dipped and scalded.

Beginners should use a thermometer to check the water temperature before scalding. This can be done quickly with a dial meat thermometer sold at restaurant supply wholesale stores. The thermometer can also be used for instant readings in incubators, brooders, egg storage rooms, poultry houses, for smoking and cooking meats, etc. A candy thermometer can be used, but is slower because you must wait for the mercury to rise.

Scalding softens and relaxes the muscles that hold the feathers into the skin, which makes feather removal easier. Adding a small amount of detergent to the scalding water allows the water to more easily penetrate the oils of the feathers for a more thorough scalding. It is easier to grasp feathers when they are wet. Soft water penetrates feathers much faster than hard water; a few teaspoons of baking soda will help soften hard water.

Use a "semi-soft" or slack-scald on young birds: Immerse them in water about 128 degrees F. (53 degrees C.) and swish around for about one minute. Temperatures above 130 degrees F. (54 degrees C.) will cause the very thin yellow outer covering of the skin to peel off on young birds, making the skin appear tattered.

Older hens and toms should be sub-scalded: Immerse in water 138 to 140 degrees F. (58-60 degrees C.) for about one minute. Stubborn feathers on older birds will be loosened with this hotter water, but the skin will have a tacky feeling because the outer skin covering is removed.

Commercially, the killing process is accomplished with an electric stunner/sticking knife. This prevents bruises and broken wings on the dressed birds and provides faster and more thorough bleeding. The birds are stunned as they are stuck and the body becomes rigid. There is no flopping around to cause bruises. Electric stunning knives are much too expensive for most small-scale butcherers.

Small-scale killing is done by severing the jugular veins in the top of the throat. Sticking (braining) can also be done (Fig. 6-2). Sticking involves inserting a knife into the groove in the roof of the mouth and thrusting backwards directly back of the eye into the part of the brain known as the medula. With a proper stick, the tail feathers will spread. This takes much experience and is not a necessary method of home killing.

The more common method is to sever the jugular veins from the outside of the throat with a knife or meat cleaver. A killing cone is a safe way to secure a turkey while using a knife (Fig. 6-3). This prevents the turkey from struggling and possibly causing the handler to get cut. A large killing cone can be made from sheet metal or purchased (Fig. 6-4). The turkey is placed head down into the mounted cone. The head is then grabbed and the neck slightly stretched while the veins are cut under the throat where the neck begins. Complete cutting through of the neck should be prevented, or liquid and materials from the crop will leak from the esophagus and contaminate the meat. If this happens, quickly hose the area off.

The use of a meat cleaver and chopping block can be dangerous if the turkey is not kept from flopping around. Tie long pieces of twine or rope

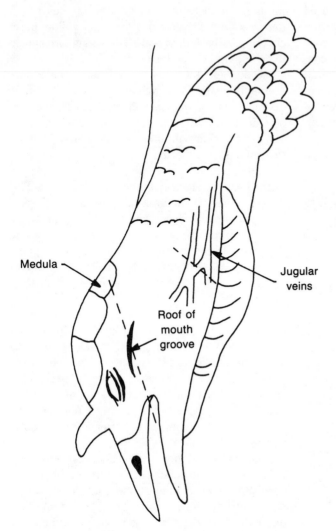

Medula

Roof of
mouth
groove

Jugular
veins

Fig. 6-2. Broken lines indicate vein cut and point to
stick. (These veins are readily seen by looking down
the throat with lights on the outside.)

around both the shanks and on the top of the neck. Have someone on each side pull downward and outward on the ropes and steady the turkey before severing the neck with a sharp cleaver.

Don't worry about messing up the neck or throat for bleeding. The important thing is that the blood begins to freely flow from the point of severing. If the turkey is not in a cone, then immediately upon severing the vein, hang the bird by the legs down into the 55-gallon drum so blood is not spattered when the bird begins to involuntarily flap

around. Gravity bleeds the bird quickly and thoroughly, so it should always be hung with the head down. Complete bleeding is necessary to prevent the skin from turning red and looking frostbitten. The skin should appear nice and yellow. Bleeding will cease in about 1 1/2-2 minutes.

After bleeding is completed and turkey has quit moving, take the turkey by both legs and lower into the hot scald pot. Slowly rotate the turkey and swish in a back-and-forth motion to assist water penetration through the feathers. Be careful to sub-

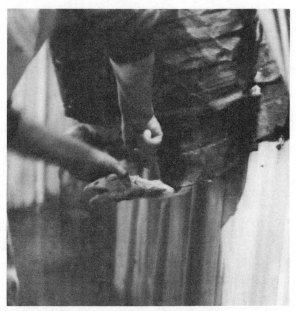

Fig. 6-3. Cutting the throat to bleed out while constrained in a homemade killing cone.

merge up past the hock joints or small feathers will remain on the bottom of the drumsticks. About one minute in the scald water is sufficient to loosen the feathers. Slowly raise and drain the bird, then either hang on shackles (see Fig. 6-4) from a sturdy tree branch, rafter board, etc., or lay it on a board or table for picking. The 55-gallon drum can be used to catch the feathers as they're removed.

Remove the large tail and wing feathers first because they will tighten up in the pores first and they are also in the way. If using a small automatic picker, these large feathers should still be hand-picked first. Large feathers cannot be removed by handfuls. Only one or a few can be grabbed and yanked off at a time.

The body and leg feathers are simultaneously grabbed, pulled, and rubbed off as quickly as possible. An automatic picking machine large enough for turkeys contains rubber "fingers" that rotate and grab the feathers from the carcass as the bird

Fig. 6-4. Use a shackle by placing the bird's foot into each larger area at top, then slide bottom of shank down through narrow end. (Cone on right, courtesy of New Delphos Manufacturing Co.)

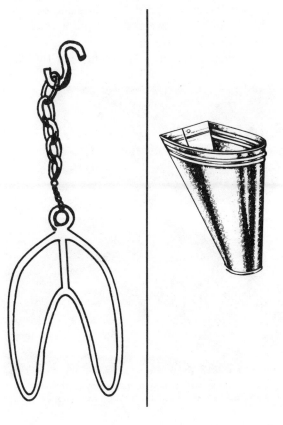

117

is held near them. To be an economically sound investment, about 112 to 150 turkeys would have to be picked for a new picker to pay for itself.

If feathers don't remove easily, either the water was not hot enough, or the dunking and water penetration was not complete, or both.

After feathers are removed, cut shanks and feet off at one time by cutting through the hock joints. Dirty shanks and feet can contaminate the carcass with bacteria. Also cut off head near top of neck (Fig. 6-5). Quickly cool the carcasses in a tub or tank of ice-cold water. Doing this before eviscerating (removing the inside organs) helps to clean the carcass and makes the job easier.

Use a clean cutting board or table to lay the carcass on for eviscerating. Large plastic cutting boards, like those used commercially, can be purchased at a butcher supply for $15 to $20 for a 2- × -3-foot size. These boards are claimed to be more sanitary than the bacteria-holding wooden cutting boards. The plastic boards must still be scrubbed with a stiff brush or debris and bacteria will be contained between the cutting marks that appear after the first use.

To eviscerate, cut a small slit over the skin

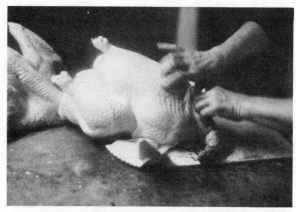

Fig. 6-6. One method to remove the crop: carefully through a neck slit on breast side to avoid breaking crop open.

where the neck meets the body and remove the crop (the bag-like sac) and the hollow tube called the windpipe. Point the sharp side of the knife upward to avoid tearing into the crop and spilling it's contents. Grasp the crop and gently pull it out through the slit skin (Fig. 6-6 and Fig. 6-7). Cut the crop and the windpipe loose as close to the body as possible.

Make a shallow slit with a small knife just below the pointed rear of the breastbone (also called the keelbone or sternum). Widen the slit, being careful to not cut into the intestines that lie just below the skin. If the intestines are accidentally punctured, the fecal contents will leak into the cavity to contaminate the meat. If this horizontal slit is not wide enough to admit your hands, make a vertical slit from the horizontal cut toward the vent, being careful not to puncture the intestine that leads to the vent. When the slit is wide enough, reach into the carcass and place your hand over the top of the mass of viscera (all the internal organs) and move the fingers back behind the entire mass. Gently pull the mass back toward the opening to work it out. The mass will still be attached by one intestine to the vent (Fig. 6-8). Push the mass of viscera to one side of the vent. Cut a circle around the vent without cutting the attached intestine. Most handlers also remove the oil gland at the base of the tail by cutting a V-groove (Fig. 6-9).

The lungs will still be attached, sometimes with the heart and part of the windpipe. The lungs lie

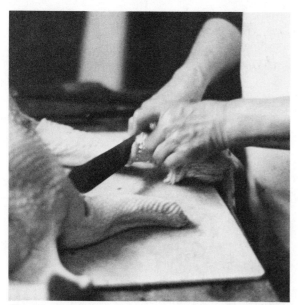

Fig. 6-5. A large, sharp knife (or a large chisel and hammer) should be used when cutting through neck bones.

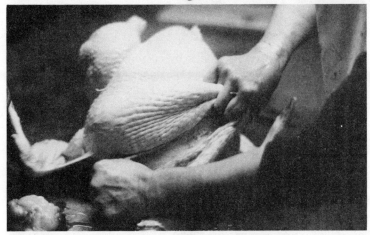

Fig. 6-7. (A) If you want a nice neck flap with no cuts, for stuffing later, cut neck on backside. (B) Stretch neck skin open. (C) This shows skin neatly folded down to back.

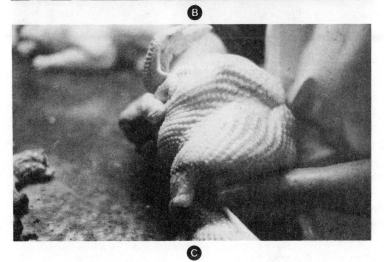

Fig. 6-8. The final step to eviscerating is to remove the attached intestine and vent.

far up into the cavity along each side of the backbone. Use the fingers to loosen the pink and spongy-looking lungs. Kidneys and sex organs are sometimes left attached to the backbone in young birds; in older birds they should be removed.

Separate the giblets (the liver and gizzard) from the viscera. Cut the gizzard loose. The liver has a green bile sac (gall bladder) attached which must be removed carefully. Using the index finger and thumb, pinch this sac tightly near it's bottom where it's attached to the liver, and pull off. If not pinched tightly, the sac will break and its greenish-yellow contents will contaminate the meat. Remove the heart, which is either attached to the viscera or sometimes remains way up inside the cavity near the neck. Mature hen turkeys will usually be full of yellow egg yolks from small to large.

Clean the gizzard by removing the interior sac. Begin by first cutting on one side while holding the gizzard with a thumb over the hole. Cut down slowly and carefully until the white lining is first noticed. Cut about 1/16-inch more, and the sac will be visible. Pull apart on each side of the slit to open and remove this sac in one neat wad. The sac is usually filled with grit, stones and grain. At commercial plants, the entire eviscerating is done using a conveyor.

The neck can be removed now or after chill-ing. Remove neck by cutting as close to body as possible. Breaking the bones must usually be done to facilitate cutting. Neck removal will give a nice fold of skin over front of carcass.

Finish chilling the carcass in ice-cold water to

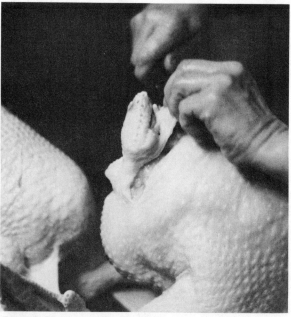

Fig. 6-9. It's believed that the oil gland near base of tail will release its oils during cooking and give a bad flavor if not removed.

120

Fig. 6-10. A livestock tank makes a good chilling vat for turkeys.

extract all body heat that could cause bacteria to grow. A stock tank can be used when a dozen or more turkeys are butchered (Fig. 6-10). It can take as long as a full day to bring large turkey carcasses to a temperature below 40 degrees F. (4 degrees C.). Again, the meat thermometer can be used to check this by inserting it into and between the thigh and body. Keep fresh ice water poured over or constantly running over the carcasses until chilled completely.

No job is complete until clean-up is done. Wash and sanitize all tables, cutting boards, etc., with diluted household chlorine bleach.

CUTTING, STORING, USING TURKEY MEAT AND PRODUCTS

After the turkey carcass is butchered, dressed, and completely chilled, stand it on end to drain away water before storing. Cutting into pieces, boning, and grinding turkey meat will take up considerably less room in a freezer. Large turkey-size freezer storage bags can be hard to find locally, so cutting into pieces solves this problem. The Kuhl Company has turkey-size freezer bags available.

Also, if turkeys are large, say 30 pounds dressed, most of today's modern ovens will not accommodate them. If turkey meat is to be used fresh, refrigerate and cook by the fourth day.

All turkey parts except the drumsticks can be used exactly as chicken parts. Drumsticks must have the ligaments removed if they are to be used whole because these ligaments are very hard to chew or cut around. Cut completely around drumstick bone about 1 inch above the hock. Then use a large knitting needle or a similar tool with a small hook to grasp a ligament at a time and pull out. Figure 6-11 illustrates the cuts from a 25-pound eviscerated turkey.

Boning and Cutting

Turkey meat that is boned can be canned, ground, frozen, or smoked. Use a boning knife so as much meat as possible can be cut from the bones. The blade on a boning knife is very narrow and about 5 inches long. Excellent boning knives are available at butcher supply stores.

Begin boning a whole turkey by making an incision down the center of the backbone or breast

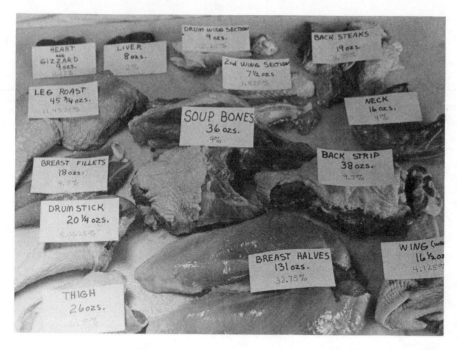

Fig. 6-11. Various cuts of meat and their individual weights from a 25-pound eviscerated turkey.

The following labels appear in the photograph:

HEART AND GIZZARD 9 ozs.

LIVER 8 ozs.

DRUM WING SECTION 9 ozs.

2nd WING SECTION 7½ ozs.

BACK STEAKS 19 ozs.

LEG ROAST 45 ¾ ozs.

NECK 16 ozs. 4%

SOUP BONES 36 ozs. 9%

BREAST FILLETS 18 ozs.

BACK STRIP 38 ozs. 9.5%

DRUM STICK 20 ¼ ozs. 5.0625%

BREAST HALVES 131 ozs. 32.75%

WING 16 ½ ozs. 4.125%

THIGH 26 ozs.

(Fig. 6-12.) Loosen the skin and peel it back from the body, cutting it loose from the meat where it might be attached (Fig. 6-13). Repeat on the other side of the backbone. Next, remove the wings by bending back, exposing the ball sockets, and cutting them from the body (Fig. 6-14). Be careful not to cut much from the breast meat when cutting wings loose. The wing tip can be brought back be-

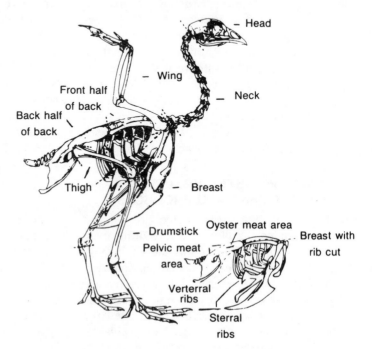

Fig. 6-12. Skeleton of fowl showing points to sever for cutting into pieces.

Labels on the skeleton diagram:

Head

Wing

Neck

Front half of back

Back half of back

Thigh

Breast

Drumstick

Oyster meat area

Pelvic meat area

Breast with rib cut

Verterral ribs

Sterral ribs

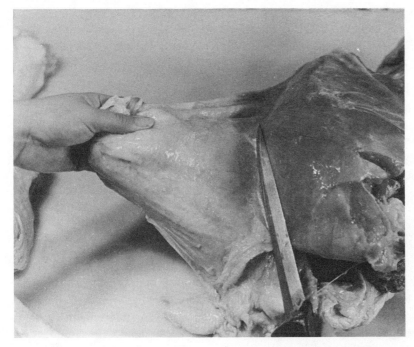

Fig. 6-13. Removing skin from breast when boning.

hind the larger bone to make a neat, attractive piece of meat. Wings can be cut in half across the joint to make four mini-drumsticks. Wings are actually white meat.

Remove the thigh and drumstick in one operation. Bend the thigh backwards and cut into the groove where the thigh meets the body. Pull the drumstick and thigh further away until the joint

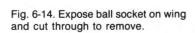

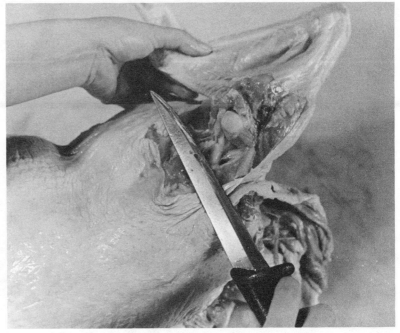

Fig. 6-14. Expose ball socket on wing and cut through to remove.

breaks. Finish cutting the thigh loose from the body through the broken joint by slightly pulling outwards on the drumstick (Fig. 6-15).

Separate the thigh from the drumstick by first laying the piece skin side down. Cut through the thin yellow fat line between the two pieces. Bone the thigh by laying skin side down with the largest end of bone towards you. Cut downward over the fat line running the length of the bone. With the tip of the knife, cut along each side of bone to loosen meat, but do not cut through to other side. Stand the thigh up on the large end of bone and scrape the meat away with the blade of the knife. Finish meat removal by cutting around the cartilage at each end of the bone. Remove the skin.

To remove skin from drumstick, cut a slit around the bone about 1 inch above the hock joint. Either pull the skin off over the hock joint or slit the skin lengthwise and remove. Boning drumsticks will be easier if the ligaments are removed first.

The breast meat can be removed two ways. Starting on the back, just beyond the spoon-shaped bones called the oyster cavities (Fig. 6-16), slice toward and up to the breastbone on each side, following the contour of the body cavity bones. Remove all the meat in one piece by cutting through the length of cartilage along the breastbone (keel-

bone). To form two breast halves, cut along each side of the breastbone beginning at the neck cavity and extending to the end of the keelbone. Cut as close to the length of the bone as possible. Pull the meat away from the breastbone using your fingers to loosen (Fig.6-17). Cut loose near bottom edge (Fig. 6-18). For roasting, smoking, or barbecuing, leave skin intact. When slicing or cutting into chunks, or rolling into roasts, remove the skin.

The meat can now be rolled into the skin and tied for a boneless turkey rolled roast, if desired. Stretch the skin out and place the meat on one side (Fig. 6-19). Roll and tuck and finish rolling firmly. To facilitate tying, place cotton string or stainless wire lengths horizontally and vertically across and down into a bread loaf pan. Put the rolled meat into the pan with the skin edge up. Firmly tie each string or wire around the roll. The roll can now be removed and frozen for later use or cooked skin edge down. Two rolled roasts can be easily made from one whole turkey. Once cooked, the roast can be neatly sliced.

Cutlets and steaks can be sliced from skinned breast halves. After thoroughly chilled for ease in cutting, slice across the grain in 1/4-3/8-inch slices for cutlets or 1/2-3/4-inch slices for steaks. Cutting into cubes will give you nice pieces for shish-kebabs

Fig. 6-15. Finish thigh and leg removal by breaking joint and cutting loose.

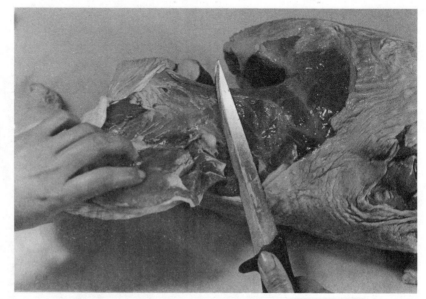

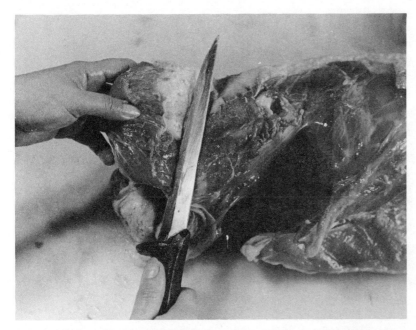

Fig. 6-16. Cut the oyster meat away and use as turkey steaks.

or Fried Turkettes (see following recipes).

Extra boned pieces of meat can be canned, ground, frozen or smoked. Follow pressure canning methods and recipes in Kerr or Ball brands canning books. Giblets can also be canned if desired. Wa-ter is not used for canning poultry meat. The pure stock and small amount of fat that constitutes the canned product can, when later opened, be used to make gravy by adding flour and water.

A convenient way to freeze cuts of turkey is

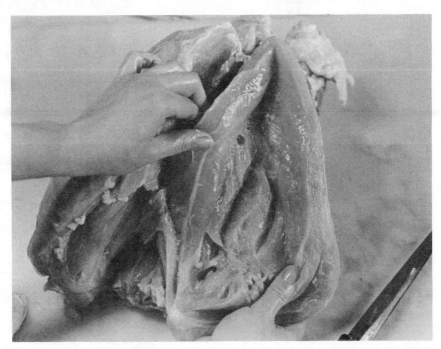

Fig. 6-17. Removing breast meat actually reveals two large fillets on each breast half.

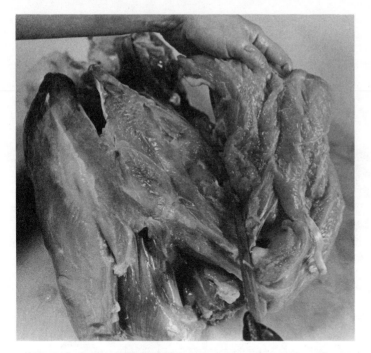

Fig. 6-18. Removing one breast half from keel-bone downwards.

in heavy-duty, zipper-lock freezer bags. After filling the bag and partially sealing, squeeze out all excess air with your hands. Finish sealing and freeze.

Grinding

Ground turkey meat is very lean. The best ground meat product should contain 20 percent fat and 80 percent meat to retain moisture, hold together when cooking, and have a good flavor. If desired, beef or pork fat or suet can be added and ground with the turkey meat to prevent it from drying or falling apart when cooking. If additional fat is not

Fig. 6-19. Meat for rolling into roasts can be white or dark pieces, or both.

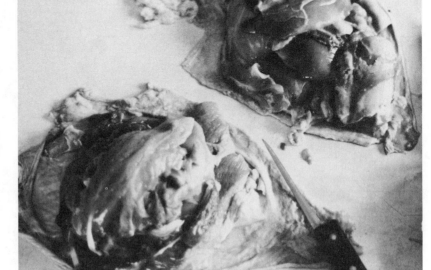

desired, be sure to grind the turkey meat very fine to help mold and hold it together.

Ground turkey meat can be used as a meat loaf, meatballs, and cooked loose for Sloppy Toms served on hamburger buns (see following recipes). Fresh breakfast sausage can be made simply by mixing the chunks of meat with seasonings and grinding through a 3/16-inch grinder plate. It can be shaped into patties or stuffed into 28-30-mm hog casings or 20-22-mm lamb casings. Ground turkey meat can be made into Kielbasa (fresh Polish sausage) and fresh Italian sausage either sweet, mild, or hot.

If seasoned turkey sausage will be frozen longer than six weeks, it's best not to season until thawed and used. Keep a jar of the mixed spices on hand and season the meat just before using because the seasonings will lose their flavor when frozen.

When meat is to be ground, it must be thoroughly chilled from between 32-35 degrees F. (0-2 degrees C.) for proper grinding. If warmer than this, the meat becomes soft and does not go through the grinding plate easily. It will bind up and grinding will take longer.

Following are some fresh turkey sausage recipes for bulk use. The sausage can also be placed into casings for link sausage.

Fresh Turkey Breakfast Sausage. Use 8 pounds turkey meat ground with 2 pounds of pork fat. Add 4 tablespoons salt, 1 tablespoon ground white pepper, 1/4 tablespoon ground, dried hot red pepper, 1/2 teaspoon ground ginger, 2 tablespoons fresh rubbed sage, 1 tablespoon ground nutmeg, 1 tablespoon crushed thyme and 1/2 teaspoon garlic powder.

Fresh Hot Italian Sausage. Use 8 pounds turkey meat ground with 2 pounds of pork fat. Add 4 tablespoons salt, 1 tablespoon sugar, 1/2 teaspoon garlic powder, 1 tablespoon coriander, 1 teaspoon caraway seeds, 1 tablespoon cracked fennel seed and 3 teaspoons crushed, dried hot red peppers.

Fresh Kielbasa (Polish Sausage). Use 8 pounds turkey meat ground with 2 pounds of pork fat. Add 4 tablespoons salt, 1 tablespoon coarse black pepper, 1 tablespoon sugar, 1 teaspoon gar-lic powder and 1 teaspoon marjoram.

Some recipes which utilize leftover cooked turkey or uncooked boned parts are as follows:

Save 'Dem Bones Italian Turkey Soup. Place broken turkey carcass in large pot and cover with water. Bring to boil and simmer covered up to three hours. Strain broth through strainer and return broth to pot. Pick any remaining meat from bones and add to broth. Add 3 teaspoons chicken flavored bouillon concentrate, 2 chopped onions, 2 stalks chopped celery (or 2 teaspoons dried celery leaves), 1 four-ounce can undrained mushrooms, 1/2 teaspoon oregano, 1/2 teaspoon garlic powder, and pepper to taste.

Prepare a dumpling batter by combining 1 1/2 cups milk, 4 cups flour, 3 beaten eggs, 1/2 teaspoon baking powder, 1/4 teaspoon salt and some pepper. Take metal teaspoon and first dip into broth to coat spoon. Then, take one teaspoon dumpling batter on spoon and lay into simmering broth until batter comes off spoon. Continue until all batter is used. Simmer covered 15 minutes. Uncover and simmer 15 minutes more.

Fried Turkettes. Beat one egg, 2 cups water, and half of one small package dry Italian seasoned salad dressing together in a bowl. Mix 4 cups dry pancake mix with the other half of the dry salad dressing mix in a shaker bag. Cut one 4-pound breast half into 2-inch chunks. Dip breast chunks in the seasoned egg and water mixture first. Then place a few pieces at a time into the seasoned pancake mix in the bag and shake to coat. Set on wax paper or toweling for about 10 minutes so the coating has time to set up.

Heat cooking oil until small bubbles appear and place the Turkettes into oil, a few at a time, and cook until light and golden brown. Drain on paper toweling. Serve with dipping sauces (following). 6 servings.

Tangy Barbecue Sauce. Mix together 1 cup prepared ketchup, 1/4 cup brown sugar, 1/4 teaspoon garlic powder, 1/4 teaspoon onion powder and 1 tablespoon hot sauce.

Sweet-N-Sour Plum Sauce. Mix together 1/2 cup heated, melted plum or apricot jelly, 1 tablespoon vinegar, 1/2 teaspoon grated green pepper and 1/4 teaspoon grated red pepper.

Turkey eggs are nutritious and should not go unused. Treat turkey eggs the same as any other eating egg. Collect them often, cool immediately, and refrigerate. When properly collected and stored, turkey eggs will keep under refrigeration for nearly a month. They are not considered to be strong flavored; eating quality is good. They're the same as chicken eggs in any recipe and when cooking and frying.

If you feel turkey eggs are too expensive to produce and simply eat, you might be able to find another handler who will purchase them from you for hatching purposes. In this case, store no longer than two weeks and do not refrigerate. A temperature of 50 degrees F. (10 degrees C.) is a good storage temperature for hatching eggs. A relative humidity level of 75-80 percent should be contained in any egg storage room. Humidity levels above 85 percent cause molds to grow within the egg, especially if the storage area is not ventilated. If hatching eggs are stored longer than one week, the eggs should be tilted in opposite directions daily after the first week to prevent the yolk from adhering to one spot within the shell. When this happens, the poult becomes stuck and is unable to completely hatch after incubation.

PREPARING TURKEYS FOR SALE

Processors slaughtering more than 20,000 birds per year are required to be federally inspected. It is only federally inspected turkeys that can move in interstate commerce. State-inspected turkeys can only be sold within the boundaries of the state.

When planning for Thanksgiving sales, you should consider the average size of ready-to-cook (RTC) turkeys that consumers usually desire: The average RTC hen weight is 12 pounds and the average RTC tom weight is 18-20 pounds.

Feeding a cracked corn or scratch feed supplement one month before butchering seems to place a nice layer of yellowish fat over the carcass, which gives it a more plumped and fleshed appearance. Remember that turkeys will not eat fat-producing grains well until the weather begins to cool.

Be sure to stop administering any drugs well in advance of butchering to prevent residues in the meat.

Turkeys for Thanksgiving can actually be advertised and sold any time prior to Thanksgiving. Any local newspaper with livestock ads is a good place to advertise. A deposit should be requested when a bird is ordered for Thanksgiving. A handler can sell the birds by the live weight. A handler should not try to compete with supermarkets during this time or he will come out at a financial loss—just as the supermarkets do. Supermarket retailers purposely sell turkeys during Thanksgiving at a loss to lure customers into the store so they will purchase all the fixins' for the holiday meal— cranberries, sweet potatoes, pumpkin pie, fruits, nuts, vegetables, etc. Many consumers who purchase only holiday turkeys believe the prices during Thanksgiving are the year-round prices. When they later see higher prices they conclude the turkey industry is out to exploit them.

A handler's pricing for his birds should include *all* costs plus profit. This is where good record keeping can help you to avoid unintentional economical losses. If customers want to come and look the turkeys over beforehand, be sure the birds look clean and are on a good bed of straw. And remember, never let anyone into pens or on grounds the turkeys walk over. One turkey can be caged to be used for window-shopping purposes.

Chapter 7

Turkey Problems
and Home Remedies

Spotting symptoms of disease and stress early will avoid many losses with your turkeys. Keeping accurate records will help detect future problems. Certain problems appear at a particular age and can therefore be suspected first. For instance, when a number of three-day-old poults die and they were smaller than the others, had dried, shriveled-looking legs, were sitting with eyes closed, heads drooping and chirping a lot, they most likely were stressed or chilled during shipping. This caused them to want to stay under the heat. If waterers were not placed under the heat source, the poults no doubt became dehydrated from a lack of water. The handler could have noticed the stressed symptoms the first day and avoided the poult losses by placing extra waterers under the heat source. Shipping stress, chilling, and confined overheating causes most losses in the early part of brooding. Dehydration can be indirectly caused by these conditions.

After three weeks of age, coccidiosis is the major cause of mortality in poults. Check the droppings regularly for signs of diarrhea or blood.

Rickets also appear about this time. Note the symptoms. How could these problems have been prevented? Could management practices be improved to provide more sanitary conditions? Was equipment disinfected routinely? Was cod-liver oil fed in the right proportions to prevent rickets? How much was given to how many birds and how often? If birds appear stunted in growth, could it be from parasites, overheating, the wrong type of feed, absence of grit, previous disease, or not enough good feeders and waterers in crowded conditions? Always look for the obvious problem.

Following are some of the most common problems that turkey raisers are confronted with. Do not let the extensive listing scare you—the more you know about potential problems, the more likely you are to isolate the cause.

AMMONIA BURNS
(KERATOCONJUNCTIVITIS)

Both the respiratory mucous membranes and the translucent part of the eyes in all poultry can be damaged from the ammonia gases created in damp litter. Turkeys and other confined poultry are most susceptible because litter may never have a chance to dry. Using a built-up litter system in poorly ventilated houses can prevent litter from drying. The built-up system consists of adding fresh litter material on top of the old, with thorough litter removal done only a few times per year.

Turkeys are usually not as susceptible as chickens to this ailment. This might be because many more chickens than turkeys are confined throughout the winter, when ventilation is at its worst and ammonia fumes build up. Also, chickens scratch around in their litter more than turkeys do.

Ammonia burns of the eyes can be noticed by a lopsided shape of the eyes, continual watering of the eyes, and some facial swelling. Occasionally it is mistaken for another disorder such as coryza, and the offending ammoniated litter might not be removed. Advanced cases will cause birds to move slowly because of impending blindness. All confined birds including waterfowl can be affected.

Prevent this ailment by keeping litter dry and ventilated. To treat, remove damp litter; replace with fresh, dry litter; and improve ventilation. Feed vitamin A until damaged eyes appear better. Without treatment, blindness could result.

ARIZONA INFECTION (PARACOLON)

This is an egg transmitted disease. Poults are more commonly affected than chicks. Pet birds and pigeons are also susceptible. Turkey hens carry the bacteria in the intestinal track, and when they lay the egg, the bacteria goes through the shell to the developing embryo. Many other hosts spread the disease. They include: feeds that use meat by-products in processing, infected chick culls, feathers, rodents, pets, flies, wild and domestic birds, reptiles, mammals, incubators, chick boxes, etc. Birds that recover remain as carriers and spreaders of the disease and are usually stunted in growth.

Symptoms in poults includes listlessness, no appetite, increased thirst, nervousness, pasted vent from diarrhea, ruffled feathers, sudden deaths. Darkness around eyes may develop (Fig. 7-1) and blindness could occur. Deaths continue to about

Fig. 7-1. Typical eye lesion in Arizona Infection. (Courtesy of L. Dwight Schwartz, D.V.M., Senior Pathologist, Michigan State University)

fourth week. The most susceptible age is 8-20 days old. Symptoms are similar to brooder pneumonia (aspergillosis) and partatyphoid (salmonellosis), except for the darkened eyes and blindness.

Do not use survivors for breeding. Bacteria can be destroyed by disinfecting and fumigating. Medication will control mortality. Use one of the following: nitrofuran compounds, dynamyxin, gentamicin, spectinomycin, sulfadimethopine, sulfamerazine, sulfamethazine or sulfaquinoxaline.

AVIAN INFLUENZA

This is a respiratory virus that mainly attacks matured turkeys, chickens, ducks, geese, and pheasants. There is a mild form and a severe form. Mild forms show diarrhea, some respiratory distress, listlessness, slight drop in egg production, and lowered fertility. The more severe form, shows watery eyes and nostrils, difficult breathing, swellings below the eyes, and eyes filled with a thick, white or yellow hardened substance. This substance will block air passages, causing suffocation in young poults. Hemorrhaging appears in the respiratory tract and gizzard.

The disease is spread by contact with other infected birds. Sometimes recovered birds are carriers and can infect others. Vaccinating is not relied on because there are too many strains that can be responsible for a specific outbreak. Treatment is not reliable, although broad-spectrum antibiotics can be given to control further mortality. The temperature in their building should be raised also, because stressing the birds from exposure to cold can cause a more severe outbreak.

AVIAN TB

This is a slowly transmitted bacterial disease of chickens, ducks, geese, guinea fowl, pet birds, pheasants, pigeons, turkeys, swans, and wild birds. It is most common in chickens over one year old. Infections also occur in livestock such as cattle, rabbits, sheep and swine.

The disease is spread by infected droppings, other birds, animals, rodents, and the carcasses of infected dead birds and animals. The ailment is spread slowly, so a small number of birds appear sick at various times. Early stages show loss of weight, pale and shrunken wattles and combs, and unthriftiness. Later stages include diarrhea, extreme loss of weight, slow death. Lameness occurs in TB of the bones. Chickens and pigeons will develop infections in the joints. Humans are resistant to this organism, which is closely related to human and bovine TB bacteria—although a few humans have been infected.

Treating the ailment is regarded as uneconomical and inadvisable because of the danger of humans becoming infected, and because the high level of medication needed might be toxic. Infected poultry should be destroyed and incinerated and buildings cleaned and disinfected. Dirt floors in buildings should have several inches removed and replaced with clean dirt. Do not reuse infected grounds for ranging birds acquired later.

BEAK TRIMMING

With small-scale raisers, trimming beaks of chicks is more common than trimming the beaks of turkeys. Commercially raised turkeys, however, are beak-trimmed regularly. Proper management methods and practices outlined in this book should make beak-trimming rarely necessary for the small-scale grower.

Beak trimming is performed commercially for various reasons. Usually it's done to prevent cannibalism, because debeaked birds are unable to grasp the feathers and skin of the other birds when a portion of upper beak is removed. Breeder toms are less inclined to fight with and hurt each other. Ordinarily, toms need their entire beak for successful mating, but since commercially raised hens are artificially inseminated, they can be beak-trimmed to avoid problems and harm to others breeders. Small-scale raisers who will be keeping turkeys for breeding and who will not be using artificial insemination, should not permanently beak trim. Because one good tom is enough for up to 15-20 hens, there is no need to keep more than one or two toms—thus fighting is reduced.

Beak trimming also supposedly quiets the birds and prevents feed wastage because birds cannot bill out feed from feeders as easily. Egg-eaters should be debeaked to save eggs, but hen turkeys don't engage in this bad habit as often as chickens do.

Occasional beak trimming of specific troublemakers in a brood of poults is essential if cannibalism starts, which can happen even while using proper management methods. Beaks can be carefully trimmed by using ordinary nail clippers any time from one week of age through adult. It's not advisable to trim day-olds' beaks before they're steadily eating and drinking well. Manual trimming is not as severe as the mechanical method—that is, less of the upper beak is removed when using nail clippers. Trim only the lighter colored tip of the upper beak. This shows as white on the beak tip of white turkeys and light brown on bronze turkeys.

By trimming just below where the lighter portion ends, bleeding will be avoided. Inexperienced handlers should take very small amounts off first until they feel confident. If bleeding does begin, quickly dip beak into fine feed mash until blood clots. If a number of poults are done, place each into a box with one or two clean thick towels bunched up so beaks can be dabbed of any blood. Manual trimming is not permanent. The beak will eventually grow back.

Some small-scale handlers insist on beak trimming *all* poultry they raise. In this case, it might be to their advantage to purchase a beak trimming machine. It will be an accurate, permanent, and cleaner method and there will be no worry whether a specific hatchery performs the service or not. The following is reprinted with permission of Lyon Electric Co:

TURKEY BEAK TRIMMING: Beak trimming of turkeys is similar to beak trimming employed for chickens. While turkey beak trimming was not done until 3 to 6 weeks of age in the past, there have been numerous cases of the operation being performed between 1 to 3 weeks of age and more recently a trend to trim beaks at one day of age. One of the methods being used at day-old is a sear cut of the upper beak shown in Fig. 7-2. This method is accomplished using a powered Super Debeaker® with a special attachment no. 940-25. There is also a Super V and Dual Debeaker® model for this method. The beak is seared a dimes width in front of the nostril leaving a small portion of the beak with its tip. The seared beak section normally drops off in 10 to 15 days, long enough for the bird to learn to eat and drink properly. When turkey beaks are trimmed at 1 to 3 weeks of age as shown in Fig. 7-3, common practice is to remove 5/8 to 3/4 of the upper beak. Growing birds

Fig. 7-2. Sear-cut beak trimming at day-old. (Lyon Electric Co.)

Fig. 7-3. Beak trimming at one to three weeks of age. (Lyon Electric Co.)

Fig. 7-4. Beak trimming at three to six weeks of age. (Lyon Electric Co.)

Fig. 7-5. Beak trimming of mature birds. (Lyon Electric Co.)

3 to 6 weeks of age have 1/2 to 3/4 of the upper beak trimmed as shown in Fig. 7-4. Mature birds' upper beaks are trimmed by removing 1/2 or slightly more of the beak Fig. 7-5. When beak trimming turkeys it is common to use one of the heavier blades on birds 3 weeks and older such as the H, S and OE blade. Thinner blades tend to warp and dull quicker on turkeys so the heavier blade is used to retain sharpness and extend blade life.

BLACKHEAD (HISTOMONIASIS)

This is a parasitic disease of chickens, guinea fowl, grouse, partridge, pea fowl, pheasants, quail, and especially turkeys. Turkeys are more susceptible than guineas and guineas are more susceptible than chickens. It usually occurs in birds less than 12 weeks of age. Cecal worm eggs and earthworms harbor the blackhead parasite. Cecal worms begin the cycle of infection when they pick up the parasite from the intestine of an infected bird. The cecal worm then produces its own infected eggs. Earthworms feed on the infected cecal worm eggs and when poultry eat the earthworms they become infected. Then the cycle repeats itself as the bird's droppings infect the ground with cecal worm eggs. The parasites contaminate the ground and winter over and handlers don't know if their grounds are contaminated until they have problems.

It has long been suggested that handlers keep turkeys away from chickens and off grounds that have been used within the past three years for chicken ranging. Very healthy chickens can harbor the infected cecal worm eggs and contaminate the soil or litter material. A handler would not know if the soil or litter was infected unless turkeys developed blackhead. Chickens *can* become sick but mortality is usually low and symptoms not as obvious.

Symptoms are the same in all poultry: increased thirst, weakness, decreased appetite, drooping wings, fluffed-out feathers, watery (yellowish white) droppings, and occasionally the head may appear dark blue—hence the name blackhead. The name is actually misleading because this coloration does not always appear. A dead bird can be cut open and observed for blackhead lesions on the liver, lower intestine, and ceca. The liver will have yellowish-green circles that are depressed in the center. The small intestine and ceca appear thickened and contain a yellowish-green fluid or later a cheesy looking core.

Range distance may have a lot to do with turkeys contracting blackhead. Prevention is the key. Turkeys can be moved to new areas every three to four weeks to reduce chances of becoming infected. Cecal worms should be controlled in all poultry by proper and regular worming. Turkeys can be raised on wire platforms. A blackhead medication can be fed continuously after the brooding period between six to eight weeks of age and until the withdrawal time listed on warning label. The medication is called histomonastat. The most commonly used for both treating and preventing blackhead is a liquid mixed into drinking water called Emtryl (Dimetridazole). Another called Ipropan (Ipronidazole), is available in commercially prepared turkey grower feed. Blackhead can be effectively treated, but to prevent further outbreaks, continuous low-level doses of the histomonastat should be given.

BLUE COMB (CORONAVIRAL ENTERITIS)

This is a highly contagious virus disease of turkeys, mainly young turkeys. It's transmitted by eating contaminated substances, or direct contact with infected birds and droppings. Recovered turkeys can shed the virus for months.

The virus appears suddenly and spreads rapidly. Birds feel chilled and want to huddle under the heat constantly. Other symptoms include loss of appetite, weakness, constant chirping, rapid loss of weight, profuse, watery diarrhea containing mucous threads, dehydration from lack of drinking, depression, below-normal body temperature, and a bluish-colored head. Adult turkeys show similar symptoms but mortality is lower. In poults mortality may reach 50 percent, in adults from 1 to 5 percent. Disorders that can produce similar symptoms in poults are poor management, hexamitiasis, paratyphoid, Arizona infection, reovirus enteritis, and water deprivation. In adult turkeys, symptoms can look like those of fowl cholera and erysipelas.

Break the cycle of infection by getting rid of all birds on the farm, clean and disinfect all buildings and equipment, and leave premises vacant of all poultry for 30 days. To treat, raise temperature of brooder or room until birds appear not chilled. Birds on range must be protected from inclement weather. Antibiotics used are bacitracin, neomycin, penicillin, streptomycin, tetracycline including chlortetracycline. Give a supplement of multiple vitamins in drinking water.

BREAST BLISTERS

These can occur as early as six weeks of age. The

blisters appear as a soft swelling on the breast or near the neck. At first the swelling contains clear or blood-tinged fluid. Later the contents are a thick pus.

Battery brooders and growers can cause the blisters due to constant irritation from sharp edges on feeders and waterers. All sharp edges in batteries should be bent smoothly back to prevent this condition. If floor-reared poultry get the blisters, check feeders and waterers for sharp edges.

Heavy-type birds such as turkeys and broilers seem more susceptible. To treat, use a sterilized syringe and needle to draw out fluid and drain. When blister has turned to pus or continues to fill with fluid, the area should be lanced. Use a sterilized razor blade and cut a small incision over and through the skin only. After draining completely, rinse and flush out well with a diluted solution of potassium permanganate—using the syringe to squirt the liquid into the cavity (potassium permanganate is also used with formaldehyde to fumigate incubators for disease). It can be purchased in tiny purple tablets at drugstores. A 300-mg (5-gr.) tablet is diluted with 1 quart of boiled water to make a stock solution. It will take a few hours to completely dissolve. Mix 1/2 cup of this stock solution with 1 cup of clear, boiled and cooled water. After wound drys, spray top of wound with a methyl violet or gentian violet antiseptic to kill bacteria. Blu Kote brand is good. The blue spray will also show you at a glance which bird was operated on.

BROODER PNEUMONIA (ASPERGILLOSIS)

This is an infectious respiratory disease caused by a fungus. It's transmitted to all types of poultry, birds, animals, and humans by breathing in the fungus spores from litter material. Poults, quail, ducklings, and goslings are more susceptible than chickens. In humans, this can become farmers lung disease.

Very dry conditions let the fine spores filter through the air easily to be breathed in more easily. Spores appear in any moldy material such as feed, litters, straw, hay, peat moss, bark, sawdust, and peanut hulls. Never use feed that looks or smells moldy. Moldy bales of straw will appear dar-

kened, and one sniff will tell you it's moldy. Do not use no matter how much you hate to waste the material or you may risk your health and your birds' health. Use clean, bright golden straw and nondusty by-products for litter.

Symptoms in poultry will show as gasping for air, sleepiness, loss of appetite, twisted neck, nervous disorders, dehydration, and bluish-colored skin. The brain can become infected, which will show as convulsions or paralysis, and the bird could die.

Raise humidity to lower spore infection. Remove offending litter or feed. Wear a mask while removing it. Medicate entire flock with a fungastat such as calcium or sodium propionate, gentian violet, mold-curb and mycostatin in feed, copper sulfate in water using a non-metal container, or Rocon in water for 3-5 days.

BROODINESS

This is when a hen turkey feels inclined to sit on eggs in order to incubate and hatch them. This tendency has not yet been bred out of turkeys as it has with many chickens. A hen turkey might want to set after each clutch of eggs is laid or sooner. Turkeys lay in clutches—they lay steadily for two weeks, stop for about one to two weeks, and begin again. With each successive clutch of eggs, the turkey should be "broken" of her broodiness if more eggs are desired from her. A broody hen will not lay eggs.

Breaking the hen consists of confining her to a large cage up off the ground with no litter available to nest in or pick from the ground. Supply water and grain. Another method for breaking is to pen the broody hen without much litter material and no nest. Leave her there with a tom. The nonseclusion and pesty tom will usually take her mind off motherhood. You must try to upset and break the broody trance she is in. Usually simply removing nest boxes or barrels will work; then she'll drop her eggs on the floor. On occasion, there can be very insistent broodies who will continue to set anywhere and forever—even without eggs. Sometimes it's best to let these hens hatch something or they can go without eating and drinking and die on the spot they're setting on. This is rare, but it does happen.

Help prevent broodiness by checking nests early and often. If the same hen is seen on the nest a few hours later, shove her off the nest each time. A turkey hen who is going to lay an egg and leave, gets it over and done with quickly. Do not leave eggs in a nest; collect often. Placing hens in different pens often will make them feel less at home and broodiness will not occur as often. Be sure to provide roosts so the hens do not become accustomed to floor areas for setting.

BUMBLEFOOT

This is a staph infection of foot pad injuries and occurs mostly with large, heavy birds. The bottom of the foot can be injured if the turkeys must jump down from high roost, and the constant impact can be damaging to heavy birds. Eventually the turkey becomes lame as the injury becomes abscessed with staphylococcal bacteria.

The swelling must be lanced to prevent lameness. Drain the hard core or pus and apply pressure with rag to control bleeding. Then flush out thoroughly, pat dry, and apply an iodine tincture. Large cavities can be packed with an ammoniated mercurial or sulfathiazole ointment. Keep bird on very dry litter until completely healed.

Supply roosts only 1 foot high for large, heavy birds. Check equipment for sharp objects that can injure feet.

CANNIBALISM

This must be remedied as soon as you notice it. White-feathered birds seem more susceptible because every speck of feed and debris can be easily seen on the white feathers. Other birds peck at the specks and eventually bleeding occurs. Those seen pecking at others on wing shoulders and vents should be marked. If they do it a few more times within a half hour or so, trim the top beak. Turkey poults always peck others' eyes, beaks, and toes— you should not be concerned over this. However, those which consistently peck at the wing shoul-

ders or bend their heads down to purposely peck the vent area, are potential troublemakers. Even in a brood of 100 poults, only one to three poults will usually be found to start cannibalism.

Causes of cannibalism are: bright brooding lights, a larger ray of sunlight coming into the brooding area, overcrowding, high temperatures, a change of housing or environment, new, smaller birds introduced into a flock, insufficient feeders or waterers, lack of entertainment, injuries not quickly attended to, lack of variety in feed consistency, and a sodium deficiency.

Adult turkeys rarely engage in this vice. If chickens are with adult turkeys, they will usually be the cause.

Immediately remove any injured or dead birds. Spray the wound with an antiseptic wound dressing such as methyl violet or gentian violet. Keep injured bird away from others until healed. With small wounds this is about five to seven days. An extremely deep and large wound on an adult turkey might take a month to heal completely if it continues to break open. Occasionally spray with antiseptic until healed.

When moving poults to new quarters, as from a brooder to a building, do it as quietly as possible. Move poults preferably in a darkened container to the new surrounding, also darkened. Keep bright lights including sunlight out of area. Poults can be given vitamin D_3 and occasionally taken outdoors if a handler does not care for the darkened atmosphere. The poults should be supplemented until they are outdoors for considerable lengths of time. Be sure there are plenty of feeders, waterers, and roosts to keep them busy.

COCCIDIOSIS

This organism mainly infects young poultry. It thrives in damp litter and is spread by the droppings. Adult birds eventually build up an immunity to the organism. Poults brooded on litters build up an immunity faster than those from battery brooders. Birds must be in contact with the coccidia organisms continually to become immune. Only specific coccidia species infect certain species of birds. They do not interact between species—the turkey's species does not infect chickens and visa-versa.

Symptoms include a noticed increase in thirst, weakness, stunted growth, lack of appetite, ruffled feathers, and possibly blood in the droppings. Coccidia invade the intestines and ceca of the bird. If examined, the intestine would appear engorged with white matter with a red and or white speckling from thickened blood (Fig. 7-6).

If the droppings have been watched carefully from two weeks of age, there should be no serious problems with coccidiosis. This is when most infections begin. Droppings will be watery, pink, or contain bright red spots of blood. It's at the later stage when most of the other symptoms show too.

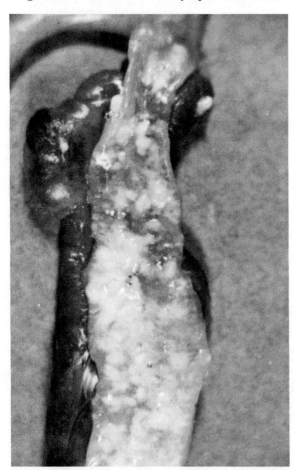

Fig. 7-6. Appearance of intestine of wild turkey with coccidiosis. (Courtesy of L. Dwight Schwartz, D.V.M., Senior Pathologist, Michigan State University)

The increased thirst can usually be noticed when birds are first infected.

When the looseness of droppings is first noticed, use plain vinegar in the drinking water before poults become run down and die. Use about 1/4 cup of vinegar to each gallon of water for three days or until droppings are no longer watery or contain blood. Do not feed cod-liver oil during this time, because too much cod-liver oil can also cause loose droppings. Droppings containing blood are usually caused by an irritation of the ceca.

Coccidiostats such as Amprollium, which are found in commercially prepared starter and sometimes growers feeds, will bring on an attack of coccidiosis at about four weeks of age. The way the medication works is that it gives the disease to the birds which builds an immunity. If handlers aren't aware of this, they will wonder why their birds are infected while they were faithfully feeding the medicated feed. They might even dangerously try to treat this coccidiosis infection with more Amprollium in the drinking water. Feed manufacturers say a handler is suppose to ride out the induced infection unless the birds are really uncomfortable, at which point they could administer a sulfa-type drug.

Amprollium is also a vitamin B_1 (thiamin) antagonist because it interferes with the function of the vitamin. This will create a vitamin B_1 deficiency which causes the birds to become flighty and excitable, and reduces the appetite so birds eat even less. A prolonged B_1 deficiency will cause lameness and paralysis from degenerated nerves. A severe deficiency will require an injection of vitamin B_1. Mild deficiency requires only extra B_1 in the drinking water.

If a coccidial infection occurs and you want to medicate, sulfadimethoxine, sulfaquinoxaline, and liquid Amprol can be used. Good sanitation must be practiced, along with paying attention to the earliest symptoms. Keep litter dry and prevent wet spots around waterers. Replace damp litter after an outbreak, which will dilute the amount of infective sporulated oocysts that begin the infection.

CURLED TOES

Occasionally heavy, fast-growing fowl such as turkeys will have one or two crooked toes. This usually is from slight injury and is of no concern. The turkey will still breed well. Turkeys are not disqualified at shows for a few crooked toes, but they can lose some judging points. True curled toes is a paralysis caused from a riboflavin deficiency. To test for the paralysis, stretch the legs outward. If toes curl halfway toward the other foot, this is curled toe paralysis. Before the exaggerated toe curling appears, the young poultry will be seen resting back on their hocks with only slightly curled toes. Other symptoms are stunting of growth, diarrhea, weakness, and mortality. One or both feet can be affected.

When the first poult is noticed with the symptom, add riboflavin to the diet and the rest of the brood will respond without mortality. Most ingredients used to prepare poultry rations do not contain enough of this B vitamin for poultry. It is usually added as a supplement to commercially prepared feeds. If problems arise, put a supplement of multiple vitamins in the drinking water when the next brood is raised.

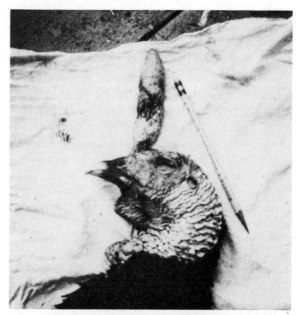

Fig. 7-7. Swollen snood and darkened skin of a Bronze turkey having Erysipelas. (Courtesy of L. Dwight Schwartz, D.V.M., Senior Pathologist, Michigan State University)

ERYSIPELAS

This is an infectious disease mostly of four-to-seven-month-old turkeys caused by bacteria from the soil. It also infects sheep, swine, and humans. The bacteria enters through skin lesions and can be spread by biting insects such as mosquitoes.

Symptoms include a yellowish-green diarrhea, loss of appetite, painful and swollen joints, swollen face, difficult breathing, low fertility, listlessness, nasal discharge, internal bleeding, enlarged liver and spleen, blush-purple skin and swollen snood (Fig. 7-7). It infects toms more than hens because of lesions caused from fighting.

Yearly problems with erysipelas calls for vaccination with E. rhusiopathiae bacterin injection. Separate sick birds and treat outbreaks with the same bacterin plus procaine penicillin and potassium penicillin. Continuous outbreaks can be stopped by decontaminating and cleaning buildings.

EXTERNAL PARASITES

These are parasites that bite the skin and suck the blood of poultry. Some remain on the poultry constantly while some visit the body only nightly or occasionally to feed. They are spread from other poultry, wild birds, equipment, litter material, pets such as cats and dogs, and even handlers can carry parasites from coop to coop. The following eight parasites are the most common pests of turkeys.

Bed Bugs

Adult bed bugs are about 1/4 inch long, flat, oval, wingless and reddish-brown in color. When filled with blood they are red and fat. They feed on poultry only at night. Bed bugs breed, hide, and lay eggs in cracks and crevices in walls, ceilings, boards, roosts, and nests. Tell-tale signs of bed bug infestation are small black specks of excrement near cracks. Handlers may discover itching welts on themselves. Bed bugs infest both humans and poultry.

Bed bugs thrive in warm temperatures. They can survive for long periods without feeding. Their eggs hatch in 6-17 days into nymphs. They remain in this immature form for one to two months but continue to feed at night with the adult bed bugs. The blood loss can cause anemia in birds.

Black Flies (Turkey Gnats)

These small, black, humpbacked flies are sometimes seen outdoors flying around the heads of poultry. They bite and suck blood. They can spread the leucocytozoon disease to chickens, ducks, geese and turkeys. Their eggs hatch on rocks, branches, etc., near streams of swift water. If these flies are plentiful in area, it's best not to range birds. Confining the birds will help prevent the disease from being spread. It's too hard to control these flies outdoors.

Chicken Mites

These eight-legged, 1/35-inch-long, gray-colored pests are also called red mites, gray mites, roost mites and poultry mites. Perhaps the various names occur because the grayish mite appears to be red to black when filled with blood. This mite feeds on poultry at night and lives hidden during the day in cracks and crevices of walls, ceilings, floors, boards, and roosts. Occasionally the pest visits setting hens during the day.

Examining the birds at night with a flashlight detects the presence of the mites. Other signs to look for are mite masses, black and white specks of excrement, silver skin casts, and small eggs near secluded cracks in the poultry house.

Young poults and setting hens can die from the continual loss of blood. Heavily infected birds will become weak, stunted, droopy, have pale head parts, and their egg production will drop. Chicken mites can spread the highly fatal bacterial disease—spirochetosis—to chickens, geese, guinea fowl, and turkeys. This disease produces a yellow-green diarrhea, droopiness, weak legs, fever, thirst, and a catarrhal enteritis.

Numerous generations of chicken mites can occur throughout the year, although they won't be active in cold buildings in the winter. They are able to go dormant for 4-5 months in the summer if the building is kept free of poultry. In the winter this dormancy can last even longer in an empty building.

Chiggers (Chigger Mites)

These bright red, figure-8-shaped pests are about 1 millimeter long. Their larvae are reddish to yellowish and about 1/150 inch long. They are not noted for burrowing into the skin or sucking blood, but they do attach themselves in clusters on the breast, thighs, vent, and under wings. They inject a substance into the bite that allows the tissues to soften and liquefy for absorption by the chiggers. Chiggers are mainly only a problem with turkeys and fowl that are ranged. Range areas can be periodically dusted with Sevin for control of these chiggers.

Fowl Ticks (Blue Bug, Chicken Tick)

These are mainly a pest of chickens but will also attack turkeys. The adults are flat, thin, egg-shaped, reddish to bluish-black, have eight legs and are 1/4 to 1/2 inch long. Their larvae have six legs and are 1/10 inch long and appear dark blue or black. Their nymphs are gray, eight-legged pests. All feed by sucking the blood of the poultry at night. Ticks can live for up to two years without feeding. They can be difficult to eradicate when infestation becomes bad.

Small birds can die from the constant loss of blood. Birds will also appear unthrifty, lose weight, have weak legs, drooped wings, pale head parts, loss of appetite, and egg production will drop in breeders. Like the blood-sucking chicken mites, fowl ticks can spread fowl spirochetosis to chickens, geese, guinea fowl, and turkeys.

Northern Fowl Mites

These mostly infest chickens and occasionally turkeys. The adult mite is a bit smaller than the chicken mite. It's about 1/26 inch long with eight legs (Fig. 7-8). Adults are dark red to black but can vary in color and appear banded. These live on the birds continuously and lay two to five eggs in the fine feather fluff. Because the life cycle is only five to seven days, birds can become badly infested even with only these few eggs laid at a time. As many as 20,000 mites can accumulate on a bird in 10

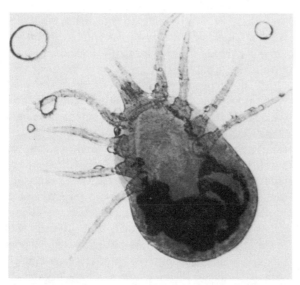

Fig. 7-8. Magnified view of a 1/26-inch long Northern fowl mite. (Courtesy of L. Dwight Schwartz, D.V.M., Senior Pathologist, Michigan State University)

weeks time. Heavier infestations occur in winter.

The mites can be seen by examining the bird's back, neck, tail, and vent. Whitish egg masses and excrement can be seen stuck and near the base of soiled-looking feathers and fluff. Scabs may appear on the skin. Fertility will be lowered because the mites affect breeding. Because these mites remain on the birds all the time, dusting the birds is the best solution.

Poultry Lice

These are wingless, flat, 1/8-inch-long, six-legged pests of chickens and turkeys. They have a round head and a set of claws at the bottom of each leg. They chew on the skin, feathers, and dry skin scales and scabs of poultry with their serrated teeth. The young nymphs are transparent looking and also feed. They can be active all year, but mostly during the summer.

Their presence makes birds nervous, lowers egg production, causes them to set less, have diarrhea, and prevents them from sleeping. This stress is enough to lower the birds' resistance to disease. Young poults and chicks can be killed by great numbers of lice if not kept in check. Most transfer

is from older birds to younger ones. Birds should be dusted with Sevin.

Scaly Leg Mites

This is an eight-legged, pale gray mite with a 1/100-to-1/50 inch-circular form. A magnifying glass must be used to observe them. The mites burrow under the scales of the shanks and feet, which causes intense itching, scabbing, and some bleeding. A white dust is seen under the scales that become raised or detached. If not treated, birds become lame, can lose some toes, lose weight, go off feed, egg production drops, and death ensues.

If not severe, scaly leg mite infestations are fairly easy to remedy. Dip the bird's legs into motor oil, fuel oil, or kerosene. Be careful not to get the oil on the feathers or skin. Dipping in oil will smother the mites by not allowing air to enter under the scales. One treatment is usually all that's needed. Repeat in one month for heavy infestation.

Because poultry lice and northern fowl mites remain on the birds all the time, dusting the birds is best. Pests such as the bed bugs, common chicken mites, and fowl ticks that feed in poultry houses during the night, are controlled by dusting the building and litter paying careful attention to all cracks and crevices. Range-related pests such as chiggers and black flies are controlled by dusting range areas. For thorough protection with all pests, birds should be dusted too. Sevin (carbaryl) is the most commonly used pesticide for all these pests. Walls, ceilings, ranges, and cages can be sprayed by using the wettable powder form. Birds and floors are usually dusted with the 5 percent Sevin powder, making sure powder filters down into feathers—especially under wings and around vent area. Withdrawal is usually seven days before butchering. Read all warnings and precautions carefully. Dust and spray on calm days so wind does not carry the pesticide. Cover feed and water so it does not become contaminated. Use face masks and avoid inhaling the sprays and dusts.

FEATHER PULLING

This is a bad habit that can occur with poults and

mature turkeys. To prevent it from becoming a long-standing habit, it must be looked for and remedied early. Feather pulling can lead to cannibalism and then lost birds. It can start when one or two poults peck at bits of feed or debris on the shoulders and backs of other poults. Soon they learn to grab individual feathers and pull them completely out of the skin and eat them. Bleeding can occur at the pore that held the feather. If this blood attracts other birds, injuries and death can result from the constant pecking.

Distinguish feather pulling from poorly feathered "barebacks" by observing the pores. Small pinfeathers can be seen protruding from the pores of barebacks. In feather pulling, no part of the feather quill is seen at all. Dim lights, preferably red, will help to prevent poults from seeing bits of feed and debris on others. Beak-trimming the offenders, both with poults and mature turkeys, will also help. Barebacks in turkey broods are usually caused by improper management—that is, too much heat, not enough humidity, and crowding. External parasites could also be the cause.

FOWL CHOLERA (PASTEURELLOSIS)

This is an infectious disease of all fowl, especially chickens, ducks, and turkeys. It's caused by a bacteria spread in a number of ways—strange birds introduced into home flocks, rodents, predators, wild birds, infective droppings, dead birds, contaminated feed and water, and nasal secretions.

Symptoms include some or all of the following: greenish-yellow diarrhea, increased water consumption, loss of weight, ruffled feathers, rattling noise in throat, discharge from mouth, joint infections and lameness, decreased feed consumption, fever, birds sit around more than usual, and some hens might even die on the nest. The heads of dead birds will turn bluish-purple. Blood appears in the tissues, intestinal lining, nostrils, throat, fat, and heart. Bottom of feet and joints are usually swollen from fluids. The liver becomes dark and swollen with small points of decay. The disease can appear suddenly and kill birds without symptoms being noticed.

If problems of fowl cholera have existed on premises, it is advisable to vaccinate at 10-16 weeks. Clemson University has come up with an effective freeze-dried live culture vaccine, for use with turkeys only, that is given in the drinking water. It should be given at onset of the disease to prevent a serious outbreak. It's not advisable to vaccinate unless fowl cholera has been a problem. Sulfa drugs, preferably sulfadimethoxine, (or sulfamerazine, sulfamethazine, sulfaquinoxaline and sulfanamides) can be used alone or with the vaccine at the time of outbreak to stop mortality. It must be remembered that sulfa drugs cause residues in meat and eggs, although there is a withdrawal period. Prolonged use is toxic to birds and lowers their ability to lay. As further treatment and prevention: keep rodents and predators under control, use ordinary disinfectants to kill the organism, and provide dry conditions, heat and sunlight to buildings, equipment and birds.

FOWL POX

This infectious, slow-spreading disease caused by a virus is one of the oldest diseases of poultry. It can affect all birds and water fowl of any age, but mainly chickens and turkeys. Its spread is by air through skin lacerations. Several species of mosquitoes are the main mode of spread, especially with ranged poultry. Infectious mosquitoes can also winter over in the poultry house to infect the poultry during winter or early spring.

There's both a wet and a dry form of fowl pox. The wet form produces lesions in the throat. These lesions can eventually suffocate a bird. The dry form produces lesions on the unfeathered parts of the body, including the nostrils, feet, shanks, mouth, eyelids, upper neck, vent, and head. On young chicks and poults, the feet and legs are usually the only parts that develop lesions.

There's actually two other similar strains of this disease: pigeon pox and canary pox. These can cross over to infect other species. These diseases are not related to the chicken pox of humans. The first symptom will be lesions resembling warts. A lesion will appear at each spot a mosquito has bitten, and can be so small they might just look like those caused from fighting. The lesions will turn yellow, then form a dark-colored scab. Other symptoms will be stunting of growth and overall unthriftiness.

Vaccination is recommended only if fowl pox has been a problem on the premises or in the area. If chickens and turkeys are on the same farm with pigeons, the pigeons can be vaccinated with the fowl pox vaccine too. A pigeon pox vaccine used on pigeons will not fully protect pigeons from outbreak of fowl pox. In severely affected areas, day-olds should be vaccinated. Being vaccinated before 6 weeks does not provide extended immunity, so they should be vaccinated again at 8-10 weeks. If less than 20 percent of the flock have lesions, giving the vaccine will usually limit the spread of fowl pox.

Do not use the wing-web stab method of vaccination for turkeys because they sleep with their head always under wings and this will cause pox infections of the eyes. Use the feather follicle method—pull a feather out and place the vaccine into the follicle pore.

To treat the disease, paint the lesions with silver nitrate. Use an antibiotic in the drinking water for two to three days. Use a pesticide to kill mosquitoes in the building.

FOWL TYPHOID

The bacteria that causes this disease is identical to that of pullorum. They produce the same symptoms and are sometimes confused. A blood test is needed to distinguish the two. Fowl typhoid is not limited to, but is mostly found in growing or mature birds over 12 weeks of age. Pullorum occurs in poultry under three weeks if the usual egg transmission mode of infection is responsible. Both diseases can appear at any age. Ducks, guineas, peacocks, pheasants and turkeys are not as susceptible to fowl typhoid as chickens are.

Recovered birds remain carriers and are not to be used for breeding because the disease will be transferred through the egg to the poult or chick.

Symptoms include: droopy heads, listlessness, loss of appetite, increased thirst, paleness, huddling from chilling, diarrhea, white droppings sometimes with green bile stains, weak knees, gasping for air,

pasted vents, and sleepiness. Upon opening a bird, small points of decay are found on the heart, liver, lungs, and other organs. The ceca is enlarged and contains a yellowish curd-like substance. Small hemorrhages appear in the muscles, fat, and intestines. The liver is enlarged and takes on a mahogany color. The gall bladder is distended. In mature birds, the ova (egg) are deformed and green-colored and the testicles are shrunken.

Medication interferes with a positive diagnosis of the disease. With small-scale raisers it's best to destroy the entire flock, disinfect, and sun the entire poultry house and equipment, and start with pullorum-free, tested birds. The organism is difficult to eradicate in the soil, so you should refrain from ranging for at least a year.

If the flock is to be butchered at home, a handler might want to treat the disease to avoid a large loss. This may prove difficult, however, because usually sulfa drugs are used and these leave residues in meat. An antibiotic such as streptomycin or erythromycin can be used instead. Remember the disease is not eradicated with medications—the birds still can infect eggs laid.

GANGRENOUS DERMATITIS (WING ROT)

This is a disease that is caused by bacteria and occurs suddenly. The bacteria is found in soil, dust, droppings, and litter. The disease is contracted individually by each bird from the litter or soil and through skin injuries. The disease affects chickens and turkeys mainly from two to eight weeks of age, but can infect birds up to 16 weeks of age. Two types of bacteria seem to be needed to bring on the disease.

Symptoms include unthriftiness, lameness, dehydration, depression and paleness. Dark reddish-black, dirty-looking areas appear over the breast, thighs, feet, lower abdomen, wing tips and wattles. The feathers in these areas look dark and dirty and the skin darkens and begins to flake off. The areas become swollen and contain fluid that begins to smell bad. Usually some birds suddenly die before symptoms are noticed. Birds die within 8-24 hours after showing depression, dehydration, and lameness. In the dead birds, look for decay of skin deep in tissues of breasts, thighs, legs, and wings and swollen bloody, bubbly fluid. The liver and kidney might be swollen and dark with bits of decay.

Because deficiencies of selenium, vitamin A, and vitamin E can bring on an attack, administer supplements of these while treating with medication. Administer oxytetracycline or chlortetracycline. Prevent introduction of the infection by controlling cannibalism, maintaining dry litter conditions, and protecting birds from injuries caused by sharp edges on equipment and fencing. The floors and ground remain infected for long periods—try thoroughly cleaning and disinfecting and dispose of the flock. Dirt floors cannot be thoroughly disinfected as concrete floors can.

HEMORRHAGIC ENTERITIS

This is an infectious intestine disease of turkeys between 4-13 weeks of age, caused by a virus. It's characterized by sudden death and blood from the vent. It's spread from turkeys eating infected feed, water, litter, and droppings. It can be brought on by hot weather and sudden changes in the consistency of a feed—as from mash to grain.

A major symptom is that the intestines appear dark and are filled with blood (Fig. 7-9). Sometimes the liver will be bloody and have decayed areas.

A vaccine might be available in areas where the disease is more commonly found. A serum given no later than the fourth day of an outbreak will reduce mortality. Antibiotics should not be given because they can cause a more severe form of the disease. Prevent spreading the disease by using chlorine and iodine to disinfect hands and boots when tending the sick birds.

INFECTIOUS CATARRHAL ENTERITIS (HEXAMITIASIS)

This is an intestinal disease of chukar, ducks, peafowl, pheasants, quail, and turkeys caused by a parasite that lives in the upper intestine of poults. A different species of the disease infects pigeons. Infection has not been observed in chickens although they might be carriers. Mortality is highest in one-to-nine-week-old birds. Poults of 10 weeks

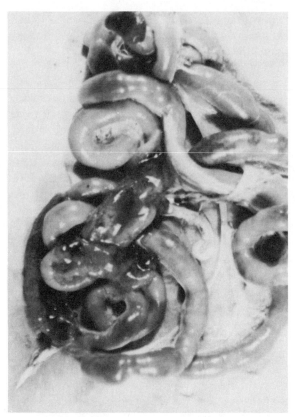

Fig. 7-9. Blood filled intestines in hemorrhagic enteritis. (Courtesy of L. Dwight Schwartz, D.V.M., Senior Pathologist, Michigan State University)

and over become resistant.

Symptoms are chilling, ruffled feathers, listlessness, good appetite but rapid weight loss, watery diarrhea, huddling, dehydration, stiff walking, nervousness, sometimes convulsive deaths. The intestines contain a foamy, watery substance. Symptoms can be confused with those of Blue Comb.

Provide sanitary quarters, food, and water and treat with Emtryl (as for blackhead), oxytetracycline, or chlortetracycline. Small-scale raisers are not advised to keep recovered birds as breeders because it's difficult to keep healthy birds from disease carriers.

INTERNAL PARASITES

There are at least 60 species of worms that infect poultry in the United States. It is better to prevent and control worm problems by management rather than to wait until worms are evident or suspected and then treating. Breaking the cycle of infestation by keeping litter dry is the main method of prevention. Controlling the source of the infection is important too. Many worms are spread by intermediate hosts such as earthworms, flies, beetles, grasshoppers, sow bugs, cockroaches, snails, and fish.

The signs of worm infestations are similar in all poultry. These include an unthrifty appearance, paleness, stunting of growth, lowered feed intake, inactiveness, decreased egg production, and loss of weight. Sometimes there are small amounts of blood in the droppings from irritation of the intestinal lining. Be sure to use the correct wormer medication for the type of worms and observe doses, schedules of doses, and withdrawal times carefully. Large amounts of worms can easily kill young poults. Periodic worming should be done to keep poultry free from the following worms most common to turkeys:

Cecal Worms (Heterakis Gallinarum)

These infect chickens, guinea fowl, pheasants, quail, and turkeys. The main problem in turkeys is that these worms spread the blackhead parasite. Infective cecal worm eggs are eaten by turkeys and earthworms. If turkeys eat the infected earthworms, the turkeys are also infected. Infective droppings help spread the worm and the blackhead disease.

The 3/8-to-1/2-inch-long worm is found in the cecum of the bird. It's suggested that turkeys be kept from chickens and off grounds used by chickens within the last three years. Chickens usually show no signs of blackhead infection but can easily transmit infective cecal worm eggs by way of their droppings. Eliminate cecal worms by worming with phenothiazine, hygromycin B, or Meldane-2, and the chances of blackhead disease are lowered. After worming, move the birds to clean, uninfected pens.

Roundworms

These infest mainly chickens, guinea fowl, and tur-

keys. The species ascardia dissimilis is the type that infests turkeys. Turkeys are infected when they ingest infective roundworm eggs from the litter. Infective eggs are those which reach a larval stage. Noninfective eggs and adult worms don't do damage if eaten. Flies can transmit roundworms to the poultry house. The infective roundworm eggs hatch within the bird and 35 days later are adult worms that lay eggs and remain in the intestine (Fig. 7-10). Eggs are passed in the droppings and the cycle begins again in the litter. Two-to-three-month-olds develop resistance to the effects of the worm.

Worm medication should be given periodically to eliminate worms, but its effect will not last unless sanitation, rotation, cleaning, and adding new litter material is practiced. The most common anthelmintic to expel roundworms is piperazine. This is also used for other livestock and pets. Types used in feed or wet mash preparations are hygromycin B, Meldane-2, and Wormal.

Tapeworms

These are flat, segmented, ribbon-like worms. Depending upon the species, the whitish or yellowish worm can vary in length from 1/16 inch to several inches. As the worm grows, the tail end, filled with eggs, breaks off and is passed in the droppings.

Tapeworms spend their immature life in intermediate hosts such as ants, beetles, earthworms, grasshoppers, houseflies, slugs, snails, etc. These hosts are then eaten by the turkey. The type host depends upon the species of tapeworm.

A specific remedy for tapeworms of turkeys is Tinostat, a butynorate compound. Efforts should also be made to rid the premises of possible hosts.

Threadworms

These capillaria worms are commonly called threadworms because they are long and thread-like in appearance. Six species infect domestic poultry. Capillaria annulata and C. contorta infest the crop and esophagus, C. retusa infests the cecum, C. bursata, C. caudinflata, and C. obsignata infest the duodenum and small intestine.

Treatment is Meldane-2 (Coumaphos). Other

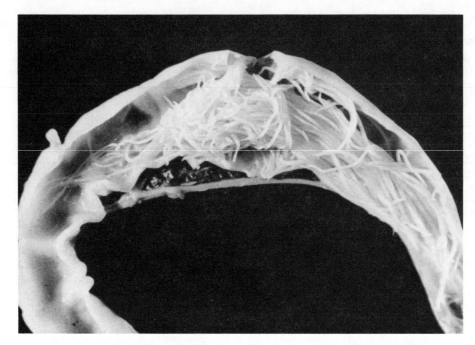

Fig. 7-10. Intestine cut open to reveal heavy roundworm infestation. (Courtesy of L. Dwight Schwartz, D.V.M., Senior Pathologist, Michigan State University)

treatments are not as effective, or they might have a long withdrawal period with residues remaining in meat. Gentian violet prevents the eggs from reaching the larval stage. Vitamin A supplements can help repair damage in the tissues.

Steaming a building at 136-141 degrees F. (58-60 degrees C.) will destroy these worm eggs. Other measures in prevention are disinfecting, fumigating, practicing clean management, flock isolation, and sanitation.

MYCOPLASMA DISEASES (MG, MM, MS)

These are three related contagious diseases caused by mycoplasma organisms. Most commercial turkey breeding flocks are tested for Mycoplasma gallisepticum (MG). Many are now tested for Mycoplasma meleagridis (MM). They can be tested for the third, Mycoplasma synoviae (MS) but it must be done every four weeks for the life of the bird. Furthermore, if MS is found, the breeders cannot be used for eggs used to hatch poults.

With MG and MM, hatching eggs can be treated before setting by heat treating, antibiotics, and egg dipping. Tylan is frequently used commercially for egg dipping in vacuum chambers to pre-

vent MG and MM from being passed in the egg. Large chambers, hatchers, or incubators are usually used to heat treat thousands of eggs at one time to kill the MG and MM organism. The eggs are heated to 115 degrees F. (46 degrees C.) for 11 hours then cooled quickly and set. Chickens are frequently tested for MG and MS; they do not get the MM disease.

Mycoplasma gallisepticum is also called Infectious Sinusitis in turkeys. MG infects chickens, ducks, peafowl, pigeons, and turkeys of all ages. Turkeys do not have antibodies to protect against MG, so outbreaks are more severe than with chickens. At one time MG was spread freely from eggs. Management at hatcheries has changed this. Now MG is spread mainly by infected birds coming in contact with others. MG is also spread by careless humans, contaminated equipment, and vehicles.

MG symptoms of turkeys in the upper form of the disease are watery eyes, noisy breathing, unthriftiness, water discharge from nostrils, and swollen sinuses below the eyes (Fig. 7-11). Discharge becomes thick and firm, and eyes can swell shut. In the lower form, only a slight rattling might be heard in the throat, caused by a thick yellow exudate in the air passages. MG can take a long time to spread through the entire flock. Mortality varies. Recovered birds remain as carriers. MG must be distinguished from Newcastle disease and other mycoplasma diseases.

MM infects the lower respiratory tract of turkeys only. Poults are most susceptible, although it can infect at any age. Its spread is by hens contaminating eggs (producing infectious poults), contaminated equipment, visitors, vehicles, etc. In mature birds, transmission is usually by genital contact of birds.

MM symptoms are high mortality in very young poults, stunted growth, unthriftiness, difficult breathing, low egg production and poor hatchability of eggs.

Mycoplasma synoviae has both a synovitis and respiratory form. MS is called infectious synovitis (not to be confused with Infectious Sinusitis of MG infections) when referring to the joint infection form. This disease infects chickens and turkeys of all ages, but mainly chicks and poults from 4 to 12 weeks of age. The respiratory form can be found in both young and adult birds. It is spread by eggs, direct contact, equipment, and humans.

The synovitis form causes swollen hocks, joints, stiff walking, lameness, weight loss, breast blisters, yellow- or orange-colored fluid in keel, bursa, hock, and wing joints. Other signs are dehydration and a greenish diarrhea. Signs internally are enlarged liver and spleen, and stringy discharge around heart. The respiratory form may go unnoticed because the thick yellow discharge is hidden in the air passages like MG. Recovery is slow for both forms. Recovered breeders infect eggs, so they should not be kept for breeding.

Antibiotics used for mycoplasma infection are tylosin, erythromycin, and spectinomycin.

NEWCASTLE

This is a contagious respiratory disease caused by a virus. It can infect any bird of any age, as well as mammals and humans. In humans it can cause a severe eye infection. The disease spreads rapidly and is transmitted in the air on equipment, crates, dead birds, wild birds, boots, and by humans. It takes five to seven days to appear after exposure.

Symptoms are sudden with hoarseness in young poultry, watery nostrils, difficult breathing, chilling, paralysis, trembling, and total discomfort. In young poultry the face swells with fluid. Nervous symptoms show a twisting of the neck. There's discharge in the windpipe and lungs, redness in the mouth and throat. Egg production drops and there is a decrease in water and feed consumption.

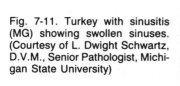
Fig. 7-11. Turkey with sinusitis (MG) showing swollen sinuses. (Courtesy of L. Dwight Schwartz, D.V.M., Senior Pathologist, Michigan State University)

The virus remains infective in litter for two months. It can live in dead birds for one year.

There's no particular treatment other than feeding an antibiotic for a few days and raising the temperature so birds don't feel chilled. A Newcastle vaccine is available. It should be given at 10 days, again at 35 days of age, at three months, and every three months thereafter. A small amount of the vaccine is placed in the eye or nostril. Vaccines can be administered in the drinking water but are not as reliable because the dose cannot be measured exactly.

OMPHALITIS (MUSHY CHICK DISEASE)

This is simply an inflamed, infected navel caused by bacteria. The bacterias are present in incubators and hatchers that are not disinfected regularly. High humidity, high temperatures, or too low a temperature in incubators can induce the infection. Thin, porous, unsanitary shells can allow the bacteria to penetrate the pores and cause infection.

Symptoms are an enlarged, soft, mushy-feeling abdomen. The navel is wet and inflamed. Chicks die within a few days if not disposed of. Part of the unabsorbed yolk may be seen protruding from the navel because of incomplete absorption and closure.

Dispose of infected day-olds, and execute sanitation and disinfecting procedures if incubating in machines.

ORNITHOSIS

This is a highly contagious disease that infects turkeys and many other birds, pet birds, some animals and is an occupational disease of humans who work around turkey growing and processing plants. Humans infected will develop a fever of up to 104.2 degrees F., and have headache and pneumonia symptoms. Older individuals are more susceptible than children. In poultry, young birds are more susceptible. Chickens aren't usually bothered by the disease.

The disease is spread in five to seven days by actual contact of infected birds, and contaminated clothes and equipment. It's not passed in the egg but recovered birds are carriers. They should not be used for breeding but can be butchered for food.

In turkeys, symptoms are loss of appetite, yellow or greenish diarrhea, dullness, loss of weight, weakness, depression, resting with bottom of keelbone on ground and lesions on heart and liver.

Use Aureomycin in feed for three weeks. Prevent the disease by screening wild birds out of poultry house, do not mix different ages or species of birds, and keep animals and humans from poultry house.

PARATYPHOID

This is a blood poisoning disease of chicks and poults caused by a Salmonella bacteria, the same group that causes food poisoning in humans. All poultry can become infected, including game birds, pet birds, pigeons. Domestic animals and humans are also susceptible.

Poultry houses, feed, water, incubators, chick boxes, rodents, flies, pets, by-products of animals, wild birds, and direct contact can all spread the disease.

Symptoms are similar to pullorum. There is diarrhea, pasted vents, increased thirst, decrease in food consumption, chilling, chirping, listlessness, weakness, and joint swelling. Autopsy shows swollen pale-yellow spotted livers, bloody intestines with a thick yellow core, and decayed spots on organs (Fig. 7-12).

Treat with medications used for pullorum and fowl typhoid. Injectable spectinomycin and gentamycin can be used. Do not use infected recovered birds as breeders. Incinerate dead birds. Prevent through hatching sanitation and by not mixing different age or species of birds.

POISONING

Rather than list a miriad of poisons and their toxic tolerance levels for poultry, it's best to describe general symptoms and how to decide whether poisoning might be the cause. Birds are usually less susceptible to poisoning than mammals are. Depending upon the toxin, chickens are more susceptible to some than turkeys and visa versa.

There are a number of toxic substances which

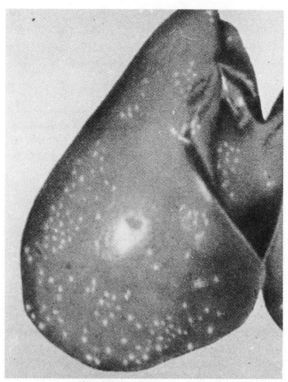

Fig. 7-12. Paratyphoid liver showing focal lesions. (Courtesy of L. Dwight Schwartz, D.V.M., Senior Pathologist, Michigan State University)

affect poultry. Signs of toxic poisoning vary but include circling, convulsions, depression, difficult breathing, dilated pupils, fluid in the abdominal cavity, internal bleeding, leg deformities, listlessness, loss of weight, loss of balance, malformed eggs, nervous symptoms, prostration, reduced hatchability, retarded growth, soft-shelled eggs, thirst, tremors, uneasiness, vomiting, watery droppings, wing paralysis, and of course death.

Most inexperienced handlers are too quick to blame the feed when symptoms arise. Although this could be the problem, there are a number of ways birds can become poisoned. Careful management will help to eliminate these other sources. Soybeans, for example, contain a tryspin inhibitor that causes an enlargement of the pancreas. The pancreas normally secrets tryspin in the intestinal tract, which neutralizes acid secretions and breaks down fats, proteins, and starches for further nutrient ab-

sorption. If this process is disturbed, slow growth can result. Soybeans must be heat-treated to inactivate this tryspin inhibitor.

Cottonseed meal contains large amounts of gossypol, which will cause a swelling around the heart, labored breathing, weakness, and lack of appetite. Many rapeseed meals contain compounds that can depress growth rate and lower egg production. A rapeseed called canola, has been developed in Canada. It contains very minor amounts of the toxic compound.

When large amounts of protein by-products such as feathers, fish scales, hair, and hides are used in a feed, a deficiency of the amino acid tryptophan will result. This deficiency can cause abnormal feathering, small eggs, low egg production, weight loss, depressed growth, reduced feed intake, and reabsorbed egg yolks in hens.

Toxic fats have been found in poultry feed. Chemical elements contained in the fats have been known to cause liver decay, and fluid retention and swelling in the abdominal cavity and heart. Hemorrhages on the heart and enlargement of the bile duct can occur.

PCB's (polychlorinated biphenyl) have been found that are in excess of the 5 ppm permitted in turkey and chicken meat, and in excess of the 0.5 ppm permitted in egg products. The PCB's were traced to heat-exchange fluid and plastic wrappers from bakery goods that were ground into the feed. The poultry would not show internal symptoms other than reduced hatchability and egg production because up to 40 ppm does not show changes in the tissues or organs. PCB's are found in the fat of birds.

Molds can contaminate feeds and cause hemorrhagic disease and prevent proper absorption of nutrients from the feed. Even small amounts of molds in a feed can be dangerous. Ducklings are the most susceptible to mold toxin.

Poisons can be introduced into feeds in a number of ways. If a fumigant such as EDB (ethylene dibromide) is used to treat grain or Thiram is used to treat seed corn, they can inadvertently get mixed into poultry feed. Either can cause problems with birds. It's not only commercially prepared feeds but also those a handler might have ground at a granary that can become contaminated. Be observant as your feed is being ground.

Treatment for most poisonings requires simply removing the offending substance after investigating the cause. When any unusual symptoms occur with your birds, think back to any methods of cleaning, disinfecting, or parasite control that was recently done. Nicotine sulfate is still used in some areas for painting roosts for external parasite control. At high temperatures it becomes gaseous. Birds can have wing paralysis, dilated pupils, become nervous, vomit, and show dark blood spots in the heart and lungs. Some compounds can cause burns on the face, feet, and wattles. Coal-tar products containing carbolineum are sometimes sprayed in poultry houses to disinfect. Besides burns from the fumes, the abdominal cavity fills with fluid, the liver deteriorates and swells, and the birds have difficulty breathing.

Check if medications or wormers could have been overdosed. When antibiotics are fed, the intestinal lining becomes thinner. Overuse of these medications can eventually cause bleeding. Be sure fly and insect baits are placed where poultry can't get to them. Keep rodent poisons out of reach. Usually a lot of arsenic must be consumed by some poultry before deaths occur, but rat poisons with arsenic will cause symptoms in the birds if eaten. The birds can lose their balance, have jerking movements of the neck, become nervous, have inflamed gizzards and crops, degenerated kidneys, and enteritis. Misuse and overuse of some chemicals, either organic or inorganic, can be toxic. It's best to keep poultry out of crops and orchards that were recently sprayed.

PULLORUM

This disease was first reported in 1900. Once a common, very dreaded disease, pullorum has been nearly eliminated in the United States due to constant blood testing of commercial breeder flocks and the destruction of infected birds over the years. Some states require a pullorum test be done on individual birds or all birds be certified that they are from a pullorum-free flock before they can be exhibited at fairs or poultry shows. The requirements are occasionally revised; check with your state university veterinarian or the NPIP state representative for revisions to the plan. Both the National Poultry Improvement Plan (of 1935) and the National Turkey Improvement Plan (of 1943), now working under a combined titles as The National Poultry Improvement Plan since 1971, works with USDA to help individual states carry out regulations of the plan.

Mainly an infectious bacterial disease of chicks and poults under 14 days of age, pullorum is usually spread from infected hatching eggs. Recovered birds remain as carriers and infect the eggs they lay. Upon hatching, the infection spreads quickly in incubators and hatchers. The bacteria can live up to one year in a poultry house, so contaminated buildings and equipment help spread the disease. Poultry by-products used in poultry feeds, carrier birds, and chick boxes also are a mode of spread.

Symptoms in infected chicks and poults include huddling near heat, no appetite, depression, sleepiness, droopiness, diarrhea, white pasting around vent (sometimes containing green bile material), difficult breathing, and weak knees. Deaths begin at 5-7 days and mortality peaks at 9-12 days of age. Internal symptoms show points of decay over the heart, liver, lungs, and other organs; blisters on leg and wing joints; and unabsorbed yolks. In adults, greenish, irregular-shaped ova are found with decay in the center of the liver.

Sulfa drugs or antibacterial drugs are used for treatment, but small-scale raisers should dispose of the birds because treatment can be economically unwise. The birds cannot be used as breeders anyway.

Pullorum testing can be done at home by purchasing the pullorum-stained antigen and bleeder loop. The bleeder loop punctures the skin over a vein and a small amount of blood is retained in the loop. This blood is then mixed with a drop of the antigen on a glass plate and compared with illustrations (supplied with the antigen) of negative and positive samples after two minutes of drying. The antigen can only be purchased in a 1000-dose bottle (about $30), but it can be recapped with the dropper and refrigerated.

RICKETS

This is a preventable, but not a curable, nutritional disorder of young poultry. It's caused by a deficiency of vitamin D_3 and calcium, or an imbalance of calcium and phosphorus. For proper metabolism, calcium and phosphorus should be present in poultry feeds at a ratio of 2:1. An excess of either also causes rickets—with the bones becoming soft and rubbery. Other deficiencies cause crippling as well (Fig. 7-13).

Vitamin D_3 is needed for calcium to be absorbed and used by the body. If vitamin D_3 or both calcium and vitamin D_3 are deficient, the young growing bones of poults will become soft and spongy. The bird becomes crippled as a result.

Rickets in turkeys is noticed as the poults begin to put on weight at about four weeks of age. Any bird can get rickets, but fast-growing poults

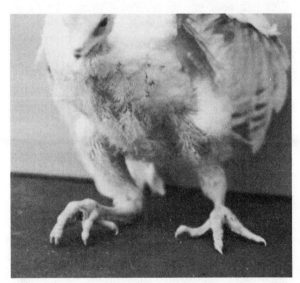

Fig. 7-13. This crippling (perosis or slipped tendon) due to a manganese deficiency results in swelling and flattening of hock joint and can be aggravated by excessive calcium and phosphorus. (Courtesy of L. Dwight Schwartz, D.V.M., Senior Pathologist, Michigan State University)

and other heavy, fast growers such as Cornish Rock Cross broilers, Mammoth Pekin ducks, and Langshan chickens are more prone because of the extra weight their legs must carry. The birds become top-heavy.

Rickets must be prevented because once symptoms show, it cannot be corrected. A bird with slightly bowed or crooked legs will not sufficiently grow out. The legs are no longer perfectly set and balanced to support the body weight evenly. Crippling prevents the birds from getting around normally and properly eating, so growth becomes severely stunted. It's best to dispose of this bird when symptoms are first seen. Keeping the birds around in hopes they'll get better is economically unfeasible. The first symptom is a slight bowing of each leg.

Commercially prepared turkey starters seem to have enough calcium but not enough vitamin D_3. There is no way of knowing how much calcium and vitamin D_3 is contained in the feeds because companies do not list the amounts. They claim this would be giving away their trade formulas. It's best to assume the feed is deficient in vitamin D_3—this is what I've found most lacking in various brands—and supplement the vitamin on your own. Do not supplement the calcium because, as mentioned earlier, an excess can cause rickets.

Administer the vitamin D_3 in the form of a good poultry grade of cod-liver oil in the water beginning at five days of age (from the actual hatch date, not the days after they're received or shipped). The hatch date should be stamped on the shipping box. Waiting until after the 5th day is often too late. It must be started no later than the 5th day of age. Starting it sooner usually causes loose droppings because the oil is a laxative. If purchased at a feed store, it would be wise to start the oil when the poults are brought home—just be sure to check the droppings for looseness which indicates that a young digestive system is having trouble handling the oil. Then cut back on the oil for a few days and the droppings should become normal again.

If poultry cod-liver oil is unavailable or only available in 1-gallon cans, the oil can be purchased at a drug store but will be higher priced per ounce. Because only four ounces is needed for 20 poults for four weeks, a 1-gallon can might become rancid before it is used up by a small-scale raiser. From the 5th day of age up until poults are out into the direct sunshine, place a small amount of the oil onto the surface of the drinking water. Do not place into filled mason jars used with base founts and then turn the jar over—the oil will float to the top of the jar and become unavailable to the poults. Place the oil on the water surface after the fount is upright. Watch the condition of the droppings later that day to tell if the right amount has been given. If droppings are loose simply use less of the oil the next day.

Poults also get vitamin D from the sun, which is why it's called the "sunshine vitamin." The vitamin is synthesized from sterol in the skin when poults are exposed to direct sunlight. Do not count on the sunlight that comes through panes of glass; poults must be in direct sunlight to absorb the vitamin from the rays. Give the cod-liver oil until poults have access to direct sunlight. This might be six weeks or more depending upon how long the birds are confined. If turkeys will be confined until market age, give the oil up until a few weeks before butchering so a fishy taste does not remain in the meat. For show birds, give the oil up until four weeks and then before the show and allow the sun to bleach the feather to white because the oil yellows feathers. Ultraviolet lights will also help synthesize vitamin D_3. Vitamin D_2 is not as effective.

SPRADDLE LEGS

The legs of day-old poultry will flex sideways if they are allowed to walk over slippery surfaces before the leg cartilage and bones have hardened enough to support their weight. Tall-legged breeds and species are more prone to this management injury—this includes turkey poults. New poults should always be placed on top of a bunch of rags or towels until they gain their footing for about seven days.

If newspapers are to be used over battery brooder wire floors to prevent the poults legs from becoming caught down in the wire, avoid leg sprains by lightly spraying the top of paper with water until the paper becomes soiled by droppings and feed. Also sprinkle crushed feed or sand lightly over the top of the paper. Be sure to keep slightly bunched-up rags back under the heating element as it won't become as soiled there. Towels can be used over the floor in the cool part of the brooder, but might have to be replaced frequently. If straw is used for litter, use a thin, rough type rather than a wide, smooth type because the wide bands of straw become slippery.

If a handler wants to try and save day-olds who are spraddle-legged, he can try tying both legs together with a very thick string. Leave a space of about 1 inch between the legs so the poult may walk normally. Place a knot in the center of this space. Do not tie too tight at the bottom of shanks. Chick-size plastic coil leg bands can be used to secure the string on each end. This method doesn't always work but if a handler has time to do it and make sure the poult gets to the water and feed, it might be worth his time and patience.

STREPTOCOCCOSIS (STAPH INFECTION)

This is a noncontagious disease caused by avian strain of the staphyococcus aureus bacteria. A selenium deficiency, dirty drinking water or mudholes used for drinking, and injuries allow the bacteria to infect the bird. All species are susceptible but chickens, pheasants, and turkeys are most affected.

At first, birds affected become listless, depressed, run a fever of 109 degrees F. (42 degrees C.), have no desire for food, droppings are watery and joints can be swollen. Later, birds become lame, lose weight, have ear infections, and acquire breast blisters. Movements will appear to be painful because birds prefer to sit rather than walk. Internally, the liver will be dark, swollen, and bloody. The contents of the intestines will be watery. Infected joints will contain thick yellow pus.

Bumblefoot can also appear if the staph is running rampant as it's a soil-borne germ. If bumblefoot is present, treat as outlined earlier in this chapter.

Treat with erythromycin or penicillin in the drinking water for 3-5 days.

The bacteria is resistant to disinfectants, but keep available drinking water sanitary. Check for sharp objects that could pierce the skin and allow the bacteria to enter. If a selenium deficiency might exist, correct the ration.

TOE TRIMMING

This is practiced on a commercial scale by many growers. It is claimed that removing the nail and a bit of the middle toes from each foot makes the birds more calm and quiet later. Personally, I have found no big difference, but if the turkeys are to be marketed or held as breeders, this practice can be somewhat beneficial. It can help reduce scratches on the skin of dressed birds caused when the birds are rounded up and caged for butchering, and can reduce the scratches breeder toms inflict on hens. Toe trimming can also be used as a permanent marking system when handlers want to keep track of their turkeys.

VACCINATING

The more money a handler has invested in his flock, the more he may be inclined to vaccinate. If a particular disease is prevalent in the area, it would be wise to vaccinate. The choice to vaccinate home birds is entirely up to the handler. Birds to be entered in fairs and shows need the combination Newcastle-Bronchitis vaccination before exhibiting.

There are some things that might deter a handler from vaccinating. One is the cost and waste. Although most vaccines are fairly inexpensive, they are only available in 500-dose and 1000-dose containers. The unused portion must be properly destroyed because the contents, once open, become ineffective with age. They can be dangerous if stored or disposed of improperly if the vaccine is a live agent as most are. This means the vaccine will actually cause the disease. Groups such as 4-H clubs can purchase the large-dose containers and share the contents among their birds to minimize costs and waste.

Another factor for handlers to consider before vaccinating is whether the vaccines and vaccinated birds will cause a sensitivity reaction in humans.

A handler sensitive to a particular vaccine can be affected by handling the live vaccine or by eating vaccinated birds. The symptoms can vary but might include pains in the joints similar to arthritis. I'm not sure this has ever been made public (or even proved by testing), but it should be considered.

Vaccines are made from large quantities of the organism or virus that causes a particular disease. Most are made of a live virus, so the poultry actually gets a mild case of the disease. Unvaccinated birds must be kept from those being vaccinated or they can become sick with the disease.

Few vaccines are inactivated, so they should be handled with extreme care. Burn, incinerate, or disinfect all opened containers to avoid accidental spread of the disease to other birds. Keep container sealed until ready to use.

Various methods are used to administer vaccines. Sometimes they are sprayed and thus are inhaled by the birds. Some are injected subcutaneously (under the skin). Others may be dropped into the eye or nostril or placed into a feather follicle after a feather is removed as in the wing-web stab method. Drinking water is sometimes used for mass inoculation when many birds are involved. This method is not as reliable because it's unknown as to how much each bird receives. Vaccines such as for coccidiosis, Fowl Cholera and Erysipelas are available only to commercial growers.

Always be sure instructions are included with the particular vaccine purchased. Follow directions as to handling, preparing, administering, etc., exactly. Keep hands washed before and after vaccinating. Keep away from your mouth, nose, and eyes. If possible, have some help with the job. If not, large turkeys can stand on the ground firmly held between your legs and with one hand holding the part to receive the vaccine (see Fig. 3-4).

Agricultural extension agents or state poultry science pathologist can answer specific questions pertaining to vaccinating schedules for your particular area.

VENT GLEET (CANDIDIASIS)

This is a digestive tract disease caused by a fungus

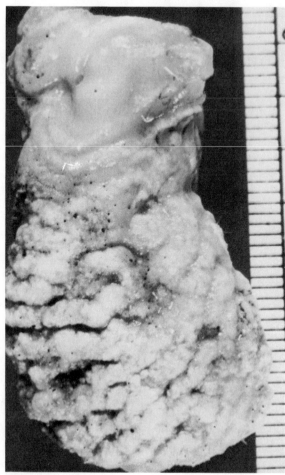

Fig. 7-14. Thickened crop of vent gleet. (Courtesy of L. Dwight Schwartz, D.V.M., Senior Pathologist, Michigan State University)

weight. The dryed, white droppings around the vent area can be a disease in itself or be combined with the intestinal symptoms of the disease.

Treat outbreaks with an antimycotic drug to control the infection. Do not use antibiotics because they feed the fungus and make it worse. Mycostatin-20 or gentian violet can be used. Copper sulfate is also used, but take care when disposing of the droppings because the copper is toxic to sheep and other ruminant type livestock who graze over these droppings.

Prevent and treat by keeping drinking water sanitary. Use iodine sanitizers in the water a few times a week or use household chlorine bleach. For older birds, mix 1/2 ounce of chlorine with 4 gallons of drinking water, preferably in a glass, porcelain, or stoneware waterer. For poults, mix 10 drops of chlorine with each gallon of drinking water.

WING CLIPPING

One wing is clipped on each turkey to throw them off balance and thus prevent them from flying over the tops of pens. Unless wild turkeys are raised, the only time a heavy breed turkey needs its wings clipped is when young. Even then, wild turkeys prefer to run rather than fly. Most adult turkeys get too heavy to do much flying. Some lighter breeds such as Bourbon Reds might need to be clipped if they manage to fly up and over a 6-foot fence. Be sure to provide low (1-foot-high) roosts for wing-clipped adults.

If breeders are kept, do not clip the tom's wings later than the fall season or toms might have difficulty breeding. The males of most species use their wings for balancing while mating. A tom doesn't use his wings for mating as much as other birds, but it's still better not to hinder his efforts.

Turkeys that are allowed to fly up into trees will make nightly roosting there a habit. This is dangerous because they become easy prey for wild animals such as owls. Also, landing continuously from great heights will cause injury to the feet of heavy turkeys, which can lead to bumblefoot.

Young poults who always appear to be loose should have wings clipped to keep them under con-

that can affect chickens, grouse, pigeons, pheasants, quail, turkeys, mammals, and humans. It does not spread from contact with other birds, but from the presence of the yeast-like fungus in feed, water, or the litter. Moldy, lumpy feed can be a source of infection because corn can contain this fungus.

Symptoms are listlessness, ruffled feathers, paleness, increase in feed consumption and white, dryed accumulations of droppings at the vent area. Interior signs are erosion of the gizzard lining, inflammation of the intestines (enteritis) and white, thickened areas of the crop (Fig. 7-14). Long-standing vent gleet shows birds who become over-

trol if outdoor pens do not have tops to keep them from flying over. With one wing fanned out, use sharp scissors to trim off the one row of primaries up to the middle axial feather (refer to Fig. 17-1). Trim only one wing on each bird. The primaries are the largest feathers furthest from the body.

Trim just below the next row of feathers. There's no need to cut close. Cutting into the hollow part of the quill can cause bleeding. Never place a bleeding bird back into the flock until complete healing has taken place.

Part 2

Guinea Fowl

Chapter 8

Choosing, Managing, and Feeding Keets

ORIGIN AND HISTORY

There are actually seven species of wild guinea fowl. The common and most well-known is the Helmeted guinea fowl (Fig. 8-1). The Helmeted guinea fowl is known to have been kept in captivity since the 4th century B.C.. At that time it was raised mainly for meat. Today it's raised for meat, utility purposes, and pleasure. It is a native to the southern two-thirds of Africa, including the island of Madagascar and Morocco in the northwest tip of Africa. It was from these areas the guinea fowl was first imported.

Guinea fowl are related to pheasants, quail, turkeys, and domestic chickens. They all share numerous characteristics and behavior patterns. They are all galliformes but are members of individual families.

Guineas are very versatile and somewhat seasonal in production. They lay eggs about as regularly as a chicken, but only from April or May until September or October, depending upon the climate. Warmer climates will have earlier and more productive guineas if not closely confined. The average amount of eggs laid, for a season of six months, is 50 to 100. Although their eggs are very good and can be used the same as chicken eggs, most guineas are kept for their meat and watch dog characteristics.

Many handlers agree the somewhat dark meat of a guinea tastes like pheasant. A guinea does not have white meat like a chicken, but the lighter colored feather varieties do have lighter meat. The meat tends to be a bit dry in texture because of a guinea's lack of body fat.

Today's handlers are also keeping guineas to ward off rats and to alert handlers when something is amiss in the poultry house. To keep rats from your poultry house, you must have a small flock of guineas. One or two usually won't do. Over the years I've usually advised my customers to keep at least six guineas for this purpose. Furthermore, the guineas must be dispersed and confined. If you have a severe rat problem in a sectioned building that is quite long, it's advisable to place guineas in

Fig. 8-1. Pearl Helmeted guinea fowl. (Courtesy Leon Zimdars, Wis.)

both ends of the building. If not, the rats feel safe enough to inhabit the ends of the building where guineas are not housed. This would not be of concern in a one-room house where the guineas would naturally be dispersed. Also, you cannot expect to keep the rats out of the poultry house if the guineas are allowed to roost outdoors at night. In addition to keeping a rat-free environment, guineas will call your attention to any intruders.

Guineas allowed to range will devour hundreds of grasshoppers, which can be very destructive to crops and gardens. Guineas also group together and attack snakes.

VARIETIES

There are at least 10 varieties of the domestic Helmeted guinea fowl although the majority are rare to come across at all. These varieties are: Pearl, White, Lavender, Coral Blue, Royal Purple, Blue, Dundotte, Buff, Red, and Silverwing. These come in the white-breasted varieties, sometimes called Pied. The Pearl and White varieties are the oldest, and the Pearl is always a great favorite. Most of the varieties have the characteristic minute white dots over the entire plumage, which gives the guinea a unique appearance. Male and female resemble each other in plumage coloration and

markings, so sexing guineas is a rather difficult task.

Pearl. The Pearl variety is thought of as black with white dots, but the background color can vary from slate-blue to purplish dark grey. This is the original color of the wild Helmeted guinea fowl.

Although many handlers contend that all varieties are alike in body conformation, I've found the most commonly raised Pearl variety grows faster and larger for meat purposes. The few commercial growers of guineas that exist in the United States raise the Pearl almost entirely because of this. The only objection might be the dark pigment oils in the pores and any pinfeathers left after butchering. Another plus for the Pearl is it's hardiness. Possibly because of more extensive breeding, Pearl strains can tolerate various climates and temperature fluctuations better than the others.

White. This is a pure white bird (Fig. 8-2). Even a newly hatched white keet is snow white with tiny orange-red shanks and beak. Many people find it interesting and unusual that they do not hatch yellow as other white-feathered bird species do.

The bright orange-red wattles and helmet contrasted with the pure white plumage of the adult birds is very striking and showy. The eggs of the white variety tend to be cream-colored rather than dark tan. With guineas, it is usually the case that the darker the bird is, the darker the eggs and meat will be. Most Pearl lay a very dark reddish-brown to dark tan teardrop-shaped egg about the size of a large walnut. These are sometimes finely speckled. All guinea eggs are very hard and thick-shelled.

Lavender. This variety is a light lavender with white dots throughout.

Coral Blue. The coloring on a Coral Blue is a beautiful irridescent blue with no dots.

Royal Purple. This is a blackish-purple bird with a purple sheen. It has a few scattered white dots but not as many as the Pearl.

Dundotte. The Dundotte is a light tan with white dots over the entire body.

Buff. This is a solid buff color with no dots.

Red. This is a fairly new color handlers are working on. It has a beautiful red color throughout with no dots at all. Coloring can be achieved by breeding the darkest Buffs possible. The resultant color should be a deep, rich red similar to a Rhode Island Red chicken.

The Pearl has always been the most popular variety. The other varieties are considered fancy by many handlers and are a bit harder to obtain. Because of this, they are usually higher priced than the Pearl.

The white-breasted guinea is brought about by crossing varieties. Along the west coast it's common to call crossed varieties with white wings a Splash. Some handlers purposely cross the varieties. Crosses usually grow faster, larger, and are hardier. A Pearl and White cross brings about birds that have the more desirable yellow skin of the Whites rather than the common dark purplish skin of the dark varieties.

PERSONALITIES

Even though guineas have been domesticated for many years, they still maintain some of their wild traits. This is not necessarily unfavorable; it is this nature that makes them special, and the reason they are very good "watch birds". Unlike most geese, which squawk at everybody and everything all the time, guineas squawk mostly during their breeding season and when something is definitely wrong.

Guineas seem to know who belongs where. For instance, years ago our guineas were allowed to roost outdoors in their attached pen. During one night they squawked up a storm. Knowing something had to be wrong, I checked and found one of our rabbits had gotten out of it's hutch and was hopping around the yard. The incredible fact behind this story is that these guineas were quite ac-

Fig. 8-2. A flock of market White guineas. (Courtesy of Pietrus Foods, Inc., Sleepy Eye, MN)

customed to the many wild rabbits that roamed the yard nightly. Yet, they were able to distinguish the wild rabbits from the tame.

Guineas are as tame as their handlers will allow them. It takes patience and careful handling to get them tame enough to fly down onto your shoulders while you scoop feed out of a drum. They must be able to trust their handler, which involves months of getting to know each other. It further entails cautiously walking up to and around them. Startling guineas with sudden movements or trying to catch them constantly will only cause them to fear you.

Domestic guineas are territorial. A flock allowed to roam during the day will walk single-file around a part of the perimeter of their yard. Ours have always used the front five acres to take their daily walk. This they do twice daily except when confined in the winter.

HOW MANY?

Deciding upon the amount of keets to purchase initially will depend upon their intended purpose. If your goal is to supply meat, then purchase the amount desired plus 10 percent extra for mortality. The losses shouldn't be that great, but because keets must sometimes be shipped in from long distances, this can stress keets and cause more deaths. Keets don't ship quite as well as other poultry. Also, having keets shipped means you will have to purchase at least 25 birds. This allows for a minimum of body heat to accumulate in the shipping container to safely sustain the keets during shipment. If 25 keets is more than you need, a small classified ad in your local newspaper should take care of the extras—you should even make a small profit for your time.

When keets are to be used as watch birds you should plan on keeping at least three grown birds. If only one is kept it will cry more often because of being lonely, even if raised with chickens. The third is an extra for that unforseen loss which can occur. When starting out, one or two extra keets should be raised, so a goal of three adults means four or five keets should be started. If your goal is to use guineas to keep rats from the poultry

house, keep at least six adults.

The cost to purchase, feed, brood, and keep guineas the first year will be about $12 each. The following years would cost about $10 a year per confined bird or about $60 for six guineas. You must decide if your rat control is worth $60 a year.

If you don't think rats are a costly problem, consider the following facts and example: Imagine your buildings are housing a total of six adult rats. Methods are not undertaken to eliminate them. Three of the rats are females. These three each produce three to five litters of young within the next year. Each litter will consist of from 8-14 young. This means the three adult females will produce from 72-210 this year. Adult rats require 3/4 ounce dry feed and 1 1/2 ounces of water every 24 hours. No feed for three to four days and no water for one to two days will cause them to become very weak. This amount is not the total they eat, but only what is required to keep their bodies functioning. Assuming all the rats will eat one ounce per day, the 78 rats (72 offspring plus the original six) will consume 1,779 pounds of feed in a year's time at a cost of approximately $216. If the population goes to 216 (210 offspring plus the original six) they will consume about 4,927 pounds of feed. This can cost a whopping $600 in lost poultry feed for a year! There are other methods to control rat populations. I would suggest using these combined with your guineas for added protection.

SEASONAL AVAILABILITY

Because guineas begin to lay eggs in April or May, naturally, keets are not available until a month later. You must figure on the days needed for the breeder farm to collect good fertile eggs and the 26 days needed by the hatchery to hatch them. This will mean keets become available for shipment in May or June.

This late start in production has caused keets to become unavailable at hatcheries that shut down in June. Guinea keets come from the hatcheries that ship baby chicks all year. These hatcheries will have keets available for shipment until October. Keets received this late in the season will need additional brooding and care in keeping them from inclement weather. If you live in a cold fall and winter climate, you should obtain your keets as early as possible.

WATERING TECHNIQUES

If day-old guinea keets are not watered properly when received, many can be lost in a matter of hours. First, prepare mason jar fount waterers by filling the entire water-filled base with marbles or small rocks. The water should not extend over the tops of the marbles, so use plenty. Energetic keets scramble over the surface of their drinking water. In the process, they become wet. Because wet down does not quickly dry, keets become chilled. A keet chilled in this way will become stressed and will not survive long.

Most keets will begin to drink on their own when first placed under the brooder. Because it is not always easy to tell whether keets were stressed during shipping, it's a good idea to tip their beaks into the water founts individually as they are placed under the brooder. It will be a lot harder to round up all keets and do this later if you decide they're stressed. Keets do not like to be held and their incessant wiggling will prove to be a chore when beak dipping. Be persistent; make sure each one actually swallows the water. Do this by watching their throat. Warm sugar water will more easily be accepted. Use 1 teaspoon of sugar per quart of warm water. For the first three days, place some of the water founts directly under the heat—either in the back of a battery, under brooder lamps, or under a heated hover.

BROODING TEMPERATURES

Keets like it warm. The temperature must not go below 90 degrees F. the first week. If your brooder does not have a thermostat, as with ordinary brooder lamps, try to keep the keets in a room where the temperature does not fluctuate. If this is not possible, as with outdoor brooding in buildings, use a brooder with a thermostat. A thermostat will command more heat if the temperature falls below the set temperature. Keep in mind that battery brooders will not function well if kept in a room

of 50 degrees F. or less. Do not count on these if nighttime temperatures in the summer are this cool.

If you must use brooder lamps without a thermostat in an outdoor building, make a rectangular box-like structure from solid plywood, making sure all corners are tight. Tight corners help prevent keets from escaping and predators from entering. This box must be large enough for keets to lay comfortably side by side on one end under the brooder lamps. At the opposite end keep most of the feed and water. Allow enough room in between for keets to sleep if the area beneath the lamps becomes too warm. The size of this wooden box should be as follows:

- Day-old to 2 weeks—1/4 square foot
- 3, 4, 5 weeks—1/2 square foot
- 6 weeks—3/4 square foot
- 7 weeks—1 1/4 square feet
- 8 weeks—1 1/2 square feet
- 9 weeks—2 square feet
- 10 weeks—2 1/2 square feet
- 11 weeks—2 3/4 square feet
- 12 weeks—3 square feet each

Plan the box size for the length of time the keets will remain in this container.

Each week lower the temperature 5 degrees. If brooder bulbs are used for heat, either raise the height of the bulbs or change to a lower watt bulb to reduce heat in the brooder area below.

SPACE REQUIREMENTS

Day-old keets are tiny creatures when compared with baby chicks the same age. They are in between the size of a standard and bantam chick, but will pretty much keep up in growth rate to a standard chick such as a Leghorn.

The brooding space is totally different from the non-brooding space—which is needed beginning at around six weeks of age. The brooding area is confined, and smaller than the final grow out (non-brooding) area to help hold heat near the birds and the birds near the heat. A separate brooding house might be just big enough to confine birds for brooding only. This will require extra labor to move the birds to larger quarters when brooding is over.

Commercially, chickens are brooded and finished in the same building. This is accomplished by closing off a portion of the building for brooding with plastic curtains. A 500-foot-long poultry house may be closed down to 100 feet in one end for brooding purposes. When the birds are fully feathered, the curtain is removed to expand the growing area. This can be done on a small scale as long as space requirements are kept in mind in relation to the brooding size and the finished size of the keets. For keets, the bottom edges of the curtain must be tight to the floor because keets will wiggle under. They might not be able to get back to the heat source and will become chilled and possibly die. Besides saving labor, this system will save on additional lighting and electrical systems and feed storage space.

The total space for brooding and growing guineas, whether using separate buildings or the curtain system, can be figured the same as for heavy-breed chicks. The per keet requirements are:

- Day-old to 2 weeks—1/2 square foot
- 3, 4, 5 weeks—3/4 square foot
- 6 weeks—1 square foot
- 7 weeks—1 1/2 square feet
- 8 weeks—1 3/4 square feet
- 9 weeks—2 1/4 square feet
- 10 weeks—2 3/4 square feet
- 11 weeks—3 1/3 square feet
- 12 and over—up to 4 square feet

To brood in any outdoor system other than a temporary box when keets must later be moved, have the total brooding area the size required at six or seven weeks of age. For example: A six-week-old keet requires 1 square foot of space. Fifty would require 50 square feet. An area of approximately 6 × 8 square feet is needed for brooding up to six weeks of age.

Use a brooder guard to keep the keets close to the heat source for the first two weeks. A guard is something placed on the floor around the keets and brooder to keep them from straying. It must be sturdy and taller than that used for chicks because keets will jump up and over, especially when scared. An 18-inch or taller continuous brooder guard is recommended. Because this size is not normally sold, one will have to be made. Welded galvanized cage wire with 1/4-inch spacings can be purchased in 36-inch widths and cut in half lengthwise to encircle the brooding area. Fasten both ends securely together with clips or wire so no space remains for keets to slip through. Wire with 1-inch spacings, such as chicken wire, should not be used because keets will squeeze through. One-by-eight-inch boards can also be used to make a brooder guard by cutting four sections to size and hinging together. This will create a foldable brooder guard to be reused later.

Once the brooder guard is removed, the inside corners of the rest of the pen should be rounded out to prevent keets from congregating and piling on top of each other in these corners. Corner guards should be installed. They can be made by attaching stiff 1/4-inch welded wire, 18 inches wide across each corner. Each side of the wire should be attached about 12 inches from the inside of the corner. The height should be at least 12 inches tall, and pack straw firmly behind the guard to prevent keets from jumping over and becoming trapped.

BOX AND BATTERY RAISING

Brooding keets artificially is a fairly recent practice. Most keets were brooded with hens even up to the 1950s. Because of their natural wildness, keets were considered more trouble to brood artificially. With a bit of knowledge, however, keets can be successfully brooded in a heated container.

Keets can wiggle in and out of the smallest exit hole they can find, which is one reason their first home should be some type of box or a battery brooder. Another reason is the quiet way in which they accomplish their escape. Unlike chicks, most keets will not cry much when away from the others and they can become lost forever. The box does not need to be very large at first. A 1- × -2-foot box is large enough for a dozen keets plus their feed and a quart-jar waterer. For day-olds, line the bottom of the box or battery with bunched-up rags or towels to assure good footing. Keep dry rags or towels in there for at least five days.

In boxes, place a small hanging reflector lamp for heat in one end. A clip-on reflector lamp will work too. The bulb size needed to keep the one end of the box at 90 degrees F. (32 degrees C.) the first week will depend upon the temperature of the room they are in. You might want to begin with a 75-watt bulb placed about 7 or 8 inches above the floor of the box. Use an oral thermometer laid on top of the rags to check the temperature. Be sure to shake the mercury down below 70 degrees F. before a reading is taken. If the temperature is not 90 degrees F. directly below the lamp, and you're using a 75-watt bulb, change to a higher watt bulb. If too hot, use a smaller wattage for less heat.

At the opposite end of the box, place a quart mason jar waterer with the fount portion filled with small rocks or marbles. The energetic keets scamper over the surface of the water without regard to getting wet. The marbles will keep legs and bodies out of the water. If keets are found wet, quickly dry them with a blow dryer.

Do not use battery water troughs until about two weeks of age. Most grills over feed and water troughs have large enough openings to allow keets to squeeze through. Use wide strapping tape to narrow the openings.

Keets scratch around in their feed even more so than chicks, but as adults, they do not scratch around as much as chickens. The feed will be scattered all over no matter what type feeder is used. For convenience and to save space, just a simple mason jar fount without the jar can be used for their feed the first few weeks.

OUTDOOR SHELTER FOR STARTED KEETS

If a handler does not have a building to brood in he will not want to keep the keets in his own home for the total brooding period. After a few weeks of age, they will begin to annoy your sense of smell. I do suggest keeping small broods of keets in the house near your watchful eyes and attentive ears for at least one week. This helps calm the keets and a handler's conscience. Inexperienced handlers can keep track of the results of equipment purchased, heating requirements, feed and water intake, and care procedures. Getting to know your keets is part of the fun of raising them and the only way to acquire total knowledge about their care and personalities.

An outdoor box brooder can be built to house keets during the all-important brooding period. These consist of a roofed wooden box with ventilation and heat. The heat is usually provided by light bulbs, but an additional brooder heater unit with a thermostat can be installed to regulate the heat better. A sliding door can allow older keets access to a screened wire porch on warm days to help harden them off and enjoy the sun's rays.

This type of brooding can be safer for vulnerable keets because it affords more protection from predators. The brooder box can be placed near a window of your house for better inspection or set up inside an outdoor building. This outdoor brooding system can also be a healthier set-up for handlers, keeping much of the harmful poultry dust created away from the handler. Precautions should still be taken, however, when opening the box and tending the keets.

It's best to include a porch. This can create some entertainment for the keets and help ward off cannibalism caused from boredom. The porch should be the same dimensions as the box. Allow 1/2 square foot per keet for brooding up to six weeks of age. Twenty-five keets will need a brooder box of approximately 3- x -4 feet and a porch of 3- x -4 feet. For the best protection from predators both the box and porch should be erected on legs or set up on blocks. A wire screened porch floor will allow droppings to fall through (Fig. 8-3).

This is not to be considered a fool-proof method of brooding to protect the keets from predators. Raccoons and dogs can quickly tear into the most well-constructed boxes. Even rats will chew through to gain access if hungry enough. This brooder, however, is much safer than placing defenseless keets into a building on the floor and out of sight for 18 hours (and usually longer) each day.

CULLING

Keets aren't culled to the degree chicks are, mainly

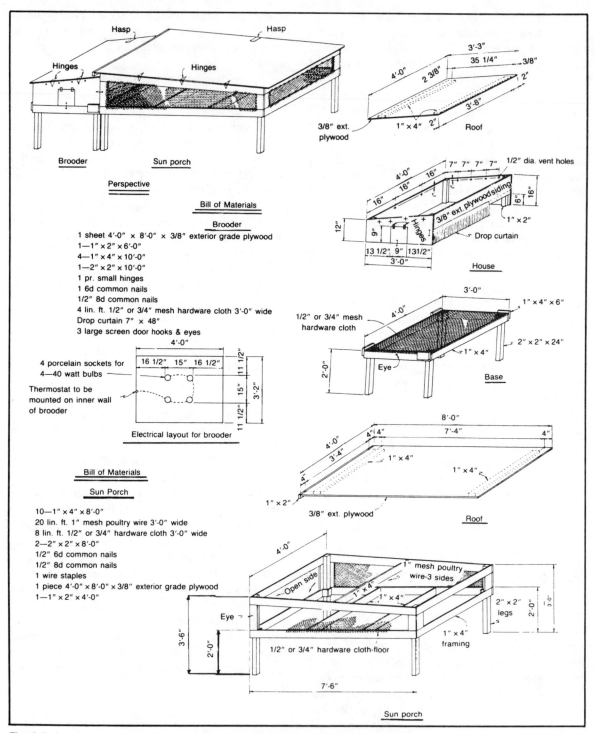

Brooder   **Sun porch**

Perspective

Bill of Materials

Brooder

1 sheet 4'-0" × 8'-0" × 3/8" exterior grade plywood
1—1" × 2" × 6'-0"
4—1" × 4" × 10'-0"
1—2" × 2" × 10'-0"
1 pr. small hinges
1 6d common nails
1/2" 8d common nails
4 lin. ft. 1/2" or 3/4" mesh hardware cloth 3'-0" wide
Drop curtain 7" × 48"
3 large screen door hooks & eyes

4 porcelain sockets for
4—40 watt bulbs

Thermostat to be
mounted on inner wall
of brooder

Electrical layout for brooder

Bill of Materials

Sun Porch

10—1" × 4" × 8'-0"
20 lin. ft. 1" mesh poultry wire 3'-0" wide
8 lin. ft. 1/2" or 3/4" hardware cloth 3'-0" wide
2—2" × 2" × 8'-0"
1/2" 6d common nails
1/2" 8d common nails
1 wire staples
1 piece 4'-0" × 8'-0" × 3/8" exterior grade plywood
1—1" × 2" × 4'-0"

Fig. 8-3. A good outdoor brooder to construct for guinea keets. (Courtesy of USDA)

164

because keets are more expensive to purchase than most chicks and because keets are not usually raised in great numbers.

If keets are to be used as breeders more culling will be in order, but not until they are fully grown. Then a handler should cull on the basis of nice feather coloring, size of bird, and aggressiveness of males. The largest guineas are best kept for breeding because they are hardier and will pass this trait on to their offspring. Aggressiveness in the males can be a problem, especially when guineas are housed with chickens or other male guineas. Although aggressive male guineas don't do much bodily harm to each other, they do cause a constant ruckus in the poultry house if confined during the breeding season. They will constantly chase other male guineas and chickens away from the guinea hens. This gallant behavior keeps everyone excited, and excited birds aren't conducive to egg-laying.

The only problem in culling out these aggressive individuals is many will not exhibit their aggressiveness to the fullest extent until the breeding season begins. But since only a few—perhaps one in three—become overly aggressive, a handler can keep an extra male or two just in case. When their breeding season begins in April or May you'll soon be able to spot a bully. After watching him a few days to confirm his aggressiveness, he should be culled from the flock immediately.

If a handler has many males and wants to cull out only the aggressive ones, it's a good idea to spray-mark them. Using a blue methyl-violet spray—such as Blu-Kote used for wounds—spray one area on the middle of the back in a good continuous stream to be sure the mark shows up. If you're fast this can be done while a guinea is cornered. Guineas are too hard to handle for other types of marking. The marking should be done in a way that will enable the handler to immediately spot the bird without further handling.

Keets are usually only culled out of the brood if they clearly show they are not doing well. A severely dehydrated and weak keet usually warrants culling. This type of culling takes place the first week. If the keet is not culled, nature will take care of it on her own. Later culling of an occasional runt can be done when sorting out breeders from those that will be butchered—keeping the largest for breeding.

NUTRITION, GROWTH, AND FEED CONSUMPTION

Because guineas seem to be low on the totem pole, researchers have not studied their nutrient needs nor the consumption of these needs at great length. Commercial guinea raisers have pretty much had to experiment on their own flocks in order to find the ideal requirements.

Where heredity factors are mainly responsible for the highly researched and genetically bred chicken growing at a certain rate, this is not true for guineas. Naturally, there are different strains of guineas but none within the same variety grows noticeably more faster than others. A fast-growing guinea is mainly the result of the handler's management and feed practices. Some difference in growth rate is noticed between light- and dark-colored guineas and crosses, but not to the degree noticed between broiler and egg-laying chickens.

Commercially raised keets are fed a 24 percent protein ration during the first four weeks because they grow extremely fast during this time. Between four and eight weeks of age a 22 percent protein ration is fed. The keets are then finished on an 18 percent protein ration up to 12 weeks of age. At this time the guineas should dress out at 1 1/2 to 2 pounds each.

In commercial feed the protein comes from meat scraps, soybean meal, and alfalfa meal. This is close to the natural food values of guineas in the wild. They are meat-eaters and will consume a large amount of insects, including grasshoppers and Japanese beetles. One large breeder claims his guineas will each consume 2 pounds of grasshoppers daily. The alfalfa meal will replace the grass and weeds guineas love to eat.

The secret to extremely plump, tender market guineas is said to be in the way they are raised. Commercially raised guineas are raised in full light the first four weeks while feeding a 24 percent protein ration. Then the lighting is reduced until the houses are dark. They are confined to these dark houses after four weeks of age in order to keep them quiet. A 22 percent protein ration is then fed for the next four weeks, followed by an 18 percent protein ration. The lights are dimmed on for feeding and drinking several times daily, then gradually dimmed off again to darkness. This method requires plenty of cod-liver oil to prevent rickets from occurring because of a lack of sunlight. A quarter cup of the cod-liver oil should be given in each 1 gallon of drinking water. This method might sound a bit cruel, but for economy and great plump meat birds it's worth a try. The conventional raising methods will not produce a plump bird because guineas have small bones and the tendency to have a fat-free carcass. Guineas allowed to range won't acquire body fat and the drumsticks will stay thin and small because of the extra energy burned.

It's best to feed keets a non-medicated ration because keets have been known to die from these. If you are not concerned with maximum growth rate—that is, if you're raising guineas as breeders for eggs or their watch bird qualities—the keets can be fed a duck starter ration for the first two months. These usually contain 20-22 percent protein and a large amount of alfalfa meal. An 18 percent chick starter is then fed the next two months. They can then be maintained on a regular 14 1/2 percent protein layer ration. This might be the only choice a handler has if a 24 percent starter ration is unavailable. Most handlers will not find it feasible to custom mix a higher protein ration for only one month's feeding. Breeders have found the 14 1/2 percent chicken layer ration keeps guineas in good condition and keeps them laying during the breeding season.

The high protein of a game bird feed is not necessary with keets as some handlers believe. They grow extremely well on less protein; money will only be wasted on this higher-priced feed. Besides, it can be hard to obtain in many areas and often must be special ordered. Trying to grow out birds faster than they are genetically bred to grow can become a waste of money and cause problems—including leg weakness. Keets are meant to attain market size by 12 weeks of age and

no sooner. Some handlers foolishly believe protein is their answer to the best production. More important is good management and a good environment—keeping the birds quiet, not letting them run out of feed and water, providing clean litter and water, and not crowding. Research has shown that if these conditions are not met, smaller birds always result.

Always supply grit to keets beginning at one week of age and beyond. This helps keets break down the feed in their gizzard for better assimilation of the nutrients, thus better growth. Use starter grit the first four weeks, then grower grit the next four weeks. Layer grit can be given beyond eight weeks of age.

If guineas are confined and very fertile eggs producing strong keets are desired, I recommend feeding additional vitamins prior to and during the breeding season. Eggs may be very fertile, but this is not a guarantee that strong, healthy keets will result. Breeders should always have their feed supplemented. Oyster shells must also be fed free-choice for good, tough, hatchable eggs. Guineas allowed to range frequently prior to and during their breeding season will usually produce strong keets.

Healthwise, ranging is not necessary. My totally confined breeders have always fared well and produced 90 percent hatches. The breeders were given cod-liver oil once a week throughout the year. Multi-vitamins in their drinking water was given daily two months prior to the expected breeding season and for as long as I wanted to collect hatching eggs. When hatching eggs are no longer wanted, there is no need to supplement their diet further with the multi-vitamins.

Without the specific research given to other poultry on feed consumption and nutritional requirements, basic guidelines can only be suggested for the feed consumption of guineas. Guidelines for Pearl guineas follows:

0-8 weeks = 5.68 pounds total consumption each
8-12 weeks = 4.33 pounds total consumption each
10.01 pounds total feed to market age.

(market age weight = 2 1/2-3 pounds liveweight, 1 1/2-2 pounds dressed)
Confined breeders = 2.17 pounds feed per bird per week
(Note: Feed consumption will vary with environmental temperatures and fat content of ration.)

When guineas are producing eggs, extra energy is needed. Cold temperatures will also call for extra energy to keep the body warmer. Guineas will eat more at these times.

Feeders for keets should be those that do not allow keets to crawl into them. Slide-top feeders should not be used with keets, but any other type should work well. As the birds grow, self-feeding feeders can be used. Feeders used during brooding should hold at least a day's supply of feed. Figure on using a feeder that will hold .13 of a pound of feed for each keet brooded. This size feeder will take care of keets up to eight weeks of age if feeders are filled daily. Twelve keets would need a feeder holding 1.56 pounds of feed. A feeder for guineas up to 12 weeks of age that are only to be filled once weekly should hold 1.22 pounds of feed per bird. Twelve guineas to be fed once per week would then need a feeder that holds 14.64 pounds of feed. Figure 2.17 pounds per adult breeder guinea per week.

DRINKING WATER REQUIREMENTS

Drinking water is more important to a bird's existence than feed. Birds can actually go longer without feed than water. Water works with feed eaten by softening it for easier digestion. More important, water helps maintain the normal body temperature and prevents dehydration of the tissues.

Excessive heat, humidity, and some rations will cause keets to drink more than usual. Stomach disorders, including coccidiosis, can also cause increased thirst. Consumption of more or less than the usual amount of water can be relied upon as a symptom of disease or discomfort.

Ice-cold water is not favored by keets; warmed water should always be given so keets drink it freely and it does not upset their digestive tract.

Ice cold water also chills keets. Clean drinking water must always be available. Keets will not drink water fouled by feed, droppings, and litter, and it eventually will cause health problems.

Keets will drink about the same amount of water as egg breed pullets. The majority of birds drink two to three times as much water in pounds as the amount of feed consumed in pounds. Table 8-1 can be used to estimate water needs. By referring to this table, the correct size and amounts of waterers can be supplied for any age guinea. Waterers for keets must be those that prevent the keets from getting wet. Small mason jar founts can be used if the fount base is filled with small rocks or marbles. Older keets can use a simple pan for their water as long as it's not too deep. A 4-inch-deep pan will prevent 6-week-old keets from drowning. Poultry should never be without drinking water. Use plenty of waterers so there is always a good supply.

FOOD AND WATER ADDITIVES

Feed manufacturers and store owners are great at insinuating a need for various types of medications. Rarely do they suggest a non-medicated feed or simply extra vitamins. If their own ground brand of starter feed has no medications, it might be because they have not acquired the necessary license to incorporate the medications into the feed. Commercially medicated starter feeds are purchased by handlers either intentionally or unintentionally. By becoming aware of what type feed is needed and learning to read tags a handler will not unknowingly purchase wrong or unnecessary feeds.

Medications can harm keets and ducklings. It's a handler's responsibility to purchase non-medicated feeds for them. Do not rely solely on your dealer. Many clerks have not raised poultry. Unless they have followed up on the results their customers have attained, they have no way of knowing if the feed purchased was the best type for the species of bird. Guineas, especially, seem to confuse some clerks. Since there is presently no guinea starter, grower, or layer feeds, clerks must sometimes second-guess what might not be in a feed manufacturer's literature. When keets get coccidiosis, dealers are quick to suggest drinking wa-

Table 8-1. Daily Water Consumption by Guineas.*

Age (weeks)	Amount of birds 10 guineas		Amount of birds 25 guineas	
1	6.4 oz.	(192.0 mL)	16.0 oz.	(480.0 mL)
2	12.8 oz.	(384. mL)	32 (1 qt.)	(960.0 mL)
3	15.36 oz.	(460.8 mL)	38.4 oz.	(11.52 liters)
4	21.76 oz.	(652.8 mL)	54.4 oz.	(1.63 liters)
5	28.16 oz.	(844.8 mL)	70.4 oz.	(2.11 liters)
6	32 (1 qt.)	(960. mL)	80.0 oz.	(2.40 liters)
7	35.84 oz.	(1.06 liters)	89.6 oz.	(2.68 liters)
8	38.4 oz.	(1.14 liters)	96.0 oz.	(2.88 liters)
9	44.8 oz.	(1.32 liters)	112.0 oz.	(3.36 liters)
10	48.64 oz.	(1.44 liters)	121.6 oz.	(3.64 liters)
12	51.2 oz.	(1.51 liters)	128 (1 gal.)	(3.78 liters)
15	53.76 oz.	(1.58 liters)	1 gal. 6 oz.	(4.02 liters)
20	57.6 oz.	(1.7 liters)	1 gal. 16 oz.	(4.32 liters)
Laying, Breeding	64 (1/2 gal.)	(1.9 liters)	1 gal. 32 oz.	(4.70 liters)

*Will vary considerably depending on temperature and diet composition.

Adapted from (Daily Water Consumption by Chickens) *Nutrient Requirements of Poultry, 8th Revised Edition*, copyright 1984, National Academy of Sciences.

ter medications. This is what they've been taught.

If keets go down on their legs, many dealers are liable to think the cause was too much protein or not enough. Do they ever ask how the birds are being raised? Do they suggest the cause might be rickets from a lack of Vitamin D_3? Many handlers purchase the feeds confident they contain everything their birds require.

Water systems can inadvertently provide harmful or useful additives. Some water supplies on a farm or ranch can contain high concentrations of nitrates, sulfates, or sulphur—along with trace minerals. Most are absorbed from the intestine but toxic levels do exist for poultry. If levels are more than 3,000 ppm of the total dissolved solids of various concentrations, problems such as reduced growth can result.

Although sodium and chloride are required by all animals, large amounts contained in drinking water can cause excessive water intake. Then a handler is faced with extra moisture in the building from wet droppings. Toxic levels will cause reduced growth. Some mechanical water softeners leave salt residues, which could be harmful to any poultry.

Antibiotics are usually classified as additives (or growth promoters). I think it's wise to classify anything other than the feed itself as an additive. Vitamins and minerals added to feed to enhance the food value are supplements. Hence, vinegar added to water for coccidiosis should be classed an additive; sugar for energy or cod-liver oil placed in drinking water should be classed as a supplement.

Chapter 9

Mature Guinea Fowl Management

PURCHASING AND HANDLING

Although guineas are believed fairly disease-free, the same precautions and considerations should be taken as with any poultry. Some disease germs are carried and spread by humans, animals, and equipment. If guineas are purchased as adults, it only seems safe to assume guinea fowl can transport disease to your flock of turkeys, chickens, etc.

If the guineas in question were raised with other type fowl, scrutinize the birds they lived with. These will usually be chickens. Look for signs of watery eyes, discharge from nostrils, coughing, smeared fecal matter on hindends, and a dumpy appearance. Insist that you see the birds the guineas were housed with. If the other types of poultry seem fine, you should still isolate and confine your new guineas to a separate house for at least two weeks to observe any signs of sickness that might develop. If guineas are to be ranged, they must be confined at least two weeks anyway or they usually run or fly off— never to be seen again. Before confining, clip one wing to prevent escape. This will prevent

actual flying for a whole season. The appearance of the bird will not be adversely affected by this wing clipping.

Many handlers do not know how to handle grown guineas. Perhaps they have not found a need to if the guineas were allowed complete freedom and never had to be moved around much from pen to pen. It would be wise for any handler contemplating the purchase of grown guineas to be assured they are or were captured safely. Guineas are not picked up by their wings as chickens may be. There will be a loss of feathers if this is attempted because the feathers are loosely attached in the follicle. Also, if handlers practice the unnecessary and absurd habit of catching fowls by their legs, the guinea can become lame. A guinea's legs have a more delicate bone structure than other poultry. If the guineas you are to purchase have already been caught and penned, observe carefully how they walk. There should be no evidence of limping. It would be better if the handler captures the birds so you can avoid getting into strange pens yourself, which could spread disease from litter and footwear to your birds at home. Suggest the following method of capture:

To grab a guinea safely, quickly reach down with one hand, placing it firmly down and over one closed wing while gently pushing it's body toward the ground. Just as quickly, place your other hand firmly over the other closed wing. While still grasping firmly, lift the guinea straight up. A guinea's main defense is his long beating wings and his incessant leg kicking. When handled in the described way, the wings cannot beat and the legs do not interfere. Furthermore, there are not many feathers lost and no injured guinea legs.

It is not easy to tell the age of adult guineas when purchasing. They do not show their age as well as chickens. Second-hand purchase of guineas is not usually for food or egg production. In fact, the age of a guinea does not commonly reflect the purchase price unless the seller believes it should— as with chickens. Most adult guineas are purchased because they are deemed an oddity. If you are only interested in "fooling around" and hatching a few keets, the odds are good that second-hand guineas will serve this purpose. If you want to get into guineas in a big way by hatching hundreds, and raising and selling large flocks for profit, you are better off beginning with keets from good stock.

An aged guinea, one over two years old, will have only slightly rough, hardened-looking legs and slightly faded coloring with long claws. Older birds have rounded ends on the outer wing feathers. In young birds, these feathers are more pointed.

TRANSPORTING

Guineas must sometimes be transported in a vehicle to poultry shows, custom butchering headquarters, or to a new residence. Wherever they are destined they should arrive uninjured, free of bruises and with feathers in good condition. A rough trip can mean bruises and badly damaged feathers.

To transport safely, the guineas should be discouraged from standing while in transit. Most injuries occur when standing birds are thrown off balance because of the vehicle stopping, starting,

and turning. Birds are then thrown into each other and into the walls of cages. Most chicken crates will prevent standing. If it's an older type with more headroom, simply add more straw to the floor of the crate. If it's of the type with a wire floor for droppings to fall through, most wire floors can be raised by placing blocks of wood underneath and making sure they're secure. The ideal height for guinea containers is 8 inches. The new plastic crates designed for game birds such as pheasants have a headroom of 8-9 inches.

Ordinary cardboard boxes can be used to transport guineas. They should be lined with clean rags or rough straw to prevent guineas from slipping and injuring their legs. Again, the height should restrict full standing. The only drawback to using boxes is the difficulty in placing guineas into the box and getting them out without them escaping. For ease in placing the guineas into the box, use this method: Cut a flap 6-7 inches high and half round in one side of the box. Make a small hole on the outside edge in which to pass some twine through for use as a handle to close the cut-out door. Tape the lid of the box shut. With wings closed, firmly grasp the guinea's body and shove head first through the hole, pushing flap inwards. When all guineas are inside box, close flap by tying shut (Fig. 9-1). If guineas must be removed from box individually rather than releasing into a pen (as at a poultry show), make another flap on the side large enough for the handler's hand and arm to enter. The guinea can then be coaxed to enter a cage.

All containers for transporting birds must be ventilated. Cardboard boxes must have holes cut in all sides for this purpose. Closely confined birds give off an enormous amount of combined body heat. This excess heat must be able to escape or birds will become overheated, suffocate, and die. Do not be stingy when making ventilation holes in hot weather. Even winter transportation in the bed of a pickup truck requires ventilation. In cardboard boxes it's better to cut 1-inch holes than small punctures. Any larger and guineas will push their head through and catch their helmet on the edge of the holes. Use a wide, stiff knife or scissors, puncture the box, twist in 1-inch holes. Don't worry about

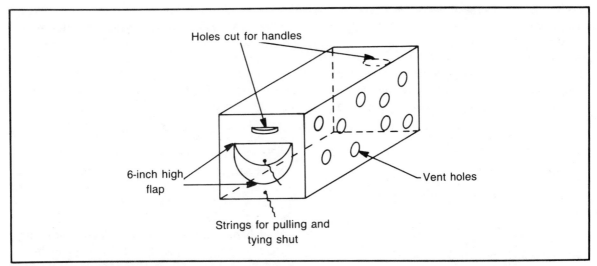

Fig. 9-1. Homemade cardboard carrier for guineas.

making too many holes because extras can be covered over with good tape after birds are placed inside.

With birds inside and all flaps and lids closed, allow body heat to accumulate a few minutes. Then slide your hand into box and feel the air between the guineas. It should not feel overly hot. If it is too hot usually dampness can also be felt from the birds' respiration.

Until you gain experience with "feeling" their comfort, a thermometer can be used to measure it. Grown birds are comfortable at about 65 degrees F. (18 degrees C.) During hot weather it will be tough keeping the temperature this low. In this case more vent holes should be cut and/or fewer birds transported in each box. At no time should the accumulated body heat bring the temperature above 80 degrees F.

Poultry do not have sweat glands. Excess heat is diffused mainly through their respiratory system, causing them to pant when overheated. Do not let panting continue long. You might need to remove some birds and cut more vent holes to maintain a comfortable environment. The correct amount of guineas in the container in relation to the temperature surrounding box and the amount of vent holes are relevant to the proper transporting temperature.

Too much ventilation can also be detrimental,

as with crates and cages. In the open bed of a pickup truck, cover such cages lightly with a porous type tarp or drop cloth. A porous material "breaths." Plastic tarps do not allow built-up heat and carbon monoxide to escape and birds can suffocate. Be careful when loading by making sure space is provided between and around all containers so ventilation is not restricted. Most chicken crates have built-in spacers so stacking does not restrict ventilation. Cages and boxes should have bricks, rocks, or wood between to keep them apart while the vehicle is moving. Enclosed vehicle transportation such as vans or truck toppers will usually need windows to be cracked for added ventilation.

The all-time favorite for some handlers is transporting birds in a feed sack or burlap bag. I do not recommend this unless it is a last resort. Sometimes guineas are purchased unexpectedly without crates, boxes or cages on hand. Be wary of using the woven plastic feed bags because they do not ventilate well. Also, if holes are cut for ventilation, they unravel and can entangle the bird. A paper feed bag with holes cut for ventilation is much better.

Do not under any circumstances tie a guinea's legs together as is sometimes done in transporting chickens. Their legs are too fragile for this treatment. And never transport in a closed car trunk in hot weather. You would think this danger would be obvious but I've seen many birds suffocate in this manner.

When birds are transported comfortably, they can travel safely for many hours without feed and water. If the trip is long and in hot weather, the birds should be checked and given an occasional drink of water so dehydration does not occur.

SIGHT SEXING

Both sexes of guineas in any given variety are exactly the same in color and possess similar characteristics. This can lead to much confusion in sorting the roosters from the hens. There *are* differences, however. With close observation and practice, any handler can become adept at picking out guinea roosters from guinea hens.

Visually, there are differences in appearance of the wattles, helmets, neck skin, size of the body, and personality. Wattles on a mature guinea rooster will be thicker and larger than the hens, and will stand out perpendicular to the head. A guinea hen's wattles are smaller, thinner, and fit closely to the head (Fig. 9-2). Both sexes have helmets but the hen's is usually much smaller. The practically bare neck skin extends a bit lower down the neck of a rooster. The majority of adult roosters are larger. With only a few guineas, this may not be an accurate sign because of the chance they are all one sex.

Some strains of some colors such as Dundottes have been sexed by color at hatching. With some Dundottes, with darker stripes over the back usually indicate hens while the lighter stripes usually indicate males.

There are personality differences that are usually noticed only on casual observations. It is the rooster who stands more alert with head up outdoors, while hens range. A rooster will also act strangely by running backwards and forwards quickly on his toes while raising his wings at the shoulder.

The most positive and earliest determination of sex is accomplished by listening to the sounds guineas make. This is only reliable if you have the time to listen, because guineas don't always make their sounds when you want them to . You might have to wait around awhile to distinguish the hens. Both sexes will scream a shrill one-syllable shriek, mainly when excited. This shriek can be deafening. But it is only the female that makes a two-syllable sound consistently. This she does even while quietly ranging. This sound goes something like: "buck-wheat, buck-wheat, buck-wheat." A male guinea *never* screams, shrieks or utters any two-syllable sound.

Inexperienced handlers have often asked me whether the term "guinea hen" pertains to both sexes or to females only. They have even ordered guineas believing they would all be hens because they heard somewhere that guineas are called guinea hens. This is not the case, and the misconstrued term placed on all guinea fowl should be thrown out with the many other myths that exist in the poultry world.

SPACE REQUIREMENTS

The housing space required for adult guineas will depend upon whether guineas are confined, or have access to outdoor pens, or range. If guineas are allowed outdoors slightly less housing space is needed for eating and sleeping purposes. If cold weather seasons necessitate partial confinement, be sure housing space is provided for in advance. Very cold weather might mean guineas are confined for many days. Very warm climates will allow the guineas to be outdoors most of the year. If guineas are housed with other poultry, their space requirements must also be considered and added to the space requirements of the guineas.

For totally confined adult guineas, allow no less than 2 square feet per bird. This is the same amount for floor-reared lightweight breeds of chickens, such as Leghorns. General-purpose breeds of chickens, such as Rhode Island Reds or White Plymouth Rocks, require 3 square feet per bird. Very large cochin type breeds of chickens should have 4 square feet per bird. Add these figures for confinement-reared chickens to the space requirement figures for your guineas to come up with total housing space for mixed species flocks. These figures will provide a comfortable environment in cold weather without crowding, as long as ceilings

Fig. 9-2. Male yearling guinea fowl with protruding larger wattles (top). Female yearling guinea fowl with small wattles close to head (bottom).

173

aren't much over 7 feet tall and there is proper ventilation and insulation.

SHELTER REQUIREMENTS

Guineas are hardy creatures and they will endure very cold weather, but it would be cruel to think they do not need shelter. Remember that they originated from a warm climate. A small shelter with attached pen will do. (Fig. 9-3).

Shelter should always be provided for guineas, and they will do well if you decide to keep them totally confined as long as the following requirements for housing any poultry are adhered to.

Living Space. This not only means floor space but total cubic space when ceiling height is considered. The very tall and open ceilings in some sheds and barns do not allow body heat to accumulate in the winter for warmth and they allow too much ventilation and drafts. A ceiling just high enough to allow a handler to stand on 2 feet of packed litter is a good height. The ceiling height can be reduced by stapling chicken wire with plastic over the top across pens. More ventilation is needed in buildings where the cubic footage is reduced in this way. Guineas will winter well in even a doghouse but they will not lay eggs well in a small area.

Ventilation. No matter how many cubic feet exist in any building, it is only through proper ventilation that the environment can be kept comfortable and dry. The droppings of guineas are a lot drier than those of water fowl, chickens, and turkeys, so a building housing only guineas requires slightly less ventilation. This would only be noticed in large flocks.

Drafts. Guineas are more immune to drafts than turkeys and chickens, but occasionally they will develop respiratory problems. A handler is gambling if he does not check his guinea house for drafts.

Predators. All buildings housing poultry should be predator-proofed. This should be done before poultry are housed in the building.

Location. If guineas are kept for the purpose of alerting you when intruders are near, do not place them out of your range of hearing. Remember, guineas can be heard for almost a mile in open unrestricted grounds, but insulation, siding, build-

Fig. 9-3. These guineas will sleep outdoors on the ground during summer unless locked in at night.

174

ings, hills, and trees interrupt the sound that is carried to your ears.

Buildings should be situated on high sloped ground so water drains away. Inside floors will stay drier, and it helps prevent a handler from tracking mud into the building. Damp grounds are breeding places for disease, they attract flies, and can cause rusting and rotting of buildings and equipment.

Access. Although there might not be constant walks to a guinea house to collect eggs—as with chickens, it's no fun trying to get straw and feed to the building in deep snow and mud. Plan on placing new buildings as close to access drives as possible. With existing buildings invest in road gravel and snow fencing to at least make a plowable access drive. The drive should be built up slightly and crowned so water drains off.

CONFINEMENT AND RANGING

Total or partial confinement, free ranging, or a combination can be utilized for guineas. All work fine if certain measures are taken in order to make the system work smoothly.

Total confinement, without any attached pen, works very well even for the breeders if they are not crowded. Eggs are more fertile if guineas are given more room. It is not true that confined guineas will not lay or eggs will not be fertile. They will breed well when given only 2 square feet per bird, but fertility and production is greatly increased when they are given 4 square feet per bird.

Guineas like seclusion for nesting on floors, so provide secluded corners. Tree branches and brush can be placed into these corners to enhance them. I have had guinea hens even become broody enough to set on eggs when these conditions are provided. Additional vitamins in the drinking water, especially D and E, will also help fertility and health of the birds. An occasional handful of weeds and grass clippings will make the guineas happier. Guineas that are usually confined will go back to their pen or house if they escape.

Partial confinement refers to housing the guineas with an occasional ranging period. It also includes a poultry house where guineas can freely enter an attached outdoor pen. It is not necessary to let guineas outdoors at all. This is a preference on the handler's part. The attached outdoor pens can be used to allow guineas to bath in the sun's rays. It's wise to chase them indoors at night. Some will find comfort sleeping on the cool ground during hot summer nights even if roosts are available indoors.

Another method that is considered partial confinement is to let the guineas out occasionally to range. Wings should be clipped to persuade guineas to go back into building at dusk. If they begin flying into trees and atop buildings for roosting, the habit will become hard to break and the guineas harder to retrieve.

Free ranging means the guineas come and go as they please without being penned. Again, unless wings are clipped, guineas allowed free range will be inclined to roost outdoors during the night. They are then in danger because they are easy prey to predators, especially owls, who simply pick them from the treetops. Guineas with clipped wings are trained to go into the poultry house easier if chickens are given the same freedom during the day. Monkey see, monkey do—the guineas will follow the chickens into the house at dusk.

If only guineas are ranged, it might be necessary to provide an attached feeding pen to the poultry house. At about the same time each day, near dusk, place a scoop of feed into the pen and stand back to allow the guineas to enter. Be sure other poultry cannot enter the pen from the building or they will get out of the pen and upset the whole plan. *Never* chase guineas into a pen. They thoroughly dislike being chased and will avoid the pen and you altogether for days. Guineas can be "walked" into a pen or house but never with quick, jerking movements on your part. Make slow steps to their side or behind them to direct them into the pen door.

Dirt floors are good for guineas. They like to take dust baths and will use the soil on the floor for this. Any clean, dry litter material can be used over the floor. Guineas don't scratch and dig as much as chickens do. If litter completely covers a dirt floor, the guineas will not usually attempt to dig a dust bath hollow from the soil. A separate shallow pan can be used to supply soil for dust baths, but do not make it too deep or they will nest in it instead.

ROOSTS

Guineas love to roost. They also should be able to sleep up off the floor for safety from predators. Place a sufficient amount of roosting poles into their building to meet these needs. Guineas that are forced to sleep on the floor are prone to frostbitten feet more so than roosting guineas. A guinea's feet will freeze when the temperature drops below 10 degrees F. When a guinea (or any roosting bird) is perched off the ground on a pole, he fluffs out his feathers to air-condition his body. This can either allow the body's heat to encircle the entire bird or allow air to enter between the feathers to cool the bird. If a guinea sleeps on cold, damp litter, the temperature of his body and feet will be affected because his feathers are prevented from fluffing out under him.

Unlike with chickens, it does not matter at what height these roosts are placed. Guineas will use low chicken roosts of only 2 feet if that's all that is available. Wing-clipped guineas can still reach a 5 foot-tall roost easily. When measuring roosting lumber, allow 7 to 10 inches in length per guinea. If enough roosting space is not allowed, the guineas will push and shove each other to get space, causing quite a ruckus at night.

The lumber used for roosts should not be too wide. The guinea's toes should be able to curve around the roosts naturally for balance. This calls for lumber 1 1/2 inches wide. Two-by-four-inch stock can be used with the narrow side up. Old wooden rung ladders can be recycled into roosts by sturdily suspending them from the ceiling. Nailing them firmly lengthwise to a wall and using heavy wire to suspend the front only from the ceiling will prevent the roosts from swinging.

Many types and combinations of roosts can be designed, including side-by-side and stair-step style. Whichever type is constructed, be sure the design does not cause the droppings from the roosting guineas to fall onto other roosting guineas. Drop-ping boards and pits are sometimes used in small-scale set-ups. Placed under roosts to collect drop pings, boards are usually constructed of sheets of plywood that are scraped clean as the manure accumulates. Pits are box-like structures under roosts. For easier manure removal, pits should have an access panel or door that runs lengthwise along the adjoining wall. Manure can then be forked or scraped from the outdoors. The same principle can be used with dropping boards if they are constructed on a level plane rather than on a slant.

Because of the small area under roosts, manure builds up quickly just from the hours the guineas remain on roosts during their sleep period. This will be the area in the building needing the most frequent manure removal. If clean litter is simply added to the litter below roosts when needed it will not take long for the built-up litter to reach a 2-foot-tall roost. This is the reason dropping boards and pits are good ideas. Whatever system is used, the birds should be prevented from gaining access to the manure area below roosts. Guineas will voice their enjoyment about roosting as they noisily chatter with each other for 10 minutes before calling it a day.

GROOMING FOR SHOW

A guinea is a beautiful, striking bird with it's red-orange legs, beak, wattles, and helmet set against a polka-dot or pastel-colored plumage. This alone has prompted many handlers, including 4-H children, to want to show off these interesting birds at various fairs and shows.

Most guineas feather out beautifully on their own. They also seem to maintain the clear, sharp characteristics of a good-looking show bird on their own. It is mainly the job of the handler to pick and choose those showing the best qualities.

A good bird is the result of good breeding and care. Because guineas are not bred to conform to any set standard or production to the extent chickens are, it's more of a job to check out the results of the breeding behind a strain of guineas. In most cases you cannot simply purchase a certain strain of guineas that outperforms the others. A handler might try to obtain photos of the strain he has in mind from the breeder or hatchery. Explain why you are concerned. This is most important in the rarer varieties that have been bred even less extensively than the Pearls or Whites. You might come across a show judge who cuts severely for faded coloring and pearl dots.

If guineas are to be entered in a meat pen, check with officials or 4-H leaders as to the age requirement for guineas to be shown. Market guineas are considered to be from 12-16 weeks of age. Order keets early to be assured of receiving them exactly when they should be started. Time their delivery to coincide with the age they should be at fair time. Raise enough so the best can be chosen for the show.

Use your own discretion in choosing the color variety to raise for a meat pen. Either Pearl, White, or a Cross are generally used. The Pearl and the Cross usually get larger and plumper, but the dark feathers might be objectionable to a buyer. If time is short for raising, a light variety should not be chosen for a meat pen because they usually take longer to finish out properly. White guineas tend to be smaller, but if you can flesh them out good they should bring a higher price.

Most birds entered as fancy are allowed to be older because they are not being shown or purchased for meat where tenderness is of concern. Fancy pens usually require a pair (male and female) or a trio (one male and two females). You should check on the requirements ahead of time so you are prepared. Also check if wing-clipped guineas are cut in points.

Proper diet and management are needed for good results. To add sheen to feathers, feed 4 teaspoons of cod-liver oil in a gallon of drinking water to the keets up until three weeks before the show. Feeding the oil beyond this time might produce a fishy taste in the meat and a yellow cast in white feathers.

Ranging always helps make birds look better, but be wary of predators and guineas that won't go back into the building at nightfall. Unclipped guineas might not be able to be caught in time for the show. I've known of guineas that could not be caught for weeks and were shot and butchered in desperation. It's best to confine them in deep litter in an indoor pen (Fig. 9-4).

Sunlight will whiten white feathers. Allow white guineas to be exposed to the sun during the last month of preparation. This can be done without ranging by using a pen. Be careful: overexposure to the weather can cause brassiness in feathers. Colored varieties should be kept from direct sunlight to prevent fading and irregular tones. Feeding supplements of iron will enhance the buff- and red-colored guineas, but it can bring about an auburn tinge to the dark varieties.

Begin actual grooming one week ahead of show time. Place the birds that are to be shown in a pen with plenty of soft, deep, clean litter material. Never raise or keep show birds in a cage. Cages damage feathers as the birds move around, and helmets and wattles can be cut and rubbed, turning into unsightly sores. The deep litter will help clean and groom the feathers with gentle abrasive action.

Guineas do not like to be bathed, and their wishes should be respected or you'll be fighting them all the way—damaged feathers and bruises will result. Besides, bathing only causes the natural feather oils to be lost, and this oil is what makes

Fig. 9-4. A pen built into corner of a building can confine guineas until they're taken to the show. (Courtesy of Pietrus Foods, Inc., Sleepy Eye, MN)

177

feathers shine. A dirty area on the feathers can be spot-shampooed. Use ordinary shampoo because it's less harsh and will not dry up oils as readily. Its best if two individuals work on this job—one to hold the guinea and one to clean. With wings folded in naturally, wrap both hands firmly around the wing joints near the body to prevent wing flapping. Keep the guinea's feet away from you so he does not have a surface to push against. Rub the shampoo gently and sparingly in the direction of the feather grains so the feather barbs are not broken. Rinse thoroughly. If very wet, partially blow dry, then air dry.

White guineas can be cleaned using ordinary cornmeal. Powder the cornmeal down through all feathers and place the bird back into the pen. The guinea will work the powder out by shaking the feathers. Later, cornstarch can be powdered over the bird to help whiten.

Some raisers whiten feathers by submerging birds quickly into diluted, thoroughly mixed laundry bluing. Use very little at first because too much cannot readily be removed from the feathers and you can end up with a blue guinea—pretty but not too impressive to judges. With guineas, this procedure is a bit tricky because the wings should be open slightly to allow solution to enter underneath. It's wise to have two persons do this job too. One person must grasp the wings over the joint near the body and hold on very firmly. The other person grasps the body with two hands from behind on both sides of the bird. The bird is then lowered into the blued water without the white neck skin becoming wet. A thick ring of petroleum jelly placed around the perimeter at the base of skin will help avoid mishaps. Rub the jelly off immediately after wetting bird. Do not accidentally rub the jelly onto the feathers or it will make them appear stringy and wet.

The day before the show, use a soft nail brush (available at cosmetic counters) and plain water to gently clean around beak, face, eyes, wattles, and helmet.

The cleaning of the shanks, feet, toes, and nails can be a one-man job by wrapping the guinea's body in a towel to prevent wing flapping. Allow the shanks to remain free and lay the guinea on his back on your lap sideways or with his head towards you. Mix a capful of peroxide with 4 cups of warm water and use a soft nail brush to gently scrub dirt from the top of shanks, down over the top of the feet, around toenails, bottom of feet, and under toenails. Scrub only in one direction down over the top of shanks and toes to avoid loosening leg and toe scales. Rinse thoroughly with clean water. The peroxide water helps soften dirt and dead skin, and is not used as a bleaching solution.

The final touch is grooming the helmet, wattles, head, and neck. Apply a very small amount of mineral oil, vegetable oil, or even cod-liver oil with a soft cloth. The beak and toenails can be buffed to a greater shine with a nail buffer.

Practice placing your guineas into a cage with a guinea who is not to be shown. Guineas do not always like going through a cage door. Grasp the body firmly with two hands around both closed wings. Point the head downward to help prevent feet from grabbing hold and pushing against the cage opening as you place the guinea through head first. All birds are placed into a cage head first so feathers aren't caught and damaged.

Routinely handling your guineas will help make them more manageable during show time. I say "help" because it would be a rare guinea that would stand quietly to pose without holding him as chickens can be trained to do. A training stick for guineas is a useless piece of equipment. Usually if you try to raise a guinea's head up to look proud, he'll pull his head down. Pull his head down, and he'll move it from side to side. Try to hold him in one spot and he'll try to dart forward or backward.

When transporting, be sure to use the previously mentioned guidelines for transporting and be cautious in removing them from their transporting container into the show pens. You do not want to chase your show bird through show exhibits.

Figure 9-5 illustrates the body features of a Helmeted guinea fowl.

SECURING AND HATCHING EGGS

In the wild, guineas mate in pairs, but a good quan-

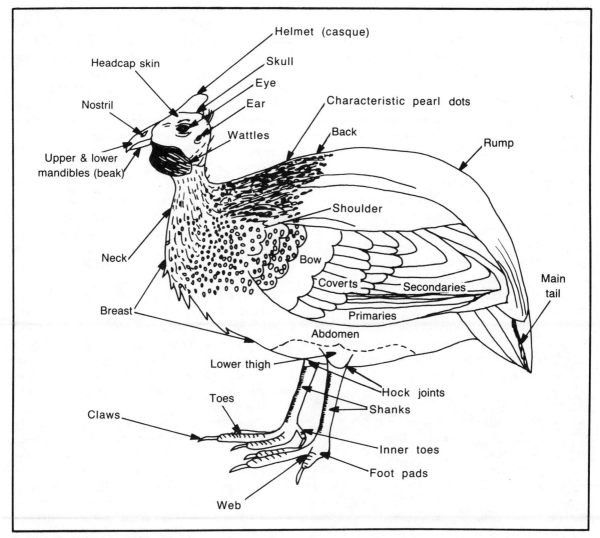

Fig. 9-5. Body features of a guinea fowl.

tity of fertile eggs can be obtained when mating one male with four to five hens in captivity. Guineas allowed to roam outdoors will definitely prefer to lay eggs in a hidden nest. Almost all the hens will take turns and use the same nest. It's not uncommon to find a small flock's concealed nest containing 24-30 eggs.

Guineas nest on the floor, although I have had a few that used chicken nests (when not bothered with constant egg collecting). Confined guineas can mate, lay eggs, nest, and incubate eggs very well.

Do not expect high fertility in the first few eggs laid in the season. After two weeks, guinea eggs are usually very fertile and proper incubation will produce excellent hatches. Considering the high fertility it's odd that guineas are not often seen mating. First eggs are usually smaller than normal. Small eggs produce small keets, so it's wise to collect hatching eggs a few weeks after laying begins. Depending upon the climate and weather, guineas begin laying in April or May. Warmer temperatures promote the earliest laying. Laying will continue until about September, depending on the climate and weather.

A guinea egg can be easily distinguished from the eggs of other poultry (Fig. 9-6). Their shape is unlike any other being "teardrop"-shaped and very pointed on one end. Most are a very dark reddish-brown and speckled with minute dark brown spots. White and lavender guineas tend to lay light-colored eggs—some absent of any dark speckles. The shell of a guinea egg is very thick in comparison to other poultry eggs.

Guinea eggs need a slightly higher humidity than other eggs during hatching. In incubators, raise the humidity a few degrees higher than for chicken eggs. If chickens or guineas are to hatch the eggs, dampen the nest with a hand-mist sprayer. Ducks have also been used to successfully hatch guineas—the eggs are naturally dampened by the ducks as they wet themselves and carry the moisture back to the nest.

Guinea hens are relatively poor mothers. Unless a handler has oodles of hens laying and hatching all over the property, the chances are good he'll end up with few feathered-out offspring. Not be-

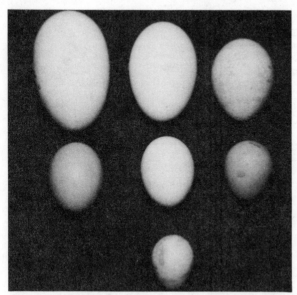

Fig. 9-6. From top left to right: goose egg, turkey egg, peafowl egg, chicken egg, duck egg, guinea egg and on bottom, pigeon egg.

ing too patient, the guinea hen will immediately lead her little troopers from the nest early in the morning through dew-soaked grass. The keets then become wet and chilled. The mother leaves them behind and does not prod them to hurry and catch up. Nor does she bother to cover and warm them whenever they want. These wet little keets find themselves left yards behind their mother and often die right there. When ducks are used to hatch keets, it's best to brood them yourself after hatching because a duck's waterer could be responsible for drowned keets.

Predators and warm weather will cause many egg losses unless eggs are collected daily. Stored hatching eggs can almost always be placed under a broody guinea or chicken later. For optimum results, it's best to store the hatching eggs in a damp area that is 50 degrees F. (10 degrees C.) Many basements fit this need. Store no longer than two weeks. If stored this long, occasionally turn the eggs to prevent the yolk from sticking to the inside of the shell, which causes the developing embryo to stick and not be able to free itself for hatching. Eggs can be placed in egg cartons and the cartons are simply tilted daily in opposite positions to keep the yolk mobile.

A few marked eggs should always remain in the nest to keep the guinea hens from laying elsewhere. There is no need to worry about touching the nest or eggs. Just collect eggs as usual.

Outdoors, guinea hens will prefer to lay eggs in low brush or under the branches of evergreens. A nest is not made in the sense that materials are brought to the site and arranged, but hens will make a round indentation with their feet in the existing material. Indoors, the hens will find a secluded area on the floor. Brush and twigs can be set into corners to accommodate her need for privacy. The laid eggs are usually, but not always, covered with litter material to hide them. Guineas lay about the same time daily, usually late morning to early afternoon. Outdoor nesting sites can be found most readily by looking for the males. The male guineas stand within a few feet of the nest while the hens lay. Upon being approached, the male will let out loud shrieks and the hen will crouch down to avoid being discovered.

Guinea eggs are scheduled to hatch in 26 days of incubation. The first few may hatch on the 24th day, the majority hatch on the 25th day, and the remainder on the 26th day. Newly hatched keets appear as brown and tan striped puff balls. With a clean cut around the shell, they seem to pop right out. As soon as they dry they become lively and get around better than most baby poultry.

Because of the size and shape of a guinea egg, I suggest the eggs remain in an upright position (air-cell upwards) during the last five days of artificial incubation. This will prevent many keets from hatching from the wrong end of the egg. It seems they don't turn around and position themselves within the egg as early as chicks do to prepare for hatching. Perhaps the shape makes it difficult to easily turn around. It's not unusual to find some eggs completely pipped but the keets still stuffed inside. On small hatches, a handler can "pop" the top half of the shell off and bring the keets' heads out to prevent crooked legs and toes.

To prove how adaptable guineas really are and how confined conditions do not interfere with their laying abilities, consider how guineas are raised in France today. Both breeder hens and cocks are kept in cages. Layer cages are similar to those used commercially for laying chickens. The compartments are larger, allowing four hens per section. The hens are artificially inseminated and they produce an average of 170 eggs per hen during a 36-40-week lay period. This is accomplished through a completely controlled management practice. The temperature, humidity, and ventilation are controlled by the handler. Windowless or completely shaded windows are used in the house, and lights are used to obtain and maintain production. The lights are gradually dimmed or turned on so the layers are not startled. The guineas are kept as calm as possible in order to increase egg production.

Conventional floor-reared breeders can be expected to lay between 50-100 eggs per season. An average season is 24 weeks. Breeders can be used with good results for about three years, although five-year olds can be used for laying and hatching. Occasionally guineas will cross with chickens when their own species is not available. The resulting off-

Fig. 9-7. Barred Plymouth Rock rooster and guinea hen with their crossbred progeny on right. (Courtesy of USDA).

spring has been termed a "guin-hen". (Fig. 9-7).

BUTCHERING STEPS

The average Pearl guinea should weigh about 2 1/2-3 pounds by 12 weeks of age and dress out at 1 1/2-2 pounds. They are usually butchered and dressed out the same as broiler chickens and similar to turkeys. Most small-scale raisers begin butchering guinea fowl when the weather begins to cool. As with any butchering, have a fairly clean and sanitary work area. Some handlers do the actual killing and bleeding outdoors and the eviscerating indoors where they can work more comfortably.

You might want to collect the guineas the night before from the roosts, which will make catching them much easier. This must be done in the dark with only a flashlight shining away from the birds so they cannot see. If they are able to see at all, they will scamper away from you when approached. Confine them to a cage for the fastest removal during butchering. Do not do night collecting if the birds will not be butchered early in the morning unless you can supply them drinking water and keep them comfortable. They should never be allowed to become overheated during confinement. Large, airy cages are best. Also do not crowd the birds. This can cause overheating and scratched and bleeding carcasses. About 1 square foot per market-size guinea would be sufficient confinement area for most conditions. To save time, confine the birds where the butchering will take place. If birds can be grabbed quickly, everything else will seem to run smoothly and quickly.

Prepare a large kettle of scalding water. Having the water the right temperature is the most important rule for success during this operation. Above 130 degrees F. (54 degrees C.), and the water will remove the very thin yellow outer covering of the skin. This protective covering helps keep the meat from drying out immediately after butchering, and the carcass will look less attractive if it's removed. A semi-soft or slack-scald of about 128 degrees F. (53 degrees C.) should be maintained. Because feathers are more difficult to remove from the skin of older birds, the scald water must be hotter. This is called a sub-scald. Use a temperature

of 138-140 degrees F. (58-60 degrees C.) for this. Older birds do not usually appear as nicely dressed as younger birds because of the hotter water that is used.

The tight feathers of a guinea can be somewhat harder for the water to penetrate. You can add a few drops of liquid dishwashing detergent to the scald water, which helps penetrate the feather oils and allows the water to reach all the way to the skin. Soft water also facilitates feather removal because it allows better water penetration. A few teaspoons of baking soda softens the water.

Killing cones do not always work well with guineas because they can sometimes manage to wiggle out of position. A cone that is smaller than those used for broilers works best. With a cone, a sticking method can be used to stun the bird after bleeding out. This prevents the inevitable flopping around which can bruise the meat. Some handlers simply slit the throat across the bird's left side where it meets the neck, then thoroughly bleed, scald, pluck, eviscerate, and chill. A more thorough explanation on these procedures can be found in Chapter 6 in the section entitled "Butchering Steps."

After bleeding stops, immerse the entire body into the scald water by holding onto the legs. A stick can be used to help hold the body under the water. If the bird has been stunned, a period of 30-40 seconds should be enough time in the water—otherwise, about one minute is required. Then lift the bird from the scald pot, drain a few seconds, and proceed as outlined in Chapter 6. Final chilling will usually take a few hours in order to extract all body heat from the guinea carcass.

STORING AND USING GUINEA FOWL MEAT

Guinea fowl meat can be frozen, canned, and smoked. Any canning recipe for chicken can be used with guinea. The versatile guinea can be used in any cooking recipe calling for chicken or game birds.

One young butchered guinea will weigh about 1 1/2-2 pounds. This will yield two to three servings. Because guinea meat is somewhat drier and body fat is practically absent, guineas are cooked with the addition of lard, shortening, fat, or bacon. Roasting guineas with slices of cured bacon or thinly sliced pork fat laid over the carcass is considered to be what the English recommend.

If guinea meat is to be ground, beef or pork fat strips should be evenly ground with the meat. If the meat is to be kept as fat-free as possible and will not be molded as for cooked patties or luncheon meat, then the fat is not needed. To prevent drying of the meat during freezing, use a thick zipper-locking freezer bag. Squeeze all excess air out of the bag before sealing.

Guinea meat is firm and fine-textured. The breasts are very large in comparison to the rest of the body. This description fits most game birds. The breast meat cooks up a yellow color while the rest of the body parts remain dark. Light-colored varieties have a lighter skin; the breast meat is almost white. The following recipes are especially suited for guinea fowl meat:

Braised Guinea with Mushrooms. Brown one guinea (1 1/2—2 pounds) in 1/4 cup butter. Place breast side down in a pan or casserole that has a tight-fitting cover. Spread 1/4 cup butter over bird. Add one finely chopped medium onion, some salt and pepper. Cover, place in a 375 degree F. oven for 30 minutes. Season 3/4 pound sliced mushrooms with salt, pepper, and lemon juice. After cooking time is up, turn breast side up and place the mushrooms all around the bird. Season the breast and replace the cover. Bake another 30 minutes. Remove cover and finish baking an additional 10 minutes or until bird is done and lightly browned on top. Carve the bird into four slices of breast, two drumsticks and two thigh pieces. Arrange on a platter with drained mushrooms. Season the gravy to taste and pour over bird. Serves 2.

Guinea and Kraut. Combine one 27-ounce can drained sauerkraut and one 13 1/2-ounce can drained pineapple tidbits. Spread in bottom of shallow roasting pan. Salt cavities of two guineas (2-2 1/2 pounds each), truss, and place breast side up over pan mixture. Lay 4 slices bacon strips over breasts. Cover loosely with foil. Roast one hour (or until tender and done), uncover during last 20 minutes of roasting. Remove bacon. Blend 1 table-spoon flour with water; stir until mixture thickens and bubbles. Serves 4-6.

GUINEA FOWL PROBLEMS AND HOME REMEDIES

Not many problems exist with guinea fowl. They can contract some of the diseases listed in Chapter 7. Following are the most common problems affecting guineas:

Aggressiveness

Although not a disease, aggressiveness can become a severe problem with guineas. Male guineas will chase other fowl and even prevent roosters from mating hen chickens. This is their nature, but some are more aggressive than others. The only thing to do, besides getting angry, is to choose the seemingly less aggressive males in the spring for breeders. This is the time they will begin to exhibit the trait most.

Blackhead

This is a parasitic disease. Turkeys are more susceptible than guineas, but guineas are more susceptible than chickens. It's claimed that range distance has a lot to do with contracting blackhead. Guineas range further, which controls their contact with organisms responsible for the disease. Cecal worm eggs and earthworms harbor the blackhead parasite. The guineas eat infected cecal worm eggs or the infected earthworms and they are then infected. Symptoms are the same in the guinea as for the turkey (Fig. 9-8). See Chapter 7.

Nonfertile Eggs

Do not expect very fertile eggs when the guinea hen first begins to lay. It takes about two weeks for eggs to get really fertile. One male should be allowed with four to five hens for good fertility. Confinement should have nothing to do with nonfertile eggs, nor should the males be blamed. It's rare for a male to be sterile. The most common causes are improper storage of eggs and poor management. Eggs should not be kept at temperatures above 55

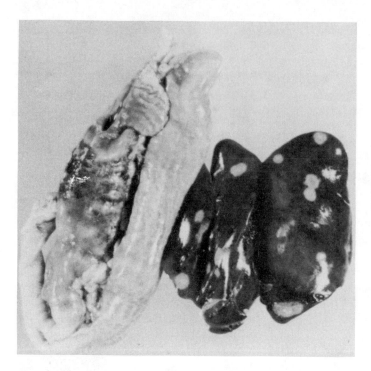

Fig. 9-8. A gut and liver of a guinea infected with blackhead. (Courtesy of L. Dwight Schwartz, D.V.M., Senior Pathologist, Michigan State University)

degrees F. A ranged guinea's nest is not always the best suited to keep the eggs this temperature. If eggs are not collected often, but rather left until a pile of 20-30 eggs are found, they cannot be assured of hatching. When many guineas are using the same nest, which is a common habit of theirs, the eggs are then constantly being warmed up again.

Confined guineas can be given extra vitamins to boost fertility. Egg production can be increased when artificial lighting is used and secluded areas are provided for laying. The hens should not be startled, but kept as calm as possible. Also see "Securing and Hatching Eggs."

The following problems and diseases can also affect guineas and are described in detail in Chapter 7: Ammonia burns, avian TB, blackhead, breast blisters, broodiness, cannibalism, coccidiosis, external parasites, feather pulling, fowl typhoid, hemorrhagic enteritis, internal parasites, Newcastle, Omphalitis (mushy chick disease), poisoning, pullorum, rickets, spraddle legs, vaccinating, and wing clipping.

Part 3

Pigeons

Chapter 10

Choosing Your Pigeons

ORIGIN AND HISTORY

The first pigeons marketed for human consumption in the United States were the Passenger pigeons (Fig. 10-1). Originally, their numbers surpassed any other bird in the entire world. Early Audubon records estimated an average flock of Passenger pigeons consisted of a billion and a quarter birds. It was also estimated a flock this size consumed more than eight and a half million bushels of beechnuts and acorns per day. Their numbers were so great that the Audubon Society concluded only a reduction of forests could diminish the birds. This happened—to a point of extinction. The last Passenger pigeon in the world died in 1914. They did not become extinct overnight. Around 1850, millions were slain and marketed or used by sporting clubs for trap shooting. The last large migrations and nestings occurred in 1878 in Michigan. Even though their numbers became fewer and fewer and large nestings and flocks were no longer seen, the pigeons were still trapped up until 1886.

Besides shooting, netting was one way of col-lecting many live pigeons at one time (Fig. 10-2). In this way the birds could be kept until the market showed a need for the birds. The top net contained pulleys and a rope that led to an attendant hiding in a brush-covered structure under a tree. As the pigeons flew down into the nets, the rope was pulled and the top net immediately fell and captured the whole struggling flock. From 800 to 5,000 per day could be caught this way. Pigeoners traveled far and wide, following the migrating flocks. Word got around quickly among these individuals of new nesting sites, market reports, and prices.

The term "stool pigeon" came from the decoy pigeons many professional pigeoners used to lure flocks down into the nets. A live pigeon was tied to a small platform, or stool, of wood or woven wire, which was attached to the end of a long, thin, flexible pole. The trapper moved the pole up and down by holding an attached cord, which caused the pigeon to flutter and attract others.

To the eyes and ears of those who appreciated these creatures of nature, one can now only imagine

Fig. 10-1. "Martha," the last Passenger pigeon in the world. (Courtesy of John A. Ruthven)

the feeling upon coming into a nesting site of Passenger pigeons. Trees contained from 5 to 50 nests, each with various age squabs. Nesting sites were sometimes 40 miles long and 10 miles wide.

The enactment in 1913 of the Federal law for the protection of migratory birds was too late to stop the shameful slaughter of the Passenger pigeon, but it helped save the wild Band-Tailed pigeon (C. fasiata) in the western U.S. from near extinction. The Band-Tailed pigeon is now considered a common wild breed.

The Rock dove (pigeon) so commonly seen on city buildings, in parks, and in farm country, is the ancestor of today's domestic pigeons. The Rock dove (Columba livia) is native to Europe and Asia. They are deemed a nuisance in many locales and efforts are regularly made—using poisoned bait or other methods—to rid cities of them. Building owners claim the pigeons make a mess with their droppings, requiring frequency cleaning and painting. Many people, however, enjoy sitting on benches and watching and feeding the pigeons. The birds represent one of the few forms of nature they can relate to in the bustling city atmosphere.

The first domestic pigeons are thought to have

Fig. 10-2. Type of net used by "pigeoners" to capture many Passenger pigeons at once during the mid-1800s.

been brought to America by colonists. Since then, pigeons have been bred to over 200 varieties, have been used as message carriers during war time, as research tools, as racing and game competition, as enjoyable hobby prospects, as a trade industry, and as a very digestible form of nourishment for convalescents.

Pigeons have been raised for food and hobby for many centuries. Five-thousand-year-old records show that pigeons were raised and used as food by the Egyptians. In ancient Greece, homing pigeons were used to relay information of the Olympian games. In 1849, they were used to carry messages between Brussels and Berlin when telegraph service was temporarily interrupted.

Many Homer pigeons, a famous domestic breed of the Rock dove, have been bred, trained, and drafted by the United States Army Signal Corps as message carriers during both World Wars and the Korean conflict (Fig. 10-3). One famous pigeon, named Cher Ami, traveled 2,300 miles to its home loft. Another famous pigeon was G.I. Joe. He is credited with making the most outstanding flight of any United States Army homing pigeon in World War II. On the morning of October 18, 1943 the British 56th Infantry Division at Colvi Vecchia made a request for air support to aid in breaking a heavily upheld German position. G.I. Joe flew 20-odd miles under extremely trying conditions in the same number of minutes with the message. The Allied XII Air Support command was ready to bomb the town five minutes later. G.I. Joe thus saved the lives of at least a thousand allied soldiers. In 1946, G.I. Joe was awarded the Dicken Medal for gallantry by the Lord Mayor of London (Fig. 10-4).

Before chicks were routinely hatched in incubators around 1920, pigeons were the birds of choice for research and laboratory experiments. Many such experiments concerned the effects of diets deficient in vitamin B_1.

There seemed to be no need for a commercial squab raising industry before 1900 because of an abundance of wild game and a lack of hunting laws. Although many squab farms have come and gone throughout the past 50 years, many more still spring up. It's estimated that over 2.5 million squabs are commercially marketed each year in the United States. Marketing difficulties were curtailed when cooperatives such as the Squab Producers of California organized in early 1943. This has helped producers in the Central Valley of California where more than 35 percent of the squabs are produced in the United States. Several of these producers keep 1,500 to 2,200 pairs of pigeons to produce squabs. This cooperative has also built their own processing plant within the last few years. Squabs are shipped throughout the United States and abroad. When a cooperative works together to produce uniform, high-quality light-skinned squabs, they are better accepted by the public. Cooperatives can adopt aggressive methods of marketing and additional outlets for selling. Their combined ideas for storing surplus squabs during the high production period in spring and summer help bring fair market prices to the producers.

It's estimated that 90 percent of the pigeons raised in the United States are for show, hobby, and pleasure. Commercial production of squabs, where 1,000 or more breeder pairs are kept is still a young market. Success in this industry is possible where markets have been established demand high-quality squabs.

The squab's popularity as food increased as the production size of the bird increased from 12 ounces to 16 and even 24 ounces. Various areas respond differently, it all depends upon where aggressive sales tactics have been aimed to bring a growing awareness of the virtues of this delicacy. Foods termed as a delicacy are often regarded as too unique to be consumed for everyday meals. Goose and duckling are still regarded as only holiday feasts. To gain in popularity as an everyday food, the turkey industry has had to expand it's horizons by offering cuts of meat similar to those of pork and beef.

BREEDS FOR SQUAB PRODUCTION

Squab is the name given to baby pigeons that are about one month old. Squab has been popular as a very digestible, tender, and rich source of meat for centuries. Squabs' quick growth and fleshing

Fig. 10-3. A Homer pigeon with a message container strapped to back. (Courtesy of USDA).

has also been an asset to their popularity. A handler can actually watch the squabs grow by the day. The average just-hatched squab weighs less than an ounce. By four weeks they can weigh up to 24 ounces. They must be butchered just as soon as the pinfeathers disappear on the sides of the body under the wings. If the squabs are allowed to leave the nest and walk and fly around, they very quickly lose weight and the meat toughens.

Pigeons bred to produce squabs are called utility breeds or squabbing breeds. A good pair should produce at least 12 squabs per year. Overestimating production is one of the largest mistakes beginners are prone to do. They become disappointed in their birds and begin to wonder what is wrong. They might even waste money trying more expensive feeds or purchasing new replacement breeders who prove to be no better. Actually, most any breed of squab can be used for food. The difference in a utility breed for squabbing is in the size and amount of the squabs produced. Some of the breeds are as follows:

White King

White Kings seem to be the pigeon of choice of most of today's commercial squab producers (Fig.

10-5). Originally the White King was created in the United States about 1891 for commercial squab production. It was created by crossing white varieties of the Runt, Homer, Maltese, and Duchess. The White King became so popular that many breeders began exhibiting it. This caused production capabilities to be sacrificed in favor of a beautiful body. The result is that today there is an exhibition White King and a commercial producing White King. The exhibition type should not be purchased if economical squab production is your goal. A well-bred squabbing pair of White Kings will produce 12 to 20 squabs a year, which weigh from 16 to 24 ounces live weight each by four weeks of age.

The White King is the most popular variety of any breed of pigeon. Other varieties of Kings include the Silver, the Blue, the Dun, the Red, and the Yellow. The Silver is also extremely popular

Fig. 10-4. G.I. Joe in cage with Dicken Medal awarded for gallantry hanging above cage. (Courtesy Paul Cooney, Detroit Zoological Park)

Fig. 10-5. White King female pigeon. (Courtesy of USDA)

for both show and utility. Silvers were created much later in America by crossing the Runt, Homer, Maltese and Mondain. The Silver is a bit more docile and slightly larger than the White King, although type and production remains the same. In the utility varieties, the Dun is the latest to be introduced.

Adult utility Kings weigh between 26 and 35 ounces. (Exhibition types weigh from 28 to 37 ounces.) They are prolific producers of large, full-breasted squabs. They are considered a medium-sized pigeon. The legs are beet-red in all varieties. They have light pinkish-white skin. Kings are a tight-feathered breed with a short, blocky body, deep well-rounded keel, a very broad breast, and a moderately large, well-rounded head.

Carneau

The Carneau is another utility breed (Fig. 10-6). It originated in the northern part of France and southern Belgium. It was brought to the United States around 1900. These early imports were red with white markings. Then, as the Carneau rage brought many to shows, a standard for all red plumage developed in 1910. It produces squabs slightly smaller than those of the King. This too is a very popular breed for show and utility. Those bred for show only are usually poor producers.

The Carneau is close-feathered. Its body is compact, solid, broad-breasted. It has a very erect carriage. The dip over the back of the neck is absent, making the Carneau appear proud and upright. Wings and tail are moderately short, yet slightly longer than those of the King. Carneaus weigh from 22 to 26 ounces. The Carneau is bred in black, dun, red, yellow, and white. The white and red pigeons are very hardy as squab producers. All other varieties are considered to be mainly show birds. The black and dun have unappealing dark

192

Fig. 10-6. Red Carneau male pigeon. (Courtesy of USDA)

skin when bred for squabs.

Mondain

Mondains are utility breeds that were originally bred in France and Italy. Mondain means "earthy" in French, as the Mondain prefers to walk rather than fly. Today's varieties are the large-sized Giant American Crest, the French Mondain, and the Swiss Mondain (Fig. 10-7)—all developed in America.

The Giant American Crest was officially recognized in 1940. It is so closely related to the French Mondain, it was originally called the French Crested Mondain. It is the second largest American utility breed next to the Runt. It has a straight back, similar to the Carneau, rather than the slight saddle-back of the French Mondain or the King. The Giant American Crest is unusual in the utility breeds because of a small upright crest it sports toward the back of the head. It is a close-feathered

Fig. 10-7. Swiss Mondain male pigeon. (Courtesy of USDA)

bird. Older birds range from 30 to 40 ounces. They are bred in all colors including white and black. Most are bred for show, although they are classed as a utility breed. If chosen for production, it's best to obtain proven strains.

The White Swiss Mondain was the first Mondain to be developed in America from Mondain imports. The White Runt was used to create the Swiss Mondain. The breed was very popular in the 1920s. The exhibition weights vary from 30 to 40 ounces. This breed has a large, deep, broad body and is longer than the King. It's not as cobby as the King and carries it's tail much lower. It has tight-fitting white feathers.

The French Mondain is a newer variety than the White Swiss Mondain. They have never been widely raised commercially, although they are found at shows. It's similar in shape to the King, being large and having a deep blocky body, short keel, and broad breast. Birds vary from 30 to 40 ounces. Colors are andalusian (midnight blue), ash-red, black, blue, brown, recessive red, silver, yellow, and white. Some colors include checkered and splashed patterns.

Homer

There are various types of Homers (see Fig. 10-3). The Giant Homer is the squabbing type. Other types include the exhibition, genuine, English Show, German Beauty, and Racing Homers. The Giant Homer is of American origin. It was admitted to the Standard in 1929. The Giant Homer was bred for squabbing rather than for it's homing instinct or speed of flight. It was developed in the United States by breeding the Racing Homer for production and size. It is a fairly prolific breed but produces squabs that are smaller than King squabs. Little attention has been devoted to breeding for color and the squabs have a tendency to dark skin, especially when the blues and blacks are mated together. Pairs should be bred whose skin is white and contain a fair amount of white plumage. Giant Homers are bred in a variety of colors, with the blue checks and silvers being the most popular. There is no standard set weight, but they should be solid and heavy, and weigh an average of 30 ounces.

Fig. 10-8. A Black Hungarian male. (Courtesy of USDA)

Hungarian

The Hungarian and the Maltese are two more utility breeds of a more unusual form. They have long legs and necks, high tails, and short, solid bodies. They have been crossed with other breeds to produce squabs with very plump breasts. The Hungarian is believed to have originated in northern Austria, created by crossing the Florentine, the Swallow, and a breed from India called the Kalpotia. The Hungarian is smaller than the Carneau, King, and Mondain. Its squabs are yellow-skinned. Because American markets still demand white-skinned squabs, the Hungarian is raised mainly for fancy exhibition. Hungarians average 24 to 28 ounces with oversize being better than undersize. They are bred in striking white with contrasting color combinations of black, dun, red, yellow, blue with black or white bars, and silver with dun or white bars, and blue, black, silver, dun, and white checkers. The Black Hungarian is the most popular (Fig. 10-8). The blacks having white feathers do not have dark skins. This breed is very hardy and pairs make good parents.

Maltese

The Maltese is more recent and was created in Austria and Germany. Like the Hungarian, the Maltese is a very tall bird, but because it was bred for height, the 15-inch bird has become a poor squabber unless crossed with another breed. Because of it's extraordinary breast development, the Maltese was used to develop the White and Silver King. Breeding the Maltese alone for production is economically unwise unless it is crossed with another breed in order to bring hardiness, a solid, firm body, and short, tight feathers to a breed that lacks these features. This utility breed is now most commonly used as fancy exhibition. They are bred in solid black, blue, dun, red, silver, white, yellow, and any other color.

Florentine

The Florentine was created in Florence, Italy over 200 years ago. It is an ancestor to the Hungarian. It is rarely seen in the United States because it never became very popular even for show purposes, perhaps because of its aggressive fighting nature. It is almost as large as the Carneau or King, and is solid-bodied and hard-feathered. Florentines are colored on the head, wings, and tail, and the body and neck plumage are pure white. They are bred in black, blue with black bars, blue checkered, brown with bars, lark, red, yellow, and various mottles and pieds. This breed is not recommended for beginners.

Strassers

Strassers originated in Moravia, Austria as utility pigeons, but are raised here as a fancy breed. This is a newer breed that never became very popular in the United States because other larger breeds already existed for squabbing. Strassers weigh 20 to 30 ounces after being outcrossed with the King to increase size, and are now almost as large as the King. The colors are solid black, brown, dun, red, and yellow. Checkered colors are black, blue, and brown. There are blue and silver barred varieties, and black and blue white-barred varieties, as well as blue and silver barless varieties. Tiger spangled varieties are bred in all colors. The squabs are white-skinned. Although it could be a good squabbing breed, it is not popular as such. Because of a lack of good production birds, beginners should not start with Strassers.

Runt

The Runt is surprisingly the largest and oldest breed of pigeon in the world (Fig. 10-9). Large show specimens have been 4 pounds in weight with wingspreads of over 36 inches, although the average is 2 1/2 to 3 pounds. The Runt is a utility breed, but it produces squabs over the preferred 1 pound, so it is not commercially raised. They have been used

Fig. 10-9. White Runt male—runts are the largest pigeons in the world. (Courtesy of USDA)

as outcrosses to increase the size of other breeds, and is an ancestor to most of today's commercial breeds. It was called the Roman Pigeon in early European times and is still termed as such in France and Germany. Latin writers described the Runt over 2,000 years ago, and excavations have unearthed bones of the Runt, showing that it was bred even before this time. The Runt is presumed to be of Spanish origin. Squabs weigh 1 1/2 to 2 pounds, but the Runt is a slow breeder.

The original color of the Runt was the wild pigeon blue with dilute silver. Pearl eyes are standard in all colors and bull (black) has been the standard eye color for whites since about 1910. Standard colors today are black, blue bar, dun, red, silver, yellow, and white. The White Runt is the most common variety. Beginners should not start with Runts. Experienced breeders may use the Runt to increase the size of other breeds, but it will not produce better than the other commercial breeds.

Runts are quite cumbersome and therefore do not fly much. Most are bred in pens rather than a loft and flight pen. Pens should be about 6 × 8 feet and about 6 feet high. Nest boxes should be 15 inches square each.

Other utility breeds that are not used much are the Lark of Germany, the Lahore of India and the Polish Lynx of Poland.

Squabs can be obtained by crossing. This involves mating one breed or variety of cock with a hen of another breed or variety. This first cross usually produces squabs that are healthier, more vigorous, and better producers. These crossed squabs should then be mated to a pure breed. If they are crossed with a cross, the desirable characteristics deteriorate. Crosses are hybrids. Hybrids should never be bred to other hybrids unless you're trying for a new breed. Hybrid squabs are usually of a mixed color. In the showroom these are not approved, but they are excellent producers. Hybrids can be obtained for less money because of lower demand.

BREEDS FOR PLEASURE

Pleasure breeds are those pigeons that look fancy and those termed flyers, that are kept for their tumbling, racing, and flying abilities or homing instincts. There are many fancy wild breeds as well (Fig. 10-10).

Some of these breeds cannot feed their babies successfully because they have very short beaks. The eggs or babies of these breeds are often given to foster parents with long beaks. Those requiring foster parents are: African Owls, Blondinettes, Budapests, Long Face Tumblers, Vienna Tumblers, and any short-beaked Tumblers. Some breeds are just not good parents; they seem to lack responsibility. These are more difficult to raise and include: Bokhara Trumpeters, Frillbacks, Jacobins, Nuns, Show Kings, and some Pouters.

It's wise to choose pigeon breeds the first time that are not difficult to raise. Some of these include: Chinese Owls, English Trumpeters, Fantails, Helmets, Indian Fantails, Lahores, Modenas, Rollers, and Tipplers. Pigeons that are easier to raise and more popular are described below.

Chinese Owl

There are several varieties of Owls. The African Owl is the smallest domestic pigeon bred today. Owls originated in Asia. African and English Owls have been bred for years in England. The Chinese Owl is between the size of the African and English Owls. Chinese Owls differ in that they have a frill of feathers that extends over the breast and up the sides of the neck, and frilled feathered shanks. Because the Chinese Owl has a longer beak, it can better feed its squabs. It's bred in almond, ash-red, ash-yellow, blues, brown, grizzles, indigo, khaki, saddles of all colors, recessive reds, recessive yellows, silver white, pied, and splash.

English Trumpeter

These are medium-sized pigeons that are gentle and prolific. They sport a crest and mane and have muffed legs. Body feathers fit close to the body. Specimens should appear proud and powerful. Colors are black, white, silver, cream, red, dun, yellow, lavender, almond, splashed, marked, mottled, and barred. There are also so-called genetic colors

Fig. 10-10. A fancy-looking wild breed of pigeon, the Crown Victoria. (Courtesy Paul Cooney, Detroit Zoological Park)

which are now classed as experimental until they are placed into the Standard. These include saddles, barless recessive traits, muffed, marked, andalusian blue, magpie, and white bar.

Fantail

These are performing pigeons. They strut and dance about on tiptoes, holding their heads back and fanning their large tails out. It's one of the oldest, most familiar, and most popular of the fancy breeds. This dainty-looking pigeon originated in India and is also known as the Broad-Tailed Shaker. White is the most popular color. Other colors are brown, dun (gray brown), cream, checkered, grizzle (a peppered combination of white with color), saddle (ten outside primaries and the underside of body is white, the rest is colored), tailmark (a white body and colored tail), body-mark (a colored body and white tail), pure white, black, silver, powdered silver, blue, powdered blue, andalusian, almond, red (chestnut), yellow (golden-buff), splash (colored body with 25-75 percent splashed with white), AOC (any other color) and NCC (a color not yet recognized as standard).

Fantails are hardy and prolific. Some strains are not good parents. It's best to clip the tail feathers of breeders because they interfere with breeding, which can cause many infertile eggs.

Indian Fantails are similar to the other Fantails but they sport a crest on the head and have muffed legs.

Helmet

These are used by many fanciers as a "coopie" (decoy) to lure racing pigeons to the loft. They have been Europe's most popular flying breed for centuries. They are sprightly, active birds and should never appear frightened. Helmets are crested or plain-headed. The colored head with the contrasting crest gives the Helmet its name. Helmets are bred in black with a green sheen, blue, dun, silver, red (chestnut), yellow, cream, mealy (lavender-gray) and AOC such as almond, brown, indigo, and khaki.

Lahore

This breed resembles a penguin in color. It has short feathers on its legs and feet. Its origin is Iran and it is sometimes called Shirazi (Shirazi is a city in Iran). It's a medium-sized bird that has been used for squabbing, but the squabs are small compared to commercial utility breeds.

Modena

This is a very popular exhibition breed and breeder that originally was a flying pigeon bred in Modena, Italy in the 14th century. Modenas were popular for pigeon napping. This is where a handler flies his flock in order to entice another handler's pigeons into his own loft. This thieving still goes on occasionally.

Modenas are bred in four basic color patterns: barred, checkered (tri-marked and T-pattern), and the rare barless. There are at least 150 different color variations.

Roller

Some pigeons are bred and kept strictly for the stunts they perform. This includes Rollers, Tipplers, Tumblers and Pouters. Many theories exist as to what causes these pigeons to tumble or roll. Some claim it's a nervous spasm, others think it's just a display of excitement, self-confidence, and the need to show off. These performance traits are hereditary, although practice does improve their performance.

Rollers are tight-feathered performing pigeons of which there are the American Rollers, the Birmingham Rollers and the Oriental Rollers. The Oriental Roller is a rare flying and rolling breed in ash-red, black, dun, red, almond, yellow, white, checked, grizzle, T-pattern, and AOC. The Ameri-

can Roller is bred in any shade or blend. The Birmingham Roller is probably the most popular. It was originally bred in Birmingham, England as a flying pigeon. It's able to tumble or spin instantly in the air in a series of backward somersaults until it almost reaches the ground. Competitions are held for the best performers. They are small to medium-sized. Cocks are 11 ounces and hens are 9 ounces. Cocks should appear masculine and hens feminine.

Tippler

The Flying Tippler was developed from the Flying Tumbler, but the ability to tumble has been bred out. Their performing feature is their ability to stay in the air: they have been known to stay up for 20 hours at a time. Head types and beak lengths vary according to the strain. Their basic color is a rich, deep, metallic copper.

Pouter and Cropper

Some breeds that frequently interest pigeon handlers are the Pouters and Croppers. These pigeons have large globes (crops) which they amusingly inflate to show off. They are comical attention-getters and are a popular attraction wherever they are shown.

Tumbler

Tumblers were developed as a flying pigeon able to reach great heights and quickly descend in a series of somersaults. Some simply roll along the ground in a long straight line. They are an old, large family of domestic pigeons that have always been popular, and are in the same family as Rollers and Tipplers. There are over a dozen varieties of Tumblers—some for show only and some for performance.

Nun

These are friendly, attractive pigeons who become quite attached to their owners. They can be allowed freedom and will still come to their owner to greet him. The most popular color is white with a black head, bib, flight feathers, and tail.

Knowledge in purchasing wisely applies to pleasure breeds also (Fig. 10-11). The *Book of Pigeon Standards* by the National Pigeon Association will help determine good specimens.

PURCHASING WISELY

When choosing a squabbing pigeon, remember that the larger the breed, the larger the squabs will be.

The average demand is for a 14- to 18-ounce dressed squab—which is 20 to 22 1/2 ounces live weight. The squabbing pair should weigh from 26 to 30 ounces each in old birds and from 24 to 26 ounces in young birds. They should produce heavy, full-breasted, plump, and meaty squabs with light-colored flesh. Purchasing the best of the correct type of breeders is the first step to success.

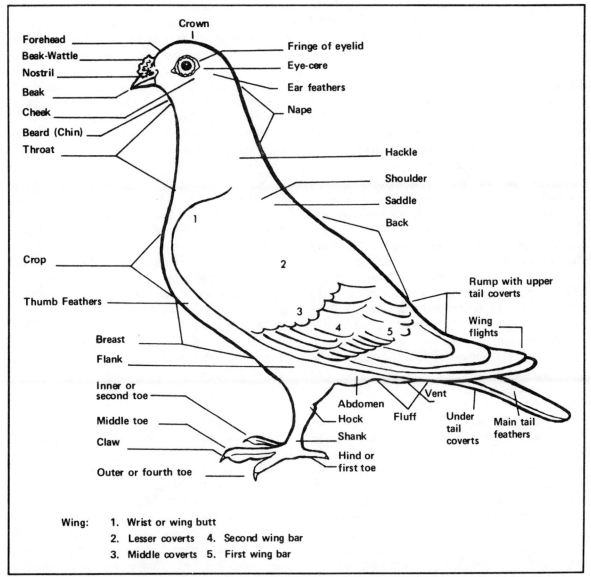

Fig. 10-11. Exterior features of a pigeon. (Courtesy of Dr. John L. Skinner and University of Wisconsin Cooperative Extension Service)

199

Avoid purchasing old birds just because they are a bargain. Their production period may be almost over. Older pigeons will usually have darker eye ceres. Although some pigeons have been known to live and breed for up to 20 years, the average production limit is 5 years for hens and 7 years for cocks. This does not mean a good pair can't produce 15 to 18 squabs per year for 8 years—some do. Cocks generally breed and live longer than hens. Old cocks can be mated with year-old hens. Hens that do not produce at least 12 squabs a year should be disposed of if economy is important. Young mated pairs can cost twice as much as 3-year-olds because they have more productivity ahead of them.

Many pigeons are sold because they are poor producers, or with show types, they might not have been up to the standard. Never purchase these culls. It's wise to purchase breeders from a well-known, experienced breeder. Good mated pairs from good stock, purchased from a reliable breeder, are well worth the money.

Many beginners sometimes unknowingly purchase a male and female pigeon and believe they have a "pair." A pair of pigeons does not simply mean one of each sex, it refers to one of each sex that have already been mated and preferably leg-banded. Official seamless leg bands are used to prove age. Pairs should contain the same numbers on the bands. Unmated birds cause a lot of trouble in a loft when other pairs are present. They will steal mates, fight, and cocks will scalp babies. Lone hens will cause parent cocks to flirt rather than tend to their babies. Pigeons mate for life. They mate in pairs and remain together for life unless they are forced to be separated by removal or death. Once they have gone through the stages of courting, mating, and nesting, they remain true to each other as long as they're allowed to remain together. If introducing new birds, the original birds must be removed for at least two months. The removed birds must be completely out of sight or new mating will not take place.

It's difficult to determine the sex of pigeons until they are a few months old and are ready to mate. Even experts cannot quickly do this as there are no distinguishing characteristics of the sexes as with other birds and poultry. With adult birds you must look at both their appearance and their behavior. Cocks are usually larger and more rugged or masculine looking than hens, with thicker legs and necks. With a producing female, the two vent bones are set further apart than the male's to allow for egg laying.

Behavior is more important than appearance in determining the sex. Males are usually more aggressive. Cocks "drive" the hen when the nest is being built. This means the cock becomes very jealous and keeps the hen from other birds. He tries to keep the hen on the nest by chasing and pecking after her if she leaves it. He'll do this until she returns to the nest. This driving is about the most positive way to clearly determine the sexes. The driving is stopped once the second egg is laid. Vigorous and continuous driving usually proves the pair are very good producers.

Most hens do not help to carry nesting materials to the nest. This is left to the cock. Cocks help incubate the laid eggs. They are usually seen sitting on the eggs from about 10 A.M. to 3 P.M., and occasionally during the night.

One male characteristic seldom displayed by females is constant cooing and strutting. The strutting includes turning around and or fanning the tail to the ground.

Billing can also help determine the sexes. "Billing" is the word for pigeon kissing. The hen places her beak into the mouth of the cock and he feeds her small amounts of feed regurgitated from his crop. This is true love and mating soon follows. When pairs are mated, the hen will preen the feathers on the neck and head of the cock. During mating, the male usually mounts and the hen crouches with her wings slightly up and out. I say usually, because sometimes in young pairs the hen tries to mount the cock.

It's not uncommon for a pair of the same sex to build a nest together, so this cannot be relied on to determine a pair. On the other hand, if a nest is built and no eggs are laid, the pair are both males. If eggs are laid, more than two eggs will usually be found in a nest made by two females.

There are sex-linked matings that produce squabs that can be feather-sexed or color-sexed as with chickens. In feather-sexing, hatchlings with short down are hens and hatchlings with longer down are males. Only certain breeds and strains mated together will produce this effect. Most of this sexing is the result of a criss-cross inheritance where female squabs feather like the father and the males feather like the mother. Any short-downed cock can be mated to a normal-downed hen. Certain chromosomes must be present in the breeding pair for sex-linkage to occur. These matings can be tried for fun or profit. Some examples are: A short-down White Carneau cock (banded for short-down when hatched) mated to a normal-downed White Carneau hen will produce squab hens with short-down. All the squabs will be white. These hens should later be mated to normal-downed cocks because mating to short-downed cocks will result in offspring that are not hardy.

Another mating for feather-sexing is a White Carneau cock mated to a blue or black Homer hen. All squabs with short-down will be hens. These hens will usually be white with specks of yellow. They are slightly smaller than a White Carneau hen but they are hardy squabbers. They can be mated successfully to White Carneau or Silver King cocks.

Color-sexing consists of mating certain colored pigeons together to produce squabs of a different color or marking. A sex-linked mating might be: A yellow cock bred to any red hen; A brown dun or silver cock bred to a red-barred, red-checkered, blue or black hen; A blue or black cock bred to a red-checkered or red-barred hen.

Safeguards include not purchasing from a breeder who has any canker prevalent in his flock. Also, never place new birds immediately in pens with the old birds because an unnoticeable disease could be present. Always segregate the new birds from the old in a separate building for at least two weeks. During this time, most any disease will begin to show itself. If birds look fine after this period, introduce them into the pens of the older birds. Don't go walking into another handler's pens or allow others to walk around in yours. This helps prevent the spread of disease.

Handle pigeons correctly by holding wings to their body. New pigeons often fly off before they're settled into their new quarters—and sometimes afterwards. Shut doors and windows.

Chapter 11

Pigeon Management

HOUSING, YARDS, AND FLIGHT PENS

The pigeon house is called a loft,. The typical loft or dovecote consists of a building for shelter with an attached flight pen for exercise. Some handlers keep their pigeons in hutches (Fig. 11-1) or cages in a covered area (Fig. 11-2).

Plan on plenty of space because you'll usually end up with more pigeons than you started with. Furthermore, crowded quarters can lead to mortality—especially if a young squab accidentally strays to another nest where it will be soon picked to death. Crowded cocks and hens are apt to fight, which leads to squabs being pushed from the nests and broken eggs. Crowded quarters will mean disposing of extra pigeons even if it breaks your heart, or building extra housing even if it breaks your budget.

Determine the total amount of pigeons you might want to raise in the future. Allow 5 square feet of floor space for each pair of regular-sized breeds. A small feed and storage room with a table for banding and a place to keep records is a very

nice addition to any loft. Plan on using a double nest consisting of two compartments 11 inches square, for each pair to be housed (Fig. 11-3). The nests are usually placed on a back wall. A typical series of nests is 4 feet high, 8 feet wide, 15 inches deep (allowing for a 4-inch landing board). Begin the series of nests 20 inches from the floor and only as high as your eye level (Fig. 11-4). The space under the nests above the floor will help prevent floor nesting. The eye-level height will dispense with a need for using a ladder to check on nests and squabs.

A landing board or perch should be in the front of the nest so birds aren't forced to fly directly onto nests. The landing board should be the width of the nests and at least 4 inches deep, making the total depth—including the nest—15 inches. Provide a 5-inch safety board along the front of each nest to keep squabs and nesting material in place. A removable bottom can be made by attaching an extra nest floor to the safety board. The safety board is then lifted out along with the nest floor for cleaning and scraping. Nests of this type do not require nest bowls.

Handlers have, and still do, use single nest boxes or orange crates, but this is unwise (Fig. 11-5). The reason is simple. Before the first set of squabs are fully grown and still in the nest, the parents will usually begin to construct another nest and lay a second clutch of eggs. Sometimes the young squabs are pushed from the nest to make room for a new brood. When a duplex nest is used, the squabs remain in their original nest while the parents lay eggs and tend the nest next to them.

Nest bowls are made of disposable wood pulp, crockery, and sheetmetal. They are available at most pigeon supply houses. Bowls make cleaning the nests easy. Woodpulp bowls eventually become deteriorated from droppings and crack into pieces—and they are extremely inexpensive to use. Other types will last much longer. Crockery bowls break easily if dropped, but they clean nicely. Nest bowls made of rugged plastic are also available. They are similar to the clay bottoms now available for under flower pots, but they do not tip. Most nest bowls measure 7 1/2 inches at the top and are 2 inches deep.

Besides the nests, perches, and landing boards, extra perches can be placed in the house if the breeds are not production birds. Inverted V-shaped perches or 2-inch-wide, flat boards running horizontally can be made (see Fig. 11-5). Utility breeds need no additional perches because most of their time will be spent up near the nests.

Nest fronts with built-in landing perches can be purchased (Fig. 11-6). The perch also folds upward to close off the entrance when nests outnumber the breeders or when a pair is to be confined for a forced mating. Removable, slatted nest fronts can also close off nests that are not being used (Fig. 11-7). The upper 7 inches of the fronts of nests can be screened with wire with a 4-inch hinged landing board below (Fig. 11-8). The nests then become a compartment for confined pairs when forced or controlled matings are attempted.

Although pigeons should not be allowed to nest on the floor, some insistent pairs will continue to do so. In this case, give them a nest box on the floor to save squabs and eggs that could otherwise be pushed onto the floor.

Lofts should preferably face south—especially in cold climates—to make use of the sun and block north winds. Some producers section long lofts into pens with chicken wire (Fig. 11-9). In commercial operations, housing for 2,200 breeding pairs may consist of 18 houses, 80 feet long, sectioned into 8 pens—producing 144 pens (Fig. 11-10).

Most pigeon breeds need a flight pen (Fig. 11-11). This is an attached covered outdoor pen where pigeons can exercise and soak up the rays of the sun. Use chicken wire with spacings no wider than 1 inch so sparrows and rats do not enter. Wild birds and rats spread disease and parasites. Rats will also go after squabs and eggs. The flight should be the same width as the loft but no higher than 7 feet. If higher, pigeons have too much freedom and will be hard to tame and catch. Many handlers now provide 1-inch, 16-gauge wire floors in the bottom of flights. The wire floor should be 12-36 inches above the ground and supported and framed well with 2- x -4s. A board can be used to form a bridge so a handler need not walk on the wire floor and bend it. Another floor treatment for flights: sand or gravel spread 4 inches thick. Gravel will provide good drainage, especially if a layer of sand is first spread underneath.

To help keep predators from burrowing under into flights, those that meet the ground should have the wire extend 12 inches below ground level, bent at right angles away from the flight, surrounded by a 12-inch strip of wire.

Horizontal, flat running boards should be placed at each end of the flight, 6 inches from the wire. They should be 8-12 inches wide and at least 1 inch thick. Because they are exposed to the weather, they should be of cedar or redwood. Keep the board low, about 4 feet high, so birds are more apt to become tame by being closer to your level.

If the pigeon exits to the flights are any distance from the flight floor, a landing board should be attached to the bottom of the exit door and extend into the loft. In milder climates, both commercial and small-scale handlers sometimes omit flight pens by providing wired, open-front lofts. In the winter

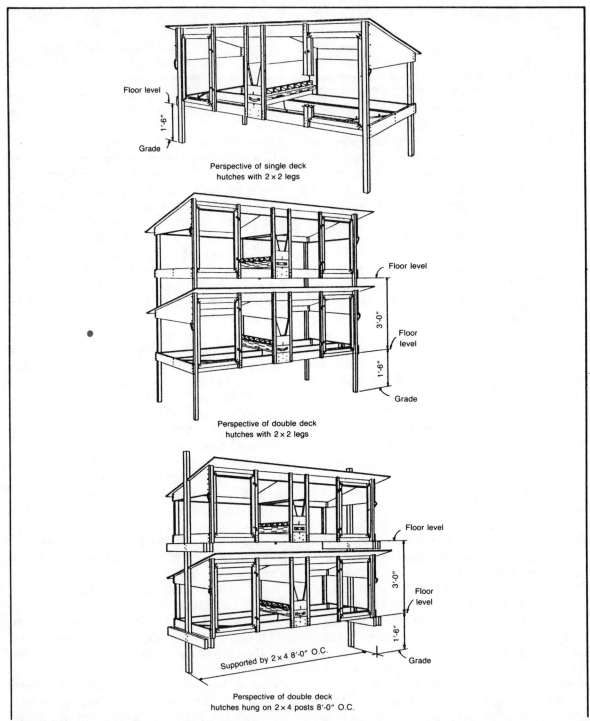

Floor level

1'-6"

Grade

Perspective of single deck
hutches with 2 × 2 legs

Floor level

3'-0"

Floor
level

1'-6"

Grade

Perspective of double deck
hutches with 2 × 2 legs

Floor level

3'-0"

Floor
level

1'-6"

Supported by 2 × 4 8'-0" O.C.

Grade

Perspective of double deck
hutches hung on 2 × 4 posts 8'-0" O.C.

Fig. 11-1. These rabbit hutches with feeders can be adapted to pigeons by adding nests. (Courtesy of Michigan State University Agricultural Engineering Dept.)

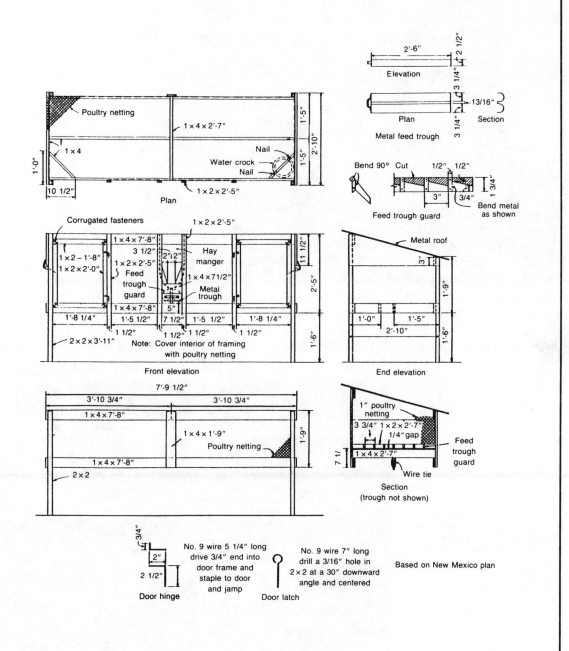

Poultry netting

1 × 4 × 2'-7"

1 × 4

Water crock
Nail
Nail

1'-0"

10 1/2"

1 × 2 × 2'-5"

1'-5"
1'-5"
2'-10"

Plan

2'-6"

2 1/2"

Elevation

3 1/4"

3 1/4"

13/16"

Plan

Section

Metal feed trough

Bend 90°   Cut

1/2"   1/2"

3"   3/4"

1 3/4"

Bend metal
as shown

Feed trough guard

Corrugated fasteners

1 × 2 × 2'-5"

1 × 4 × 7'-8"
3 1/2"

Hay
manger

1 × 2 – 1'-8"
1 × 2 × 2'-5"
1 × 2 × 2'-0"
Feed
trough
guard

2" 2"

1 × 4 × 7 1/2"

Metal
trough

1 × 4 × 7'-8"
5"

1'-8 1/4"   1'-5 1/2"   7 1/2"   1'-5 1/2"   1'-8 1/4"

1 1/2"   1 1/2" 1 1/2"   1 1/2"

2 × 2 × 3'-11"

11 1/2"

2'-5"

1'-6"

Note: Cover interior of framing
with poultry netting

Front elevation

Metal roof

3"

1'-0"   1'-5"

2'-10"

1'-9"

1'-6"

End elevation

7'-9 1/2"

3'-10 3/4"   3'-10 3/4"

1 × 4 × 7'-8"

1 × 4 × 1'-9"

Poultry netting

1 × 4 × 7'-8"

2 × 2

1'-9"

1" poultry
netting

3 3/4"   1 × 2 × 2'-7"
1/4" gap

7 1/

1 × 4 × 2'-7"

Feed
trough
guard

Wire tie

Section
(trough not shown)

3/4"

2"

2 1/2"

Door hinge

No. 9 wire 5 1/4" long
drive 3/4" end into
door frame and
staple to door
and jamp

No. 9 wire 7" long
drill a 3/16" hole in
2 × 2 at a 30" downward
angle and centered

Door latch

Based on New Mexico plan

Fig. 11-2. A pair of young Racing Homers housed in a 3- × -3-foot cage with bathpan, plastic fount, and attached feeder.

these wire fronts are covered with plastic to reduce drafts and retain the temperature (Fig. 11-10). In very cold climates where squabbing is done throughout the year, some handlers heat the lofts so squabs do not become chilled.

A loft need not be fancy or expensive, but it should provide protection from inclement weather and predators. A dry loft is essential for raising

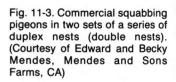

Fig. 11-3. Commercial squabbing pigeons in two sets of a series of duplex nests (double nests). (Courtesy of Edward and Becky Mendes, Mendes and Sons Farms, CA)

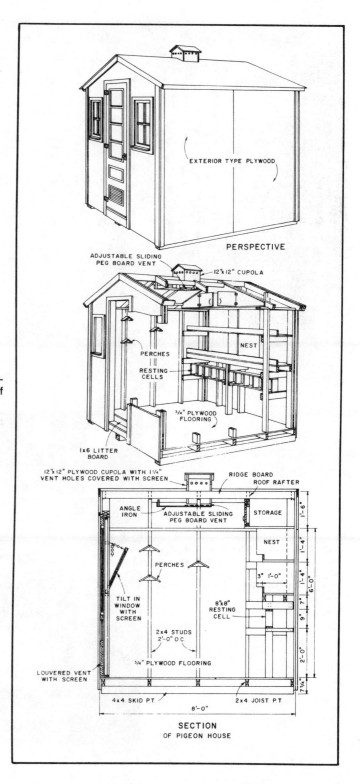

Fig. 11-4. A small pigeon house to construct, showing placement of nests and perches. (Courtesy of Texas Agricultural Extension Service)

207

Fig. 11-5. Interior of an old pigeon house showing feed hopper, V-shaped roosts, single-nest boxes, and nest pans (bowls). (Courtesy of USDA)

Fig. 11-6. Manufactured nest fronts, such as these with folding perches, are simply installed over the front of open-nest holes. (Courtesy of Foy's Pigeon Supplies)

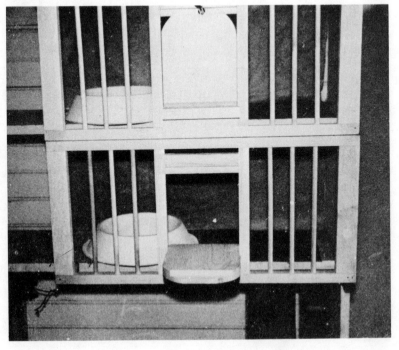

Fig. 11-7. Homemade slatted nest front, on right center, closes off a vacant duplex nest to restrict its use. (Courtesy of Edward and Becky Mendes, Mendes and Sons Farms, CA)

healthy, disease-free pigeons. Organisms that cause disease and parasites all breed freely under damp conditions. The loft should stand on high and dry ground. Do not allow drafts to blow through the house and over the floor.

Solid flooring is best to keep rats and mice out of the building. A foundation rat-wall is recommended but not always possible. An earth floor can

Fig. 11-8. Double nest boxes with wire fronts may also be used as "forced-mating" compartments. (Courtesy of A.R. Lee and S.K. Haynes, USDA)

Fig. 11-9. Commercial squabbing loft sectioned into 10- × -10 pens with chicken wire. (Courtesy of Edward and Becky Mendes, Mendes and Sons Farms, CA)

be made fairly predator-proof by lining it with good-quality 1/4-1/2-inch wire, and securing it tightly at the junction of walls. Cement floors might seem ideal, but they can cause Bumblefoot with heavy squabbers such as Kings. Cement floors also stay cold and damp longer and can cause respiratory problems.

Cleanliness can be overdone. When birds must constantly be moved around, losses can occur. A thorough cleaning once a month is plenty. Loose feathers can be raked from sand floors once a week. If the lofts are clean and dry, the droppings will dry

Fig. 11-10. Looking down one sectioned 80-foot-long commercial squabbing loft, of which there are 18, housing a total of 2,200 pairs of squabbers. Note accessible grit boxes placed in front of each pen and removable, plastic-covered frame fronts for wintering squabbers. (Courtesy of Edward and Becky Mendes, Mendes and Sons Farms, CA)

Fig. 11-11. Flight pen yard of 1-inch chicken wire showing gravel floor and roosts. (Courtesy of A.R. Lee and S.K. Haynes, USDA)

faster and will not become offensive. Excess feed scattered throughout the loft and surroundings will surely provide a fine diet for rats and mice. Rats will eat eggs faster than they can be laid. They also are known to eat small adult pigeons. The inside of the lofts should be occasionally whitewashed or painted. Whitewash formulas can be found in Chapter 18.

Some commercial and small-scale producers like to give their pigeons more freedom than is wise or necessary by allowing their birds to fly free. This causes a drop in production. Confined pigeons will keep themselves busy producing eggs and squabs. Also, if the breeders don't return home, their nested squabs will die unless the handler resorts to hand-feeding the babies.

If pigeons are to be housed in cages, a size 18 inches wide, 24 inches deep, and 24 inches high will be sufficient for most breeds. Two nests should be installed off the floor of the cage on the back wall. Two nestbowls can be set on a suspended 12-inch board, which will leave 12 inches in front of the board for easy access to nests. To save space and labor, feed, grit and water containers should be hung on the outside of the cage with access holes cut in the wire. Cages can be suspended from the ceiling with heavy wire. Be sure they do not sway or nests and water will be upset. Cages can be placed one on top of another by using trays 6 inches

below the wire floors to catch droppings.

Cages used for laying chickens can be used by pigeons if wire cutters are used to remove every other partition. Feeders and waterers will need to be adjusted. Grit can be supplied in one side of the feeding trough right next to the feed grains. When secondhand cages are converted, be sure the sliding door front operates smoothly so pigeons aren't disturbed when you open the door. Provide nesting material in the cage.

Caged birds do not need bathpans, but the birds should be regularly treated for lice and mites—being careful not to contaminate the feed, water, and grit. Squabbers (and the young birds too) will enjoy the bathpan and carry moisture back to eggs for better hatching. Any type pan will do as long as it's kept clean, because pigeons might also drink from it (Fig. 11-12).

FEEDING

Feeding pigeons is simpler than feeding other types of poultry. Feed does not have to be crumbled, pelleted, or ground. There are two basic ways in which to feed pigeons: Twice a day by hand or by using cafeteria-style self-feeders.

Pigeons have a tendency to overeat and to overfeed their squabs, so feeding should be restricted. Handlers who have only a few pairs of pigeons usually hand-feed them. A pair of 2-pound pigeons

Fig. 11-12. Even young pigeons begin bathing as part of their grooming procedures.

and their squabs will consume approximately 4 1/2 ounces (126 grams) of feed per day. Such would be the case for a pair of Carneau and their squabs. A pair of 32-ounce pigeons such as Kings and Mondains with their squabs will consume about 5 ounces (140 grams) total per day. This amount of feed is divided in half and given in two feedings each day. Troughs or feed pans should be used because they are more sanitary than floor feeding. A rule of thumb is to feed as much as the birds will consume in 20-30 minutes twice daily.

Cafeteria-style self-feeders should have at least four compartments. Five compartments will allow for grit feeding also. The feeder is divided to keep individual grains from being mixed. As the birds feed, gravity brings more grain trickling down into the trough.

Because pigeons will overfeed with a cafeteria feeder also, the feeder should have a flap that can be closed from dusk to dawn. Regular single-compartment self-feeders where grains must be mixed should not be used because the birds will pick out the more desirable grains, causing wasted and scattered feed. Scattered feed greatly attracts

rodents. Cafeteria feeders can save hours of work for those with many pigeons. If you want to vacation for one or two weeks, the feeders can safely be left open. Be sure plenty of water is present by calculating their drinking water needs. A 30-ounce pigeon will consume about 2 ounces (56 grams) of water daily.

As with any poultry, pigeons require feeds that supply energy, protein, vitamins, and minerals. The energy requirements will depend upon their activity, production, the temperature of the environment, and their metabolism—the body's ability to use and convert feeds into energy. Colder temperatures will cause them to eat more to have the energy to keep the body warm. Energy comes from starch which is present in grains. Fats also satisfy energy requirements.

The need for protein is actually a need for the essential amino acids contained in the protein. The requirements for amino acids in the way they work are similar to chickens. Table 11-1 shows recommended percentages of protein and calories per ounce of feed for various production stages and activities of pigeons.

Table 11-1. Suggested Calorie and Protein Intake for Pigeons.

Situation	Calories per oz. fed	Percent Protein
Spring	90	15
Summer	86	16
Autumn	90	15
Winter	92	14
Molting	86	16
Prebreeding	80	18
Squabs under 6 weeks	82	17
Squabs over 6 weeks	86	16
Racer Homer training	82	17
Pre-race	92	14
After race	90	15

Commercially prepared feeds contain ingredients such as yellow corn, popcorn, Canadian peas, Austrian peas, maple peas, wheat, hulled oats, vetch, buckwheat, safflower, and the sorghums (kaffir, millet and milo). These grains can be purchased and fed by the pigeon handler. Grains should be whole and hulled if pointed, hard husks are present (as with oats). Cracked grains cost more and there is no need to feed them. Corn is the largest amount of grain used in the diet. A winter diet should have slightly more corn to generate energy and heat.

A good basic formula to go by is equal parts of corn, peas, hard red winter wheat, and Kaffir corn, milo or millet. Kaffir and milo may be more difficult to purchase separately than millet. If unavailable locally, they can be shipped. Many handlers feed nothing but this type of diet and have good results, but as shown in Table 5-7, it can lack the amount of protein needed for performance and production. If you feel your birds should be doing better, you could try a higher protein pellet-type feed. These feeds can be fed as a supplement to whole grains or visa-versa. When completely changing from grains to pellets, do it gradually over a two-week period or the body functions and production might be upset. Do this by replacing one-fourth of the grains with the pellets the first three days, 50 percent the next three days, 75 percent the next three days, then 100 percent. Also, gradually withdraw the pigeon health grit and any

vitamin supplements, and supply regular chicken grower grits instead.

From time to time, various other grains can be used in place of the basic four. For instance, as a substitute for peas, use peanuts, vetch or heat-treated soybeans. Other substitutes are hulled barley, hulled oats, rice, buckwheat in small amounts, rye, flaxseed and the hard-to-find "pigeon candy" called hemp seed (cannabis sativa). Pigeons love hemp and many handlers give some during the molting period. If you want to give hemp as a treat without getting some raised eyebrows and snickers at the feed store, a sterilized hemp seed can be obtained from a company who deals in wild bird seeds and odd grains. Hemp is a drug, and the seed is sterilized so it cannot accidentally or illegally be planted and harvested. Hemp seed is very palatable but is relatively low in protein and high in fiber and fat, so it should be fed sparingly. Polished rice is low in protein too.

When only a whole grain diet is fed, the ingredients will be deficient in some vitamins and minerals. A water-soluable vitamin mix can be given in the drinking water. This is available at most poultry supply houses and feed and grain stores.

It's best to purchase grains which have been mechanically dried in a grain dryer. Field dried grains appear dry but contain enough moisture to quickly mold. Do not feed damp, dirty, musty, discolored, vermin-contaminated, or mildewed feed. Spoiled feed can cause diarrhea and even kill the pigeons. Molds are toxic enough to kill also.

Grains are generally deficient in micro and trace minerals. These should be supplied daily free-choice in the form of a pigeon health grit mineral mix. These can be purchased already mixed and prepared, or a mixture can be made at home. See Table 11-2.

Besides providing minerals for the utilization of energy and protein, pigeon grit supplies the necessary calcium for good hard eggshells and aids the gizzard in crushing feed for proper digestion. Grit is a must. If not fed, birds will not be as healthy and will lay soft-shelled, easily broken eggs. Prepared health grit is inexpensive. When grit dries

Table 11-2. Pigeon Health Grit Formula.*

40 %	medium-sized crushed oyster shells
35 %	limestone or granite grit (a grower-sized chicken granite grit can be used)
10 %	medium-sized hardwood charcoal (if feed store doesn't stock, try pet shop)
5 %	ground bone
4 %	salt
1 %	calcium sulphate and red iron-oxide supplement

Combine and mix thoroughly.

*Adapted from USDA formula.

out, it is less palatable and pigeons will be less inclined to eat it. Grit should be moistened with water. Insoluable grit particles are naturally passed in the droppings. Small breed pairs with squabs will consume about 16 pounds of grit per year. Larger breeds such as Kings require about 20 pounds per year.

Never feed loose salt, only proper mixtures with salt. Too much salt will kill pigeons.

Sufficient quantities of clean drinking water are essential to the pigeon's health. Pigeons will consume twice as much water as feed. Excess heat and certain rations can cause an increase in water consumption. A 30-ounce pigeon will consume about 2 ounces of water daily. Water should be kept clean so pigeons consume it. Water aids a pigeon's digestive system in that it softens the feed, helps maintain the normal body temperature, and prevents dehydration of the bird's tissues.

When pans are used for water, grills and cone tops should be used over the pans so the pigeons cannot use the water for bathing. Only the pigeon's head can poke through the grill for drinking.

Galvanized duplex founts made specially for pigeons can be purchased with a single hooded access hole or double access holes (Fig. 11-13). Both come in two pieces—the top slides down over the bottom. The hoods prevent pigeons from entering and bathing. The double fount can be set in partitions to serve two pens at one time. Ordinary 1-gallon plastic chick founts can also be used to prevent pigeons from bathing in their water.

The newest fount on the market is a sturdy plastic 1/2-gallon funnel fount (Fig. 11-14). The unit can also be used as a feeder. It's base design prevents pigeons from entering and bathing.

A worry-free system for watering pigeons is an automatic fount that supplies a constant supply of fresh water. These will not work in freezing temperatures. Ordinary water pressure systems can be used to operate the fount. Homemade waterers can also be made from gallon vinegar or cider jugs by inverting them over a dish and holding them in place by a stand (Fig. 11-15). Yet another waterer is a coffee can with a grill and cone top (Fig. 11-16). If you find an adult pigeon who is a bully and has taken over at a fount, provide an extra fount.

Electric fount heaters are available for use with pans and galvanized duplex founts. Some operate strictly from electrically heated and thermostatically controlled bases, and some are heated by an ordinary light bulb screwed into the base. Birds can go longer without feed than water. Also, the smaller the bird, the sooner the effects of water deprivation become apparent. Hence, the need for a constant supply of fresh water during freezing weather too. See the section entitled "Fount Heaters" in Chapter 4.

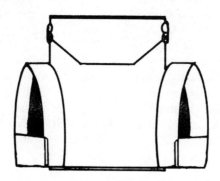

Fig. 11-13. Pigeon founts showing single-hooded style on left and twin-hooded style on right. (Courtesy of Foy's Pigeon Supplies)

Fig. 11-14. Base of this plastic fount allows bird to reach only its head inside to keep water from becoming dirty. (Courtesy of Kuhl Corp.)

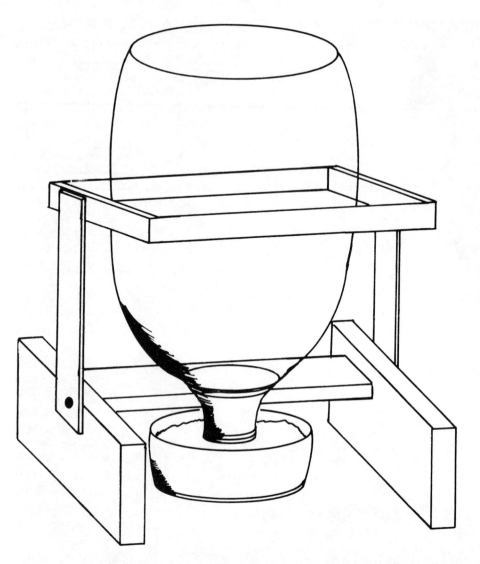

Fig. 11-15. Homemade jug waterer in stand with pivot top.

Some knowledge of the way pigeons drink and eat will help you understand your birds' habits. Unlike most birds who dip their beaks into water, lift their heads, and let the water run down the throat, pigeons drink as humans do. They immerse their beaks up to the nostril and sip the water without raising their heads. This is known as the vacuum pump method. Because of this, be sure the water level is at least 3/4 inches at all times.

Pigeons feed sporadically throughout the day between other activities. Pecking at feed is a part of this feeding. Pigeons eat by what is commonly termed the "slide and glue method," in which the grain is positioned between the tops of the beak and moved backwards by lingual protraction after it becomes "glued" to the tongue.

MOLTING AND MATING

There is no special season for breeding and mating pigeons. They are able to produce and raise squabs throughout the entire year except when going through their molt. During this time old feathers are shed and new ones come in.

A pigeon's first molt actually occurs at about

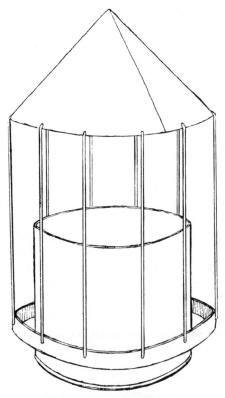

Fig. 11-16. Coffee can with a grill and cone top for watering or feeding pigeons. (Courtesy of Dr. John L. Skinner and University of Wisconsin Cooperative Extension Service)

six weeks of age when the squab plumage is shed and the adult plumage grows in. Adults molt once a year in late summer or early fall. Some pigeons do breed even during their molt, so many commercial breeders continue breeding well-nourished squabbers at this time.

Some handlers separate the pairs from June until after the fall molt so squabs are not raised during a molt. If economics are not involved, a handler with show or racing stock might wish to rest their pairs this way. Beginners might also wish to follow this practice at first. Most handlers who raise show or racing pigeons will control breedings so squabs are not present when the molt is to occur. The length and time of the molt is determined by the seasonal changes, daylight hours, diet, breed and strain of bird, climate, disturbance, disease and parasites.

A forced molting can be accomplished by separating the cock from the hen and withholding feed for 24 hours. Always keep drinking water available. Another method is to separate the pair and then reduce the amount of feed by half. The first method is more disturbing and will cause a quicker molt. Forced molting is only called for if a handler is scheduled to exhibit his pigeons when the normal molt would occur. It is done about two months before the normal molt or scheduled show.

When a handler is breeding his own stock or when he has purchased young, unmated and also unbanded birds, he can place an even number of males and females all three to five months of age into an empty loft or breeding pen. They will then select mates and can be captured and pair-banded to identify the pairs.

Breaking up pairs is done when a handler wants to upgrade his stock. This is called a controlled or forced mating. Breeders are chosen by qualities characteristic of the breed or variety: hardiness, docility, largeness or smallness, good squab breeders, productiveness, long life, or color. Use pairs that have as many of the desirable qualities as possible. Some qualities are recessive, however, and all the squabs can be poorer in the certain quality than both parents. It can sometimes be trial and error. Forced and controlled matings are the only way a loft will ever contain an excellent full flock of birds. This is how your own strain of pigeon breed is produced.

There are four methods in choosing and mating the pairs: Outcrossing, linebreeding, inbreeding, and crossbreeding. All will produce or set various traits.

Outcrossing is when an unrelated pigeon is bred to an inbred, linebred or crossbred strain to introduce new blood. This should be done occasionally or constant family breeding will result in weak squabs and mortalities.

Linebreeding is when offspring are bred back to a distant relative of several generations who has sought-after qualities. All birds then eventually become closely related. The usual matings are son to great-grandmother, son to great-great-grandmother, daughter to great grandfather, daughter to great-great-grandfather. Results can be excellent to very poor; again, it's trial and error. Linebreeding is a form of inbreeding.

Inbreeding is the continual mating of individuals of the same or closely related stock. Such is the case when matings are father to daughter, mother to son, grandfather to granddaughter, grandmother to grandson, cousin to cousin or brother to sister. Inbreeding does have it's place in the animal world. It tends to fix certain qualities or characteristics. Inbreeding also pronounces both good and bad traits in the resulting squabs. Again, it's trial and error. Matings without plan or records—where pigeons mate at will—are often termed as inbreeding.

Once the pairs are chosen, they should be first placed in wire cages next to each other. (A fish net can be used to catch pigeons safely.) Even better is a cage with a removable partition. Confine both with feed and water for 2-14 days until the birds show an interest in each other. Some only take a few minutes, others require days. Be sure the previous mate is out of sight and sound. From the start, a cock may begin continuous cooing, strutting, prancing, bowing, ruffling his feathers, fanning his tail and wing feathers to the floor, or blowing up his crop with air. This prancing back and forth and circling should soon spark the hen's interest. The hen will respond with a little dance of her own. She will bob her head up and down and swell her neck until it can be seen pulsating. When this occurs, remove the partition the next day and watch them. If they are still interested in each other for two more days, then they can be color-number banded and released into the loft. Billing should then take place. Pigeons can be considered mated when this occurs because unmated pairs do not bill.

Nest building begins within a week. The hen will sit on a selected nest and the cock will bring nesting material to the nest a piece at a time (Fig. 11-17). Be sure nest material is provided somewhere in the loft. A slatted orange create turned upside down will allow nesting material to be pulled through the slats. Excellent materials are long pine needles or tobacco stems, oat or wheat straw can also be used. The hen takes each piece of nesting material into her beak and arranges it into a cup shape. A handler can help by placing loose sand or sawdust in the bottom of the nest because pigeons are not as adept as other birds at nest building.

Keep "bully" pigeons under control. These are

Fig. 11-17. A cock pigeon brings nesting material to a hen—a piece at a time. (Courtesy of Edward and Becky Mendes, Mendes and Sons Farms, CA)

cocks who want to rule near feeders, waterers, and nests. An aggressive, strong cock will keep pairs from taking a nest. He'll chase other cocks and production will be hurt. Pen the bully up with his mate for a few days so other cocks become more confident and take on a nest.

As soon as the nestmaking begins, the cock begins his driving. This involves pecking and flying at the hen in order to keep her constantly at home on the nest. The poor hen is constantly chased even when she tries to get a bit to eat or drink. But this is all a good sign, because a very vigorous driver will usually result in a good producing pair. The first egg is laid in the late afternoon. Three hours later a new ovulation occurs and the sperm penetrate the ova at about the same time. As soon as the second egg is laid, in the afternoon two days later (or precisely 40 hours later), the driving stops. A normal clutch is two eggs. Any more or any less means the hen's reproduction organs are not functioning properly. A hen with this problem should be culled immediately. Eggs are about half the size of a standard chicken egg.

Serious brooding to incubate the eggs does not commence until the second egg is laid. Beforehand, they just stand over the single egg so it does not prematurely begin to incubate ahead of the second laid egg. Both the hen and cock incubate the eggs. The eggs are not left alone for longer than a few minutes, or they will cool down and the embryo will die.

Pigeon eggs hatch in 17 to 19 days. That is— the first egg will hatch about 18 1/2 days after being laid and second about 17 days after being laid. Occasionally both hatch at the same time, but usually there is a lapse of 6 to 16 hours between hatches.

The eggs should be checked for fertility and development on the fifth or seventh day of incubation. If the pair is very young or the weather has been cold, the eggs can be infertile or dead. The earliest determination of good or bad eggs should be done by candling. Reach under the hen at night when birds are the quietest and calmest and remove the eggs, protecting them in the palm of your hand. A startled or nasty hen (or cock) can knock the eggs

from your hand if not careful. With lights off, hold a flashlight to the egg. A good egg will contain a series of red blood vessels radiating up the inside of the shell. Infertile eggs will be clean, showing only a tinge of the yellow, floating yolk. If eggs look clear on the tenth day or have not developed further, dispose of the eggs so the pair can start over. When consistently bad eggs are laid, remate or dispose of the bird if it's an old one. As the embryo develops, the egg begins to take on a dark cast because of the larger embryo.

If pigeons do not have a bathpan, use a small hand mist sprayer with warm water to lightly (very lightly) spray the nest material the day before hatching. Do not spray the eggs in case any are just hatching. Spraying water over the faintly pipped hole can clog the hole and suffocate the squab about to hatch. Do not dampen sooner because the cuticle substance can be removed that protects the embryo by closing off the shell pores to germs during incubation. When squabbers have access to bath pans, they bring some of the moisture back to the nest with them because it clings to the feathers. This moisture softens the eggshells for easier pipping and hatching.

Anxious handlers can check for pipping by listening to the eggs the day before hatching. Remember you always chance accidental breakage when removing eggs. Place the eggs up to your ear and the baby about to hatch will be heard pecking away at the inside of the shell.

HATCHING AND REARING SQUABS

Newly hatched squabs are very tiny, weak, nearly naked, and helpless—they cannot walk, hold their heads up, or feed themselves. Their eyes are not open. They remain wet for a few hours.

Both parents begin to feed the squab a white, mushy, cheesy substance called pigeon milk (also referred to as crop milk), three to four hours after hatching. Pigeon milk is produced because of a hormone secreted called prolactin. The hormone is secreted in both sexes when they begin to incubate the eggs. On the eighth day of incubation, the crop lining thickens and slightly bulges. Blood vessels grow in the lining and by the fourteenth day the pigeon milk is produced in the crop.

By the time the squab is fed, the yolk sac is absorbed and the squab gains strength, raises it's head, and searches for food. The male pigeon and dove are the only male birds (or mammal) who develop milk. The squab is fed by the parent who happens to be on the nest when the squab shows it's hungry. The squabs place their beak into the parent's and the parent then regurgitates the contents of the crop into the squab's mouth. This procedure causes the forehead and chin feathers of the squab to grow out last because of the constant abrasion. The pigeon milk is fed the first 7-10 days. At seven days, predigested, regurgitated food from the parents' crops is given with the milk. The eyes are now open and the pinfeathers appear along with the plumage color.

Seamless aluminum leg bands should be placed on the squabs' legs at 7-10 days of age. Hold the back toe up along the shank. Slide the band over the foot and up past this back toe. The toe is then let go and the ring band lies loosely around the bottom of the shank until the squab grows into it. Seamless leg bands are always placed on young squabs and remain on the leg for life. It's a permanent identification necessary in any successful pigeon program. It's used as a means to transfer numbers and hatch years to a loft register. A loft

register is a pocket-sized book for pigeon handlers to record dates eggs are laid, dates squabs hatched, sex, color, seamless band number of each squab, etc. Records are extremely important when certain matings are to take place or certain colors are to be bred, etc. The leg bands are purchased by size according to the particular breed to be banded. Numbered identification bands must be used at shows. Bands can help recover stolen (or lost) pigeons.

In addition to seamless aluminum leg bands, seamless plastic bands are also available. These colored bands can be more easily seen and sexes or pairs can be color-coded. Many handlers use these for Racing Homers when sight distance and quick identification become more of a problem.

Squabs grow fairly slowly up to about the fourth day. After this point they gain rapidly; the changes can be observed on a daily basis (Fig. 11-18). By the sixth day they weigh about nine times as much as they did when hatched.

At 10 days, squabs begin to assert some independence, they are aware of anything and anybody who comes near. They will hiss and snap (this does not hurt). Squabs develop a ravenous appetite. If they show a lack of appetite, it means the squab is ill. At 10 days, the squabs are quite large. The pinfeathers will usually look partially broken off.

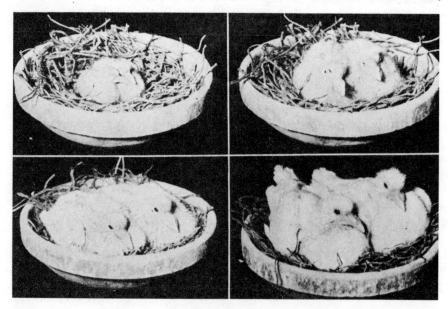

Fig. 11-18. Top left, squabs 24 hours old; top right, one week old; bottom left, two weeks old; bottom right, three weeks old.

Fig. 11-19. White King squabs still in nest and about ready for market. (Courtesy of USDA)

It's not until the fourth week the squabs are able to stand up.

When squabs are about four weeks old, they are fully feathered and very fat and clumsy (Fig. 11-19). This is the peak of growth. The first hatched squab is sometimes larger than the second hatched because it might have been more demanding of food. An occasional squab might be underfed and die when the other has been tended to more. Squabs must be removed from the nest when this peak of growth is reached for two reasons: First, the prolific parents will begin nesting again when squabs are between two and three weeks old. The parents lay a second clutch of eggs in a nest next to the first (Fig. 11-20). If a duplex nest is not provided, parents may shove squabs out of the nest and onto the floor. They immediately begin to incubate this second clutch. The cock then assumes most of the duty of feeding the first squabs. About the time the second clutch hatches, the first clutch should be weaned or removed because the parents will be busy feeding the newly hatched squabs. In a com-

mercial squab plant, the squabs are removed and butchered before they leave the nest on their own.

The second reason for removing the squabs from the nest has to do with meat quality. If squabs are allowed to leave the nest the exercise of walking very quickly diminishes the body fat and the flesh begins to harden. They are then no longer a tender, marketable squab.

Squabs are prime and ready between 25 to 32 days of age depending upon the breed, strain, and management. To check accurately for the prime time to market, lift the wings and check for pinfeathers. Look on the underside of the wing and on the body under the wing for the shiny pinfeather shafts that contain a small bristle on the end. Squabs that have pinfeathers are very difficult to dress; wait a few days longer until no pinfeathers are seen. At this point, feathers are long enough to be easily plucked without using a knife. Squabs can attain a live weight of 20-22 1/2 ounces at this age.

Keep records of those pairs that produce slow-

Fig. 11-20. On left side of duplex nest is father peering out with a squab behind. Other compartment shows squab ready for market with his mother to right. (Courtesy of Edward and Becky Mendes, Mendes and Sons Farms, CA)

and fast-feathering squabs. Pairs consistently producing slow-feathering squabs should be culled.

If squabs are to be kept and raised as future breeders, they must be weaned. The next eight weeks can be the most difficult adjustment for any squab. They must now learn how to eat and drink. This includes learning where the feed and water are located. The cock will usually continue to feed the squabs for perhaps another 10 days and will protect them somewhat from other birds. Clumsy, inexperienced squabs meet much opposition when they often get into the wrong nests, they can be injured or scalped by adult birds. The squabs must learn to keep to themselves in this new, unsociable world. The squabs will imitate the adult birds and find the food, water, and grit. Some handlers clip their tails 1 or 2 inches so they can be readily distinguished when the time comes to remove them from the loft. If left until the mating age of five to seven months old, the squabs will interfere with adult matings and production.

If the loft is crowded, or if very many squabs are to be raised, they should be removed as soon as they leave the nest. Place squabs together in a grower cage, battery, or small empty loft until breeding is desired. Do not use regular nesting materials or the matured squabs will begin to mate

before you want them to. You must wean the squabs yourself if they are thus caged. Give small, frequent feedings of small grains the first few days. If a solid floor is not in the cage bottom, place a small piece of plywood or a large, flat dish in the center in which to scatter some grains. This will assist in getting the squabs to eat.

Use the bathpan as the squabs' first waterer. Water should be only about 1 inch deep. Change frequently because it will be fouled with droppings and feed. Within a week the squabs should be pretty well on their own and cafeteria feeding can be introduced.

At seven to eight weeks the voice pitch of both sexes changes. The pitch lowers and they begin to "whoo" almost like the adults. This is called voice breaking or vocalbreak. Up until that time the timid, inactive young emit a high peeping sound. The display "cooing" is also begun, but rarely heard.

It's best to choose breeders out of those hatched early in the year. They always seem to be hardier and will be producing squabs at a time when prices are the highest—near fall and winter.

Foster parents are used for those breeds who do not parent well or have short beaks and cannot feed squabs properly. Foster parents should be those who are hardy and long-billed. They may be kept for the sole purpose of hatching and raising more expensive and fancy types of squabs, or they may be conveniently used if there is no place to put just-hatched squabs or extra stray or floor eggs. If something happens to squab parents—if they die, are disposed of, or become ill—their eggs or babies can then be given to the foster parents. This is another area where records come in handy. By checking when individual pairs began incubating a certain clutch of eggs or hatching, a handler can then place eggs or squabs of the same in the nest with these foster parents.

If one squab dies in the nest of each of two pairs, both remaining squabs can be placed in one nest to empty the other. The pair who owns the empty nest will then commence to nest and lay again. This speeds production. Some pairs will tend to as many as five squabs successfully—these make good foster parents.

Squabs can be successfully hand-fed using a number of formulas: Mash pigeon pellets fine and add boiled water until of soup consistency for first week feedings. Feed at least three times daily, preferably more frequently. After one week of age, this mash formula should be thickened by using less water. Feeding periods can then be reduced to twice daily. Another formula is to mix canned baby formula or evaporated milk with equal parts of boiled water, and then add the mashed pigeon pellets. Still another is mixing the previously mentioned diluted milk with mashed pigeon pellets and cooked cream of wheat cereal. Small grains can also be fed by soaking them in warm water for eight hours to soften. After three weeks of age, larger grains can be soaked and fed.

Feed by using an eye dropper or syringe (with needle removed) the first week. Afterwards, graduate to a plastic squeeze bottle with a long, narrow spout. Give the squabs cooled boiled water after each feeding. By the time they're four weeks old, begin to wean them (or butcher) as when removed from the nests of parents.

Pigeon eggs can also be incubated in a small incubator. This can save expensive breeds and utilize the stray and floor eggs you're bound to get in the average loft. Most of the same principles of incubation for chicken eggs holds true for pigeon eggs. Incubate at 102 degrees F. in a still-air incubator and at 98 1/2 degrees F. in a forced-air machine. Humidity (wet bulb temperature as taken with a hygrometer) should be 88 degrees the first 15 days, then raised to 92 degrees. Eggs should first be sterilized and any parasites killed by quickly immersing them in a solution of 4 cups water and 1 tablespoon of bleach. Lice can multiply quickly and kill new squabs.

Lightly mark with a pencil the date the egg was laid. Do not press too hard or the shell will crack. While incubating, turn the eggs completely from side to side at least four times daily up until the 15th day. Calculate 18 days for hatching because you might not know the exact date the second egg was laid or for that matter, which one it was. After the 15th day, keep the eggs standing on end with the large air cell portion pointing upwards. Do not frequently open the incubator door or remove the incubator top during the last few days or moisture will be lost. Open only to add eggs or more moisture. A hand sprayer can be used with small incubators to add lost moisture. Once hatched, do not leave squabs in incubator for more than two hours. If not completely dry, use a hand-held hair dryer to quickly dry the squab down to the skin, under each wing and in the crotch of the legs. Their skin is very tender so be sure the dryer is not hot. If it's hot on your hand, it's definitely too hot for the squab.

When dry, try to find a nest in the loft containing the same age squabs, preferably where one or both squabs have failed to hatch. Otherwise, incubator squabs can be placed in a nest containing two squabs the same age.

Eggs can be continually taken from pairs on the tenth day of incubation and placed in an incubator to double production. Occasionally a pair may desert partially incubated eggs. Even if deserted for up to 24 hours in warm weather, or for up to 6 hours in cold weather, the eggs have a chance to hatch if placed in an incubator or with foster parents. If placed into an incubator, the eggs should still be quickly dipped into the chlorine solution to kill lice.

CULLING AND RECORD KEEPING

Culling should begin when you first go somewhere to choose pairs for breeding. Pick only those that are good representatives of their breed. Culling is mostly done with newly hatched squabs. Culling is selection. Selection means quality birds who will not eat up your dollars unnecessarily.

Keep only those squabs and breeders that come as close to your ideal as possible. Then control matings to upgrade this ideal and consistently cull, cull, cull. Squabs should not be raised as breeders until months of record keeping have been made. In this way, you can then choose for good production. Good producers are those which lay a clutch of eggs every 30-45 days with low mortality in developing eggs and hatched squabs. It's better to keep a pair that produces only 15 eggs but raises all successfully, than to keep pairs that produce considerably more eggs but fail to raise more than 15 squabs. Twelve squabs per year is a good average. A series of infertile eggs, dead embryos, deaths upon pipping the shell, later deaths, deformities, and thin squabs are bad traits for any breed of pigeon.

Other culling is done at about four weeks. This includes looking for dark skins; sickly squabs; slow growing, oversized, or undersized squabs; loose feathering; long bodies; and feathered shanks where the breed does not include this feature. Feathered shanks are hereditary in all types of poultry and should quickly be bred out. This means dis-posing of the feather shanked birds and not breeding them or perhaps their parents. Remate (to a different mate) or dispose of pairs that do not produce well or produce poor squabs.

Cull after the productive life of the birds is over. This varies with the bird. Some breeds and strains are very productive up to six years. Some peter out by three years. Loft records will determine who is doing what and how many times. Do not rely on memory. I know of no successful handler who has ever left details to memory.

Records involve keeping written tabs on all matings, performance, and costs. Have a separate loft record book for detailed descriptions of matings and mortalities. Then keep a book to record sales and money spent (Table 11-3). Racing enthusiasts will want to keep flight records at hand. Show records should also be kept. Experienced buyers will very often ask to see your loft records. By keeping separate records, there is no need to show others your sales or purchases. Table 11-4 shows a typical loft record. The more pigeons you keep and the more serious you are about economically raising them, the more records you should keep. This is the only way a handler can tell if the venture is paying.

Records further help to adjust good or bad management practices. A specifically important management method may not reveal itself unless written information is before you. I've seen liter-

Table 11-3. Purchase and Sales Record Sample.

	Month-Paid Out			Month-Received	
Date	**April**	**Amount**	**Date**	**April**	**Amount**
Ap-23	one waterer, plas. S & H Supply Co.	$10.00	Ap-20	pair 5 year old, no. 231	$ 8.00
Ap-29	100 # pellets L. Feed Store	12.00	Ap-20	4 six week old squabs, poor coloring	12.00
Ap-29	150 feet chicken wire S & H Supply Co.	45.00		Subtotal	20.00
	Subtotal	67.00			
Date	**May**	**Amount**	**Date**	**May**	**Amount**
Ma-14	50 # oyster shell L. Feed Store	3.00	Ma-20	3, 3- x -4 foot wire cages	$24.00

Table 11-4. Sample Breeding Loft Chart.

BREEDING RECORD									
Year _____ Pair no. _____ Owner _____									
Cock no. _____ Color _____ Markings _____ Sire _____ Dam _____									
Hen no. _____ Color _____ Markings _____ Sire _____ Dam _____									

Egg no.	Date Laid	Date Hatched	Date Banded	Band Number	Breed Type	Color	Markings	Sex	Remarks

ally hundreds of various businesses fail simply because the all important records were not faithfully kept. Depreciation of housing and equipment should also be figured.

If you really want to know how well you're doing with your squab venture, the following will help you determine how much it's costing you (in feed) to produce each pound of squab meat: (1) Take the total squabs produced during one year and multiply by their average live weight per squab in ounces. (2) Divide the total ounces by 16 ounces to get pounds of meat per year. (3) Next, multiply the total pounds of feed per year (for squabbers and their young) by the cost per pound of the feed. (4) Divide this answer by the total pounds of meat to find the cents per pound to produce the meat. Other expenses, such as utilities, can be added to the feed costs to be more accurate. Example follows:

(1) 15 squabs × 14 oz. = 210 oz.
(2) 210 oz. ÷ 16 oz. = 13.125 lbs. meat
(3) 100 lbs. feed × 12¢ = $12.00
(4) $12.00 ÷ 13.125 lbs. = 91.43 cents per lb.

Squab income from your loft must reach the total feed costs in (3) in order for a handler to break even on feed alone.

BUTCHERING SQUABS

Squabs are the "what is it" meat of most parts of the country. If there is not presently an active market in your section of the country, you can contact many butchers about obtaining squab and they'll respond: "What is it?"

Active markets exist in most large metropolitan cities and trade is mainly from restaurants and hotels. Chinese consumers represent the largest consumer trade and are concentrated largely in San Francisco, Los Angeles and New York areas. Where active markets do not exist, the wholesome, tender, delectable squab cannot even be special ordered. The main active markets in the U.S. lie along the Eastern seaboard, the Dallas-Houston area, Los Angeles, Chicago, and New York. The market continues to grow yearly.

Squab can cost about $6 (sometimes more) for one bird. This might not seem expensive since many game birds and beefsteak cuts run the same per pound on the open market. The accumulated costs of raising, slaughtering, packing, and shipping (usually by airplane) contribute to it's price.

Without constructing elaborate buildings, a small-scale handler can figure an average cost of slightly over $1 per pound for the meat acquired from raising his own squabs. Each pair of squab-

Fig. 11-21. A naugahyde folding training basket with doweled top has both single-release and multiple-release doors for releasing one bird or a basketful at once. (Courtesy of Foy's Pigeon Supplies)

bing pigeons and their 12 squabs consuming 112 pounds of feed per year should net a handler about 9-12 pounds of squab meat per year. The average small-scale broiler grower raises 50-100 chickens for his family of four per year. This is from 200 to 400 pounds of meat. To raise the same amount of squab meat, a handler will need 20 to 40 pairs of squabbing pigeons.

Usually squabs are gathered the night before or eight hours before butchering and are given water, but no feed. This allows the crop to empty and makes eviscerating easier and more sanitary. Long confinement before butchering will result in noticeable skin scratches on the carcass from the squabs climbing over one another. Also, some plumpness and weight is lost. Do not crowd squabs in a container or cage because they can suffocate. Confinement is not actually necessary at all. Crops can be quickly rinsed and flushed of feed after butchering. If the heads are to be removed, the crop can be carefully removed even if full of feed.

Collect the squabs in a small cage, a pigeon carrier, or a folding training release basket. The ideal container is only 6 inches tall, so squabs cannot freely climb over one another. The new high-impact plastic quail coops by Kuhl are idea for collecting and holding squabs. When only a few are to be butchered, the container type is of less concern.

When home slaughtering, the head is usually cut off and the carcass allowed to bleed freely a few seconds. The Chinese culture is very adamant about having the head and legs attached to their dressed squabs, and sometimes require that the birds not be eviscerated. New York dressed squabs are those that still contain the viscera. Some of these squabs are still shipped to places such as New York. Most squabs are American dressed, that is, with feet, head, and viscera removed. This is the type most small-scale handlers are interested in.

A funnel holding-rack can be constructed to hold a number of birds at a time (Fig. 11-22). The squabs are placed head down into the cone funnels so struggling is hindered. When cones are used, the most efficient, quick, and humane method of slaughter—sticking (piercing the brain)—can be accomplished. Cones will probably have to be homemade; small cones for squabs seem unobtainable. Cones should be 7 inches long, 5 inches across the top, and 2 3/4 inches across the narrow bottom. A piece of bendable sheet-metal, 10 1/2 inches by 8 inches, can be formed into a cone. The cones are then nailed onto a platform or rack a few inches apart. Do not keep the squabs alive too long in the cones or they may die. Funnel only as many as can be done in about 10 minutes or so.

Sticking is the best method for killing. This loosens the feathers so scalding is not necessary. If squabs are scalded, their tender young skin will quickly loose its bloom and can tear easily. Scalding is done at commercial plants because it's faster. If sticking is not done, the birds must be scalded. Use a semi-soft scald with a water temperature of about 128 degrees F. (53 degrees C.). When sticking, use a narrow boning knife (available at all butcher supply houses), insert the blade into the mouth, and pierce it firmly and quickly up through the roof of the mouth into the brain. Give a slight twist and quickly pull out. The squab will cease moving in a few seconds. Allow it to bleed freely and to stiffen slightly before removing from funnel.

Pick the feathers soon after killing. The sooner they are picked after killing, the easier the feathers will come out. Pull the large wing and tail feathers first, being careful not to tear the tender flesh. Pull only a few at a time, to help avoid tearing skin. Remove the body feathers next by pulling small handfuls backwards. Pinfeathers should not be present if the squabs were collected at the prime point. If some are present use a blunt butter knife or pinning knife to squeeze the feathers and grab against the thumb to remove.

The head and feet can now be removed. Cut the head off by cutting as far up the neck as possible. Remove the feet by cutting through the hock joint. Some squabs may have vestigial feathers (hairs) that should be singed off.

Because squabs are so small, it's best to eviscerate as soon as possible before the legs stiffen. When done soon, the legs can be spread easier to remove the viscera. Lay the squab on its back. First cut a slit in the neck skin to the side of the crop. Carefully pull crop through slit and cut loose. Then cut a shallow slit in the skin just below the keelbone, above the vent. Point the blade edge away from the carcass when cutting to prevent cutting into the intestines. From this slit, cut another slit down towards the vent to one side. With two fingers, reach in and pinch the intestine attached to the vent. Then, cut a circle around the vent so it comes free. With fingers inserted, reach in just above the keelbone and pull the mass of viscera out through the opening. Completely butchering eight squabs per hour is a good rate.

Chill the carcasses well by immersing in ice-cold water for 1-3 hours. It's best to run ice-cold water over the carcasses while in the container so the loose feathers and debris overflow out of the container. In warm weather, run more ice-cold tap water into the container. Chilling removes the body heat from the whole carcass all the way through to

Fig. 11-22. Rack and four funnel cones that can be hung as shown or built upon a stand.

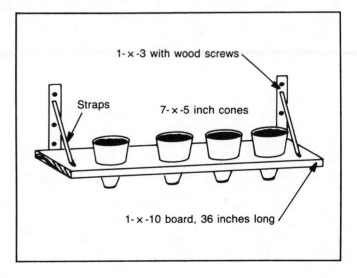

1- x -3 with wood screws

Straps

7- x -5 inch cones

1- x -10 board, 36 inches long

the inside. When chilled, remove and stand the carcasses on end so they drain well before refrigerating or freezing.

STORING AND USING SQUAB MEAT

Squab meat is almost too tender to can, although it can be done following the directions in canning books. When only a few squabs are occasionally butchered, it's usually more convenient to freeze the birds; canning requires quite a few birds. The squabs can be frozen whole or split down the breast and flattened. They can then be layered into freezing bags. Two small squabs will usually fit into a quart-size, zipper-type freezer bag.

Squab can be used any way other poultry are used. The average 14-ounce dressed squab is considered two servings. A small Homer squab of only 7-8 ounces would only be one serving (Fig. 11-23). Some squab recipes follow:

Mandarin Squab. Blend 1/2 cup of flour with 1 teaspoon salt, 1/4 teaspoon pepper and 1 teaspoon paprika. Coat two split, ready-to-cook (14-16-ounce) squabs with this mixture. Brown the coated squabs in small amount of fat. Sprinkle with 1/4 teaspoon ground cloves and 1/4 teaspoon ground nutmeg. Cover and cook until tender and done, about 25 minutes. Blend 3 tablespoons cornstarch with 1/2 cup water, then add 1 cup pineapple juice and 1 cup orange juice; cook until thickened, stirring constantly. Add 1 cup pineapple chunks and sections from 2 oranges. Pour over the cooked squab and serve with rice. Serves 4.

Almond Squab with Rice. Brown 1/2 cup blanched almonds in 1 tablespoon of oil. In another pan, combine one mashed clove of garlic, 1 teaspoon salt, and 1 tablespoon oil with one cooked and boned squab (12 ounces). Brown lightly. Add 1 cup sliced bamboo shoots and 1/2 cup sliced mushrooms; brown lightly. Add 2 tablespoons liquid from the mushrooms or bamboo shoots. Cover tightly and cook over low heat for 5 minutes. Add 1/2 cup sliced water chestnuts, 1/2 cup sliced celery, and the browned almonds; heat through. Blend 2 teaspoons cornstarch, 1/2 teaspoon sugar, 1/4 cup water and 2 teaspoons soy sauce. Add to vegetables and cook over low heat until thickened and

Fig. 11-23. Comparison size of 7 1/2-ounce racing squab to a fork.

smooth. Serve over hot cooked rice. Garnish with chopped green onions. Serves 4.

PIGEON HEALTH

Pigeons are subject to many of the diseases that affect other poultry, and similar treatments are effective. Good management and sanitation along with observing symptoms will help a handler to correct the problem. Many handlers believe canker (trichomoniasis) is the most common disease of pigeons, but paratyphoid and Mycoplasma gallisepticum supposedly affect them more. These are described in detail in Chapter 7. Following are problems particular to pigeons.

Canker (Trichomoniasis or Trich)

This is a serious disease caused by protozoan organisms. There is both an upper form and a lower form. The upper form is the disease that most affects pigeons. Adult pigeons transmit the disease to the young squabs in the pigeon milk. It's a killer of young squabs of about 2 weeks of age. The parent birds can appear unaffected by the organisms.

The organisms are present in the greenish mouth fluids and are seen under a microscope of low magnification. The upper form shows as depression, sunken and empty crops, drooling, stretching of the neck, swallowing, and a bad odor. There are lesions showing as yellowish-white pustules, crust formations, and ulcerations mainly about the mouth, esophagus, and crop. Those in the throat grow large enough to close off the windpipe opening and suffocate the bird. There are also cheesy-looking exudates in the upper digestive tract and nodules in the lungs and liver.

The most popular treatment is to swab the throat with a mild astringent when the condition is first noticed. The preferred medication is Emtryl, manufactured by the Salsbury laboratories. It's administered in the drinking water. Another medication is Enheptin, which is given in the feed, water, or individually in capsules.

Poor sanitation and management can bring about the disease. Pigeons and other free-flying birds can easily spread the disease to other poultry. It is spread from bird to bird or by coming in contact with stagnant pools of water, contaminated feed, litter, and water. Recovered birds remain carriers to infect others. Segregate susceptible birds from these carrier birds. Further management controls include screening out wild birds from the loft, segregating young birds from adults, and keeping grounds free from standing pools of stagnant water. Prevention and management for canker is the same as for blackhead in turkeys.

Cannibalism

This problem shows up as scalping, mainly of young squabs who just leave the nest. Other pigeons begin pecking at the squab until his head is raw and bleeding. Young squabs must be watched when they are about to leave the nest. It's best to remove them to a separate loft or cage before this happens. If a squab is found scalped and it's not too bad, spray the wound with an antiseptic such as Blu-Kote. Remove the bird from the loft and place into a separate cage until the wound heals completely. A pecked on bird will become shy of other birds and must be introduced gradually and watched.

Pigeon Malaria (Haemoproteus infection)

This is a malaria-like disease of pigeons, doves,

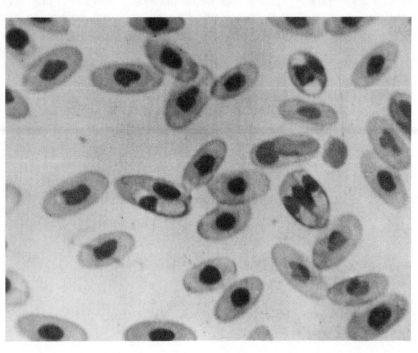

Fig. 11-24. Blood cells of pigeon as seen under a microscope, parasite showing in each cell as a dark form in pigeon malaria. (Courtesy of L. Dwight Schwartz, D.V.M., Senior Pathologist, Michigan State University)

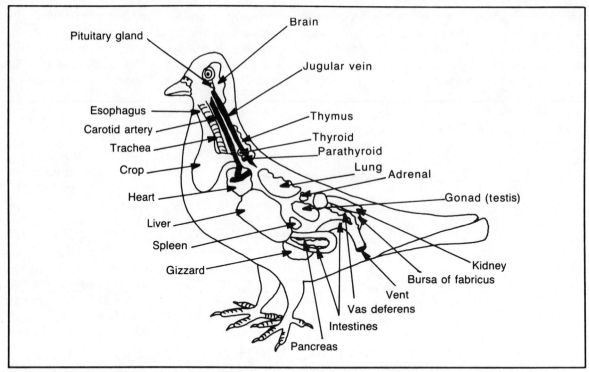

Fig. 11-25. Internal organs of a pigeon (male). (Information courtesy of Syed Bokhari)

quail, ducks, and songbirds. It is caused by a blood cell parasite (Fig. 11-24). Transmitted by blood sucking flies. Biting midges transmit disease to ducks.

Symptoms are weakness, no appetite—the same as with malaria. Use antimalarial drugs. Prevent by controlling insects and administering low-level medication.

Other problems referred to in Chapter 6 that can affect pigeons include the following: Arizona infection, avian TB, bumblefoot, cannibalism, external parasites, fowl pox (pigeon pox), infectious catarrhal enteritis (hexamitiasis), internal parasites, mycoplasma gallisepticum (MG), paratyphoid, poisoning and vent gleet (candidiasis).

Figure 11-25 can help a handler to diagnose problems by showing where the various organs of a pigeon are situated.

Part 4

Ducks and Geese

Chapter 12

Choosing Your Ducklings

ORIGIN AND HISTORY

The Wild Mallard is the ancestor to all ducks that have been domesticated for meat or eggs (Fig. 12-1). The Mallard is the only wild breed of duck that has curled sex-feathers on the tail. These are the two hard, curled feathers growing from the upper portion of the tail in drakes. These feathers grow upward and forward. The Wild Mallard occupies most of the northern hemisphere, so it's easy to see why so many of the domestic breeds were propagated from it.

The Muscovey duck is the only duck that cannot credit the Mallard for its breed. The Muscovey is a distinct species. It originated in the mountainous jungles of Peru, Brazil, Bolivia, and Ecuador near the headwaters of the Amazon River. It's thought the South American Inca Indians first domesticated the Muscovey, and when the Spaniards and Portuguese came to South America, they took some of these ducks to other parts of the world.

Muscovies are found wild in the warm regions of South America. They are called by different names throughout the world. In southern Europe and northern Africa they are the Barbary duck. In Brazil, they are simply the Brazilian duck. In the Guianas, it's the Guinea duck or Turkish duck because of the carnucled face. The Spanish refer to it as the Pato as do some handlers in the United States. Other names include the Cairon duck, the Indian duck, the Musk duck, and the Turkey duck. When called the Guinea duck in the early 1800s, the Muscovey was a very commonly served cuisine feast. The Muscovey later became known as the Barbary. French waterfowl standards still list it as such.

The mystical Muscovey has had scientists stumped for years. They cannot place it into the category of any particular species such as the duck, goose, chicken, or turkey. It has a body like a duck, it nests, attacks predators, and hisses like a goose, it roosts like a chicken, and has a plump breast like a turkey.

In early years, when game and waterfowl eggs were abundant, ducks were kept mainly for convenience. Some countries kept them for meat and

Fig. 12-1. Mallard drake (photo by Peter Carboni, courtesy of U.S. Fish and Wildlife Service)

eggs. Fancy breeds were mainly kept by royalty. With the growing civilization and declining waterfowl population, more restrictions were placed upon hunting, either voluntarily or by law. Farmers began to keep a few ducks for food. It was not until the early 1870s that Pekins, Aylesburies, Rouens, Muscovies, Cayugas, and Crested ducks were kept in any great numbers. A trade started about 1850 when the demand for duckling meat began to increase, especially among the foreign-born population.

Before duckling meat become popular, farmers declined to raise them because it wasn't considered profitable. Those which were raised were made to forage for most of their feed. Many bodies of water existed that the ducks willingly frequented. Their diets consisted of plenty of fish and other water foods. Later, around 1900, handlers began feeding grains which improved the looks and taste of

the meat. With this, the demand increased until today where more than 15 million ducklings are commercially raised for meat every year in the United States. Ducks also became a great pastime. Both poultry shows and an effort by growers to upgrade breeds for economic reasons led to many improvements.

MEAT BREEDS AND GENERAL PURPOSE

Large and medium weight ducks are raised for meat. Some people feel duck meat tastes like a cross between beef and chicken. "Duckling" refers to young ducks used for meat. Commercially, this is called "green duck." Ducks used for meat include standard breeds of the Aylesbury, Buff (Orpington), Cayuga, Crested, Muscovey (Pato), Pekin, Rouen, and Swedish. Breeds not in the Standard book but usable for meat are other varieties of the Orpington family and the Pommern duck. The largest

234

breed is the Muscovey, although it grows slower than White Pekins. The Mammoth White Pekins are more of a commercial strain of Pekins. They are similar to the famous Long Island ducks. Both Pekins and Muscovies are among the 15 million raised commercially for meat every year in the United States. This number has not changed much in the last few decades since duckling is generally regarded as a special occasion or holiday item.

Pekin

The Pekin breed is most popular with commercial growers (Fig. 12-2). The breed originated in China and was introduced into the United States in 1873. The popularity of the Pekin here is due to its fast growth rate and yellow skin. The average Pekin will reach a live market weight of about 8 pounds in 8 weeks. This is the fastest-growing duck of all, indeed it is the fastest growing of any fowl. They must not be allowed to grow past 10 weeks of age or they are extremely difficult to pick because of pinfeathers. Also, the conversion of feed to meat declines rapidly. Otherwise, their slightly cream white plumage plucks nicely and leaves a good-looking, clean carcass of 5-6 1/2 pounds (Table 12-1).

If a very yellow skin is not desired in the finished bird, pigment-producing feeds such as alfalfa meal, corn, corn gluten meal, and pasture grass should be considerably reduced in their diets toward the end of the growing period. Oats, kaffir, and milo can be substituted. It's the lutein in alfalfa meal that imparts a yellow color.

Pekins can be considered general purpose because they do lay a fair amount of white eggs. The average amount of eggs per season is 160. Some are good setters but most are not. Some good setters and hatchers will viciously try to protect their young as Muscovies do. The Pekins' natural nervousness sometimes causes them to abandon a nest if disturbed.

Muscovey

In many areas the Muscovey (Fig. 12-3) is the duck of choice because it's not fatty. It has the firmest meat of any duck, and a creamy yellow skin that looks appealing when dressed out. It has a distinct skin pattern and a plump body with dimpled breasts. The flesh has been considered to be of a higher quality than other ducks and has a more wild flavor that complements wine sauces, fruit, and rice especially well. The flesh contains barely any fat,

Fig. 12-2. Pair of Pekin ducks.

	Liveweight (pounds)	Dressed Weight (pounds)	Age (weeks)
Pekin drake	8	6 1/2	8
Pekin duck	7	5	8
Muscovey drake	10	8	16
Muscovey duck	4	3	16

Table 12-1. Average Live and Dressed Weights of Pekin and Muscovey Ducks.

so less cooking time is required. The average dressed-out weight is 7-8 pounds for a drake and 3-3 1/2 pounds for a hen (Table 12-1). The standard weight for young drakes is 10 pounds and for young ducks, 6 pounds. The drakes easily reach this weight, but it's rare for a female to go over 4 pounds. Muscovies must be butchered by 16 weeks before flesh firms. The Muscovey is highly regarded by French chefs because of its distinct flavor, firm meat, and high yield.

Muscovies lay a good amount of eggs and are very prolific, but they should not be considered for eggs only. Because they raise a large amount of ducklings, they also are very broody. When fowl are broody, they do not lay eggs, but are interested only in setting and hatching young. They succeed very well in this because they are insistent—

including the drake who very often tries to keep the hen on the nest by chasing her. From her yearly 45 eggs, the duck will hatch 30-35 and raise them all! The Muscovey incubation period is 33-35 days.

A drake will take on other animals much larger than himself, especially during the breeding season. He can truly be the bully of the farm. Some handlers call him ugly, sassy, and a pest. It's sometimes necessary to dispose of such males because of their aggressiveness and the trouble they cause. It's not good to keep more than one drake for each six hens. If kept with a flock of chickens, the drakes will sometimes keep roosters from hen chickens and beat them up in the process. Some roosters become shy and nonaggressive with their own hens. Drakes can also become quite possessive of hen chickens and will attack a handler who dares to pick one up.

Fig. 12-3. Pair of White Muscovey ducks with their brood.

236

Year-old Muscovey drakes get up to 12 pounds and are hard to handle. They are the strongest and most vicious of all domestic fowl. Although the drakes are not very friendly as pets, the ducks (hens) can be quite docile—but don't expect them to follow you like a puppy. Muscovies are very independent. To pick up a Muscovey, grasp firmly and strongly at the base of both wings using one hand on each wing with the duck's back snug to your body. Otherwise, their powerful wings and sharp claws can hurt you.

Muscovies can fly—especially the lighter weight hens. Most don't attempt to fly to any great length until close to fall. Large drakes are unable to fly. Although lightweight Muscovies can fly, they do not migrate. If their flying becomes bothersome, as when they fly into neighbors' yards, they should either be confined or have their wing feathers clipped. This flying enables Muscovies to perch on the tops of barns, houses, fences, and trees. Unlike other ducks, the Muscovey has very long, sharp claws adapted for perching. In the poultry house, the Muscovey likes a perch the same as chickens. Muscovey ducks (hens) will also very often use wall-hung nests. Generally, they make a nest as most other ducks do.

The other unusual traits about Muscovies are their absence of curled sex-feathers in the tail, their exaggerated head-bobbing, and their voice. Unlike other ducks, Muscovies aren't noisy and don't quack; they hiss. Early in the century, they were sometimes called the Musk duck because of a musk odor on the skin. Even then, it was considered a grotesque-looking, pugnacious, quarrelsome, violent bird.

Muscovies will cross-mate with other breeds of ducks, but the offspring are sterile and are called mule ducks. These hybrid mule ducks are purposely produced in some countries using female Muscovies and Mallard type drakes. Only four varieties are recognized by the Standard: White, Colored, Chocolate, and Blue. All Muscovies have a red, fleshy protuberance around the eyes and extending partially over the top of the bill. This is called a carnucle, caruncle, or tubercle. The tubercle usually refers to the small knob on the top base. The drakes have thicker and larger carnucles than

the females. At hatching time, the smallest ducklings are usually the females.

The White Muscovey is the most popular variety for meat, although any can be eaten. It has pure white feathers throughout with a pinkish bill, pale orange shanks, and very human-looking blue eyes.

The Colored Muscovey (admitted to the Standard in 1904), is mistakenly referred to by many handlers as any Muscovey which is white and another color, such as brown and white, black and white (pied) and an occasional tri-color. By standards it is an all black duck with a patch of white on the wing bows and bars (Fig. 12-4). A Muscovey resembling this is, in turn, mistakenly referred to as a Black Muscovey. A Colored Muscovey will breed true to the standard description. The Muscovies of mixed colors are at present a farm duck. This is only a problem if they are to be shown since no standard can be given to Muscovies who hatch any color.

It's interesting to see the many colors hatch. Mixed colors can even throw all chocolate, all black, all brown, all blue (slate-colored), and pure white. When later mated, these single-colored birds also can hatch any color duckling. If two whites from parents of mixed colors are mated, this can result in quite a few white ducklings, but matings of mixed colors results in very few pure white ducklings. Therefore, if your aim is for lots of white ducklings to raise for meat, seek pure white pairs.

The standard Blue and the Chocolate Muscovies are more recent introductions. The Blue was admitted to the Standard in 1950 and the Chocolate in 1982. Both are solid-colored except for a patch of white on the wing bows and bars.

Aylesbury

The Aylesbury is a 7-9-pound pure white duck that originated in England and was introduced into the United States around 1870 (Fig. 12-5). It has always been a favorite in England because of its white-skinned carcass. The yellow-skinned Pekins never went over well in England, and the Aylesbury was never popular here because of its pinkish, flesh-colored bill.

Fig. 12-4. Pair of Black Muscovey ducks. (Courtesy of Watt Publishing Co.)

Like the Pekin, the Aylesbury will reach a market weight of 7 pounds in 8 weeks. The Aylesbury usually appears larger than a Pekin because its feathers are looser and it has a much deeper keel. The keel is long, straight, and deep—nearly touching the ground. The Aylesbury has much whiter feathers than a Pekin. Their egg production is usually lower than the Pekin, although there have

Fig. 12-5. Pair of Aylesbury ducks.

been records showing 300 eggs per year. They are less nervous than Pekins but still do not sit on eggs well.

Because the pale, flesh-colored bill is preferred for exhibition, care should be taken to keep them from ranging grass and eating rations with xanthophyll pigments that will color the bill and possibly the skin yellow. This means not feeding alfalfa meal, yellow corn, or corn gluten meal for 30 days before a show or before butchering.

Buff

The Buff was admitted to the Standard in 1914 and is actually a variety of the breed Orpingtons for which four other varieties exist. Besides the American Buff of a rich fawn buff color, there is the English Buff of a rich reddish fawn color, the Black with a white bib, Chocolate with a white bib, and a Blue with markings the same as a Blue Swedish—that is, bluish-slate with white bib and two white primaries on each wing. Characteristic to all Orpingtons are blue pupils. If this does not exist, it is evidence of crossbreeding.

Slightly smaller than the Aylesburies and Pekins, the Orpingtons will lay very well if not allowed to get too heavy. They originally were considered an egg breed duck only. The Buff variety is the most popular in the United States. It will dress as clean as a white duck. It is a good general-purpose duck. The Orpington ducks were developed at Orpington, England where the Orpington chickens were also developed.

Cayuga

The Cayuga is a very handsome, all-black duck. It was produced from a strain of ducks near Cayuga Lake in New York State. The original Cayuga was slightly larger and more of a dark brown shade— long before its admittance to the Standard in 1874. It's believed that the East India duck was crossed with the Cayuga to produce more black plumage, which could account for its smaller size of 7 pounds for a young drake. Unlike the Aylesbury and Pekin who reach 7 pounds in 8 weeks, other heavy ducks such as the Cayuga take from 12 to 16 weeks to finish as a market bird. Its black feathers and dark gray to bluish-green eggs have prevented its popularity as a utility bird. Many raise the Cayuga for exhibition.

Rouen

The Rouen is very popular among duck handlers

Fig. 12-6. Pair of Rouen ducks.

and nonfarming individuals for decorating their ponds. The Rouen is colored like the wild Mallard but is too heavy to fly away (Fig. 12-6). Many beginners or those purchasing Rouens as a pond ornament, mistakenly refer to it as a Mallard.

The Rouen was developed by the English and then imported to the United States. Young Rouens reach 7-8 pounds, but the bulk isn't gained until just after 12 weeks. During the eclipse molt at the end of summer, the Rouen drakes resemble the females in color and lack of sex-feathers. The duck can lay an egg about every other day. The egg is of a blue tint. Rouens hardly ever are inclined to sit on a clutch of eggs. In fact, many are egg droppers and never nest even for laying. It was admitted to the Standard in 1874.

Crested

The Crested duck draws attention because of the puffball it sports on top of its head (Fig. 12-7). The puffball, more correctly termed the crest, is not a unique feature obtained simply by mating a pair of authentic Crested ducks together. A Crested duck is not simply a white duck with a crest; it is a defined breed of its own. Hence, it is not termed a Crested White duck, but more correctly, a White Crested duck.

A Crested does not actually breed true. The reproducing cells carry lethal genes in one-fourth of the fertile eggs, which kills the developing embryo before hatching. Only two-thirds of the remaining fertile eggs will develop ducks that have a crest. The other one-third will not develop crests and will not carry genes to produce crests in future generations. These are then simply a white duck.

Many handlers are inclined to raise the Crested duck for ornamental or exhibition purposes only. This does not have to be the case. Crested ducks lay very well. They lay better than most other heavy breeds and they can be very good sitters. This is how Nature sometimes compensates for other faults. It's important to look and breed for a good crest formation and an only slightly arched neck. A good crest should be fairly large, well-balanced, and firmly attached on the crown of the head. Some have been found attached by very lit-tle flesh, hanging to one side of the head, appearing as only small protrusions, or so large as to impede the duck's sight.

Their growth is better than many heavy breeds. The young drakes attain a weight of 6 pounds, young hens, 5 pounds. The White Crested duck has been recognized in the Standard since 1874. A more recent variety, the Black Crested, was admitted to the Standard in 1977.

Swedish

The Swedish ducks comprise two varieties: The Blue Swedish admitted to the Standard in 1904, and the Black Swedish presently not recognized by the American Poultry Association.

Similar to the problems encountered breeding a true type in the Crested duck, Blue Swedish matings do not naturally produce the desired uniform slate blue throughout. Most will hatch as Blues but Blacks and those with specks of white over the plumage will also be found. If a handler wants to combine utility with genetic improvement and breeding practice, both the Crested and Blue Swedish can be used to advantage by butchering those that don't conform, and breeding the best to upgrade the breed and flock. Poor characteristics are therefore not able to be rebred into a fowl when unthinking handlers have access to these birds.

The dark feathers of this breed have shut it from the commercial markets, but the medium size of 6 1/2 pounds for young drakes is still a very usable size for a small family's table. The ducks lay fairly well and will occasionally sit on eggs. As with other black and blue ducks, the eggs are of a gray to bluish-green tint.

EGG BREEDS

There are two main breeds of ducks that are bred for egg-laying and/or exhibition only. These are the Khaki Campbells and the Indian Runners. Both are unique in form; the Indian Runners have a much more exaggerated upright stance.

Khaki Campbell

The Campbell breed is comprised of three

Fig. 12-7. Pair of White Crested ducks.

varieties—the Khaki, which is the original variety developed by Adele Campbell of Gloucester, England around 1900; the Dark Campbell; and the White Campbell. The Khaki variety is the only variety admitted to the Standard in America. This was accomplished in 1941. Campbell's endeavors in developing the breed were for the purpose of a high egg-producing breed. She never wanted it to become an exhibition bird, although it has.

The original strains are lighter in weight than some, and their carriage is slightly upward, and a young drake weighs about 4 pounds. Other strains have weights of 5 pounds in 10 weeks, their bodies are wider, and they can be used for meat. This is good when surplus drakes must be utilized.

Laying an off-white colored egg, the Campbell can rival any good egg breed chicken. Using a lighting system, Campbells will lay throughout the winter months when daylight hours are naturally shorter. The most common color of Campbells is that of withered grass or khaki military uniforms. The head is a darker contrasting color.

Campbells are more nervous and flighty than other strains of ducks. Females rarely set on eggs. This flightiness can be bothersome to some handlers. The ducks, like Runners, will stampede together up against a fence or wall when approached. Walk slowly towards them when caring for them. Both breeds will forage, although they do well in confinement when good layer rations are provided.

Runner

This breed is commonly called the Indian Runner (Fig. 12-8). It originated in Asia. There are eight standard varieties listed in the *American Standard of Perfection*. A Fawn variety also exists which is not recognized. The Fawn and White variety were the first to be admitted to the Standard in 1898. This was followed by the White in 1914, the Penciled in 1914, and then the Black, Buff, Chocolate, the Cumberland Blue and the Gray in 1977.

Indian Runners became very popular in this country and others. In fact, Germany conducts individual Indian Runner shows consisting of

Fig. 12-8. Fawn and White Runner pair on left, White Runner pair on right. (Courtesy of Watt Publishing Co.)

hundreds of entries in all the new color varieties.

The weights of Runners are 4 pounds for a young drake and 3 1/2 pounds for a young duck.

The upright carriage is exaggerated in some illustrations. This is perhaps an effort by some fanciers to stay as close to the ideal as possible. The White variety has been bred towards this perpendicular carriage moreso than other varieties. This might be the ideal, but I've had some very good strains that were excellent layers but could not reproduce. The other color varieties with a more forward carriage always produced good, fertile eggs.

The Runner is referred to as the Leghorn of the duck family. A lighting system will keep Runners laying throughout the winter months, but the environment must not be allowed to become cold. The dark varieties lay a tinted blue egg. The Gray Runner drake is colored exactly as a Mallard drake and the duck exactly as the Mallard duck. The Gray Runner lays a tinted blue egg also. Runners run rather than waddle like other breeds. It's quite a spectacle to see a group of these ducks run to and fro in a synchronal pattern while quacking almost simultaneously. Herding dogs, such as Australian Shepherds, are frequently trained with a group of Runners. Runners can run extremely fast, and be-

cause of their tendency towards flightiness, can take days to capture by hand. They should be fenced or confined. They use their wings to balance and gain speed on the ground, but wing clipping does little to keep them still.

BANTAM AND ORNAMENTAL BREEDS

The bantam breeds of ducks consist of the Calls, East India, and the Mallard. These are only the breeds admitted in the Standard of Perfection. Some wild breeds raised are also considered bantams because they are small. Such is the case with the cheerfully colored little 24-ounce oriental Mandarins and the attractive 20- to 24-ounce Wood ducks that nest in trees. Both are harder to tame. The Harlequin has become popular with duck fanciers in recent years. These ducks are some of the most colorful of those found wild.

Call

Calls are small fellows that run up to 18 ounces. They are considered miniature breeds of ducks, and are the smallest of any domesticated or semi-domesticated duck. The Gray Call and the White Call were first admitted to the American Standard of Perfection in 1874. The Gray Call was originally developed in Great Britain and was widely used in the mid-nineteenth century to lure wild ducks to the hunter. All Call ducks are very loud when calling their mate, so the Calls made an ideal decoy.

A Blue variety, colored like the Blue Swedish Duck, was admitted to the American Standard in 1977. The latest addition in 1982 was the Snowy Call whose base plumage is white with lacings of fawn and stipplings of gray on the females and gray stippling and claret (purplish-red) lacings on the drake.

Just-hatched Calls can be quite delicate. Duck starter crumbles should be mashed and slightly moistened for them during the first week. Calls are good setters but they prefer to be alone.

East India

This is an old breed admitted to the American Standard in 1874. It's a lustrous, greenish-black duck of up to 26 ounces. The East India's origin is obscure because there are no wild black ducks it can be traced back to. It seems the only wild duck it has any link to is the Mallard. The East India duck has the same sex-feathers as the Mallard and the domestic breeds that originated from the wild Mallard. It's claimed the English developed the breed to what we know it today, although they, in turn, claim it originated in America.

The East India is a very good egg layer. The eggs are first covered with a black film over a deep blue-green, then change to a lighter blue. One strange feature of the East India is the two molts it goes through annually. Other ducks molt only once a year.

Mallard

The common Mallard is seen on ponds more than any other breed of duck, next to the Rouens. It's the favorite for those who wish to simply decorate their ponds. The standard weight for the Mallard is 36 ounces for a young drake. This entitles it to be classed a bantam. It was surprisingly not admitted to the Standard until 1961, although it is the ancestor to all domestic breeds (except the Muscovey).

The Mallard was first domesticated 2,000 years ago in China. The wild Black duck of eastern North America is often mistaken for the wild Mallard. Both sexes of the Black duck resemble only the female Mallard's plumage, but they are still frequently referred to as a Black Mallard. Black ducks are not black and the Black duck drakes do not have the curled sex-feathers as the Mallard does. The Black duck is a very wild breed that cannot be successfully domesticated.

The wild Mallard occupies most of the northern hemisphere. It's abundant where its habitat has not been destroyed. The Mallard seems to be the only wild breed that can become very domesticated. After a few generations they lose their migratory instinct, yet if previous generations are kept a few years, the urge sooner or later comes and they might fly off with the wild ones. Successive breeding also changes their looks; they become more thick-bodied and their flavor begins to lose much of the gamey taste often sought after in wild game.

Domesticated Mallards will breed freely with more than one breed or mate. It seems pairs that keep to themselves and do not care to intermate with others, are closer to the wild than the domesticated state. These drakes will stay with the female until she begins to incubate eggs and then, if wild Mallard drakes are nearby in water, they will usually spend their days with them. Many young are lost to snakes, frogs, turtles, raccoons, and hawks.

For thousands of years, the Mallard has provided mankind with meat, eggs, feathers, and domestic breeds of ducks. Thousands are raised annually to stock game preserves. The wild Mallard is very adaptable to the foods available in a given area. They eat grass, water plants, nuts, acorns, seeds, rice, fruits, bayberries, grapes, sour gum fruits, algae, dogwood fruits, hornwort, pondweed tubers, water shield, widgeon grass, reeds, wild celery, arrowhead roots, millweed, horned pondweed seeds, mermaid weed seeds, tadpoles, small fish, toads, frogs, crayfish, snails, newts, lizards, fly larvae, earthworms, beetles, baby fish, leeches, dragon fly nymphs, mussels, and mice.

In southern parts of the United States, crayfish destroy dikes and levees when they burrow into them. The Mallard is considered useful because it feeds upon these crayfish. The Mallard also cleans rice fields of volunteer and scattered rice, which improves the quality and quantity of the crop. Mallards are important in keeping over-abundant pond growth reduced, which could otherwise deplete the oxygen and kill fish. This is especially true during the middle of summer when aquatic plants grow the fastest. Many pond owners purposely keep a few ducks or geese on the water to prevent this overgrowth from getting out of hand.

Mallards are very prolific. A clutch in a nest consist of from 9-12 greenish-buff-colored eggs. If the nest is destroyed, the female will often renest and incubate another clutch. Layer rations should be fed to all breeder ducks to ensure production.

Mandarin

This is a very colorful, cobby little duck which is related to the Carolina Wood duck also kept by fanciers. The Mandarin is considered by many to be the most beautiful of the fancy breeds kept in captivity. Unlike the Mallard, Mandarins do not usually cross with other ducks. When domesticated, their colors can fade. A color-producing feed should be given. The most outstanding features of the Mandarin are the bright chestnut with blue-green, fan-shaped shields on the wings and a greenish-copper head and extended crest that runs into metallic purple, reddish-brown, and green towards the rear points. The female also has a crest, but it is smaller.

The eggs of this hardy duck can be successfully artificially hatched (and ducklings brooded), or they can be put with other broody breeds. Incubation is from 29 to 31 days. The ducks come into full plumage the first summer after hatching.

The Mandarin has been kept in the Orient for showy purposes for a very long time. It was developed by early Chinese emperors. Even though small, they can defend themselves from other much larger breeds of ducks.

Wood Duck

Some confuse the Wood duck with the Mandarin, although the Wood duck does not have fan-shaped wing shields and neck hackles. The Wood duck is also longer in body, as compared to the cobby Mandarin. The Wood duck drake sports a green, bronze, and dark purple crest. Its wings are a darker color than those of the Mandarin. Wings are mainly dark green and purplish black. Its appearance is striking because of the white bars along the sides of the breast, around the throat, up behind the face, and on the secondaries of the wings.

The Wood duck nests in the hollows of trees up off the ground, sometimes as high as 50 feet. An average clutch is 15 off-white eggs. Incubation is from 29 to 31 days. The ducklings must drop to the ground to feed. The Wood duck can be hatched and brooded artificially but the ducklings must be dropped into a pan of wet grass clippings to emulate their natural habits. If this is not done, the ducklings will consistently try to escape the brooding quarters rather than eat, and will become tired and starve to death.

Another breed of merit is the striking white and black Magpie duck which was once used as a utility breed. Also occasionally raised are the Bahama Pintail, Barrows Golden Eye, Canvasback, Gadwalls, Pintail, Red Crested Pochard, Red Head, Rosybill, Ruddy, Greater Scaup, Tufted Lesser Scaup, African Shellduck, Rajah Shellduck, Ruddy Shellduck, Shoveler, and Spotbill.

A federal permit is not required for ducks not native to North America. The federal propagating permit is only required on migratory birds of North America if you sell them, and a possession permit for migratory ducks must be obtained before receiving them. The permits required to keep wild birds will vary with the state. Contact your district office of the U.S. Fish and Wildlife Service.

PERSONALITIES

Like humans, a duck's personality varies with the breed of duck. If you want pure friendship, a duck might not be for you. Ducks hardly ever follow their keeper around unless it's feeding time and you have a pan of feed in your hand; they are quite independent. Many have no qualms about leaving their residence. If a single duck exists among a flock of other species of fowl, he will most likely prefer them to you. There are some exceptions. I once had a pair of Rouens that kept coming back home. I traded the Rouens for some hay from a neighbor living 800 feet away. It seemed every day the pair would be caught waddling up our 500-foot driveway back home. I eventually had to reclaim them and pay for the hay.

Most ducks have a nervous quality that has never been bred out. They often run when you approach them. Some, such as Runners, stampede over each other to get away from you and they run up into fences and walls if they are not approached with care. Most ducks quack if you come near and do not like to be touched. They might nervously run in circles if disturbed in the dark, which becomes a problem with a larger flock size. Dim night-lights may be needed.

There is the exception that might follow you and not mind being held. Calls, Mandarins, and Muscovey hens can become this type, along with a few other breeds. Bantam chickens and certain pigeons make much better pets.

Ducks are also greedy feeders. They can become expensive to feed as a pet, especially the larger breeds. They will hog feeders. When swans are kept in waters with ducks and geese, special feeders with swans rations must be provided a distance above the ground or water surface to allow swans to eat without competing. Swans can become undernourished because they will not compete for food.

Most ducks are very noisy, although they can alert you to the approach of strangers. This noisiness often attracts wild breeds to a pond who otherwise might not visit. The drakes have a soft, reedy voice, the females, a very loud quack. Muscovies are the exception: they do not quack but make a hissing sound.

Ducks need deep drinking water to help wash feed down and to rinse out their nostrils. This makes many handlers think of them as messy and sloppy. Confinement must be well managed to prevent overwetting of litter.

Most drakes do not protect their mates, their nests, or their offspring to any extent. Again, Muscovies are the exception. The Muscovey drake can become aggressively obnoxious and possessive.

Most domestic breeds of ducks are too heavy to attempt flying. The lighter breeds, such as Calls, Mallards, and young lightweight Muscovies, can readily fly. If they are to be kept close to home, they must be confined or their wings must either be pinioned, brailed, or trimmed. If a handler does not take the time to do these things, they can lose their birds forever.

Ducks are not the easiest poultry to raise as many beginners are led to believe. Ducklings must be prevented from choking and getting into their drinking water. Waterers must frequently be washed because of their habit of eating and immediately drinking to wash feed down. When artificially brooded, they must not be allowed to get wet—even from the dew in grass—until completely feathered out. Many beginners believe all ducklings can immediately be placed in swimming water because mother ducks are seen with their babes swimming. These handlers aren't aware mother ducks have oiled the down of the ducklings so they don't become waterlogged.

HOW MANY?

Obviously the amount of ducks to raise depends upon the purpose for which they are intended. With meat-type breeds, individual families will need to figure the total amount of meat desired. Reviewing Table 12-1 will give the estimated amount of ducks needed to meet this need. If ducklings will be purchased as straight run or are to be raised from a home-hatched brood that have not been sexed, then figure on half the amount as being drakes and the other half as ducks (females). In this way the estimate for the total dressed-out weights will be closer. You might want to figure how much the meat will actually cost by adding brooding cost, duckling costs, and feed costs. Table 12-2 will help

Table 12-2. Body Weights and Feed Consumption of Pekin Ducks to 8 Weeks of Age.

Age (weeks)	Body Weight				Feed Consumption Each Week				Culmulative Feed Consumption			
	Males		Females		Males		Females		Males		Females	
	lbs.	(kg)	lbs.	(kg)	lbs.	(kg)	lbs.	(kg)	lbs.	(kg)	lbs.	(kg)
0	.11	(0.05)	.11	(0.05)								
1	.60	(0.27)	.60	(0.27)	.49	(0.22)	.49	(0.22)	.49	(0.22)	.49	(0.22)
2	1.72	(0.78)	1.63	(0.74)	1.70	(0.77)	1.61	(0.73)	2.18	(0.99)	2.09	(0.95)
3	3.04	(1.38)	2.82	(1.28)	2.47	(1.12)	2.45	(1.11)	4.65	(2.11)	4.52	(2.05)
4	4.32	(1.96)	4.01	(1.82)	2.82	(1.28)	2.82	(1.28)	7.49	(3.40)	7.34	(3.33)
5	5.49	(2.49)	5.07	(2.30)	3.26	(1.48)	3.15	(1.43)	10.74	(4.87)	10.50	(4.76)
6	6.52	(2.96)	6.01	(2.73)	3.59	(1.63)	3.51	(1.59)	14.33	(6.50)	14.00	(6.35)
7	7.36	(3.34)	6.75	(3.06)	3.70	(1.68)	3.59	(1.63)	18.04	(8.18)	17.60	(7.98)
8	7.96	(3.61)	7.25	(3.29)	3.70	(1.68)	3.59	(1.63)	21.74	(9.86)	21.19	(9.61)

(Adapted from *Nutrient Requirements of Poultry, 8th Revised Edition*, copyright 1984, National Academy of Sciences.)

to figure feed cost for Pekins.

If ducks are to be kept for eggs only, figure five months of laying at just above 50 percent production for meat breeds. This is about four eggs per week. For an egg breed such as the Khaki Campbell, with 14 hours of lighting in a comfortable environment, figure about an egg per day for 10 months. With Indian Runner ducks, with 14 hours lighting and a temperature above 40 degrees F., figure four eggs per week for eight months. These are all averages, but you must have something to go by if the ducks are to be raised for eggs only. With these estimates in mind, figure the total amount of eggs your family will consume per week.

When ducks are to be a hobby only, the amount can suit your fancy. You may want to consider housing space, pond area, pasture availability, feed costs, brooding costs, available spare hours, and the initial costs of the ducks.

PURCHASING

After you figure how many and of what breed, it's time to look for sources of good stock. Most good meat and egg strains will come from the more well-known hatcheries. A good strain in a fancy bred is most times better purchased from a reliable breeder-fancier. Those who show their birds and take pride in what they sell would be a good bet. They upgrade their fancy stock the same as com-

mercial breeders upgrade their utility type stocks. Poultry magazines, newsletters, and poultry newspapers are good sources for fancy stock. Also of great help is the *S.P.P.A. Breeder's Directory*. Put out by the Society for Preservation of Poultry Antiquities, the organization consists of members who support, perpetuate, and improve various breeds of all poultry. By joining and receiving the directory, you can locate breeders throughout the 50 states and Canada.

Another source book is the *National Poultry Improvement Plan (N.P.I.P.) Directory* put out by the United States Department of Agriculture. You must ask for book number APHIS-91-42, which includes waterfowl. Published and revised once a year, the directory lists various hatcheries, breeder flocks, and dealers. Participants' products listed meet specific requirements for a "U.S. Pullorum Clean" classification. The type and breed of poultry they handle along with addresses are listed. Because many large commercial businesses are included, some will not sell retail. You can only find out by writing and asking. In any case, try to check out the firm or individual beforehand because no book is a guarantee of quality or service. Publications are merely a tool to be used. Use them wisely.

Other sources for ducklings can be as near as your local area newspaper. Excess ducklings from very prolific ducks are often advertised in the classified section of a rural newspaper. Many area hatcheries and breeders advertise in a local paper. Feed stores, elevators, veterinarians, farm equipment sales, farm supply stores, nearby farmers, service stations, phone books, and newspaper offices can be other sources to contact for the whereabouts of ducks. Remember that places such as feed stores or grain elevators are middlemen and usually charge a higher price for poultry.

If you're interested in just a few farm ducks for your pond, you might be able to obtain some from a hatch of a nearby neighbor's ducks. It's a good idea to let him know you'd like a few when hatched early in the season. Then live up to your word and take them when he later calls you to pick them up. He might have gone to a lot of trouble to gather up your ducklings if they were naturally hatched outdoors.

Baby duck and goose raising can be disastrous to those who are unfamiliar with their abilities and needs. As with any poultry, be sure you obtain good quality. Many times hatching eggs are available. Hatching eggs are no deal if they come from poor stock, are not highly fertile, and have not been stored properly. Even hatcheries cannot always ascertain the quality of purchased eggs. If you're not familiar with the seller's reputation, ask for a written guarantee that at least 50 percent of the eggs are fertile. In this way you should at least get your money back on those that do hatch from the fertile eggs. If the seller is unwilling to this, it's better to go elsewhere.

There are sellers who have nutritionally deprived stock who know darn well the resulting eggs are poorly fertilized, yet they pass them off to unsuspecting handlers. They hope the egg purchasers will think it was their hatching ability that was at fault. Some of these sellers know they have not stored the eggs properly but would rather get a few cents for nests full of eggs than to toss them out. A handler should not purchase eggs from nests because they are not always of a good storage temperature and the constant laying of eggs by the birds warms the eggs periodically. Eggs should be no older than two-weeks old and should have been stored in a 50-55-degree F. area.

Day-olds might not be lively, but those two days old or more must be alert, energetic, and perky. If they appear weak, do not bother with them at all. If possible, view the adult stock to see if they are well taken care of and specimens worthy of the particular breed.

Chapter 13

Choosing Your Goslings

ORIGIN AND HISTORY

Geese have been described as being somewhere in between a swan and a duck. They differ from swans in that they have the space between their eyes and bill feathered rather than bare, and they have a somewhat shorter neck. They differ from ducks because they have longer necks and their shanks are covered with hexagonal rather than clam-shaped scales.

Geese were used in Roman times as a sacred guard, because human guards could not detect the enemies' approach as well as the geese. It's rare for geese to be unable to tell the regular, everyday sounds and sights from those that are strange.

Goose raising had been practiced for centuries in the European countries. When settlers from these countries arrived in the United States, it became common here as well. Farm flocks of geese were raised for both food and feather use. Goose feather down was used for feather ticks on beds for a more comfortable rest.

As small cities begin to spring up, commercial goose raising was started to supply city dwellers with meat and feather products. Even as early as 1880, the commercial raising of geese became a significant industry in states such as Massachusetts, Connecticut and the Little Compton section of Rhode Island. Today, the U.S. census reports Iowa, North Dakota, South Dakota, Minnesota, and Wisconsin as being the leading goose production states. Next in production is California, Indiana, Ohio, Pennsylvania and Washington. Very limited research has been done in selective breeding and genetics centering around geese. Most attention has been given to chickens and turkeys.

During the Vietnam war, U.S. soldiers used flocks of geese to warn of enemy infiltration. Runs (continuous pens) 6 feet wide with geese inside encircled an entire camp.

Choosing A Breed

There are 11 standard breeds of geese in the United States ranging from 5-26 pounds, depending upon age and breed. Today all 11 breeds are raised for exhibition. All but the 5-pound Egyptian and the Canada goose can be used as utility birds. Egyptian and Canada geese lay only a few eggs per season, and are not prolific in this respect.

Unlike ducks, where the females of the colored breeds are marked and colored differently from the drakes, geese are marked and colored the same in both sexes. (The Pilgrim breed is the exception.)

The 11 breeds are separated into three weight classes: heavy—those that are 16-20 pounds for young ganders; medium—Young ganders of 12-16 pounds; and lightweight—Young ganders weighing 5-10 pounds.

Weight might not, and should not, be your top priority for choosing a breed. There are other merits and shortcomings among the various breeds to consider. A handler might not want a nasty, ill-tempered goose no matter how large he gets. Then again, this might be your trade-off if you must have a "super goose." If you're interested in plenty of goose eggs for hatching while keeping the least amount of ganders around, a lightweight domestic breed is best. Large breeds mate one male to only two or three females. The lightweight ganders, such as the Chinese, will mate with up to six females. This can save money in a flock's upkeep. Review the personalities and traits of the various breeds, then consider the weights. Note that a male is termed a gander and a female is correctly termed a goose.

In the heavyweight class are the Toulouse, Embden (Emden), and African. In the order of size, from smallest to largest, they are described as follows:

African

The African was admitted to the American Standard of Perfection in 1874, young ganders are 16 pounds, old ganders are 20 pounds. A young goose is 14 pounds, an old goose is 18 pounds (Fig. 13-1).

The African is a descendant of the wild China Swan goose. The Swan goose can be found today in the wilds of eastern Asia. The African originated in China. Over the years it was erroneously called the Barbary goose, China goose, Guinea goose, and the Muscovey goose. It was previously called the Gray African goose. In earlier years it was thought to be the most profitable because of the fast growth

Fig. 13-1. Pair of African geese. (Courtesy of Leon Zimdars, Wis.)

and weight gain. Many breeders, therefore, used to cross the African with the Embden breed.

The African has the characteristic knob over the base of the bill. The African is one of three breeds that possess a dewlap. This is a single fold of skin attached at the throat and the upper underside of the neck.

The African is mostly dark and ash brown. On the back of the neck, there is a broad, dark brown stripe the entire length of the neck. This stripe is also characteristic to today's Brown Chinese goose. The knob and bill are a contrasting pure black color. Shanks and feet are usually black when hatched but later change to a dark orange. The adults' neck is slightly arched and fairly long.

When choosing African breeders from young stock under a year old, it's best to choose those that are not too slender or the desired type will be lost. Also, choose those showing little dewlap development. The dewlap will continue to develop but to a thinner, smoother, nonpendulous type. Furthermore, a young specimen showing pronounced dewlap development will also usually develop undesirable keels and folds of skin hanging from the abdomen. These folds of skin are called paunches. The Toulouse is the only breed that should show a large paunch.

A fairly good egg layer, the African is one of the more aggressive breeds. I personally wouldn't keep Africans any place where children could come in contact with them. Although many geese become nasty from being teased, as some unthinking individuals are inclined to do, the African needs no prodding. Even if handraised from a gosling, the African can insist upon being cantankerous.

Embden

This is a pure white goose with bright blue eyes and deep orange shanks and bill (Fig. 13-2). It was known first as the Bremen, named after a port in West Germany from where it was imported. The breed was later called the Emden, or the English Embden.

Admitted to the American Standard of Perfection in 1874, the young ganders are 20 pounds, old ganders are 26 pounds. A young goose is 16 pounds and an old goose goes 20 pounds. These are standard weights. The Embden can be grown much larger, but it then becomes less productive and acquires a fatty carcass. Such was the case of a pair I obtained and tried to breed. The three-year old gander topped 45 pounds and the goose 35 pounds.

They bred very efficiently and set on clutches of fertile eggs. However, her huge body would ultimately suffocate the robust goslings upon hatching.

The Embden is a fair egg layer but not as prolific as the Toulouse. It makes up for this by being a better sitter than the Toulouse. Embden goslings can usually be sexed by observing the gray portion of the down. Females will usually show a darker gray. The Embden matures early and dresses out nicely because of the white plumage, but it has a tendency to a fatty carcass. It's best to keep Embdens away from more docile breeds because they tend to bully and dominate others.

Toulouse

This large gray goose descended from the wild European Gray Lag goose (Fig. 13-3). It was first called the Marseilles goose and the Mediterranean goose because they were shipped from this area. It was imported into England where it was developed into a much larger goose. At this time, the English breeders referred to it as the Toulouse, named after the city of Toulouse in southern France.

There is now both a gray and a buff variety. The Gray Toulouse was recognized and admitted

Fig. 13-2. Pair of Embden geese.

Fig. 13-3. Pair of Toulouse geese.

to the American Standard in 1874. The Buff Toulouse was admitted in 1977. Young ganders are 20 pounds, old ganders, 26 pounds. A young goose is 16 pounds, an old goose, 20 pounds. Of the heavy breeds, the Toulouse is the most prolific, laying an average of 40 eggs per season. This is just under what the Chinese lay. Chinese are a lightweight goose but the best layers of all geese. The Gray Toulouse goslings are predominately gray.

The Toulouse has a broad, deep body. It is loose-feathered, and this makes it appear even larger. It's colored mostly dark and light gray with some white. An authentic Toulouse must possess a dewlap, a long, deep keel almost reaching the ground, and a smooth, low paunch under the abdomen. It's good to become familiar with the Standard description of the Toulouse. It is the one breed where mongrels are constantly referred to as Toulouse, simple because they have the same coloring, size, and markings. These nonconforming types are sometimes called "farm goose,""common gray goose," "utility goose," "business goose," or simply gray goose. This is fine as long as a purchaser knows he is not obtaining a Toulouse breed, but rather a goose with no breed distinction. Most of these so-called farm geese are similar to an Emb-

den, but are gray. They do not have the massive, square, compact look of the pure Toulouse.

Toulouse do better if they are kept by themselves. When raised with more flighty breeds of fowl, the docile Toulouse will not be as productive. Also, as with any large breed, they should not be fed rich, fat-producing rations that interfere with laying ability.

The medium weight class includes the fancy looking Sebastopol, the Pilgrim, Pomeranian, and the American Buff. In the order of size, from smallest to largest, they are described as follows:

Sebastopol

This lovely curly-feathered breed was admitted to the American Standard of Perfection in 1938. Young ganders are 12 pounds, old ganders, 14 pounds. Young geese are 10 pounds and old geese are 12 pounds.

The Sebastopol has been considered a novelty breed for years, but it also lays well and dresses out nicely as a table bird. Because it is a good utility bird, raising Sebastopols is a great way to dabble in the unusual and still consider economics.

The Sebastopol is undoubtedly unique. The entire plumage, except for the head and neck, is

251

curled and twisted. The curlier and longer, the better. Even the primaries and secondaries of the wings are curled and twisted. This prevents flying, so there is no need to worry about wing clipping.

Sebastopols are hard to obtain because they are not commonly bred. Even harder to obtain is a good specimen. Many of these geese have too-short feathers with stiff primary feathers in the wings. The wing feathers should not be hard and stiff, but flexible to allow natural curling. Stiff feathers do not curl well and as a result they unattractively stick out at right angles to the body. It would be best to view the parent stock first if goslings are considered. Curling is not due to abnormal wing growth structure; be sure wings are normal. The plumage of the Sebastopol might be hard to keep clean unless it has access to a body of water for bathing and swimming.

Sebastopols are named after a Russian port in the Black Sea called Sevastopol. They are docile in nature.

Pilgrim

Pilgrims were admitted to the American Standard in 1939. Young ganders are 12 pounds, old ganders, 14 pounds. Young geese are 10 pounds, old geese, 13 pounds.

The Pilgrim is a sex-linked breed of goose developed by an American poultry and cattle judge and author named Oscar Grow. It was the first sex-linked breed of goose to be developed.

Authentic Pilgrims produce goslings that can be sexed as early as hatching by the color of the down. The male goslings are hatched dusky yellow (which is actually the color of goslings that later turn white in other breeds). The females are mainly gray. As adults, the ganders will be white with gray-blue eyes and the geese will be almost completely gray with brown eyes. They seem to be difficult to obtain at most hatcheries.

Pilgrims are fairly good layers but some tend to go broody too soon, resulting in small nest clutches. They are very protective of their nest, which can make egg collecting a bit tricky.

Pomeranian

There are two sub-varieties of the Pomeranian that were admitted to the American Standard in 1977. One is the Gray Saddleback Pomeranian. The other is the Buff Saddleback Pomeranian, which is a sub-variety of the American Buff and has been also called the Buff Pied goose. Actually, the Saddleback is a variety of the Pomeranian, but some have taken it upon themselves to turn this variety into a distinct breed. There is also a gray variety colored like the Toulouse, but with reddish-pink or flesh-colored bills, shanks, and feet. Another is the white variety with reddish-pink or flesh colored bills, shanks, and feet. The Pomeranian is not very common; the Gray Saddleback is more popular and easily found. It's of ancient German origin but is said to be a descendant of the Eastern Gray Lag.

Bill, shanks, and feet of all varieties must be the orange-red-flesh color to be representative of the breed. They must also have a broad, deep, single-lobed paunch rather than the two-(dual) lobed paunch of most other breeds. The Embden also carries a single-lobed paunch, but has an orange bill, shanks, and feet. If offspring develop dual-lobed paunches, it is usually the result of a cross of breeds on the mother's side. She should then not be used for producing if pure stock is desired. Because she will not show this fault herself, pedigree hatching must be practiced. This is done by marking her eggs, incubating them, banding the goslings, raising them, and viewing the results. It will be time well spent because dual-lobed paunches are a serious defect in the Pomeranian.

Good as a commercial breed, but only occasionally seen at shows, the standard weights for a young gander are 15 pounds, an old gander, 17 pounds. Young geese are 13 pounds, old geese, 15 pounds.

American Buff

This is a more recent addition to the Standard, being admitted in 1947. Besides the Pilgrim, the American Buff is the only other breed that originated in America. The Buff Saddleback is actually a spin-off of the American Buff. The young ganders are 16 pounds, old ganders are 18 pounds. Young geese are 14 pounds, old geese, 16 pounds.

When choosing adult American Buff breeders for color, keep in mind that constant ranging in the sun will fade the buff color. Also, the feathers loosen just before molting and tend to lighten. Usually choosing ganders a shade lighter than the standard buff color will result in goslings with very good color. To correct poor coloring in offspring because of a gray tone in the feathers of the mother parent, choose a gander mate for her of a very light buff color.

Very often, American Buffs, like some other breeds, are thought to be fancy because they are not easily obtained. As mentioned earlier, all geese except the Canada and Egyptian can be used for production to a greater or lesser degree. Unlike other poultry species, geese have been bred with utility rather than appearance in mind. The American Buff dresses out almost as nicely as any white breed.

In the lightweight class is the ornamental and unusual Egyptian, the Canada, the Tufted Roman and the unsurpassed Chinese. They are described as follows from smallest to largest:

Egyptian

This is an old breed admitted to the Standard in 1874, and is the smallest of the standardized geese (Fig. 13-4). Present standard weights are 5 pounds for a young gander, 5 1/2 pounds for an old gander. A young goose is only 4 pounds, an old goose is 4 1/2 pounds. At the beginning of the century the standard weight for an adult gander was 10 pounds and the goose, 8 pounds. It was also referred to as the Nile Goose because it's a native of the Nile region of Egypt (Fig. 13-5). It can still be found in its natural habitat and over most of Europe. It breeds in England, Scotland, and farther south.

The Egyptian is a showy, varied-colored bird. The head is gray with a reddish-brown patch around the eyes. The back is gray and black with a rich, iridescent, reddish cast. The wing shoulders are white with glossy black primaries, secondaries, and tail feathers. The breast is gray with a rich, reddish-brown center. The bill is a reddish purple. Shanks and feet are reddish yellow, eyes are orange. It has been compared to the Muscovey because of the bill shape and the small carnucle at its base. Its body shape is also similar. The plumage does not take on its full splendor until about two years of age—after the second molt.

Like the Canada goose, the Egyptian is not a true goose. It did not descend from either the wild

Fig. 13-4. Two pairs of Egyptian geese grazing. (Courtesy Paul Cooney, Detroit Zoological Park)

Fig. 13-5. A larger, old-type Egyptian, commonly called the Nile goose. (Courtesy of Leon Zimdars, Wis.)

Gray Lag (Anser-Anser) goose nor the wild China Swan goose (Anser cygnoides) as the domestic breeds have. Ornithologists class the Egyptian as a Sheldrake.

Egyptians can be very quarrelsome. The ganders have been known to fight among themselves until dead. Most of the time they are peaceful, however—it's during the breeding and hatching season when they become tyrants. The gander will protect his mate and nest to the fullest. They are monogamous in that they will breed to only one mate even when semi-domesticated. This trait can be responsible for the aggressiveness. Although small, the Egyptian can injure those who intrude because of the stiff, hard protrusions on the front base of the wings.

The average Egyptian usually lays only one clutch of about six eggs for the season. An older goose may lay eight eggs. Some have been known to lay as many as 12 eggs and hatch them while in confinement. It very much depends upon the strain you have. Some will occasionally lay another clutch if the first clutch doesn't hatch. The incubation period is 28-30 days. It also remains a migratory bird. If the wings aren't clipped, pinioned, or brailed, its migratory instincts will take it flying.

As with other fowls in very cold and inclement weather, the Egyptian needs some type of shelter for protection.

Canada

The Canada goose is a member of the Brant family. The Brant geese frequent the Arctic in the spring and summer and winters along the coasts south to California and the Carolinas. The plumage coloration and markings are similar, but the other breeds of Brant geese are smaller than the Canada goose; the Brant is the smallest of our wild geese. The Canada goose is also a migratory bird. It winters south to the northern part of Mexico and along the Gulf Coast. It can be found from Alaska, east to the Baffin Island, south to Massachusetts, further south to North Carolina, and west to California. The common eastern Canada goose (Fig. 13-6) was admitted to the American Standard of Perfection in 1874. It's described as a refined-looking goose.

The Canada goose is kept for ornamental purposes. Because they are loners during the breeding season, they should not be kept with other breeds. It is a monogamous breeder for life even while in captivity. They will take on another mate if their own dies. This is similar to the faithful matings of swans. The Canada goose can be forced to crossbreed, but the offspring are then sterile. Early in the century, they were frequently crossed with African ganders to increase the weights of goslings. This did not become extremely popular because Canadas have an aversion to mating with other breeds.

The Canada is not productive; it lays only one clutch of 4-8 eggs annually. The eggs are usually very fertile and hatch very well, however. Egg laying does not begin until the goose is three years old. Sometimes it does not begin until she's four years old. During the breeding season, the mated pairs go off on their own to look for a nesting area. The gander will viciously protect and defend their nearby nest. Although old ganders are only 12 pounds, and an old goose, 10 pounds, they are very quick and have very strong and powerful wings which they use to bat at intruders. This migratory bird must be wing clipped, pinioned, or brailed because the instinct to migrate is not totally lost under confinement.

The Canada is a hardy, independent breed. If goslings are purchased, which is rare, they are raised the same as any domestic breed. The most usual way to acquire a pair is by purchasing mated adults. If they are an older pair, breeders will not usually sell them until they have first hatched and raised their season's brood of goslings. Most breeder geese are sold in the fall after their molt.

There is a much larger version of the Canada goose which was thought to have become extinct, but there are now known to be small, isolated flocks. These are called Giant Canada.

Roman

The Roman is a breed of its own with two varieties, the White and the Tufted. Only the Tufted variety has been standardized in the United States—when admitted to the American Standard of Perfection in 1977. And the Tufted has been listed as a breed rather than a variety. Where, then, can the original White Roman (lacking the characteristic tuft on the crown as required with a Tufted Roman) fit into the Standard at a later date? The White Roman has been around longer than the Tufted. The same error has been made with the Saddleback variety of the Pomeranian breed. A

Fig. 13-6. Canada gander. (Courtesy of Leon Zimdars, Wis.)

breed should not describe color, markings, breed variances, or a group of species. Such is the case where "Turkeys" are listed as a breed in the Standard. Turkeys are a species and not a breed. Can you imagine how confused dog fanciers would be if "Dog" was the breed and all pure stock was a variety of "Dog"? There would then be many subvarieties of the species rather than varieties of the breed. Perhaps these misnomers will be taken care of in the future so there is no further misinterpretations among the poultry public.

England was the first to adopt a standard for the Roman towards the end of the last century. The market for geese was always for large breeds. This could have been because consumers had larger families years ago. The trend of smaller families seems to have given rise to a smaller market bird. The Roman can fit this need. It has done so in other countries already. A young gander is 10 pounds, an old gander, 12 pounds. A young goose is 9 pounds and an old goose, 10 pounds. It's an early-maturing goose.

The Roman's plumage should be pure white with blue eyes and orange to pinkish-orange shanks and feet. The bill should be pinkish- to reddish-orange with a white bean. This would also describe the Tufted Roman, except that the Tufted would have a cylindrical tuft on the crown. Romans have medium-length necks and a broad back that should be as wide as half the back's length.

Chinese

There is no other goose that can be utilized in so many ways as the Chinese. They are often termed "Weeder Geese" because of their voracious and active appetite for weeds and grass only. They are often used by cotton producers, strawberry growers, nurserymen, tobacco growers, and fruit and vegetable farmers to alleviate weeds, insects, and windfall fruits. They are also often called the "Poorman's Swan" because they can be an inexpensive alternative to grace a pond when swans are financially out of the question. From a distance, their long swanlike necks can give an ethereal effect to a calm, cool pond.

There are two varieties, the Brown Chinese and the White Chinese (Fig. 13-7) both of which were admitted to the American Standard in 1874. The Chinese is small, yet dresses out without fat at from 5 1/2-7 pounds—a good size for many families. The standard liveweight is 10 pounds for a young gander, 12 pounds for an old gander. Young geese are

Fig. 13-7. Pair of White Chinese geese.

Fig. 13-8. Although these goslings are incubator-hatched, this Chinese gander is quite worried over the fate of the one that is out of the box.

8 pounds, old geese, 10 pounds. The more meal-size weight of the Chinese has made it popular with many handlers who raise their own meat.

The Chinese matures earlier than most breeds. It lays the most eggs of any goose in the entire world. The eggs are slightly smaller than the large breeds but if total eggs were weighed, the Chinese would still win. Even in cold climates, the Chinese will sometimes begin laying in February. If eggs are collected so a clutch does not form, they will continue to lay until the end of May. Most lay an egg every other day without fail. They are instinctively broody enough to sit only on a clutch of eggs. It's a rare Chinese goose that becomes so broody she'll sit on nothing. This means eggs can be collected up to the end of May, if desired, for incubator hatching. Then the last week or two of egg laying, a clutch of about 10 collected eggs can be placed back into the nest. It's usually not long before the goose will become broody and sit.

Upsets and changes in the weather rarely upset their production. Because of the docile nature of the Chinese goose, eggs are easily collected even from under the goose. She will usually just lay her head down—an ancient instinct to appear less obvious—unlike most geese who try to fight you off, batting their wings and breaking eggs in the process. Occasionally you might need to hold her

neck held with one hand while you retrieve eggs with the other. Most handlers wait until she's done laying before bothering a goose, but there might be times when you need the eggs: perhaps you are setting a tray in the incubator and need one more to fill a gap. It is a good idea to candle her eggs if she's sitting. You might want to give her more eggs if she's just begun to sit.

Although they're of the lighter weight class, Chinese geese are still large enough to protect their brood. The entire flock will watch over one brood of babies. Chinese are very good babysitters. If you have a pen of chicks, ducklings, or any other poultry babies outdoors, the Chinese ganders will come sit near the pen and watch over them. They'll even chase away dogs or cats that come near the babies (Fig. 13-8).

Chinese geese have just enough aggressiveness to take care of their family, but I've never known a Chinese to attack and hurt anyone. Occasionally they'll reach out and give you a "love bite" or gently pull your hair if you happen to be bending down at their level. This is far different from the attacks most other breeds tend to resort to. With our many customers visiting the hatchery daily, our roaming flock of Chinese were completely trusted with small children, even when they had their goslings with them. Occasionally the geese would follow the cus-

257

tomers out to the drive because they heard the boxed babies peeping.

Chinese are excellent foragers. There's no need to protect any plant from them except corn which just sprouted. The corn must be at least a foot tall before it's safe around Chinese geese. But any other vegetable, fruit, or flowering plant is never touched by them. Given this fact, the Chinese can be allowed the run of the farm, if desired. They will then be able to sustain their own living and will take care of weeds, stray seeds, and insects. They do a great job of keeping the grass to a reasonable length. Our neighbors mow their lawns four times more than we do. The one plant I cannot entice the Chinese to devour is the dandelion.

The only problem a handler might be faced with when the Chinese are allowed freedom in the garden, is some trampled plants if they take a path perpendicular to the planted rows. This is easily remedied by placing a barrier of chicken wire strung diagonally across their path to redirect their route.

The Chinese geese are the most economical to feed. In fact, they'll refuse feed if they have access to any pasture at all. The only time they'll ask for feed is if a heavy snow covers the ground. They prefer grass and weeds over any grains or mash. As an example: A dozen full-grown Chinese, raised in a climate where the annual snowfall averages 39 inches, will get by nicely on 300 pounds of feed per year. The rest they'll forage on their own and hatch beautiful, healthy goslings on top of it. They usually don't need oyster shells.

Over the years, I've tried Chinese geese of various strains. I've seen no difference in their behavior. All have joined me in the garden to help pull weeds. They like you best at their level. As I sit on my milkcrate to handweed between the onions, the Chinese join me not more than a foot away. They immediately begin talking to me and reach down next to my hand to pull the next weed as if they're completely aware of what I'm doing.

The Chinese are also less noisy than larger geese. This is good to know if loud, deep honking annoys you (or your neighbors). The Chinese have a higher pitched tone, which only drowns out other

sounds when they're next to you. Their vocalizing isn't as frequent as the larger geese. They honk mostly when a strange animal comes near or you approach them. Other geese honk for these situations plus have frequent chats with one another. The Chinese rarely talk among themselves except to express delight over a new brood of goslings. Occasionally the female will call to her mate as she leaves the nest for a swimming and eating break. The gander responds in order to let her know his whereabouts.

Some years I've found it necessary to clip wings in the fall because a few females flew across the road to another nearby pond and refused to come home for five days. I now also routinely clip their wings in the fall to prevent them from flying onto our pond when it's only partially frozen. They land on the surface and could go through the thin ice and drown.

Their housing does not need to be much. A simple shed during winter blizzards will do. My Chinese have actually run into the laying house during very cold spells. Otherwise, they'll group together along a windbreak such as the side of a building.

If a handler can allow his Chinese to pasture, and does not mind goose droppings in the driveway or near the house, the Chinese geese will more than repay him for their little upkeep.

COMMON TRAITS

The good, the bad and the ugly. Geese are the one species of domestic fowl that can lift your spirits or try them. There are many handlers who aren't sure they like geese until they personally raise a few. Likewise, there are those who quickly give up their infatuation after the first brood. The problem can sometimes be due to an incompatible breed choice or that too many were raised at one time. If raising your geese seems too much of a burden, it's not fair to blame the geese. They only behave as nature has intended.

Geese are one of the most independent of the domestic fowl. If they're part of a flock, this trait will be more pronounced. This, however, is what leads them to be such good foragers. If you're looking for a pet, one you can pamper and pet, a goose is not a good choice. Geese do like people, but they show it in a different way than other fowl. They are very leery of strangers but are sociable with those who have gained their confidence. They can become very interested in a new or different task you might be performing outdoors. Many will come to investigate and "talk" to you about what you're doing.

When I say geese talk, of course I mean in their own language. When they talk their necks are always stretched out before them. This they also do when they're scared and are warning or investigating. When frightened, their necks are stretched as high as possible upwards and their voice becomes loud. Only large domestic geese or wild geese honk.

Geese are always aware of what's going on around them. If you have a good window from which you can occasionally glance out to see them, their actions will warn you of hawks, wild animals, strange dogs, strange cars, and people nearby. A few ganders in the flock become the official guards. They watch for danger as the others feed (Fig. 13-9). The ganders will then warn of approaching trouble. Because geese can distinguish between dangerous and safe sounds, they supposedly watch over a homestead better than a dog.

As if not to draw attention to themselves, they will all remain quiet, yet hold their heads high when spying a large hawk or crane flying overhead. I'm sure they would vocalize loudly should the giant, strange bird fly toward them. It doesn't quite matter if the large strange bird is mechanical or not. They act the same way when an airplane speeds overhead or a colorful ultralight glides by. When a flock of migrating Canada geese begin their triangular formation southward, the domestic geese seem intrigued over the phenomenon overhead. They seem to believe the strange geese are more of their kind. Likewise, Canada geese will often share the same water and pasture with the domestic geese and livestock (Fig. 13-10).

While a Canada goose incubates her eggs, her mate will often mingle with the domestic flock until their brood is hatched. Perhaps this is because of their need to be sociable. When their goslings hatch, the gander will then join his mate and new brood. The Chinese ganders love baby poultry when they don't have any of their own. They become extremely interested in them when they hear their peeping. Female geese, domestic or wild, will try to camouflage their nest if it's approached by laying low and stretching their necks outward.

Although they are independent, they do not do well without a mate. They will be very unhappy and restless. Geese must flock. It's their nature to want to be with others of their own kind. Unlike a duck, a single goose will not cohabitate well within a flock of chickens. Even a duck will usually cry for a mate.

Fig. 13-9. It's easy to see here which two ganders are acting as guards while the rest of the flock eats.

Fig. 13-10. A wild Canada gander grazing with cattle until his mate hatches goslings nearby.

A goose just doesn't know how to fit in; it will become lonely. The goose will eat and drink with the other species but it does not want to be bothered by them. It's loneliness can turn to aggression with the other birds. Some become overly quiet.

Wild breeds prefer to remain alone with their mate throughout the breeding season on up to the time their hatched offspring are a few months of age (Fig. 13-11). Then they'll rejoin the flock until the next breeding season. Domestic breeds only occasionally remove themselves from the flock.

Wild geese are monogamous. They choose one mate only during their life. If one should die, they will usually seek out another mate of their own kind. Wild geese rarely cross breed. This loyalty does not exist in domestic type breeds. Large breed domestic ganders will take on two or three mates. The small breed ganders will choose up to six mates.

If you want to add a female or two to your flock,

Fig. 13-11. The Canada gander stays with his mate to help guard the newly hatched goslings between them.

do not expect the ganders to like them right away. The ganders might not accept them as mates until the following year. Younger ganders, especially of the lightweight breeds, will accept them sooner than older domestic ganders (especially if they're of a heavy breed). For an easier introduction, confine the new female with the other females in a pen or building. Also confine the gander (or ganders) in a separate pen. After about five days the females will all become sociable. The males and females can then be brought together and the new female will be welcome.

Introducing a new gander into a flock that already has ganders, is a bit more lengthy. It will require removing some females from the flock which the new gander can call his own. Confine these females with the new gander until the females quit calling for their old mates and feel comfortable with the new one. When all are eventually released, there might still be some fighting among the ganders, but it's usually short-lived. Because this confinement will usually upset egg production and mate attachments, add new birds just before the season begins. Adding a male after the season will usually cause him to become an outcast by all. The confinement method will no longer work once the females have mated and layed and the season is over. Furthermore, if the entire flock must be housed and confined together any length of time during the winter, some fighting might be encountered with the newer gander.

Loyalty among an entire flock also exists. If you were to lock up half the flock, the remainder would stay on the other side of the barrier, whether it be a building or a pen. Both halves of the flock would cry out to each other for days. A pitiful sight, indeed.

Ganders can become a problem, especially during the breeding season—and every year they can become even more aggressive and belligerent. All children should be kept from large, nasty ganders. Some ganders will charge from quite a distance, even if a person is nowhere near a nest. Ganders can inflict serious wounds with their painful bites and their batting wings. Some can even become a problem with other livestock much larger than

themselves. This is why I recommend the Chinese geese for anyone with children. I have never known a Chinese gander to hurt anyone, even during the nesting or breeding.

Geese are a long-lived fowl. The females can be kept for breeding 10 years and even more. Ganders of the domestic breeds sometimes become sterile by the seventh year. A lot depends upon the particular gander and how it's been cared for. A very fat gander, for instance, will not be a good breeder for long. Geese can live up to 20, 30, 40 years; some records showing 60-year-old geese. Again, it depends upon the individual goose and its lifestyle.

Geese are the most unique of all domestic fowl.

HOW MANY?

The amount of goslings to initially raise will depend upon their intended purpose. If the goslings will later be used for meat, it's only a matter of figuring the net amount of meat your family desires. Table 13-1 will help figure those needs. Also remember the percentage of waste is greater with lighter weight breeds of all poultry, whether it's a goose, chicken, duck, etc.

Goslings are very hardy creatures. Unless you're planning on raising more than a half dozen, it's not necessary to purchase extras to make up for mortality as with chicks and poults. If you're unsure of your own capabilities when raising goslings, then include one extra for every 12 you desire. Goslings can't outlive poor management.

For a beginner, about six goslings is a good amount to practice on. More than this, and many beginners feel overwhelmed as the fast-growing

**Table 13-1. Average
Live and Dressed Weights of Geese.**

Liveweight (pounds)	Dressed Weight (pounds)
20	16
18	14-14 1/2
10	7
8	5 1/2

goslings begin to demand more care. At first, the goslings look so cute and cuddly that you can't imagine they could ever become a problem. Later, they must be fed and watered more, requiring more of your time. They must be safely housed and kept from predators. When the brooder is not heating them anymore, they'll have to be watched to make sure they don't become wet (when the brooder heat is off, they no longer have a place to quickly dry off). Larger amounts of litter material will be needed also. Just watching for the neighbor's dog while the goslings are out sunning can keep you hopping. Once you've had experience at raising goslings, even a brood of 50 will seem a snap.

If you're only concerned about obtaining a pair and the goslings aren't sexed, a good rule of thumb is to purchase four goslings. This method is not 100 percent, it's only an average. If you want a good pair for breeding stock, it's best to obtain about 12 goslings. In this way, you'll be able to pick the best pairs.

If a hatchery offers sexing, you can save time and money by ordering the preferred sexes. If you only want a pair and a sexing service is available at the hatchery, but you must purchase at least four, eight, or fifteen, ask the hatchery if they'll sex a pair and mark their heads with a black permanent marker. Occasionally a hatchery will oblige.

When your main interest is plenty of goose eggs without keeping many ganders, a lightweight breed will better fit the bill. Large-breed ganders will mate with two or three females. A lightweight-breed gander, such as a Chinese, will mate with up to six geese. This only applies to domestic breeds. Wild breeds are usually monogamous, plus lay only a few eggs.

SEASONAL AVAILABILITY

Day-old goslings can be purchased from most hatcheries starting in March on through to July. Because geese can be stimulated to lay by using artificial lighting, egg-stimulating feed, and warm housing, goslings can sometimes be obtained as early as February. This means the geese were laying prior to January. Breeders have not been able to extend a goose's laying period much past June, as they have with chickens.

For some reason, many handlers begin inquiring about goslings just when their hatching season has ended. This might be because many handlers have finished up their vacations and then feel free to raise them. Raising the goslings before a vacation usually means finding someone to care for them when they leave. Unlike chicks, which should be started early for faster growth and feathering and a supply of eggs by fall, goslings do well if started in the middle of summer. It might also be that many handlers with children wait until the children are out of school so they can help tend and enjoy the goslings.

If you will be purchasing goslings locally, you might want to inquire about the length of the laying season in your area. Most goose owners will be able to tell you. In this way you'll know approximately when goslings might be advertised in the local paper. If a handler incubates most of his goose eggs, goslings might be available early in the season. Those who hatch naturally with geese will usually let the goslings grow with the flock until fall before selling them. The important thing is to know exactly what you want and to inquire and order as early as possible. Most hatcheries are already booked for the season by May.

Chapter 14

Duckling and Gosling Management

GETTING THEM STARTED

Waterfowl have been misrepresented to many beginners as being the easiest of all fowl to raise. By far, the chicken is the easiest, but the pasturing goose is the most economical.

Most ducklings and goslings can be brooded together. Mammoth White Pekins should not be brooded with small breeds of geese. These ducklings grow so fast, and their aggressive eating and drinking nature will cause the goslings to get pushed around a lot. Likewise, do not brood any goslings or regular standard size ducklings with the tiny Call ducklings. As the others grow faster and larger, the tiny Calls will get trampled.

Never brood other species such as keets, chicks, or poults with waterfowl. Ducklings and goslings have very active eating and drinking habits, which will cause the others to get wet. After a few weeks, the stronger and larger waterfowl can easily trample them. Besides, all should have their own special feed. It takes an awful lot of experience and watching to mix them together while

brooding. Even then, the final results are not always good. All day-olds can be brooded together in an *emergency* when only a few days old, and for only a day or two. Be sure the ducklings and goslings are not given medications in the water or medicated feeds. It's best to give all the birds a duck starter during this emergency.

When bringing day-olds home, have their brooding quarters already set up so they do not have to wait to be watered and warmed. A hastily put together brooding arrangement can cause mortality. Offer them water first. They will go under the heat on their own. The most disastrous set up is one which allows the day-olds to enter their drinking water containers. Many beginners believe water is only second nature to waterfowl. They are surprised to learn they can chill and die from becoming wet or can drown if they can't escape the water. Furthermore, if they are without drinking water they can choke on feed as it compacts in the throat. Ducklings and goslings do not need their bills dipped into the water to get them started drinking, although dipping a few after shipping will show the others where the water founts are more quickly.

Raising a few day-olds in a box should not present a problem if it's large enough, cleaned often, and is very temporary. Waterfowl will not usually be tolerated in a handler's home for longer than two weeks because of their offensive odor. Their droppings are extremely wet compared to other species of fowl, so the odor is stronger. The only exception is the Call ducks. They stay small quite a while and should not be entrusted to outdoor brooding where they cannot be constantly watched. Outdoors they can fall prey to predators, and because they usually cost more than many other breeds, you might not want to chance this. Granted, any predator can kill and maime any breed, but you may want to make safer quarters until they're placed out of sight in a building. Also, to some extent, many breeds of ducklings and goslings become more tame if kept near you and handled during their early life.

Waterfowl babies should have a large enough cardboard box so the moisture from droppings and splattered drinking water is distributed. This way the bedding material stays drier. A 2- × -3-foot box will accommodate a dozen standard-sized, day-old ducklings or six large day-old goslings the first week. If kept in a box another week, increase the size by at least 2 square feet. After this time, boxes become too difficult to efficiently keep clean and dry.

In a box set-up, place a small lamp reflector in one end of the box for heat. A 6-inch reflector with an ordinary lightbulb will do for one week with 12 ducklings or 6 goslings. For two weeks of box brooding, use the standard 10-inch reflector so the bulb heat reaches all the babies. Never use the regular 250-watt bulb in this type of set-up for only this many ducklings or goslings. The heat will be too great and there's a chance of starting a fire. There are 75-watt and larger reflector floodlight bulbs that can be used, or ordinary light bulbs will work. The wattage will depend upon the temperature of the room the box is kept in. Try a 75- or 100-watt bulb first. Adjust the temperature by raising or lowering the hanging lamp. The lamp can be hung by securing a piece of wood lath across the width of the box on one end, and using a strip of wire to hang and adjust the lamp height.

For two weeks of box brooding, the simple mason jar founts will suffice, but be sure to use enough so they never run out of water. A half-gallon jar can be used with these to supply more water, but care should be taken because it will tip more easily. Do not use the larger jars with larger waterfowl because they will easily knock them over, causing everything and everyone to become wet. Place the waterers at the end opposite the heat lamp. A small bowl will be good for the feed. Try to keep it away from the waterers to help prevent the drinking water from becoming full of feed.

Always place day-olds on top of bunched-up rags or towels to prevent spraddle legs. Line the entire box floor with these rags. Day-old ducklings, and especially goslings, do not gain enough footing until about the fifth day of life to sufficiently steady their bulky bodies. If placed on newspaper and some types of straw, they tend to slip around when they walk. This slipping can injure the softened ligaments in the tops of the shanks and thighs and cause severe sprains. The injury causes one or both legs to extend horizontally to the body. The result is a crippled duckling or gosling which must usually be disposed of. After the fifth day, the rags can be removed because the ligaments and cartilage have hardened sufficiently. Then use rough straw or a thick padding of newspaper. Try not to use colored print; this can be toxic if eaten.

Battery brooders can accommodate young waterfowl if used with caution. As with box brooding, place clean, slightly bunched-up rough rags or towels over the wire grill floor. In a battery, the towels need only be placed under the heating element. In a battery, the towels serve three purposes. First, they prevent spraddle legs. Second, they help keep the heat from being lost through the wire floor. Third, they prevent the occasional mishap when waterfowl get their hocks caught down in the wire when they sit. It's best to keep the towels under the element for two weeks to prevent their legs getting caught. It can be almost impossible to remove the leg after slight swelling begins. Sometimes the wire has to be cut to avoid injury to the leg. Because the babies don't sleep much in the cooler section the first few weeks (unless the room is very warm) this problem rarely occurs over that part of the wire.

A word on grower cages is in order here if you plan on using them for waterfowl. The wire floors of most are larger spaced. A 3/4-inch spacing allows them to easily get their hocks caught. It's not safe to use these cages with waterfowl.

Water troughs that are provided with battery brooders can be dangerous. Day-olds can work their way into these troughs and become soaked. They sometimes are unable to get back out and they drown. Close off these troughs by placing the grill cover behind them. Ducklings will also slip into the empty trough and become trapped and not be able to get back to the heat. Use mason jar founts for at least the first week.

Sometimes day-olds are extremely thirsty after being shipped. Their pushing and shoving to gain access at the waterers can cause the majority to get wet. Help prevent this the first day by adding small rocks or marbles to the mason jar fount bottom. After a few days they'll shove the marbles out.

If young waterfowl ever run out of water, it must be replenished with great care. First remove any available feed so it's not gulped down and compacted in their throats during a mad rush of intermittent drinking and eating. A deep waterer is ordinarily provided so waterfowl can rinse the feed from their nostrils, but extremely thirsty youngsters will become soaked if given these deeper waterers. If the youngsters have already graduated to deeper waterers such as a trough, do not refill this, but use plenty of small mason jar founts to replenish the water. Using the smaller founts again will help prevent them from getting very wet. Be sure to use plenty of these waterers to cut down on the pushing and shoving thirsty waterfowl will exhibit. If the ducklings are outdoors, rocks can be placed into larger founts until the birds are no longer extremely thirsty—this may be 20 minutes or a few hours. It depends how long they were without water. Always use warm water with thirsty young waterfowl. If cold water is gulped down, it will chill them and upset their insides.

Because it might take them a few hours for their drinking to slow up, keep a good eye out for any that get wet, and do not let any of the waterers run dry. If any get wet, quickly blow them dry with a hand-held blow dryer. After they are no longer as thirsty, refill the original larger waterers. Also decide whether more waterers should be available to prevent them from ever running out again. Ducklings, especially can get staggers when waterers are allowed to run dry. This is not a disease but a disorder they can acquire if water is depleted for any length of time. If it does happen, removing the feed until they are fairly well watered should help alleviate this problem.

Ducklings and goslings do very well under hover-type brooders or infrared heat lamps in an outdoor building. A brooding area should first be sectioned off. Allow for expansion by using plastic curtains or removable barriers. A small single brooder house can also be used. If floor area is a bit too large, use a brooder guard to confine the day-olds to the correct floor area around the brooder heat.

Prepare the floor under hovers or lamps by first placing extremely dust-free, clean, rough straw down over the entire area. The wide strands of straw tend to be slippery and should not be used, nor should newspaper. Both can cause spraddle legs in day-olds. Bare wood floors and cement also do not allow them to gain their footing. Dirt floors are good because they dry faster and absorb brooder heat, but they should be covered with rough straw. Be sure the rough straw is not dusty or moldy. Both will easily cause respiratory problems in waterfowl. Goslings are more susceptible than ducklings. A type of pneumonia will occur called brooder pneumonia (aspergillosis). Some handlers place burlap bags down to prevent spraddle legs, but these do not dry out as quickly as straw, and usually contain a lot of dust and—if they haven't been stored properly—molds. These should not be used unless you have plenty and are sure they are clean.

Figure on using one infrared heat lamp for every 15 ducklings or goslings the first three weeks during cool weather. For the remaining brooding period, add an extra lamp and hang it about 1 foot away from the other. Use the red 250-watt bulbs in the reflectors during the early part of the brooding period. Later, especially if the weather is warm, these can create too much heat. Rather than switch to ordinary bulbs, raise the lamp's height. The red bulbs serve to prevent feather eating and should be used. Sometimes a lower wattage red bulb can be found that will also provide the correct temperature.

A small light should remain on constantly so the birds can eat throughout the night. Do not depend on the thermostat light to provide this because it does not remain on. Even a small 7 1/2-watt bulb will do. Heat lamps remain on and can be used as the eating light too.

Fill reel-type trough feeders and place them around the outside of the hover or heated area the first day. Space plenty of waterers around the area also. As soon as the day-olds are brought to their quarters, place them in the feed and water area. If they have only just hatched, place them under the heat first to allow them to fully dry. Just-hatched ducklings and goslings are not interested in eating and drinking until the second day. You can dip a few bills the second day to get them started if they seem too content to stay under the heat.

BROODING TEMPERATURES

For day-old waterfowl, adjust the brooder or heat lamps to maintain a 90-degree F. temperature the first three to seven days. At seven days of age, reduce the temperature to 85 degrees F. At 14 days of age, reduce to 80 degrees F. By the fourth week, the temperature should be about 70 degrees F. These are only rule-of-thumb temperatures. Use the ducklings and goslings as a guide to the temperature. If they are cold, they will huddle together under the heat source. If very cold, they will actively and noisily pile on top of one another rather than spreading out and quietly sleeping. If they're too hot, they will be sleeping out away from the middle of the heat source. They may also be panting.

Ducklings and goslings do not require as long a brooding period as other domestic poultry. The brooding period is the length of time they are given artificial heat. Unlike other poultry, they are not brooded until they attain all their body feathers. Complete plumage covering takes about eight weeks. Brooding is usually no longer needed by about five weeks of age or when nightly temperatures in their unheated quarters stay at about 65 degrees F. If nightly temperatures are below this, perhaps you need to supply heat during the night only. If using lamps, you must provide enough space so they can safely escape excessive heat as the day warms. Then you do not have to go out and quickly shut the lamp off very early in the morning. The extra space is a safety precaution.

On nice days, the birds can be placed in a pen on grass in the sun for short periods. Watch that the sun does not become too hot for them. Provide a shaded area to protect them. Also, they can still become chilled if they become wet—even if in the sun. They must be watched carefully. When a few are being raised, some handlers give them an outing by sitting on the grass with them. Goslings like this attention, and they become more friendly when cared for this way. As you sit by them, they'll talk their heads off telling you how great it feels to be in the warm, dry grass on a sunny day.

NATURAL BROODING

Natural brooding is when a duck, goose, or chicken hen hatches and raises ducklings and goslings. Nothing much needs to be done when a duck or goose raises them. You must only be sure deep pans of water are not around where the babies can enter and not get back out. Many are lost yearly because of this. The babies get tired from constantly swimming and eventually drown if not found right away. The mother goose or duck usually becomes frantic, but cannot usually help them out of this predicament. Even the dog's water bowl can mean doom to young waterfowl. So can large deep holes in the ground whether filled with water or not. These can include excavation or foundation diggings, and unfilled perk holes and post holes.

Other accidents occur when the babies slip through fencing housing a dog or livestock. The youngsters can get mauled or trampled. If the livestock happen to be hogs, they also get eaten. Hogs will quickly devour live poultry—big or small. Ducklings a few days old can easily slip through a chain link fence. A border of 12-inch-high plywood placed around a dog kennel will usually keep them from entering. But it's hard to keep them from entering areas with livestock. Ducklings and goslings who have freedom outdoors can never be considered safe.

Ponds can prove fatal for young waterfowl, especially ducklings. Turtles are very dangerous to small and grown waterfowl. They grab their feet from beneath the water and pull them down under to drown. If the duckling or gosling happens to get away, the leg may be too injured to heal without crippling. Geese are fairly good at being able to ward off some of these predators. They are quick to know when one of their youngsters is in trouble and the entire flock joins the fight. It's quite a spectacle—water churning everywhere, geese screaming, all poking their heads and snapping at the intruder who's under the water's surface. Once the intruder is gone, all is quiet again.

Turtles can become so overly populated in some waters that not a single duckling or gosling will be left after a few days on the water. Before the youngsters are taken to the water by the parents, you should rid the pond of these killers. If you're a good shot, a gun can be the surest way to accomplish this. Do not count on many for turtle soup if you shoot them because they quickly sink to the bottom and can be hard to find. Many dead turtles left in a pond can foul the water, which, in a small pond, can make your waterfowl sick. Trapping is a good way to get rid of turtles if you don't want to foul the water or you want to utilize the turtles for food. Be sure the waterfowl aren't able to get to the pond when you are trapping.

Hawks and owls are also a menace. Owls will get the babies at night. If some goslings are missing some morning, there will usually be quite a few feathers laying in one area from the parents or the rest of the flock trying to fight off an owl or some other predatory animal. Even the smaller breeds of geese such as the Chinese are very good at protecting their goslings. Ducks have a tougher time and lose more offspring than geese. Many domestic mother ducks must fight and fend for their offspring on their own because the drakes have deserted them. Muscovies are better able to protect their babies than other duck breeds and the drake stays with his mate, but they can't compete with hungry turtles or fast snakes. None can compete with a very large persistent attacker.

If a broody chicken hen was used to hatch goslings or ducklings, do not allow the mother to have freedom with her brood. Ducklings get carried away when they're out ranging with mother. They are more independent than goslings and can stray too far. Goslings are more behaved than ducklings, yet adult geese are more independent than grown ducks.

When chicken hens are raising ducklings or goslings, either all should be confined or the mother should be placed in a brooding coop (Fig. 14-1). This is a pen or box used to confine the mother and her brood, but allows the youngsters to exit in order for them to eat grass. They will stay near the mother if she can't leave. A portable pen with a small attached house can also be used. The pen can be moved to clean grass every few days.

Don't be alarmed if you know some have hatched and the mother does not leave with them right away to eat and drink. This is normal. She knows it takes a couple days for all to hatch and there's no immediate need for food and water. The absorbed egg yolk sac provides nutrients and moisture during this period. You should begin to worry when she leaves unhatched eggs as soon as the first few are hatched. About the only thing that can be done, if you want to salvage the rest of the clutch, is to remove the eggs from the nest and finish hatching them in an incubator. The mother will usually not go back to finish the hatch even if you take the hatched youngsters away from her. Her urge to hatch and sit is over once she leaves the nest with any hatchlings.

Finishing the hatch yourself can be done only if the eggs have not become too cold. When they get cold, the hatchling becomes stressed and weak inside the egg and does not attempt to hatch. First candle the eggs to be sure they are alive. You

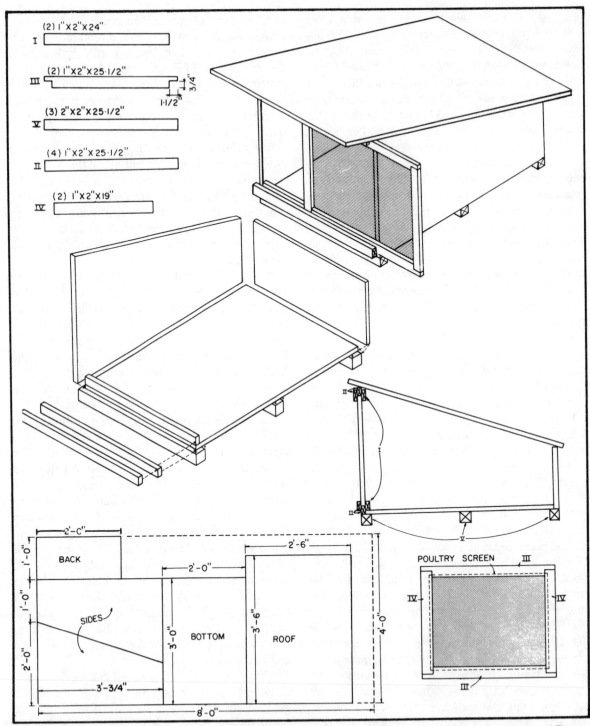

Fig. 14-1. To use this brood coop, leave sliding door open only wide enough to allow ducklings out. (Courtesy of Texas Agricultural Extension Service)

should see them moving, usually with their heads already poked into the air cell. If they are through the air cell, the air cell will appear very dark. You can also put the egg up to your ear. If they are into the air cell with their heads, you can sometimes hear some peeping.

If the eggs seem good, quickly heat the incubator if it's not already operating. Lay a warmed, wet towel in the bottom of the tray under the eggs to be hatched. This will provide the necessary moisture more quickly. Stand the eggs on end with the large air cell end facing up. You might need a few stones to prop them up when only a few eggs are being hatched. Very lightly mist the eggs with water and close the lid. Take temperature readings every few minutes while the eggs are inside if you have just started operating the incubator. In a small, still-air incubator, the temperature should be about 101-102 degrees F. at the top level of the eggs, but no higher. A forced-air incubator (one with a fan inside to circulate the heated air) should have a temperature of 95 1/2-98 1/2 degrees F. for hatching.

Avoid opening the incubator to check the temperature. Sometimes a vent hole can be used or a hole purposely placed in the top to insert an oral thermometer. Keep tabs on the temperature frequently until hatching begins. If they're in the air cell when placed into the incubator, the actual hatching would begin within 6-8 hours if the eggs were not chilled. Chilled eggs will take longer to begin hatching.

Keep the incubator shut until all are hatched. Just keep tabs on the temperature and do not let the humidity go above 90 or 92 degrees F. wet bulb reading. Use a pen hygrometer to check the humidity so the machine does not have to be opened to take the reaching. Slide it into a pencil-size hole cut in the top or slide through a vent hole. If a hygrometer is equipped on the inside glass window of a cabinet machine and can easily be read, use that. If the eggs are going to hatch, they will usually do so by the next day.

Sometimes the abandoning mother will still take these extra hatched ducklings or goslings. Because a goose will usually not go back to the nest for any reason, many times the goslings can be placed on the ground near them, then you can quickly run back so the parents take over. Ducklings can be added similarly. If the extras are going to be accepted, the mother will push the youngsters toward the rest of the brood. Don't waste time if they continually shove the youngsters away—they won't accept the youngsters. You'll have to raise them yourself.

FEATHERING AND SWIMMING

Many beginners cannot wait to see their young stock swim. Some immediately supply their day-olds with a cute little pool of water. This should not be done until the young waterfowl have actively oiled their down and have attained most of their feathers. It takes about eight weeks for most waterfowl to become fully feathered.

Some handlers assume young waterfowl can be allowed to swim because they have seen mother ducks and mother geese bring their offspring swimming. These mothers have sufficiently oiled the fluffy, water-absorbing down with oils from their own oil gland near the base of their tail. This is called the uropygial gland. The birds are frequently seen using their bill to expel the oil from the sac to groom their feathers. Almost immediately after hatching, a mother duck or goose begins oiling her babies with her bill while they are still under her.

Within a few days after artificial hatching, the down naturally contains some oils that repel water for a certain length of time. The hatchling can become waterlogged if it's left to remain in the water—for instance, if it got into a container of water with no ramp to get out. Furthermore, their down begins to lose it's water repellent oils quickly if the youngster does not frequent water, so suddenly placing young, downy waterfowl into water later can be hazardous. The down will appear soaked. This soaked down can be heavy enough to impede proper swimming and drown a heavy youngster who is far from shore. But the more often the young waterfowl are placed in water, the more the oil gland is stimulated. This is mainly because of the natural instinct for the waterfowl to bill at this gland immediately after swimming. The more they bill at, expel, and preen the oil through their down and feathers, the more active the gland becomes in producing and secreting the oil. The main reason young waterfowl who are artificially brooded should not be allowed in water is because they become chilled when the water soaks the down.

Commercial raisers vary as to their method of allowing young waterfowl access to swimming water. Some do not let ducklings into water at all. Some let them have access at one week of age. Some wait until the brooding period is over at six weeks of age.

Artificially hatched waterfowl who still have down should not be allowed to remain in downpours of rain. They will become soaked, chilled, and can even drown. If they are accidentally caught in a heavy rain they might appear dead, but many times if they are quickly gathered, brought indoors, and dried, they will be revived. Use a hand-held hair dryer and completely blow dry down to the skin. It might take awhile for them to show signs of life, so keep them under a lamp for warmth. After an hour, if there are no signs of life, you can safely give up the idea of reviving them.

Swimming is not necessary to successfully raise any waterfowl, but they will always appear cleaner and more well-groomed if they have access to water. The main reason to allow swimming is to give the birds access to a variety of natural aquatic foods. This will make any waterfowl more healthy and vigorous, which will in turn improve fertility. It's been often thought waterfowl need swimming water for mating. This is not so. Only the swan, who is surprisingly ungraceful and less agile on land, needs water to facilitate mating.

Always remember that ponds, lakes, creeks, etc., can be a good refuge for waterfowl against predators, but these waters also contain their own predators.

SPACE AND SHELTER REQUIREMENTS

Forethought should be given to shelter for young ducklings and goslings. Some handlers would not think of obtaining them without a plan for shelter, yet others purchase these eye-catching, cuddly little creatures on the spur of the moment without considering whether the available shelter is sufficient. They might only see them as they are today—not three weeks from now. Ducklings and goslings grow so fast, you can usually see the difference from day to day. They soon outgrow their little box and become large, active, messy, smelly creatures. Ducklings and goslings will usually not be tolerated in a box set-up in the home for longer than two weeks.

The best type of shelter for young waterfowl up until eight weeks, is one that has enough floor space for the entire brood until they're completely feathered. It should be ventilated because ducklings and goslings throw off a lot of moisture into their environment. A clean, dry building is essential for health. And lastly, it should protect them from the weather and from predatory animals. A simple shed can supply these basic needs for shelter (Fig. 14-2).

A very small enclosure can be used for the first few weeks with infrared lamps for brooding. To save labor and time, it's ideal to confine the waterfowl to one grow-out building that can be used for brooding and growing to a semi-mature stage—or in the case of meat ducks, to the mature and finished stage. When quite a few are raised, it can be time-consuming to move meat birds from building to building. With those to be kept as breeders, there is usually a shelter for other adult waterfowl already on the premises, or there will be a need for one later anyhow. Then moving them from a brooder house to other quarters becomes advantageous and even necessary.

For only one or two pairs of ducks, a small doghouse has been used with success by some handlers. This can cause problems with predators entering unless it's locked up tightly every night. As long as a good bedding of dry straw remains inside a small enclosure most can even be wintered without much trouble. A pen of 1-inch chicken wire should be attached for exercise and feeding and watering purposes. Waterfowl are messy eaters and drinkers. Small housing quarters will not stay dry long if they are fed and watered inside. A pair or two of young goslings can use a set-up like this until they become crowded, depending upon the size of the enclosure.

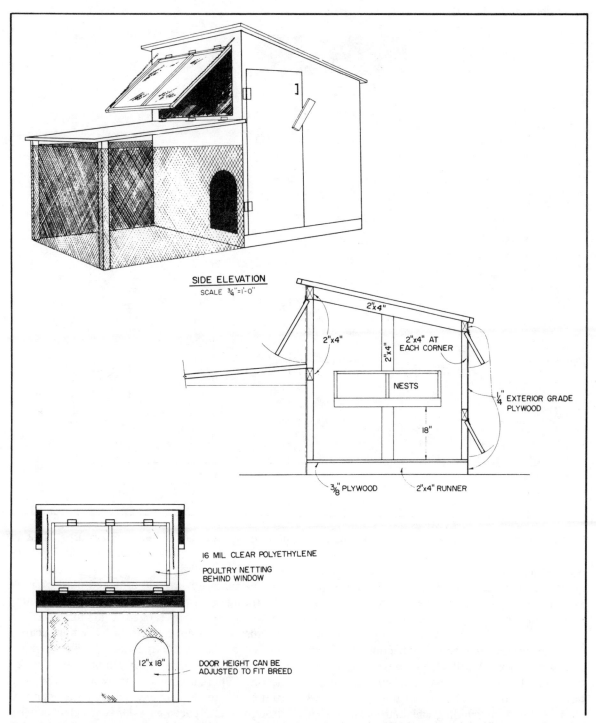

SIDE ELEVATION
SCALE ¾"=1'-0"

2"x4"

2"x4"

2"x4" AT EACH CORNER

2"x4"

NESTS

¼" EXTERIOR GRADE PLYWOOD

18"

⅜" PLYWOOD

2"x4" RUNNER

16 MIL CLEAR POLYETHYLENE

POULTRY NETTING BEHIND WINDOW

12"x 18"

DOOR HEIGHT CAN BE ADJUSTED TO FIT BREED

Fig. 14-2. This bantam house would make a fine shelter with outdoor pen for 8-10 large breed ducklings up to 8 weeks of age. (Courtesy of Texas Agricultural Extension Service)

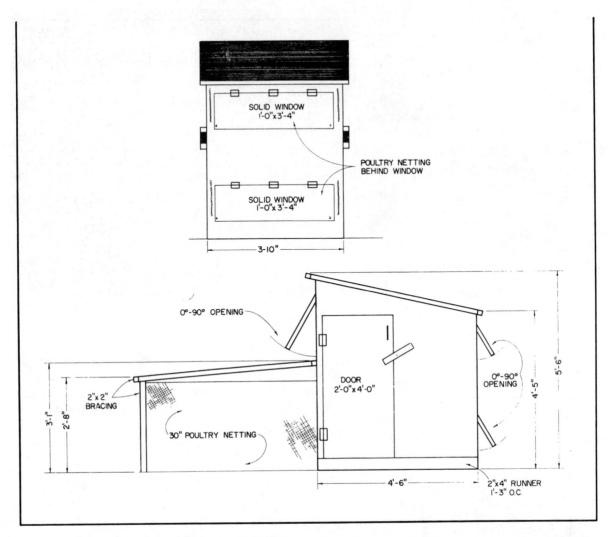

SOLID WINDOW
1'-0"x3'-4"

POULTRY NETTING
BEHIND WINDOW

SOLID WINDOW
1'-0"x3'-4"

3-10"

0°-90° OPENING

2"x 2"
BRACING

30" POULTRY NETTING

DOOR
2'-0"x4'-0"

0°-90°
OPENING

3'-1"

2'-8"

5'-6"

4'-5"

4'-6"

2"x4" RUNNER
1'-3" O.C.

A small brooding enclosure can be built into the corner of a large outdoor building. After brooding is no longer required, they can be moved to larger quarters. Or, by using short plywood walls, fencing, or plastic curtains, the barrier can simply be moved outward to allow more room as they grow.

Commercial housing will usually consist of long, narrow houses divided into sections by short, 12-20-inch plywood walls. Each section might contain from 125-200 day-olds. The building might have a series of canopy hovers running along the back length of the building which are heated with hot water pipes for brooding. The youngsters are usually moved to larger quarters every few weeks,

depending upon the outdoor temperatures. Most do away with brooding heat by the fourth week if temperatures are mild.

The majority provide attached outdoor runs from the age of day-old on up to market age. Maturing geese are usually ranged. Runs for ducklings and goslings do not need to be very tall because they will not be constantly flying over like chickens (Fig. 14-3). Almost anything can be used to make the runs. Short sections of snow fence have also been used. Remember day-old ducklings can slip through 2-inch spaced wire. One-inch chicken wire can be used. Little Muscovies very often use their sharp claws to crawl up and over barriers. They are

Fig. 14-3. Commercial duck farm showing attached outdoor runs.

also good jumpers when very small. A 20-inch, smooth-surfaced plywood barrier makes a good early run for them.

The following figure can be used to estimate needed floor space for each Mammoth White Pekin duckling and each large breed gosling: Day-old to 2 weeks—1/2 square foot; 2 to 4 weeks—1 square foot; and 4 to 8 weeks—2 square feet.

A hover or battery brooder's capacity for standard-size ducklings and goslings can be figured by dividing the rated chick capacity to half.

CULLING

Culling means eliminating undesirable individuals from a brood or flock. Culling is in order whenever any bird is in extremely poor shape. Waterfowl do not seem to need as much culling as chicks, but this could be because fewer are usually raised in a group than chickens. The larger the brood, the more that will need to be weeded out. If you want good-quality breeders and offspring, strict culling should be performed to achieve this goal. Many large breeds of ducks and geese begin to lose size in offspring after successive breedings. Matings should be chosen to keep the desired large size. The flock should not be allowed to breed at will.

It's not profitable to keep, feed, and raise birds

that are extreme runts, crippled, weak, or sick. It becomes a satisfying challenge to pamper and doctor these birds with some handlers. It should be more of a gratifying challenge to raise only good-quality birds. It costs no more to raise good stock.

The amount of culling depends upon whether the birds will be used for meat or breeding. Meat birds are culled for extreme runts, crippling, weak and sick birds. The gross amount of meat from these culled birds is always less. Their carcass is not usually filled out very well. These are the carcasses that usually keep getting pushed to the back of the freezer. These rules also apply for exhibition or breeding stock. Plumage coloring, skin coloring, markings, conformation, and breed type are also scrutinized. Personality can also become criteria for choosing good stock. The American Standard of Perfection is used in order to breed towards the ideal breed type. Those that don't conform appearance-wise can always be sold or butchered. Those that are unhealthy, weak, or runty, should be properly disposed of at the farm.

Older birds that are not producing well anymore become strictly a hobby if kept. It is a good idea to band or mark all your stock so older stock can be weeded out when production declines.

For pedigree breeding or culling of ducks, each

female can be kept in an individual pen or run. If a particular breeding is desired, a selected drake is then placed into the pen with the female for one or two hours every other day. This is a very good way to pedigree-breed because you'll know exactly who the parents are by marking it on the eggs that are produced. You will also see how her egg production is. To justly recognize the actual production, you must wait until at least two weeks after laying has started. Geese lay all through the day—ducks by 8 A.M. If you only have a few geese, you can usually tell which have gone nesting by watching them a few days. Large trap nests can be built for use with geese, of the same type used for turkey hens.

To choose general-purpose breeds from yearling stock, it's best to wait until fall when development of the bird is more complete and a wiser decision can be made as to the appearance of the bird.

When selecting meat ducks for breeding purposes, look for broad full breasts, good back lengths, and deep bodies. With egg producing breeds, look for an active, refined type. Those that lay early are good egg layers. They are also either busy eating or running from a nest. The pubic bones on the vent area of a good layer should have at least 1/2-inch space between them. The whole hind-end and abdomen should appear round and full as with chicken layers. Breeds that have orange or yellow bills and shanks will lose the pigment in these areas if they're laying. This fading is a result of the pigment being transferred to the yolks of the eggs instead. When eggs are being counted, always be sure predators and rats are not collecting the eggs before you do. You might unnecessarily get rid of very good layers because their eggs aren't being found.

Also remember that yearling ducks lay more eggs than two- and three-year-old ducks. But the ducklings hatched from the older birds are usually larger and hardier because the eggs are larger. Some commercial flocks keep their good two- and three-year-old layers because of this. When choosing drakes, as a rule, early maturing yearling drakes are best for these older females, while two-year-old aggressive drakes are best for yearling females. Good matured yearling drakes will prove to be more fertile; immature drakes used consistently will eventually lower the vitality and vigor of the flock.

Avoid keeping overly fat duck and goose layers. Larger specimens are different than fat specimens. Fat layers tend to contribute to soft-shelled eggs and double yolkers. A double-yolked egg laid by any poultry species is actually an abnormal egg. If these extra large eggs are consistently laid, they will eventually tear ligaments in the abdomen and the bird will become worthless. It's wise to begin keeping yearling breeders on a restricted diet that does not allow fat to form. Extra-large ganders are not always the best to keep for breeding. If one is desired, choose one which is active and full of vitality. Extra-large eggs will sometimes hatch, but because they probably came from less vigorous and fat geese, the goslings are usually less vigorous too. The average goose egg weighs between 6 and 8 ounces. I once hatched a 14-ounce egg, but the huge Baby Huey gosling only survived a couple hours. The egg was from an overly fat goose who consistently laid large eggs. Goslings from large eggs might hatch but be too tired to survive because of a lack of vitality in the parent stock.

EQUIPMENT

The equipment for ducklings and goslings is simple, but it should be chosen with care. The incorrect feeder or waterer can cause mortality when used with waterfowl. Knowing their habits will help you decide upon the proper equipment.

Brooders

Any brooder used for other species of poultry can be used with ducklings and goslings. Battery brooders can be used if certain precautions are kept in mind. Their limit of use is to about three weeks of age for meat ducklings and about six weeks for other standard-size breeds. Most goslings can only remain in them for about three weeks. After this time, their heads will begin to touch the brooder top and they can be rubbed raw. Calls can be kept in batteries longer, sometimes until completely feathered.

Because ducklings can easily enter the water troughs, use small mason jar founts the first week. Close off the trough waterers until then. Also, use bunched-up towels or rags over the sleeping area under the heating element for the first two weeks to prevent the young birds from getting their hocks caught down in the wire grill floors. These wires are designed for chick feet.

About 25 meat ducklings or goslings can be safely kept in a 2- × -3-foot and by 9-inch-tall battery brooder for three weeks. Keeping more waterfowl than this, or for a longer period of time, will cause the dropping pans in a battery brooder to become excessively messy and hard to clean. Battery brooders contain a sliding pan or tray under the wire grill floor. The droppings fall through the wire floor into the dropping pan below. Because the droppings of waterfowl are very wet, more thickly folded newspapers must be used in the pan than with other poultry.

Batteries operate on electricity. Most newer models contain a thermostatically controlled heating element in the rear with a curtain to help hold the heat in the rear sleeping area. A pilot bulb shows when the element is heating; the element does not run constantly unless in an extremely cold room. Batteries will not operate properly in rooms below 50 degrees F.

Young ducklings love to chew on the curtains provided in these batteries. They will chew the edges up and wreck the curtains. This can cause unraveling of the threads in the material, which can get wrapped tightly around necks and legs. Replacing the cloth curtain with a thick plastic curtain has proved to be better with ducklings. An old shower curtain cut to size can be ideal.

Most batteries today are designed as single units that can be stacked on top of each other, usually by using an optional rack. Most contain two feed troughs—one on each side, and one watering trough in the front of the unit. Game bird batteries usually do not contain these, because the birds are completely fed and watered inside by using separate feeders and waterers.

Gas or electrically operated hover-type brooders can also be used for waterfowl. Most infrared gas brooders are designed to be hung from the ceiling. Most electric models have legs and set directly on the floor, but there is one hanging model with a curtain. Gas models run on propane or bottle gas. The radiant-heated ceramic cone in the center of gas hanging dome brooders produce infrared rays that continue to heat even after the thermostat shuts it off.

Ordinary infrared reflector heat lamps are good for a few or a lot of waterfowl. These are available with a reflector shield only or a shield and guards. It's best to use a red bulb rather than a white bulb to help prevent feather eating. These bulbs should be the 250-watt type. Figure using one lamp for every 15 ducklings or goslings in early spring. Space them 1 foot apart by hanging them from the ceiling.

A four-lamp unit is also available. It is operated by a wafer thermostat. The temperature is regulated when the thermostat turns one lamp off or on. The four lamps are connected under a shield and the entire unit has legs to be set on the floor, or it can be hung. This unit will brood about 125 standard ducklings or goslings up to about the fifth week. Figure a brooder's capacity for waterfowl to be just slightly less than half of what it's rated for chicks.

Bands, Notchers and Tattoo Equipment

It will be hard to distinguish your younger stock from the older stock if they are not properly marked. Proper pedigree matings can become impossible if you do not know who is who, and very good specimens can mistakenly be disposed of.

There are various ways to mark waterfowl for identification purposes. Some ways are better than others. Web notching and bill marking do not allow easy and fast identification. Colored bands are the faster method of identification.

Notches or punch holes can be put in the web of the foot at any age. Very small notchers seem virtually nonexistent. The smallest standard livestock ear notcher makes a triangular cut, with a 5/16-inch width at the outside edge of the cut. This is too wide if a series of notches are desired on day-old waterfowl. It's better to make a short, narrow, triangular clip with ordinary scissors. As the bird grows, the mark will widen so a large clip is not needed. Various combinations of marks can denote parentage such as: one mark on left web of left foot for first-year breeders, two marks on left web of left foot for their first offspring, one mark on right foot web for the offspring of these offspring, etc.

A chick toe punch is sometimes used, but is not a permanent method of marking. This small, inexpensive tool makes a hole in the web, but the hole is too small. Later, the hole might grow together, and dirt tends to stick inside the hole, making it tough to locate.

Many types of leg bands are available. They are made of plastic and aluminum. Most aluminum types need a tool to secure and close the band. Some have an adjustable tongue and slot fastener that requires no tool; the tongue is simply brought through the slot and bent over. Other aluminum types are called butt-end leg bands. These are thicker and wider bands in which the ends are forced toward each other. A different plier is required for each size band.

Most plastic leg bands are in the form of a colored spiral or coil that are applied like a key wound on a key ring. Some are called a spiral and a half and some are a double spiral. The doubles stay put better. Most bands can be purchased with numbering, lettering, and names—except for the thin plastic spirals.

I've found many of the aluminum leg bands eventually come loose or break and become lost when used on waterfowl. The butt-end leg bands are very good; even the spirals stay on longer than most aluminum bands. All leg bands must be reapplied in a larger size as the bird grows. Seamless leg bands are tough to obtain for waterfowl. Sometimes they are available through clubs or very large poultry supply houses. This type is slipped over the folded foot when the bird is young but almost grown, and it's left on. Wing bands should not be used for waterfowl because they restrict the wing movement for swimming and flight.

If quite a few birds must be permanently marked, they can be tattooed over the web of the foot. A kit can be purchased that includes a pair of marker tongs, numbers from 0-9, and a jar of tattoo ink. For waterfowl, purchase 1/4-inch digits. A kit will cost about $35-$40.

Cages

These come in handy for moving the birds from building to building when young. Large geese are too heavy to be moved in groups, so are generally moved individually without cages. For moving young waterfowl, small cages with handles are best. In this way, only one person is needed to carry the cage. Large cages are used for travel purposes and occasionally for breaking up broody ducks or mating two particular ducks. A cage can also be used to safely let young waterfowl graze—or when raised up on blocks, it can become an outdoor pen that allows the droppings to fall through.

For traveling, a cage should be large enough to hold the fowl without crowding. It should be low enough to restrict standing while in a vehicle moves because they can suddenly be thrown off balance and suffer leg injuries.

For exhibition purposes, a cage should be large enough to hold one bird, a pair, or a trio without them having to constantly brush up against the sides of the cage. This can cause broken feathers. There should also be enough headroom to allow full standing.

Feeders

Most any feeder can be used for waterfowl. Trough types are the most commonly used for young waterfowl. Plastic or metal ones can be purchased, or a wooden one can easily be constructed (Fig. 14-4).

As the birds grow, a self-feeder can be used. This will save much labor if many birds are being raised. If they are confined, a hanging tube feeder is good. Many handlers with large amounts of ducklings and goslings, and commercial growers, use an outdoor self-feeder on range. This method of feeding keeps the indoor sleeping quarters cleaner and dryer and does not attract rodents to the shelters. Ducklings and goslings are messy eaters and most handlers prefer the mess to be outdoors rather than

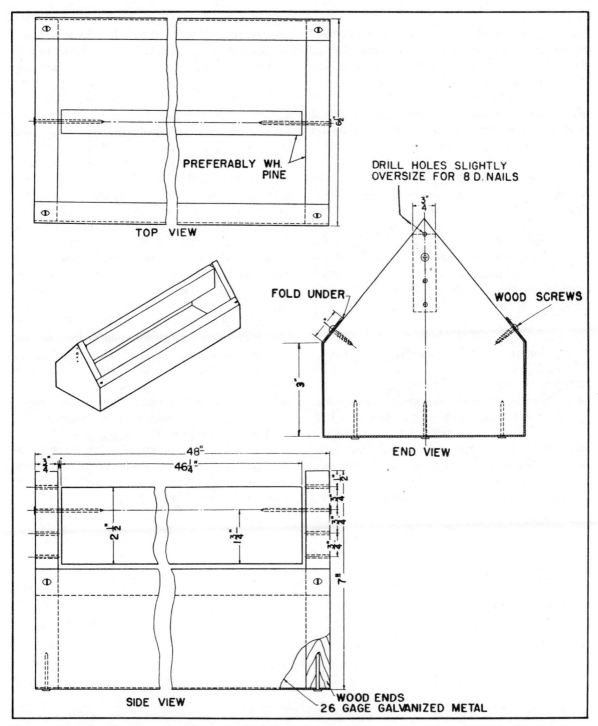

TOP VIEW

PREFERABLY WH. PINE

DRILL HOLES SLIGHTLY OVERSIZE FOR 8 D. NAILS

FOLD UNDER

WOOD SCREWS

3"

END VIEW

48"

46¼"

2½"

1¾"

7"

SIDE VIEW

WOOD ENDS

26 GAGE GALVANIZED METAL

Fig. 14-4. A homemade wooden trough feeder to make for young ducklings or goslings. (Courtesy of Michigan State University Agricultural Engineering Dept.)

277

in a building.

A wooden self-feeder for range can be built like the turkey range feeder in Fig. 3-11. A duck feeder should hold at least 500 pounds of feed. Although this seems like a lot of feed, it is only enough for 25 Pekin ducklings to finish out from 2-8 weeks with a 16-percent protein grower feed. Or, it will feed 35 Pekin ducklings to finish out from 4-8 weeks with a 16 percent protein grower feed. Approximately the same amount of feed would be figured for goslings, but if good pasture is available, they will eat less feed than the ducklings. Ducklings are good foragers but not as good as goslings.

The size of a feeder depends upon how often you choose to fill it, which in turn depends upon how many birds and at what age are being fed. Table 12-2 can help determine the feed consumption of ducklings. It can also be used to estimate the feed consumption fairly close for goslings.

Waterers

A good waterer for young waterfowl is one that is deep enough so they can completely immerse their bill up to their nostril, yet it must not be so wide as to allow them to enter and get wet. For day-olds, ordinary mason jar founts or the new plastic 1 1/2-quart waterers with the fount rim guard are ideal. They are not quite deep enough, but there is no problem in using them the first few weeks. Later, deeper founts should always be provided. This can be done by using the double-wall, cone-top fountains. They are available in 2-, 3-, 5-, and 8-gallon sizes. The ducklings should not be given any open top water pans until they are completely feathered. Even then they will want to bathe in the water and it will become fouled and dirty. Older feathered waterfowl can use water pans with an attached grill to prevent entry.

Because no fowl, especially waterfowl, should be without water for any length of time, the water supply should be kept from freezing. This can be done by using a rod heater. The cords of rod heaters are usually easily tripped over by clumsy waterfowl and should be secured. There are some heaters available that are clamped to the side of a 2- x -2-foot container for adult geese. Base heaters are not good for waterfowl because they will get wet on top and rust. A stock tank de-icer is excellent for geese that remain outdoors mostly in winter. Use these in a very large, low-sided tank for a continuous supply of water. When older waterfowl are confined, a stand should be built to hold their water containers. The top of the stand should have a wire fabric stretched across the top to allow excess water to drip into a catch pan or drain below. This helps to keep the litter material dry— a common problem when confining waterfowl.

Pond aerators can also be purchased to keep pond areas free of ice so waterfowl can enjoy swimming and have a drinking water supply at the same time. These are discussed further under "Shelters, Yards and Ponds" in Chapter 15.

Chapter 15

Mature Duck
and Goose Management

PURCHASING

It does not pay to purchase mongrel stock. The results can be poor and mongrels eat just as much and require the same care as pure-breed stock.

There are two types of adult birds to purchase: Grown birds of any sex or proven breeders. This year's birds purchased in the fall are considered grown stock. This is the type beginners should purchase. The reasons are as follows: For one, proven breeders are more costly. A beginner might not even be sure waterfowl raising is suited to him. He will not be experienced enough yet to choose the better of two good stocks offered for sale. Even poor quality is sometimes sold for high prices. Furthermore, a beginner will then have a chance to more economically get acquainted with the species and their demands before a large amount of money is spent.

Proven breeders are those pairs, trios, and flocks that have already laid and nested at least one season. Because the first season's eggs and hatches can be smaller, proven breeders are sometimes desired. These purchases should be mated pairs or

groups but are not always. This is not too important for the domestic breeds of waterfowl because they will mate up with others at least by the next breeding season. Wild breeds of waterfowl are monogamous and mate but once in their life unless their mate dies or they become separated. They will usually take on another mate, but production and the structure to their living habits will be upset. They will take longer to adjust. Mallards usually adjust quickly, and, if they are of the more domesticated type, will willingly take on many mates.

Be wary of those birds sold as utility, crosses, common, or farm stock. These birds can be anything. If the quality of the breeding does not concern you, at least be sure they are healthy. Also remember that all white geese are not Embdens and all gray geese are not Toulouse. All crested ducks are not Crested ducks and all buff-colored ducks are not Buff Ducks. Mongrel breeds exist everywhere.

When purchasing grown birds in the fall, do it as soon as possible. This way the choice will be wider and the birds will still have some pasture available. When pasture is available, this helps them to adjust to their new surroundings. If their pasture is not fenced as many farm lots are not, keep the new adult stock penned first or they may wander (or fly). This penning also helps you to become aware of any diseases that are not yet evident. Usually two weeks is enough pen-up time.

If other domestic waterfowl are on the premises, having the new birds penned where the original birds can see them will help to acquaint everyone. Never place new birds and original birds together right away. This is how disease is spread. Also, terrific fights resulting in injuries and even deaths can ensue. This can even prolong the period required in getting them to accept each other and flock together. If the new stock is not of full size yet, keep them from the larger birds until they can better defend themselves. After the pen-up period, the new birds can then be allowed to mingle. This pen-up period does not guarantee that there will be no fights, but it will lower the frequency and duration of the fighting.

When various ages of geese will be flocked together for breeding stock, it's better to have older ganders with yearling females than vice versa. Keep this in mind when purchasing extra stock. To help bring these matings together, pen the older ganders together with the yearling females in the fall or winter. Allow them to remain together until the season begins in the early spring. This must be done because often older ganders are reluctant to accept new mates.

Very large breeds of waterfowl, mainly geese, tend to deteriorate in size with each succeeding generation unless they are carefully bred up to keep the desired larger size. Large geese of the large breeds are alright to purchase as long as they have been properly nourished and cared for. Fertility is not as much of a problem with these geese as the ability to hatch. Overly heavy geese will sometimes unknowingly smother newly hatched goslings. Even if swimming water is unavailable, large breeds will produce very fertile eggs if cared for and nourished correctly. Production is usually poorer with fatty birds. Fatty birds can have health problems too. Do not purchase fatty birds, and keep in mind that there is a difference between a fat bird and a large bird. Do not buy for size alone. Also look for all other qualities.

When first releasing adult waterfowl to a pond keep three things in mind: First, choose a spot where they can enjoyably be viewed from a window in your home. You will get more enjoyment from them when you can occasionally glance at their activity. Watching them can make you forget about problems for a while, and you'll learn more about their habits when they're watched at various times. Second, the point of release should be where feed can easily be brought to if the birds are to remain near the water. It's best to use a self-feeder placed at the water's edge. This is a type of extra large bird feeder with a large overhanging top to prevent the feed from getting rained on. Both ducks and geese love to wash each mouthful of grains or pellets down with a sip of water. Having the feed out over the water will help them do this. Furthermore, the feed that falls will not become contaminated with droppings as on land. Third, choose a site that can be fenced for a few weeks to confine the birds.

Adult waterfowl and young ones just being released must be oriented to a chosen water site. This helps them to adjust to the handler and others who feed them. They will also become accustomed to the everyday noises and activities around them and will not be frightened. A good method is to fence a small area at the chosen site. Use fencing the waterfowl cannot get their heads through and become trapped and strangled. One-inch chicken wire is safe for most sizes of waterfowl. Test a piece of the wire to see if their heads can slide through. If so, it's better to use a fencing mesh with larger spacings (or stays). Erect the fence partially on land and partially in the water. Wild breeds will take longer to get used to an area; it takes domestic breeds about two weeks.

SEXING

When raising ducklings and goslings for meat, there is no need to purchase or sort them out as to their sex. Occasionally handlers want only a pair or trio. In this case, it can be worthwhile to purchase older birds so you can see exactly what you're getting. If a pair of day-olds is purchased, you can only guess as to the exact size or color they will be in the future. You should not rely on one or two pairs or trios of day-olds if this is all you'll be raising.

Then there are 4-H children who enter meat pens and pairs or trios of ducks or geese at fairs. They, too, should not rely on picking winners from only a few birds. When entering a trio (one male and two females), for instance, it's recommended that at least 12 straight-run birds be raised, and the male and two females be picked from these. A rule of thumb, if you want a pair from day-olds and cannot have them vent sexed, is to purchase four day-olds. A pair usually results from four birds chosen at random. This is not 100 percent positive, but only an average. Muscovies can fairly accurately be sorted because the larger ones are usually the males. Even this is not 100 percent positive because I've seen some tiny Muscovey ducklings that turned out to be drakes.

All domestic breeds of ducks, including the Mallard but excluding the Muscovey breed, can be accurately sexed when they acquire their adult plumage. This is done by looking for the "sex-feather." These are the two curled feathers growing from the upper portion of the tail in drakes. These feathers curl upward and forward toward the head. Muscovies are not a true duck and do not have these sex-feathers. The Mallard is the only wild breed of duck that has these feathers. If a Mallard were crossed with another wild duck breed, the offspring would have none or only a slight evidence of sex-feathers. It's this recessive characteristic which indicates that the Mallard is the ancestor to all domestic breeds. Adult ducks can also be sexed by plumage. Unlike geese, the plumage of drakes is colored and marked differently from the female's when matured.

As the Muscovey matures, the red carnucles around the face will be much larger in the drake. Any Muscovey drakes that might have appeared to be females when hatched, will become larger with age.

With adult ducks, the posture will be different between the sexes. Drakes tend to have a more horizontal carriage than the females. This is most noticeable during the laying season.

Using the ducklings' voice as a guide to sexing can be done at 5-6 weeks of age. This is earlier than the sex-feathers normally appear. The voice of a drake will be a low husky whisper, while the female will have the common loud, flat quack.

Determining the sex of geese by a glance is more perplexing than ducks because all but the Pilgrim breed are identical in color and markings. A beginner will have a very hard time distinguishing adult ganders from the female goose. After you've had a particular flock for a while, the slight differences will usually become more noticeable. Even an experienced goose handler can be fooled if he must sort sexes by sight in someone else's flock.

There are some distinguishing characteristics to be noted in both sexes of domestic geese. First, during the breeding and mating season, adult ganders will carry their heads higher, making their necks appear much longer than the females. This is noticeable when they're casually walking or swimming. When on guard or frightened, all will assume this position. When swimming, the stern (hindend portion of body) will be slightly higher out of the water than the females. Usually, but not always, a gander will have a larger body, larger head and be taller.

After laying has begun, the females will develop a more pronounced abdomen. This slight fold down the abdomen is sometimes called the "egg tract." It will make the abdomen appear lower to the ground than the abdomen of the gander. This will not be as evident in heavily keeled geese such as the Toulouse. In Chinese, this egg tract is easily seen after laying has begun.

If individuals in a flock of Chinese have fairly close strains, the size of the knob at the base of the bill will be larger (Fig. 15-1). If two separate strains of one age exist in a flock, one strain might have females that have larger bill knobs than the males of the other strain. Similarly, African and Toulouse ganders will develop larger dewlaps earlier than the females.

There is also a difference between the voice of a gander and goose at maturity. The difference is

Fig. 15-1. There are two White Chinese ganders in this picture—one is in the foreground to the right, the other in the center of background.

more noticeable when they are separated and are calling to each other. The gander will call with a more intense, honklike sound.

The most accurate method of determining sex in ducks and geese is by examining the organs within the vent. This method can be done from day-old through adult. Use a very good light to easily see the organs in day-olds. When vent sexing a duckling or gosling, hold the bird upside down in one hand with the thumb held on the side of the vent, the forefinger down behind the thumb on the bird's back, and the second and third fingers brought together to hold the bird's legs still. With the other hand, first bring the forefinger and thumb together. Then place these finger and thumb tips down over the vent. While pressing slightly downward, spread the thumb and forefinger apart slowly so the vent is fully extended and exposed. If the bird is a male, there will be a very small penis in day-olds which is absent in the female day-olds. The surrounding area is called the cloaca. In day-old females, only the pink cloaca will be seen.

If adult birds are to be vent-sexed, it's easiest by first sitting and laying the bird on your lap upside down with its head secured under one arm and the vent facing up over your knees. With both hands free, take one finger with a lubricant (such as petroleum jelly) on it and insert it about 1/2 inch into the cloaca. Move the finger around in a circular motion several times to relax the sphincter muscle that closes the opening. As the muscle relaxes, the opening will enlarge. Then apply some pressure downward and outward with the thumb and forefinger held above and below the vent opening. If the bird is an immature male, the spiral-shaped penis will protrude from a sheath of skin (Fig. 15-2, top). In sexually mature males, this organ will be much larger, firmer, rough, and reddened looking (Fig. 15-2, center). In a female there will be a small raised genital projection (Fig. 15-2, bottom). Be sure the organ of a male is fully exposed beyond the sheath encasing it or it may appear as the genital projection of a female.

TRANSPORTING AND HANDLING

Correct handling and safe transporting do not always become evident until waterfowl are grown. The birds are then much larger and harder to handle. Occasional handling is necessary sooner or

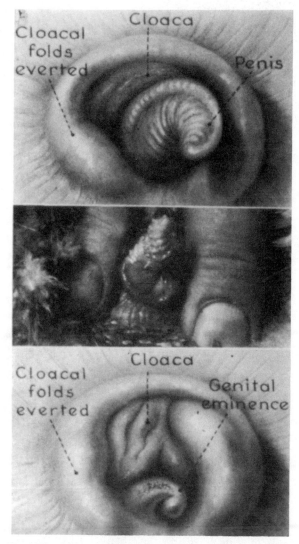

Fig. 15-2. Top—immature sex organs of waterfowl male; center—sexually mature waterfowl male; bottom—female waterfowl sex organs. (Courtesy of USDA)

to be blocked off first with a roll or two of inexpensive chicken wire and stakes. If this is not done, the birds will constantly head for the water.

Most handlers won't go through all this trouble unless there's really a need to capture the birds. There might be a time towards fall when wings must be clipped, you might decide to band the birds, sell the birds, butcher their young, change their mates, or prevent them from dying during a formidable winter. If you have predator problems, you might need to confine the birds.

If the birds become evasive, you might need to resort to extra manpower plus a long section of chicken wire to corral them. Using a person on each end to hold the wire (and someone in between if the flock is large and the chicken wire must be longer), the birds are rounded up and grouped toward a large entrance to a building. The entrance should have barricades to direct the birds.

Breeds and strains of ducks and geese will vary as to how elusive they become. It helps tremendously if a handler periodically treats his waterfowl to some grains and attention. Geese love to be talked to. If they've been teased by people, harassed by dogs, or totally ignored and left to fend for themselves, their survival instincts will become stronger. This means they'll avoid you even if they are a domestic breed. Ducks can be much more difficult to coax into trusting their handler, but if they are regularly fed and not constantly chased about and frightened, they will learn what you want of them and can be trained to go into a pen or building when slowly herded.

When geese must be manually picked up and handled, reach from behind them with the right arm and place your right hand over the front of the top of their breast. This stops them from going forward. At the same instant, grab the top of the left wing where it joins the body with your left hand. Then you can immediately do one of two things: 1) Slide the right hand back towards the right wing and lift the bird by firmly holding both wings near the body. 2) Bend down and slide the right hand from the top of the breast down to the bottom of the keelbone, almost to the legs. Then take the left hand from the left wing and grab the neck firmly but gently

later, even for completely ranged birds.

Waterfowl which have had nothing but freedom can be very tough to confine. They can get wild enough to evade their tired handler for days on end. To save wear and tear on everyone concerned, a handler must have a good strategy. He must think about his waterfowl's future moves—for they have their own strategy. For instance, if the waterfowl have a pond or access to other water, this will need

near the throat. Stand up and carry the bird against your body in this position. Never grab their legs to catch them because their legs can become injured. A sprained leg in a goose can be very difficult to heal.

Ducks are handled similarly. From behind the duck, take your right hand, grab the right wing where it meets the body while gently pushing the duck to the ground to hold him still. Then take your opened left hand and slide it to the left side of the duck's body, holding the left wing against the body at the same time. This will keep the wings from flapping. Then, immediately do one of two things: 1) While still holding the duck, bring it up to your body with the left wing against your chest. Slide your right hand out from the right wing, but place your palm down over the wing to keep it still. Place your left arm around the top of the breast and bring your left hand over the right wing. Ducks are most comfortable when handled this way. 2) This is used mainly for large, amazingly strong Muscovey drakes. Serious injury to a handler can easily occur when a Muscovey's trenchant wings begin flapping. As before, grab the right wing near the body with the right hand, coming from behind the bird. Use the left hand to grasp the left wing near the body. Lift the bird and firmly hold his back up to your chest and against your hands. This will protect you from the Muscovey's kicking, jerking legs and scratches from his long claws. A large man can have trouble holding on to a Muscovey drake. If you don't want to bother handling him at all, a harness can be made of baling twine by looping around the base of both wings and around the breast. He can then be walked, but not willingly.

The 4-pound Indian Runner and Khaki Campbell ducks can move quickly. Grasping them around the base of the neck near the body and lifting will not hurt them. This is much faster and easier than ordinary methods. Calls can just be grasped around each side of the body over the wings to keep wings still.

As with all other poultry, when transporting, use a container that prevents the tall birds from completely standing. This avoids injury should the birds lose their balance in a moving vehicle.

SHELTERS, YARDS, AND PONDS

Of all domestic poultry, geese need the least amount of shelter. In fact, geese prefer to be outdoors. Most will not indicate they want shelter unless the weather is extremely cold with blowing winds and snow. In severe winter areas, most need only occasional shelter. If a full-size building or shed is not available, a 3-foot-tall roofed structure should at least be provided with plenty of deep straw to help keep feet from freezing. If the geese can come and go as they please, this shelter can be used in combination with a large compost pile. Waterfowl will use a large, rotting compost pile of vegetation, straw, and manure to keep their feet warm when they climb on top. The compost pile must be started and actively generating heat before severe cold approaches. A compost pile that is generating heat will usually melt snow that begins to collect on it.

The side of a building protected from direct winds is sometimes used by the geese as a windbreak. A handler can help by placing bales of straw out from the wall and perhaps a tarp draped over to form a more comfortable shelter.

Geese not accustomed to shelter might refuse to enter buildings even when very cold. You can try placing pans of grain or pellets and drinking water near the building for feeding. Every few days move the feed closer to the building until the feed ends up inside the building. Be sure to have the feed setting indoors where it can easily be seen by the geese through an open door. The geese will eventually go into the building on their own. If your plan is to lock them in, however, they must be going in the building for a few days or they'll run out the moment you attempt to close them in. Many geese are afraid of buildings they've never entered. If they can become accustomed to a certain building in the spring by being allowed to lay and incubate eggs there, they will often use the building on their own in severe winter storms.

Ducks need more adequate shelter than geese. In areas that go below freezing, there are two good reasons to keep ducks confined during the winter. First, ducks cannot take the cold as well as geese. Their webbed feet will get frostbite and the toes will wither off. Frostbite is very painful, and the duck might become lame. The second reason is predators. Food is more scarce and predators will pick out these ducks as their easiest, most available prey. If open water is iced over, the ducks don't even have this chance to get away from four-legged predators. With owls it makes no difference. They will fish ducks out of ponds during the night. Some, such as the Great Horned owl, have their offspring in the midst of winter, so they hunt more than ever to feed their babies.

Most housing suitable for chickens is good for ducks. It's best not to house the ducks with chickens, however, because the ammonia from the litter of chickens will build up and burn the eyes of ducks and cause eventual blindness. It's better if they have a building of their own. If you want to conserve body heat for winter comfort of all the birds, and do not have extra housing for the ducks, it can be done using a few precautions: section a separate area off to keep the chickens separate from the ducks. Be sure to provide adequate ventilation, either with properly placed openings in eaves, or—if necessary—by using fans.

Because a floor drain is not always available, although practical, a provision should be made where spilled drinking water can collect under the duck founts rather than in the litter. If this is not done, much unnecessary litter will be needed and the environment will become too humid. The fount should be on a screened stand, and the stand should fit over a container to collect spilled water.

A water heater should be used to keep the water for ducks and geese from freezing. Once they are without open swimming water, they are entirely dependent upon their handler for drinking water. If their nostrils become packed shut, they cannot breath and eat properly. The debris must then be carefully picked out with a toothpick. Even if geese are outdoors during the winter, a rod heater can be secured in a large container of water to keep it ice-free outdoors. Just be sure to protect the electrical connection over the plug from water. These heaters do not cost much to operate, and they can save on water because there's no need to dump thick clods of ice out of drinking pans before refilling. Be sure the drinking containers are large enough to supply

at least 1 1/2-2 days worth of water. If not, the heater will continue to operate full blast when water isn't covering it.

If ducks and geese have access to open water in the winter, they are able to keep their feet from freezing, oil glands functioning, and can avoid some predators. Where temperatures reach 50 degrees below zero and a large area of open water is desired, this can be accomplished with a wind driven (Fig. 15-3) or motor driven (Fig. 15-4) pond aerator. These units will cost over $400 with shipping charges, but they do have advantages. They enable waterfowl access to open water, prevent winter kill in fishponds, and can provide water for other livestock. Also, if used along a beach, they can prevent ice heaving, beach damage, or damaged boat docks. In light of all these advantages, they could be a worthwhile investment for some handlers. Also consider the man hours involved in hauling drinking water to the birds. One unit comes in two sizes and operates by the wind to agitate and therefore aerate and oxygenate the water. It will keep an area 10-12 feet in diameter free from ice. When the wind is absent, the water will freeze until the unit has available wind again, but the ice is gone in a few minutes. The motor-driven units have a submersible stainless motor that thrusts the water to keep a 40-foot circle free of ice. A large version of this unit keeps the St. Lawrence Seaway open throughout the winter.

For small areas of open swimming water or low, large water drinking tanks, a stock-tank de-icer can be used. These are sold at most livestock supply stores, and are available in 1,000- and 1,500-watt units. Some use a float, some function with the temperature of the surface water, some lay in the bottom of the tank and others hang on the side. These units are under $50.

When laying ducks are housed, the same consideration should be given to them as is given to laying chickens. That is, comfortable quarters, dry litter, ventilation, constant drinking water supply, layer feed, and artificial lighting. When only a pair of ducks is to be housed, they can mingle with the chickens—but there are a few drawbacks. The ducks will lay eggs on the floor and egg-eating

Fig. 15-3. Small wind-driven aerator to keep a circle of pond ice melted. (Courtesy of Wadler Manufacturing Co.)

chickens will eat them if they are not covered by the ducks. Also, egg-laying ducks such as Indian Runners are very nervous and flighty, which can cause your chickens to become more flighty. It's better if the ducks have an area sectioned off to themselves.

Confined ducks and layer ducks should have at least 4 square feet of floor space. If placed in a separate shed, a few egg-laying ducks will not generate enough body heat to warm the shed in very cold weather, so do not expect as many eggs. The temperature for all layers should be above 40 degrees F. In cold sections of the country, this will not be possible unless a certain amount of birds are housed together, and the building is ventilated and possibly insulated.

It doesn't hurt ducks to be totally confined if they are given an adequate housing environment.

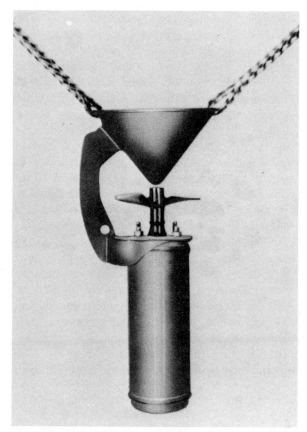

Fig. 15-4. Motor-driven pond aerator. (Courtesy Air-O-Later® Corporation)

tached across the top of the entire length to make it sturdier.

Sometimes females use the same nest and will wait until the nest site is empty before laying. This causes the eggs to be sat on constantly and they never have a chance to cool down. This can cause eggs to go bad. Separate stall-type nests 3 × 3 feet square should be sectioned off against a wall for geese. They might all still insist on using one nest, so place eggs or dummy eggs in all available nests, or close off a nest or two every few days so all nests get used.

If a penned yard or run is to be attached to their house, have it as large as possible. Grass won't continue to grow in stationary pens and runs anyway, but the larger the yard, the more sanitary and healthy it will be for the waterfowl. With ducks especially, it's important to cover the tops of these pens and runs to keep predators out. Unless ducks are chased into the house every night, most will remain outdoors in the pens on cool summer evenings. Then they become good prey for nighttime visitors. Simple 2-inch chicken wire will keep most predators from entering the top of pens.

A system of small portable houses and pens can be successfully used for pairs and trios of ducks and geese. These small units can be moved every few days to clean grass areas. The waterfowl will do very well in these when only a pair or trio are housed in each unit. They will also lay well and will hatch and raise broods of babies under these housing conditions. Be sure to keep the spacings of the pen wire to 1 inch if ducklings will later be brooded by the parents in them. Ducks do far better than geese in these pens during the breeding season.

Although swimming areas such as ponds are not absolutely necessary for waterfowl, the birds will be healthier, lay more and more fertile eggs, have cleaner plumage, and will require less feed and shelter from you. Ranged waterfowl will also be safer from predators when water is near. There is something tranquil and relaxing about watching waterfowl break the glassy surface of a calm pond.

Swimming keeps the waterfowls' oil gland functioning. This oil gland is used to waterproof their feathers as well as insulate their bodies from

Geese, on the other hand, will only survive. They will not be thriving to their capacity. Some will even hold up eggs and not lay regularly unless given plenty of room and privacy from other fowl. Adult geese in winter confinement should have 8 square feet of floor space each. If they must be totally confined during the breeding season, allow at least 12 square feet per goose. A dirt floor is best for all waterfowl. The cool, damp earth helps make a good nest site too. Most commercial raisers, especially of breeding ducks, supply individual wooden floor nests along the length of a wall. Duck nest should be 14 inches wide by 18 inches deep by 14 inches high. A 6-inch board should run across the front to keep eggs and litter material in the nest. The nests need not have tops, but if a long length of sectioned nests are constructed, a narrow board can be at-the cold. Just a small area to take a plunge will serve this purpose. Open water will protect waterfowl from stray dogs. Dogs are the most common threat to geese and about the only threat to swans. Because geese are such good watch birds, a single goose will warn all other waterfowl when danger is near and all will immediately head for the protective waters.

An open, three-sided shelter should be near the water for summer use, and/or winter use. In summer, the waterfowl might conveniently use the shelter for laying. Shelter from the sun should be available to all waterfowl, but those that have water for swimming will barely use it. In winter, the shelter can be used to escape winds and snow storms. If the water area is not sheltered, large clumps of branches and evergreens can be tied together and set into the ice during winter to help break driving winds.

A feeder should be placed out over the water's edge. This is nothing more than an oversized birdfeeder with an overhanging top to keep rain out. The feeder is hung on a post driven into the pond bottom. If geese or swans are in the pond with ducks, have the feeder only high enough for swans to reach because they will not compete for feed. If geese and ducks only are in the pond, the feeder should be tailored to the height for geese. The ducks will take care of all the feed that drops from the feeder. If fed on land, this feed spillage would become contaminated with droppings.

Wild breeds of ducks and geese and most domestic geese (as well as swans), have an instinct to nest on protective islands. Island nesting protects them from stray dogs, raccoons, egg-eating skunks and inquisitive people.

An artificial island can be created for peaceful nesting (Fig. 15-5). The main points to remember in construction is that they are large and sturdy enough to support the weight of the birds and that they are natural and visually appealing.

A 4- × -5-foot square platform is needed for a pair of Canada Geese. Larger breeds should have a larger platform. The platform can be secured or post driven into the pond bottom or a floating island can be made using a recycled truck or tractor tire with an inflated tube. The tire still needs to be attached to the platform. Floating islands are held stationary by anchoring to the pond bottom. Platforms can be attached to floating barrels and styrofoam. If styrofoam is used, it must be painted green and covered with 1-inch mesh chicken wire. If this is not done, the geese will "attack" it and chew it to pieces. If the platform is large enough, small shrubs and aquatic plants can be planted on the island for aesthetics and privacy. It's best to keep the nest shaded so eggs stay cool until incubated. A small island for ducks can be made by placing an 18-inch-square box on a pole sunk into the pond bottom.

Nest-building material must be placed on the islands for the waterfowl because they will not carry the material from shore. Do not use straw because it's too slippery and eggs will roll out of the nest. Also, do not use hay because it molds quickly and will contaminate the eggs. Use roots of aquatic plants, cattails, marsh grass, and muskrat house material. Place this material over dirt or sod. The dirt and sod help keep eggs cooler and prevent them from drying out.

MOLTING

All breeds of true ducks native to the northern hemisphere have two periods of molting called the eclipse molt (also spelled moult) and the nuptial molt. The Muscovey is not considered a true duck and molts only once annually. Geese molt only once a year too. After the breeding season is over for true ducks, both sexes immediately undergo the eclipse molt. This is usually towards the end of summer for most ducks and extends to about early fall. During this molt, the drakes with the color pattern of the Mallard—such as the Gray Runner, Gray Call, and Rouen—shed the brilliant male plumage and take on plumage resembling that of the female. This color is also worn by the drakes when young, until they get their first adult plumage. The neck stripe will also disappear. This change in color occurs with the other breeds to, but is less noticeable because the drakes are originally feathered similar to their female counterpart.

In the fall, this eclipse plumage is shed and the

Fig. 15-5. An artificial island built with a tire, wood platform, and shaded with bog-type plants—set into a cut-out hole in platform.

drakes regain their original male plumage. This second molt is called the nuptial molt. The flight feathers of the wings are not shed during the second molt. This regained plumage lasts until the end of the next breeding season when the eclipse molt will begin again. Both ducks and drakes complete both molts but the drakes usually complete the second molt faster. This second molt is not always noticeable in the females.

In the various breeds of geese, the sexes of each breed always resemble each other in plumage color and pattern. This is why it's harder to tell the sexes apart. The single yearly molt of adult geese can occur anytime after their goslings are being raised.

This molt begins in both sexes with the shedding of the primary and secondary wing feathers. The tertials are shed next along with the body plumage. Some fleshing loss occurs during the molt also.

Because wild geese and the lightweight domestic breeds cannot fly during this molt, they are more easily attacked by predators. Although most wild breeds will try to keep hidden during this time, handlers should pay stricter attention to safeguarding their geese from dogs and other large animals until the wing feathers grow back in. This is usually by the end of summer. If the geese are to be kept from flying by wing clipping and are protected otherwise, the wing clipping should be done as soon as the new wing feathers grow back. Unlike chickens, geese do not appear ragged during their molt.

PREPARING FOR EXHIBITION

Some handlers simply enjoy showing their waterfowl. Others do so to bring better prices on their quality geese. It can be tough to dispose of your extra adult geese and goslings at the going rate for quality stock unless some of the stock or strain has winning titles from shows. Starting with a well-known strain will help reap the higher price, but this type of buyer is more likely to be met at a waterfowl show.

It's preferable to have at least six (12 is naturally better) to choose from for exhibition purposes. Choose the specimens at least 30 days prior to the show. A handler should not worry if his waterfowl have just completed their molt. Judges are to take this into consideration. This includes any weight loss caused by the molt. During this 30-day period before the show, the birds must be brought to peak condition. Colored varieties of waterfowl should be kept out of the sun so their feathers don't fade. This will mean confining them. It's best to confine all the birds that are to be shown no matter what the plumage color. They will then become easier to handle and you won't have to go on a wild goose chase when showtime arrives.

Use plenty of clean, dry litter material to help keep them clean. Plenty of clean deep drinking waterers are also important. Waterfowl will keep their bills, nostrils, and eyes clean in the water. They can do a far better job than you. It will be necessary to prevent litter from getting wet from this water so provide a catch pan under the pan of water to receive the drippings. The drinking water should be placed on a stand first with the catch pan directly under.

Spend as much time as possible near the waterfowl. Make it a point to handle them a few times a day. Waterfowl are easily frightened and are then hard to judge at a show. Do not worry about commotion around their pens. Extra activity and noise will help to accustom them to conditions at shows and fairs.

A separate bathing pen can be very helpful if used a few days before the exhibit. In this pen place deep fluffy litter and a low wide pan or tub of clean water. Let the fowl use the water for swimming a few hours for two days. Then the day before the show, don't allow anymore swimming. Instead, go over the entire bird and remove any faded or off-colored feathers on the body by plucking. Do not cut any feathers because this can be frowned upon. Do not try to improve a bad crest by trimming either.

With clean water and a very small amount of hydrogen peroxide, take a soft-bristled nail brush and gently scrub any dirt from legs, feet, and claws. With plain water, very gently remove any dirt from the bill and nostrils. This area around the nostrils is sensitive so don't do any hard scrubbing there. Use a toothpick to gently remove dirt from nostrils.

If any very dirty areas exist on the body plumage, use only a very minute amount of shampoo and a small amount of water to lightly lather, then rinse by wiping with a wet rag. Never rub feathers the wrong way. Rub in the direction the feather grows. Rubbing the opposite direction will separate the feather webs and the feathers will look split and ragged. Once separated, these feather webs do not go together again.

Legs will show better color and gleam when a few drops of cod-liver oil, vegetable oil, or mineral oil are rubbed over them. A final buffing of the bill and claws (and knobs of African and Chinese geese) with a nail buffer will give extra shine to these areas.

Finally, do not ruin everything you've done to make the birds look great by cramping them into transporting crates and exhibition cages. If the cage or crate is too small, feathers will be broken and knobs scraped. Transporting in a cardboard box with holes is the safest container. It's less likely to damage plumage, bills and knobs. The box should not allow them to stand. Transporting in pairs and trios is best because it keeps waterfowl more calm; they get nervous when alone.

At the show, be very insistent upon using a cage large enough so the fowl do not break feathers and scrap knobs each time they turn around. Try to find out weeks beforehand whether the cages are suitable. Large geese need very large cages. If good large cages will not be provided, you may want to inquire about providing one or two for yourself. Be sure space permits their use. Extra space is a rarity rather than a rule. You might need to be very vocal over the space that should rightly be provided for large birds.

Keeping waterfowl dry while confined in a cage can become a problem because they need constant drinking water that is fairly deep. A few 26-ounce empty coffee cans secured in the corners with wire wrapped tightly around them will do the trick. Feeding pellets during showtime will keep everything cleaner and water less messy.

Figure 15-6 can help a handler to become acquainted with the outside parts of a goose. Figure 15-7 shows the parts of a duck.

BUTCHERING STEPS

It seems there's a lot of false notions over the butchering of waterfowl. Some handlers are afraid to tackle this job because they've heard how awful waterfowl are to pluck clean. The secret to dressing out waterfowl lies in timing the butchering.

The most common mistake is that birds are overly mature at butchering time. Waterfowl must be butchered before pinfeathers begin to grow from the skin. Pekins, for example, are hard to pluck clean if you wait until after they're 10 weeks old. The majority of Pekins should be done at 8 weeks of age. Muscovies are ready from 12-16 weeks of age. Most geese are ready at 5-6 months. In the commercial trade, a fairly new class of waterfowl is marketed. They are referred to as junior geese, green geese, junior ducks, and green ducks. These fowl are quickly fattened the last month on a fattening ration. This allows geese and Muscovies to be marketed at 12-14 weeks. Some are fully confined and fed only prepared feeds. Geese reared this way can be marketed at 10 weeks of age. Pekins are fattened and marketed at exactly 8 weeks.

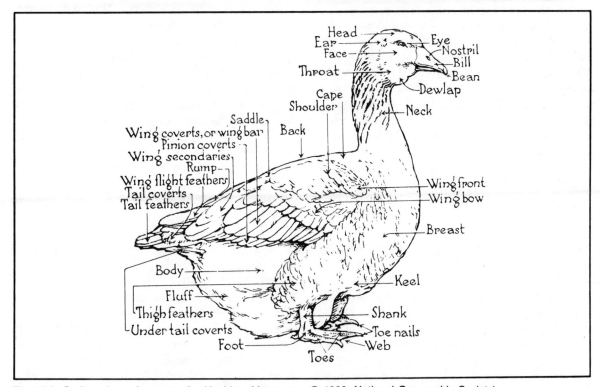

Fig. 15-6. Outline chart of a goose (by Hashime Murayama, © 1930, National Geographic Society).

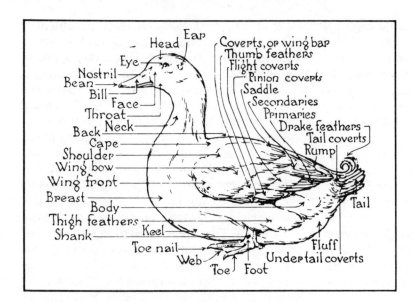

Fig. 15-7. Outline chart of a duck (by Hashime Murayama, © 1930, National Geographic Society).

With the advent of the special poultry wax and mechanical methods of plucking, the industry can whisk through processing and freezing at up to 2,000 or more birds per day. Many commercial growers have their own processing plant.

If waterfowl are butchered according to their cycle of feather growth, pinfeathers and difficult plucking will be avoided. Pinfeathers are actually undeveloped feathers just beginning to emerge from the skin. These are termed protruding pinfeathers. Naturally, they cannot be easily grasped when picking. Nonprotruding pinfeathers are evident but have not pushed through the outer layer of skin. As these feathers grow, they form a brush on the ends. This is when poultry wax must be used because the pinfeathers never really become large enough—without risking tough meat—to pluck quickly by hand. As fall approaches and the full adult plumages matures, the pinfeathers will again become less of a problem to remove. The problem, however, is completely avoided by butchering before the pinfeathers poke through the skin. If a small-scale handler will be marketing his own waterfowl and desires to do this for Thanksgiving and Christmas holidays only, the waterfowl should be raised only soon enough so pinfeathers are not present at the time they'll be dressed out. This means starting Pekins in mid-September or mid-

October. Geese would be started from mid-April to mid-June.

There is a very short time period within which ducklings must be slaughtered. With other birds, the period is longer. You can part the feathers to check for any pinfeathers to determine butchering time. They are also considered ready when the primary wing feathers are developed. During early fall butchering, your younger ducks can be sorted from your breeders by their longer primary wing feathers (if you've mixed all ages into a flock).

To distinguish the age of geese, feel their windpipes through the neck. A hard one indicates an older bird, while a soft windpipe shows it's a young bird.

When ducklings and geese are to be fattened prior to butchering, they should be penned and not allowed to range, and fed only on a fattening ration. A fattening ration consists of a moistened mash containing about 50-60 percent ground yellow corn (16-18 percent protein). Fowl consume larger quantities of mash when it's moistened. It's best to feed the moistened mash twice daily so it does not ferment. A self-feeder hopper of dry mash can remain with them for eating between the moistened mash feedings. Keep plenty of clean drinking water at hand to keep feedings constant, and because mash feeding waterfowl is a bit more messy and can clog nostrils. If a paler skin is desired, reduce the amount of corn to one-half and omit alfalfa meal the last two weeks of the 30-day fattening period. Substitute with ground oats, ground wheat, kaffir, or milo. Fattened waterfowl undergo less shrinkage than nonfattened birds. Heavy breeds have less shrinkage than lightweight breeds. Tables 12-1 and 13-1 show the dressed-out weights of some ducks and geese.

Birds to be butchered can be contained in a holding pen without feed for 8-12 hours before slaughter to help empty the crop and intestines of feed. This makes dressing them more sanitary and cleaner. Provide clean drinking water constantly during any holding period. Water also helps flush the system clean of fermenting feed.

A killing cone can be used for waterfowl. This helps prevent bruised carcasses caused by the bird's flapping. When a killing cone is not used, the bird must be hung by the feet using a shackle or rope. Keep from nearby objects to avoid bruises when the bird thrashes about.

The following method is used to bleed the birds: Draw a thin, sharp knife across the outside of the throat—high up on the left side of the neck just under the lower bill—to sever the left jugular vein and carotid artery. To control wing thrashing, the bird can be stunned after cutting the jugular vein. This is done by inserting a long, narrow-bladed knife into rear of the mouth and thrusting the point deep into the brain just behind the eyes. Some handlers hang a weighted blood cup under the severed neck to catch the blood to be later consumed or used as fertilizer because of its high protein content.

After blood completely drains from carcass, either the dry plucking, or scalding then plucking methods are used. Dry plucking is very time-consuming and is seldom done. It has the advantage of producing an exceptionally attractive carcass, but besides being slow, there is a greater possibility of tearing the skin.

For scalding, immerse the birds in water with a temperature of 150 degrees F. for 2-3 minutes or until the feathers are loosened. Add a teaspoon or so of detergent so water will penetrate the oil of the feathers. If water is hard, add a few teaspoons of baking soda to water; soft water loosens feathers better. The easiest way to immerse waterfowl is to grab the bill with one hand and the legs with the other, then immerse the entire body breast down into the scald water. Push the bird around against the lay of the feathers to force the water through the feathers to the skin. A stick can be used to ruffle the feathers and help the water penetrate.

Picking is immediately begun after this scald. First remove the large wing and tail feathers; these must be pulled almost singly in order to come out easily. Do the breast area next because these feathers are the first to tighten up again. Then finish pulling the rest of the feathers off by simultaneously rubbing and pulling. Do not grab too many feathers at once or the skin may tear. The bird can be hung or laid upon a clean work surface for feather removal. If pinfeathers are evident and waxing is not to be done, grasp pinfeathers between the thumb and a dull knife blade and pull out. Usually one good dunk and scald is all that's necessary. A second scald can be done after most feathers are removed.

In some commercial plants, wax dipping removes any traces of pinfeathers, hairs, and vestigial feathers. Don't use ordinary paraffin wax because it does not adhere well and tends to crumble. Special poultry dipping waxes are available at some poultry supply houses or through the National Wax Company.

Three pots should be used when waxing: one for scalding, one for melted wax water, and one for chill water. The wax is melted on the surface of hot water. The bird is lowered into this wax water. As the bird is brought back up through the surface wax, the bird becomes coated with the wax. Next the bird is lowered into a container of cold water to chill and harden the wax. Finally, the wax is stripped off by hand. With it go any remaining feathers—and even pinfeathers from the occasional overmature bird. To remove any traces of wax on the carcass, immerse once more in the 150-degree F. scald water. At some plants the waxing process is repeated because consumers can be very fussy.

Upon removal of all feathers, the carcasses

must be chilled to remove body heat. This is done by keeping the carcasses immersed in a container of ice-cold water. The head and feet are usually cut off before chilling, which helps avoid contaminating the chill water. While the carcasses chill, eviscerating can be done. As each bird is dressed out, they are placed back into the cooling tank to finish chilling. Chilling will take a few hours depending upon the size of the birds. To eviscerate and clean the giblets, follow the same procedure as for turkeys—outlined in Chapter 6. The finished bird is called a ready-to-cook (RTC in the trade) bird with giblets (Fig. 15-8).

STORING AND USING DUCKLING AND GOOSE MEAT

Duckling and goose can be stored and used the same as any other poultry, although there are methods that are more favored for various reasons. For instance, both duckling and goose can be canned, cut up, fried, made into casseroles, and cooked into soup. But most hear only about the roast duckling of Christmas. Furthermore, waterfowl is still thought of as an exotic dish. Therefore, the sidedishes and trimmings for waterfowl are en-

visioned as such. Plain rice, wild rice, oranges, apples, pineapple, ginger, curry, and sherry all are waterfowl go-togethers. The following recipes give some varied options for cooking:

Quick Duckling. Roast one 5-pound quartered duckling in a shallow pan in a 425 degree F. oven until browned, about 30 minutes. Use a rack so fat drains while cooking. Lower temperature to 325 degrees F. Drain fat from pan and remove rack. Sprinkle one envelope dry onion soup mix over the duck pieces in pan. Baste with 1/4 cup red wine. Cover pan with aluminum foil. Bake one hour covered; remove foil and bake another half hour or until tender. Serves 4.

Roast Muscovey Duck with Jules Bond's Beach Plum Sauce. Place one halved onion and a few green garlic shoots into the cavity of one large or two small Muscovey ducks. Rub skin of duck with a clove of cut garlic. Place duck in a roasting pan with about 1/8 inch of dry white wine or vermouth in bottom of pan. Roast in a preheated 325-degree F. oven for 2 1/2-3 hours or until meat is tender, basting occasionally. While duck is cooking, combine 1/4 cup dry white wine, 3/4 cup giblet stock (or chicken broth), 1 teaspoon Dijon

Fig.15-8. Completely dressed-out goose with liver, heart, and gizzard.

mustard, 1 teaspoon beach plum jelly (or currant jelly), and 1 teaspoon lemon juice. Bring to a simmer, stir well and simmer a few minutes.

When duck is done, skim all fat from roasting pan and add pan juices to sauce. Add 1/4 cup Curacao, 3 teaspoons cognac, salt, and freshly ground pepper to taste. Simmer another minute. If a thicker sauce is desired, dissolve 1 teaspoon arrowroot in a little water and add to sauce. Simmer until thickened. Serve with duck. Serves 6-8.

Navy Bean Stuffed Duckling. Combine 4 cups cooked navy beans, 1 cup flavored bouillon water, 1/2 pound bulk pork sausage, one chopped medium tomato, 1/2 cup finely chopped onion, 1/4 cup finely chopped celery, one finely minced clove of garlic, a small bay leaf, 1/2 teaspoon finely crushed thyme leaves, a few sprigs of freshly chopped parsley, and a dash of salt. Stuff lightly into duck and truss. Roast at 375 degrees F. for about 2 hours, then at 425 degrees F. for 15 minutes (over a rack), or until tender and golden. Serves 6.

Fruit Stuffed Goose. Stuff one 6-pound goose with the following mixture: 4 cups bread cubes, two peeled and diced apples, 1/2 cup chopped onion, 1/2 cup raisins, 1/2 cup melted butter or margarine, 1/2 teaspoon salt, 1/4 teaspoon rubbed sage, 1/4 teaspoon crushed and dried rosemary leaves, and 1/2 teaspoon pepper. Truss, place breast side up on rack in shallow roasting pan. Prick legs and wings with fork to allow fat to run out. Roast uncovered at 325 degrees F. for 2 1/2-3 hours or until tender. If wingtips brown too much, cover them with foil. Serves 6.

Some cooks believe waterfowl should be cooked fast in a hot oven for 30 minutes, then finished at a moderate temperature until done. This results in a pink-colored meat with a crisp brown crust. Another method is to cook hot 5 minutes and then reduce the temperature. If ducks have ranged much over pond areas, they might have a fishy taste as wild ducks do. To eliminate this, place celery, carrots and/or potatoes in the body cavity, simmer the bird in water 10 minutes, discard the contents, then roast as usual.

Because the legs of ducklings are set far back under the body, they have a tendency to protrude when roasted whole. This can be kept to a minimum by tying a cotton cord tightly around the legs and body. With geese, the long wings may stick out. These can either be tied to the body or twisted so the wing tips lay over the neck skin area. The loose neck skin should be brought under the bird and fastened to the back with skewers. To cut either bird into parts, simply sever each part where the parts meet over the joint. Zipper-type freezer bags are not usually large enough even for ducklings. Some handlers use a double thickness of 2- × -2 foot plastic kitchen trash bags.

Chapter 16

Duck and Goose Feeding

GROWTH AND FEED CONSUMPTION

As soon as the ducklings or goslings are hatched or placed under the brooders, their first feed should be available nearby. If naturally brooded and allowed outdoors, mothers will take their offspring to grass and pans of feed. When brooded by their mothers, it's not necessary to have starter rations available if they also have grass to graze on. But if confined with their mothers, a well-balanced, 22-percent protein starter ration should be given.

When the prepared rations for older birds will also be eaten by the babies, it should be in a form they can readily swallow such as mash or crumbles. They can choke on pellets or grains, especially if drinking water is not close by. Some commercially prepared starter rations for waterfowl are in the pellet form, but it's extremely hard for most day-olds to swallow. Usually by three weeks of age, most waterfowl can better handle the pellets. (An exception would be the tiny Call ducklings. They should not have pellets until 8 weeks or older). Many handlers also slightly moisten these with water the first

few days to assist in swallowing. This is a good idea, but moistened feed can quickly spoil and becomes a toxic substance that will kill young waterfowl. This includes feeds which have been dampened by rain or heavy dew; feed should be protected from any form of dampness.

Calls are considered to be delicate the first few days. Although dry mash is acceptable, slightly moistened mash always works better for them. At two weeks of age, they can gradually be introduced to a crumble feed and a limited amount of grass. They should not be given pellets or grains until 8 weeks of age and older. Their first waterer should be a small mason jar fount or the new plastic 1 1/2-quart waterers with the rim guard. For small amounts of Calls raised in a brooder or box, the same mason founts, without the jar, can be used to feed them. Day-old Calls have trouble reaching brooder troughs and most reel type feeders until they are almost 4 weeks of age, and because they are not aggressive feeders, they might not get all the feed they need. They should not be raised with standard-size ducklings when being brooded because they will get shoved away from feed and get trampled upon because the others will grow faster and larger.

Mammoth White Pekins grow to a live market weight of almost 8 pounds in 8 weeks. Their average live and dressed-out weights are shown in Table 12-1. Their feed-to-meat ratio is 2.82 pounds feed for each pound of gross weight. The average Pekin consumes about 21.46 pounds of feed during their first 8 weeks. Unlike other species and other breeds of ducks, the Mammoth White Pekin drakes and female ducks do not vary much in their market weight and feed consumption. Gosling sexes will not vary much in weight until about a month of age. Muscovey sexes vary in size and weight the minute they are hatched. This allows for a fairly accurate sex determination at hatching time, although it should not be relied upon 100 percent.

Muscovies are very popular for meat. In some areas, they are preferred over the Pekin. Although they take longer to mature to market age, their flesh is lean and not as fatty as Pekins tend to be. Some enjoy the Muscovey flavor more. It has a bit more of a wild taste that can sometimes be attributed to more grazing. The average market age of a Muscovey is 16 weeks, at which time they will have eaten approximately the same amount of feed as an 8-week old Pekin. Muscovey drakes will easily reach the standard weight requirements of 10 pounds for a young drake, but females hardly ever reach the standard weight of 6 pounds by 16 weeks. The females are usually only about 4 pounds. Other standard-size ducks will eat from 20-25 pounds of feed until they reach market age at 12-14 weeks. Market age is the point at which ducks or geese have just matured and their body is at its peak quality and fleshing.

Estimates for the feed consumption of geese are rarely determined because they usually range to supplement rations or visa versa. In fact, many young goslings require no rations when allowed to range in good pasture with the parents. I've raised plenty of "junior geese" without ever giving them feed at all.

Junior geese and "green geese" are those to be used for meat when they have reached a semi-matured weight and feathering from 4-6 months of age. Commercially, these geese can include all those up to December 31 of the same year they are hatched.

Goslings are usually not considered geese, until they reach 5 or 6 months of age. This is when most have attained an adult size and have adult plumage. Geese are ready to butcher when they show the least amount of pinfeathers and are well-fleshed—anywhere from 12-24 weeks of age. This large age span is due to the fact that there are various breeds, with varied ages of maturity, methods of feeding, and environments they are grown in. Usually the lightweight breeds of geese mature faster than the heavy breeds. For instance, a Chinese gander raised with its parents and feeding on grass only, will be ready to butcher at 4-5 months and have a 10-pound live weight. Its dressed-out weight will be about 7 pounds. At this age, most will pick clean easily using no wax, but only a scald to loosen feathers. The average live weights and dressed-out weights of geese are shown on Table 13-1.

Commercially raised geese are raised and fed a variety of ways. Some give a 22-percent protein starter feed the first 2 weeks and allow them to range and forage most of the rest of the time, until they are marketed at about 18 weeks of age. During the last 2 or 3 weeks, they are finished and fattened with various grains—similar to a scratch feed, which is a mixture of grain. Other growers feed limited amounts of prepared feed throughout the growing period but also allow considerable ranging and foraging. The last few weeks the birds are fed a high-energy finishing and fattening ration before being marketed at 14 weeks of age. Geese can also be strictly fed on prepared rations while in confinement. These geese can be finished in about 10 weeks.

In Europe, a common practice is to grow the geese to about 12 weeks of age and then force-feed a high grain ration (or noodle) for the production of fatty livers for "paté de foie gras." For this delicacy, livers are four times larger than normal.

The geese that produce these livers also are called "noodled geese." Years ago goose fat was in high demand. Noodling today is still practiced, but has been questioned on humane grounds because it's claimed no animal should be forced to eat. The geese are force-fed 6-8-inch noodles, four times per day for the last three to five weeks. The noodles look like small hot dogs or sausages. They are made by mixing together one-third wheat middlings or powdered oats and two-thirds of very fine ground corn and moistened with water or milk. They are then molded as with a sausage stuffer or rolled in the palms of the hands to produce 2- × -1/2-inch noodles, and are usually steamed to aid adhesion and to become more digestible. The noodles are greased with fat or moistened before feeding so they slip down the throat more easily. The geese are usually confined in dark, small enclosures. Their bills are opened and the noodle is slid into the throat. A goose can gain from 6-8 pounds of flesh and fat during three to five weeks of this treatment. Most of today's consumers want a lean carcass, but the noodling exists in those areas where there's a market for fat geese and fat livers.

Ducklings are commercially raised either in confinement where everything is controlled—from the feed eaten to the environmental temperatures, or they are raised in a building but have access to an outside pen and swimming facilities. They are very often given two or three feeds during the entire grow-out period. When only two types of feed are given, a starter ration of 22 percent protein is fed the first two weeks. A grower-finishing ration of 16 percent protein is fed the remaining weeks. Another method is a 22-percent protein ration fed the first two weeks, an 18-percent protein grower ration for another two weeks, followed by a 16-percent protein finisher ration for the remaining four weeks. If Pekins were fed a 16-percent protein ration the entire period, their early growth would be set back, but they still would reach a normal body size at market age. The typical body weights and feed consumption of Pekin ducks up to the age of eight weeks is given in Table 12-2.

NUTRITION REQUIREMENTS

The nutrient requirements for meat ducklings and goslings vary because of differences in ranging habits and growth pattern. Research has been focused on duck rather than goose requirements. Even more attention has been given to the nutrient requirements of turkeys and chickens. This is because of the birds' particular popularity in the industry. More research should be devoted to duck and goose feeding because each year consumer demand for them grows higher.

Because ducklings and goslings forage much of their own feed, knowledge of their total nutrient requirements is not so critical. In fact, most do well on an ordinary non-medicated chick starter and grower ration. Rations designed for chickens are too low in vitamin A, vitamin D and niacin; most chick starter rations do not contain enough vitamin D_3 even for chicks. Chick starter also provides extra—unnecessary—amounts of certain nutrients not fully utilized by waterfowl. Ducks are more carnivorous than geese and will eat many insects.

Duckling starter rations are available in most areas. This can be fed to goslings also. Remember to purchase and feed the mash or crumble form and not the pellets.

By looking over Tables 16-1 and 16-2, a handler will realize a substantial larger amount of vitamin A and vitamin D is required for Pekin ducks than for geese. This is due to the Pekins faster rate of growth. Rickets is a problem with fast-growing Pekins who are artificially brooded. The problem also exists with artificially brooded geese but to a lesser degree. This is usually caused by a lack of vitamin D_3. There is no way to know exactly how much of these vitamins (or any other, for that matter) exist in commercially prepared feeds because amounts are not listed on the feed tags. Feed companies insist they manufacture only nutritionally balanced feeds, but how are consumers suppose to know for sure? Many handlers are left believing the feed companies know exactly what they're doing. When their ducklings or goslings go down on their legs because of rickets, handlers then feel solely to blame, when it isn't their fault at all.

I can only suggest a handler try to choose the feed that most closely resembles the recommendations given by the National Research Council in Ta-

**Table 16-1. Nutrient Requirements
of Pekin Ducklings Up to 7 Weeks of Age.**

Energy Base kcal ME/kg Diet[b]		Starting (0-2 weeks) 2,900	Growing (2-7 weeks) 2,900
Protein	%	22.0	16.0
Arginine	%	1.1	1.0
Lysine	%	1.1	0.9
Methionine + cystine	%	0.8	0.6
Calcium	%	0.65	0.6
Phosphorus, available	%	0.40	0.35
Sodium	%	0.15	0.15
Chlorine	%	0.12	0.12
Magnesium	mg	500	500
Manganese	mg	40.0	40.0
Zinc	mg	60.0	60.0
Selenium	mg	0.14	0.14
Vitamin A	IU	4,000	4,000
Vitamin D	ICU	220	220
Vitamin K	mg	0.4	0.4
Riboflavin	mg	4.0	4.0
Pantothenic acid	mg	11.0	11.0
Niacin	mg	55.0	55.0
Pyridoxine	mg	2.6	2.6

(Adapted from *Nutrient Requirements of Poultry, 8th Revised Edition*, copyright 1984, National Academy of Sciences.)

ble 16-1 and Table 16-2. It might be to your advantage to have your own grains mixed into a 22-percent starter ration. Furthermore, I've always recommended giving artificially brooded ducklings and goslings a supplement of cod-liver oil in their water. This prevents the crippling effects of rickets. Cod-liver oil is rich in vitamins A and D_3. Without the oil, I've seen many birds cripple. Many handlers have problems with rickets. A lot depends upon where the young birds are brooded. If they're confined to a building or a battery away from the sun during the early part of brooding, for even one week, it's enough to bring on rickets at about four weeks of age.

The sun provides vitamin D_3, but do not count on this source unless it's direct. When going through panes of window glass, it is no longer direct. If you have only a few young waterfowl, some let them sun outdoors for short periods, but this must be started the first week of brooding. Natu-

rally, if the weather is not favorable, this is not possible—so administer the cod-liver oil. About 4 ounces of cod-liver oil for every 25 ducklings or goslings is enough for four weeks. It's only needed until the young birds have access to direct sunlight. Placing the oil into a plastic squeeze bottle will make less mess. A poultry grade of cod-liver oil should be less expensive but is not always available in small quantities. You can use the cod-liver oil sold in drug stores for humans, but it costs more. Purchase the plain and not the flavored types or the birds won't like to drink the water as much.

When purchasing feed for young waterfowl, do not let retailers talk you into a medicated feed. Sometimes if a duck starter is unavailable, they will suggest you use a chick starter for the waterfowl. If you must purchase a chick starter make sure it's not medicated. Some medications are toxic to waterfowl.

Cracked grains and duck pellets can be given any time after three weeks of age. Remember grain feeding will lower the total protein intake. Equal parts of cracked corn, crimped oats, and wheat will only provide 9.71 percent protein. If this is fed with a 22-percent protein starter and the birds eat one-half of each, they'll actually only be consuming

**Table 16-2. Nutrient Requirements
of Geese During Starting and Growing Period.**

Energy Base kcal ME/kg Diet[b]		Starting (0-6 Weeks) 2,900	Growing (After 6 weeks) 2,900
Protein	%	22.0	15.0
Lysine	%	0.9	0.6
Methionine + cystine	%	0.75	—
Calcium	%	0.8	0.6
Phosphorus, available	%	0.4	0.3
Vitamin A	IU	1,500	1,500
Vitamin D	ICU	200	200
Riboflavin	mg	4.0	2.5
Pantothenic acid	mg	15.0	—
Niacin	mg	55.0	35.0

(Adapted from *Nutrient Requirements of Poultry, 8th Revised Edition*, copyright 1984, National Academy of Sciences.

15.85 percent protein. This is all right for ducklings from 2-8 weeks of age, but goslings should have 22-percent protein from hatching up to 6 weeks of age. Other nutrients will be somewhat lessened with grain feeding also.

Always keep feed available. This is called free-choice feeding. The birds eat when they want and as much as they want. Never let ducklings and goslings run out of drinking water or they could choke.

To help assimilate nutrients, feed grit to the birds. If ducklings and goslings are confined and do not have access to sand or fine gravel, a starter size grit can be purchased or sand and gravel can be given. Poultry do not have teeth; grit is important because it serves the purpose of teeth. Grit need only be given until the birds have access to sand and gravel outdoors. Feed starter grit from 0-3 weeks of age. Follow with the medium-size grower grit for the next 2-3 weeks. A coarse layer-size grit is for birds who are almost adult size. Call

Fig. 16-3. Nutrient Requirements of Breeding Pekin Ducks.

Energy Base kcal ME/kg Diet[b]		Breeding 2,900
Protein	%	15.0
Arginine	%	—
Lysine	%	0.7
Methionine + cystine	%	0.55
Calcium	%	2.75
Phosphorus, available	%	0.35
Sodium	%	0.15
Chlorine	%	0.12
Magnesium	mg	500
Manganese	mg	25.0
Zinc	mg	60.0
Selenium	mg	0.14
Vitamin A	IU	4,000
Vitamin D	ICU	500
Vitamin K	mg	0.4
Riboflavin	mg	4.0
Pantothenic acid	mg	10.0
Niacin	mg	40.0
Pyridoxine	mg	3.0

(Adapted from *Nutrient Requirements of Poultry, 8th Revised Edition,* copyright 1984, National Academy of Sciences.)

Table 16-4. Nutrient Requirements of Breeding Geese.

Energy Base kcal ME/kg Diet[b]		Breeding 2,900
Protein	%	15.0
Lysine	%	0.6
Methionine + cystine	%	—
Calcium	%	2.25
Phosphorus, available	%	0.3
Vitamin A	IU	4,000
Vitamin D	ICU	200
Riboflavin	mg	4.0
Pantothenic acid	mg	—
Niacin	mg	20.0

(Adapted from *Nutrient Requirements of Poultry, 8th Revised Edition,* copyright 1984, National Academy of Sciences.)

ducks should have starter grit for up to 6 weeks of age. Feed grit by sprinkling some over the top of the feed. With confined older birds, the grit should be available in a separate container for free-choice feeding.

NUTRITION AND EGG PRODUCTION

The feeding of laying and breeding ducks and geese is different from the feeding of those raised only for meat. Tables 16-3 and 16-4 show the nutrient requirements for breeding ducks and geese. Most waterfowl are kept as breeders to produce eggs—the majority of which are used for hatching purposes. Because the shell of the egg is so important in protecting the developing embryo, the calcium content in the layer-breeders' ration is increased substantially.

When geese have good range and water, most will produce sufficient eggs and healthy goslings. Ducks are not as good foragers and benefit from a laying ration. A laying ration fed to ducks will help produce more eggs and the hatches will be healthier and larger. If you do not want to continuously feed ducks, they should be ranged and supplemented with a good layer ration. Do not expect excellent production and hatches when ducks must almost solely range for feed.

Indian Runners and Khaki Campbells can successfully be confined by supplying a layer ration and giving cod-liver oil a few times a week. Many will produce an egg almost every day. By using artificial lighting to increase the natural daylight hours to 14 total hours, over 300 eggs per year can be realized with a good strain of Khaki Campbell ducks. Indian Runners tend to be upset by cold spells and do not lay as constantly.

To prevent duck and goose breeders from becoming too fat, many handlers feed a "holding diet" throughout the winter and up until six to eight weeks before the breeding season is to start. Feed restriction is a matter of choice. It's much healthier and comfortable for any fowl if they do not carry around unnecessary fat on their carcass. Overweight birds will also produce soft-shelled and double-yolked eggs, which rupture the ovarian and abdominal walls when the abdomen muscles break down. They are then worthless breeders.

The breeder-developer ration fed during the holding period should contain less energy than starter and grower rations. If this type feed—which contains less than 2,900 calories—cannot be obtained, the feed should be restricted gradually to 70 percent of what's normally eaten. About two months before the laying and breeding is to begin, the "breed-layer" ration is fed. Those ducks used for laying throughout the year, such as Campbells and Runners, should be continuously fed a 15-percent protein layer ration. These flighty ducks are more energetic and are not prone to fatty accumulations on their carcass which would normally inhibit good production. A holding diet is mainly for the heavier breeds. As for geese, the Chinese breed is not prone to a fatty carcass either, so a holding diet is not necessary for them even if confined. Once they are ranged again in early spring, they lose any bit of fat they might have acquired anyway.

Oyster shells and grit should be fed free-choice to all confined waterfowl. Even if not laying, oyster shells are inexpensive enough to keep them supplied. The extra calcium from the shells fed a month before egg production will prevent the eggshells from being easily broken when laid, especially with ducks.

Select your breeding stock early in the fall so geese will pair up and choose mates before egg laying begins. They're quite particular about choosing mates and they need time to do this. Egg laying will be affected if this is not taken care of early. Ducks are not so particular. They can be chosen and placed together a month before egg production begins. Choose 5-6 female ducks for every drake. Geese do best in trios, although the lightweight breed ganders will accept 5-6 mates. Ducks such as Indian Runners or Khaki Campbells, which are to be kept for eating eggs only, need no drakes at all.

Most ducks and geese begin to lay the following early spring. It's not unusual for quickly maturing ducks to begin laying at five months of age, but this should be discouraged. These early eggs are not very fertile and the ducks that laid them won't set on them this early. Their strength and bodily functions should be saved for spring or winter laying. Both ducks and geese given artificial light stimulation can be induced to produce winter eggs. There's even been cases of ducks wanting to set on a clutch of eggs as early as February.

To induce early laying, provide 14 hours of total light (including natural daylight) three weeks before the date you want production to begin. Do not induce laying in any waterfowl until they are at least seven months of age. It will take 5-6 weeks before a high egg production rate is realized. The light does not need to be bright. Use a timer to turn the lights on and off automatically, unless you're positive you can do it like clockwork yourself. Most handlers can't. If the lighting is on and off at irregular hours persistently, it will affect production. Drastic fluctuations can cause a premature molt and no eggs. Besides initial purchase, timers cost a few pennies a year to actually use.

The artificial lighting can be timed to come on as soon as the sun goes down or before the sun comes out in the morning, or both—as long as the total natural daylight and artificial lighting total 14 hours. It doesn't matter much with ducks. The majority will lay eggs before 8 A.M. anyhow; only a few lay during the day. Geese lay throughout the day, but seem to prefer noon or early evening hours.

Both ducks and geese will usually take turns at nests if nest sites aren't plentiful. This can cause ducks to lay throughout the day or share a nest.

Avoid this problem by supplying sectioned nests along the wall on the floor of a building. The nests need no tops. Duck nests should measure 14 inches wide, 18 inches deep, 14 inches high. Goose stalls should be 3 × 3 feet square, and 14 inches tall. Do not make a high entrance or the eggs will be broken when the bird jumps down inside. If they are reluctant to use nests and insist upon sharing, use dummy eggs, rocks, or real eggs to entice them to the empty nests. The real eggs can be chicken eggs—they're not fussy. Just lay a couple eggs in each nest and only partially cover the eggs with litter material so they can be seen.

Sod or dirt make a good nest bottom. They help to keep eggs cool and prevent them from drying down too fast. This is important if eggs are not collected frequently. Hatching eggs keep best at 50-55 degrees F. Lay a thermometer on the bottom of nests to check temperature. If higher than 55 degrees F., it's best to collect eggs every few hours. At 65 degrees F., eggs will rot because they start to incubate but the embryo soon dies. Most basements are good for hatching egg storage. Storage temperatures for hatching eggs should be 50-55 degrees F. with a relative humidity level of between 75 and 85 percent. Humidity levels above 85 percent cause molds to grow within the egg, especially if the storage area is not ventilated. Eating eggs must be stored at temperatures between 45 and 55 degrees F. with a relative humidity level of between 75 and 85 percent. A hygrometer, such as used in incubators, will tell you the humidity level of the storage area. All eggs should be allowed to cool quickly. Do not prevent rapid cooling by piling eggs on top of one another or hastily placing collected eggs into egg cartons. Egg cartons (especially styrofoam) act as insulation and prevent rapid cooling. Do not allow many ducks to use one nest or allow broody ducks to constantly sit on eggs to be collected. This will only keep eggs warm and allow them to deteriorate more quickly.

Duck eggs seem to deteriorate faster than chicken eggs. Most times this is because the eggs are laid in damp litter (or mud). This removes the clear, protective cuticle substance, called "bloom" from the surface of the shell. Washing also removes this substance. If very dirty, let the eggs dry and rub dry mud or dirt off lightly with fingers. If the eggs have become extremely dirty, wet, or muddy, the cuticle has been already destroyed and most of these eggs will rot rather than hatch.

Duck and goose eggs for hatching must not be cracked at all. If cracked, but the membrane is intact (the contents won't be leaking), they can be used for eating and cooking. Occasionally a cracked egg can be saved and hatched by dipping the egg quickly into bleach water (1 teaspoon to 2 cups of water), thoroughly drying, then melting wax over the crack in a thin layer.

Hatching eggs are good for up to two weeks if stored properly. After this time, their hatching quality begins to go downhill. If eggs are to be incubated in a week, I've found that they don't need to be turned daily. This practice prevents the yolks and therefore the duckling or gosling, from sticking to the inside of the shell and preventing it from hatching. After one week of storage, the eggs should be turned at least once daily until set for incubation. The longer the eggs are stored, the less your total hatch will produce even under correct storage methods. Incubate as soon as possible. Goose eggs keep a bit longer than duck eggs. Usually the larger the egg, the longer it can be stored before actual incubation—but this time is only a few days longer. I would still count on only two weeks storage for goose eggs.

Some handlers leave eggs in the nest until a broody sits on them. This is done a lot with geese. I've found I can get 75-80-percent hatches from light-breed geese when eggs are collected daily and stored. Ordinarily, these eggs would only give me 35-50-percent hatches. This is because of temperature fluctuations in the nest caused by the body heat from laying geese, and uncontrollable environmental temperatures in their small building.

Some handlers house a few ducks with their laying chickens, which is usually safe even with egg-eating chickens because most ducks cover the nest with litter material. If they don't, egg-eating chickens will eat the eggs as soon as the duck leaves the nest. Egg-eating chickens are a threat to all floor-laid eggs (and nest eggs above the floor, too).

If you ever have waterfowl which appear to not lay at all, this is not normal. The first thing to consider is rats. If chickens aren't housed with the waterfowl, rats are most likely the problem in closed buildings. Rats eat more eggs than most handlers dare to imagine. They prefer the smaller eggs, but have been known to carry away goose eggs. Measures must be taken immediately to destroy these costly vermin.

When chickens are in the same building or area as ducks, many beginners are confused over whose egg is whose, especially if the ducks and chickens lay the same color eggs. It's really quite simple to tell them apart: chicken eggs have a duller sheen to them than duck eggs. Duck eggs have a waxy appearance. Chicken eggs that have been sat on and turned for a few days by the birds, will appear more glossy than waxy. White duck eggs, such as from Campbells, Aylesburies, Muscovies, White Runners, and Pekin, are not chalk white but rather a creamy white color. Those which lay blue and blue-green eggs, start off production by laying black-coated eggs. If this black coating were scraped away, you could see the blue-green color underneath. All waterfowl eggs are of one color—that is, they are never spotted as turkey eggs are. Various duck egg colors and egg weights are explained in Table 16-5. Goose eggs are white.

The majority of waterfowl will wait until their laying season is almost up before setting, although there are exceptions. The Muscovey becomes broody very early, and so do some geese. In wild breeds, the laying season is very short and only a few eggs are laid. They will sit on a clutch of eggs earlier than domestic breeds. A lot can depend upon the privacy a domestic duck or goose has. Those with more privacy from other fowl tend to sit earlier. Most ducks do not like to be disturbed. It does not take much to make them abandon a nest. Then there are some, especially Muscovies, who

cannot be prodded from their nest. It can even be tough to break up their broodiness. Yearling geese sometimes lay only one clutch of eggs and become broody. Keeping a broody goose from the nest for a few days will usually break up her broodiness so more eggs will be laid. Laying stops when birds are broody. If a broody is insistent, you can try locking her up in a pen a few days.

If a duck has begun sitting and you want to place more eggs than are in the nest, it's best to wait until she leaves the nest for a quick swim or snack. Then remove all the nest eggs and replace with only new eggs. Because it will be a few days before she decides to take this break, you cannot just add more eggs to those already in the nest because these are already partially incubated. Only the first eggs would hatch and the newer eggs would be wasted, unless artificially incubated or set under another broody who has no eggs. If this is your plan, you must mark the eggs to keep them sorted. Use an indelible marker or the markings will become rubbed off from her constantly turning them.

A standard-size broody chicken can sit on about 10 large duck eggs or 5 average-size goose eggs. With goose eggs, a rule of thumb for clutch sizes is: one goose egg for every pound of the bird's body weight. This rule can be used for any type fowl used to incubate goose eggs. For instance, a 12-pound goose can safely sit on 12 goose eggs. An 8-pound duck can sit on 8 average-size goose eggs. A 6-pound chicken hen can sit on 6 goose eggs. Treat chickens' nests for lice before setting the eggs. Lice will multiply around chickens and kill the babies.

Most waterfowl cannot have their nest moved to a more suitable location once they've begun to sit. If the area is predator-proof but is in a pen with chickens, it's usually better just to count the days to hatching and then watch carefully when the duck leaves the nest with the babies. It's then best if she's removed to a pen of her own. Most chickens won't bother ducklings after a few days of age unless one wanders into their pen alone. But chickens cannot always be trusted, so they must be watched. Father ducks occasionally help watch over their

Table 16-5. Duck Egg Colors and Weights per Dozen.

Breed	Egg Color	Egg Weight per Dozen
Aylesbury	White to greenish-white	38-42 ounces
Call	Cream-white to green	16-22 ounces
Campbell	White to cream-white	30-32 ounces
Cayuga	First, black, then blue-green	32-38 ounces
Crested	White to blue-green	32-40 ounces
East India	First, black, then blue-green	16-24 ounces
Mallard	Bluish-green	24-30 ounces
Mandarin	Light to dark tan	16-18 ounces
Muscovey	Creamy-white to greenish-white	44-52 ounces
Orpington	White to tinted white	30-32 ounces
Pekin	White to cream-white	38-42 ounces
Rouen	Light blue, light green to cream	38-44 ounces
Runner	White to blue-green	30-32 ounces
Swedish	Tinted white to light blue	34-40 ounces
Wood Duck	Buff to light brown	16-18 ounces

mate's babies. An entire flock of geese watch over all babies hatched from the flock, but they don't care for goslings who try to pick new parents.

Broody chickens can sometimes be moved to a more suitable nest site before eggs are given to her for hatching. This must be done in the dark. Lift her gently while moving her and place her in the nest with warmed artificial eggs (or the eggs she's been sitting on). To make sure her broodiness was not broken from this move, wait a day or two before giving her the new eggs you want hatched. Be sure to remove the old eggs (or the artificial eggs) at the same time. Goose eggs should not need to be turned by you if placed under a chicken hen. Most can turn the goose eggs themselves. Only occasionally will a hen not turn eggs. By first marking the eggs with a line half way around the diameter of each egg, a handler can tell if they're being turned. Do not be too hasty in assuming the hen is not turning them if you see the eggs in the same position twice. Hens turn eggs frequently. After they're seen in the same position at least seven times, it's usually correct to assume they're not being turned. Start this checking on the third day of sitting if the hen is not flighty enough to be scared off the nest. If she's flighty, she's not a good broody

and should not have been chosen for the job anyway.

Sometimes day-old ducklings and goslings can be added to a newly hatched brood. Perhaps you have extras that artificially hatched the same day and want to give some to the new waterfowl parents. The hatchlings must all be within 24 hours of age of each other and the addition must be made the first day they bring the hatchlings from the nest. Otherwise, most will refuse the additions by chasing them away, pecking at them, or killing them. Adult geese sometimes break the neck of the little "intruder." Also, if the additional goslings are older, they will not always go with the new parents. If younger, they will not be able to run and keep up. It's surprising how just one day can turn a wobbly little gosling into a peppy little runner. Even at one day of hatching, the addition might be refused. You never know for sure until you try.

When giving geese additional babies, it's safer for everyone to simply place the babies as close to the other babies as possible when the parents first bring them from the nest. Then quickly run back. To do this while the mother is still on the nest can cause her to get excited and accidentally step on and kill the other babies. The same should be done

Table 16-6. Duck and Goose Egg Incubation Periods. *

Ducks	Days of Incubation
Ringed Teal	24
Ruddy	24
Green-Winged Teal	25
Blue-Winged Teal	26
Canvasback	26
Cinnamon Teal	26
Northern Pintail	26
Sharp Wing Gadwall	26
Lesser Scaup	27
North American Black Duck	27
Domestic (Calls, East India, Pekin, Rouen, etc.)	28
Greater Scaup	28
Hooded Merganser	
Mallard	28
Red-Head	28
Carolina Wood Duck	29-31
Mandarin	29-31
Australian Wood Duck	30
Barrow's Golden-eye	30
Harlequin	30
Shelduck	30
Red-breasted Merganser	30
Muscovey	33-35

Geese	
Ross's Black Brant	23
Emperor	25
Snow Goose	25
Canada Geese (all)	28
Egyptian	28-30
Eastern and Western Graylag	28
Swan Goose	28
Domestic (African, Chinese, Embden, Toulouse, etc.)	30

*Since it takes 3 days for a clutch of eggs to all hatch, this means some hatch a day or two before the given incubation period.

with mother ducks. If the parents accept them, you'll know right away. They'll start maneuvering them with their bills towards the other babies. If rejected, they'll begin to shove them and chase them away. Time does not warm their hearts to the little orphans.

Table 16-6 shows the incubation period for various goose and duck breeds. Eggs can be candled at seven days of incubation if desired. Dark-colored eggs can be accurately candled at about ten days. Egg production will continue on the average to the end of May with geese, and to the end of summer (usually August) with ducks.

PELLETS, MASH, AND GRAINS

Adult waterfowl consume and better utilize pellets than other feeds. Grains are also good, but take longer to break down and release nutrients in the body. Mash can be used but is harder for waterfowl to swallow. It can be wasteful to feed mash because quite a bit is washed from the mouth as the waterfowl drink to facilitate swallowing. Once it's washed from the mouth into the drinking pan, it's lost forever. Bits of grain, on the other hand, can be picked out of the water and eaten.

Many handlers shy away from pellets because of their higher cost. This is fine. Everyone wants to raise their birds to be healthy yet at the lowest cost possible. If you are unconcerned with vast quantities of duck eggs, ducks can be successfully ranged and supplemented with grains only. A good scratch feed should be given. This consists of equal parts of cracked corn, wheat and oats. Grains will digest faster and be utilized in the body better if they are cracked or crimped into smaller bits.

Chapter 17

Duck and Goose
Problems and Home Remedies

Waterfowl are not immune to the ravages of disease, parasites, and other problems. As with all fowl, accurate records and observance of symptoms of problems will help a handler correct the condition. If a problem is noted one day with only one bird, it's a good idea to write it down. If any more problems show up later, a handler can sometimes put two and two together to figure out the problem.

The following extensive list can help a handler of waterfowl become more knowledgeable about problems that affect them. Although waterfowl are hardy creatures, the loss of just one bird can be devastating to many handlers.

ANATIPESTIFER
INFECTION (NEW DUCK DISEASE)

This is a blood poisoning disease peculiar to ducklings of one to eight weeks of age, caused by bacteria called Pasteurella anatipestifer. It's been reported in other waterfowl, chickens, and turkeys. Older ducks can become infected, but they do not become seriously ill.

The disease occurs rather suddenly. The earliest symptoms are mild coughing and sneezing, and discharge in eyes and nostrils. Later there is a greenish diarrhea and tremors of the head and neck. Birds lose their balance, fall into a coma, and die. Sometimes ducks lie on their back flapping their feet. Dehydration occurs and the liver and spleen may swell. There is a thick, string discharge in the area of the heart and over the liver. Pneumonia sometimes occurs.

Treat with a combination of penicillin and streptomycin, or sulfaquinoxaline which is less toxic. Keep sick flock from other pen of birds. Take precautions while tending birds so the disease does not spread to healthy pens. Always tend to the healthy birds first, and wash hands and change boots before and after tending to the sick birds.

Prevention depends on keeping ducklings or others in a sanitary environment. Disinfect brooders and pens after sick birds are gone. Keep them empty for at least two to four weeks before placing healthy birds back in.

ANEMIA

This is mainly a condition of geese whose resistance and strength has been lowered from molting, sitting on eggs, or gizzard worms.

Geese in this condition will molt very slowly, become weak, unable to balance when standing, and will lose weight. Eventually the goose dies.

Isolate the goose from the others and treat with ferrous sulfate, mixing 1 teaspoon into a gallon of clean drinking water. Also supplement with iron, vitamin B_6 and vitamin E. Treat for five to seven days and then every two days until you see a marked improvement. Because gizzard worms can produce the same symptoms and weaken a goose, use a wormer such as ivermectin, levamizole, or the over-the-counter brand Tramizole to rid the gizzard lining of the worms. Feeding a sloppy, wet mash might encourage the goose to eat more and thus recover faster.

ASCITES (WATER BELLY)

This is a condition mainly affecting ducks, and shows as an accumulation of fluids in the abdominal cavity. It can be caused by malfunctions of the organs or by overdoses of salt. The abdomen looks swelled and the duck will seem to stand more upright. It's best to destroy the afflicted duck because treating will not totally cure the ailment and it may only occur again.

BOTULISM

Also known as limberneck and western duck sickness, this is a food poisoning of either ducks or geese. It occurs when the birds eat decayed matter containing a toxin produced by the Clostridium botulinum bacteria. It is only contracted by eating the toxic substance; it is not spread from bird contact. Just ingesting a few maggots that have been feeding on a rotting carcass can cause toxic reactions in a bird. Western duck sickness is the name used in the western United States and Canada where wild waterfowl die by the millions after eating decayed vegetation in shallow marshes.

The most common symptom, occurring shortly after ingesting the toxin, is paralysis—mainly of the neck muscles. Legs and wings can become paralyzed. Frequently the feathers become loose and the bird becomes listless and sleepy. A large amount of the toxin will kill the bird in 12-24 hours.

Quick action must be taken before paralysis sets in if birds are to be saved. Lock them up until the source of the toxin is found. Stagnant ponds or other places containing decayed matter should be considered as sources to the toxin. Wet, spoiled feed is another source. Remove spoiled feed from birds. Do not feed birds for 24 hours; flush out their intestinal system by giving 1 ounce epsom salts mixed in a very small amount of wet mash or clean water for each six birds. About 1/4 cup of a stock solution of potassium permanganate mixed into 2 gallons of drinking water might help remove the toxin (a stock solution can be made by dissolving one 300-mg. tablet into 1 quart of hot water. It will take a few hours to dissolve fully). Inject each affected bird with 2-4cc of C.botulinum antitoxin under the skin of the neck. If there's no marked improvement seen in 12 hours, repeat the injection.

DROPPED TONGUE (HERNIA)

This is mainly a condition of adult geese who have dewlaps, but can occur in any breed of geese. It occurs when the inside of the lower mandible obtains a long groove. The tongue drops down into this groove and the goose cannot easily remove the tongue for proper eating. The goose loses weight, becomes weak, and dies. The cause can be an abnormally extended dewlap. Dewlaps should extend no farther than the beginning of the lower mandible under the throat. If it extends further, the weight can pull the inside of the bottom mandible downwards.

If a handler wants to save the goose, a small procedure can be performed to correct the problem. With a sterilized needle and strong cotton thread, sew very small stitches beginning under the lower mandible and across the edge of the dewlap. Have someone assist you by placing their finger under the tongue. They must keep it raised high enough so the membranes underneath are kept raised too. This is to prevent stitching into the membranes that must be left to form a solid pad on the inside of lower mandible. Stitch as small and close as you can over the dewlap next to the mandible. When you come just to the edge of the mandible, begin stitching downward and taper off for a nice-looking dewlap. It's best to restitch, taking stitches between the original stitches. This will assure that circulation will be cut off and the small section sewn off will dry up and fall off. It takes about two weeks for the part to turn dark, dry up, and fall off. If a small piece of skin remains, a thread can be tied around it to cut off the circulation. This too will dry up and fall off.

DUCK VIRSUS ENTERITIS (DUCK PLAGUE)

This is a contagious disease of ducks, geese, and swans of all ages—caused by a herpes virus. The first diagnosis in the United States was in 1967, Suffolk County, New York. It's been reported in Europe, Asia, and North America. Commercial duck growers have suffered much loss from this disease.

The disease is spread by contaminated droppings in the feed or bathing water of the waterfowl. The virus obtains entry into the body through the mouth, nostrils, cloaca, or through lacerations and cuts on the skin.

Symptoms include extreme thirst, watery or bloody diarrhea, listlessness, lost appetite, drooped wings, soiled vents, swollen eyelids, nasal discharge, drop in egg production, high mortality, sudden deaths, hemorrhages and decay in the internal organs. Very sudden high mortality is usually the first sign of this disease. Birds do not even have time to waste away; they die with a good, fleshed body. Ducklings will show dehydration, weight loss, blood on vents and bluish colored beaks. It is fatal to Muscovies more than other breeds.

Treatment is not successful. Prevention is the best plan of attack. Keep pens sanitary, and incinerate any dead birds or slaughter remains. Keep visitors away from your pens and keep away from other ducks. Thoroughly clean and disinfect pens and buildings before replacing with new stock. Vaccinate with the modified live virus vaccine to prevent further losses.

DUCK VIRUS HEPATITIS (BABY DUCK DISEASE)

This is a highly contagious, very fatal disease mainly in ducklings under four weeks of age. It is caused by a virus. There have been minor outbreaks in Mallard ducklings and goslings, and it is highly fatal to Pekins. After contact with contaminated surroundings or infected ducklings, the disease makes its appearance in only 18-48 hours. The virus is contained in the droppings of infected birds. It amazingly doesn't spread easily to other nearby pens, but is highly contagious within the same pen.

Symptoms become obvious suddenly. An affected duckling will lie on its side with its head drawn back towards the tail, paddling its feet in spasms and dying within a few minutes. Within 3-7 days 95 percent of the ducklings are dead. Some have reported 75 percent mortality in 48 hours. Internally the liver will be enlarged and covered with spots of blood. The spleen is slightly enlarged and of a dark color, and the kidneys can be swollen.

Treat at onset of symptoms by injecting 1/2 ml. of antiserum into a muscle. Contact state poultry science laboratory if you are unable to obtain the antiserum. Prevent outbreaks by vaccinating breeders with attenuated or killed vaccine. Ducklings from the breeders will have parental immunity for three to six weeks. Ducklings can also have lifetime immunity by vaccinating with attenuated vaccine. Keep ducklings in sanitary living conditions.

FEATHER EATING

This is a bad habit occurring mostly with ducklings kept in crowded conditions. It begins when ducklings preen feed that has fallen on the backs of other ducklings. The down soon comes away with the feed and becomes another substance to satisfy their appetite. Soon the entire backs of most all the ducklings are bare. These barebacks must be brooded longer, and the feathers that eventually grow in can be pinfeathers, which cause difficulties at butchering time. Birds become somewhat stunted.

Some preventative measures should be taken

because this problem is easier to avoid than cure. Provide more than enough feeders and waterers because the habit can begin when ducklings are looking for feed. Place the feeders as far from the waterers as conveniently possible. This will help prevent scattered wet feed from appearing on the backs of the ducklings. Also, in the busy process of running from feeder to waterer, waterer to feeder, etc., a lot of the particles of feed fall from faces and bodies. Use feeders the ducklings cannot crawl into. Use waterers that allow complete immersing of bills without ducklings being able to crawl in. Feed a crumble-type feed to day-old ducklings rather than a mash. Do not keep ducklings on the crumbles longer than two weeks. At two weeks switch to the grower pellets. This will help avoid scattered particles of feed at the time many ducklings begin the vice of feather eating. In the beginning (or when feather eating has become a problem) brood under red lights so feed specks aren't as easily seen.

FLYING

This only becomes a problem when lightweight breed ducklings such as Mallards and some Muscovies or goslings such as Chinese are nearing the fall season. If the fowl are around this long, it usually means they're being kept for egg production or reproducing. Then it's usually wise to clip wings. Even if kept confined, some breeds might accidentally get out and fly from your reach. Runner ducks do not fly although light in weight, but they're excellent at outrunning you—which you can't do anything about. The majority of ducks that can fly, except for the Muscovey, are more wild in nature. Once they fly into some comfortable brush, they are usually content there.

There are obvious and not-so-obvious dangers in ducks and geese being allowed to fly about the premises. They can land suddenly in a roadway and be run over. Neighborhood dogs might spot them before you do. If a pond or lake is near or on the property, large turtles can pull lightweight ducks under and drown them. Turtles prefer ducklings, but will also take bites out of mature duck legs or

feet, crippling them. If ponds or lakes are just beginning to freeze over, geese will fly toward them to land. The impact breaks the ice and the goose slides helplessly through the hole and under the ice, and drowns. Birds can slide into strings of barbed wire fencing. Geese, in particular, can easily sprain their legs if they land on iced and slippery ground.

Wing clipping prevents ducks and geese from flying and can prevent harm from coming to the bird. Use ordinary sharp scissors to clip breeder's wings. Fan out one wing and evenly cut only the row of primaries off (Fig. 17-1). Do not cut into the hollow quill because this can be like cutting into the quick of your own fingernail. Clip one wing only; this throws the bird off balance. Clipping both wings allows them to fly because balance is again even. It's best to do wings on the same side of all birds to avoid later confusion should you want to check the wing. One clipping will last a full season. This means clipping is only done once a year—in the fall when birds get their winter plumage.

FOWL CHOLERA

This is sometimes referred to as goose septicemia because of the blood poisoning involved. It is an infectious disease of birds usually over six weeks of age, caused by a bacteria called Pasteurella multocida. Chickens, ducks, and turkeys are the most susceptible. Muscovies seem less resistant. It is spread from carrier birds, contaminated buildings, predators, rodents, dead birds, infectious droppings, nasal discharge, and contaminated feed, water and equipment.

Dead birds might be first sign of the disease. Other symptoms include yellowish-green diarrhea, fever, depression, thirst (from fever), ruffled feathers, discharge from mouth, watery eyes, fast breathing, and lowered feed intake. Later there is weight loss, lameness, joint infection, a rattling sound in throat, swollen joints and footpads. Internally there are small hemorrhages on the tip of heart. The intestines appear inflamed, and there's pinpoint decay on a swollen, dark liver. There can be hemorrhages elsewhere as in the fat, inner eyelids, and mucous membranes.

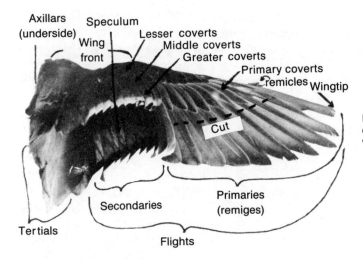

Axillars (underside)
Speculum
Wing front
Lesser coverts
Middle coverts
Greater coverts
Primary coverts
Remicles
Wingtip
Cut
Tertials
Secondaries
Primaries (remiges)
Flights

Fig. 17-1. A Mallard wing extended with dotted line over primary feathers showing where to cut for wing clipping.

Treat with a sulfonamide such as sulfadimethoxine. Double the dose the first day, medicate at recommended dose for four days, then medicate twice a week until the disease seems to be under control. When first diagnosed, vaccinate all birds to prevent serious outbreak. Use vaccine preferably from duck cultures. Remember sulfa drugs can cause residues in meat and eggs. Recovered birds remain as carriers.

Prevent the disease by rodent- and predator-proofing buildings and grounds. Disinfect buildings and equipment. If the disease has been a problem on the premises, vaccinate all future replacement birds.

GOOSE INFLUENZA

This is also called goose pneumonia or goose septicemia because of the characteristic blood poisoning. It is a contagious disease of geese caused by a bacteria called Pasteurella septicaemiae. It is a very serious disease in goslings and young geese. It's believed that ducks can become infected, but no major outbreaks have ever been reported.

The disease comes on suddenly with coughing, sneezing, and eye and nasal discharge. Later, the disease weakens and dehydrates the bird and it becomes uncoordinated and dies. Transmission is by contact with infected birds, discharges, feed, and water. (Do not confuse disease with watering eyes and sneezing of geese housed with chickens in the presence of strong ammonia fumes.) Internally there are lesions around the heart, liver and respiratory membranes.

Treat with sulfadimethoxine; this is the safest sulfa drug for waterfowl. Effective treatment is dependent upon quick action when symptoms begin. Observe withdrawal times.

Although not spread from the egg, it's been suggested the recovered birds not be kept; they should remain isolated and confined until butchered. Thoroughly clean and disinfect pens when geese are disposed of and leave them empty a few weeks until new birds are placed into pens.

IMPACTED CROP

This is an infrequent condition of waterfowl. The only physical sign is an enlargement over the crop area that does not go away. This is caused by the crop being packed with feed and not emptying, which prevents the feed from continuing on through the digestive system. Very long, coarse, fibrous materials such as dead vegetation, and occasionally mash fed without drinking water, can—especially with goslings and ducklings—cause feed to stick and cake in the crop.

In mature birds, first relieve the crop of any gases that might have formed from fermentation by mixing 1/2 teaspoon of sodium barcarbonate (baking soda) in 1/4 cup of warm water. Use a syringe and slowly release solution into the fowl's throat with his neck and head extended. Follow with 2 tablespoons of mineral oil or cod-liver oil, using the syringe to release down the throat. Massage the crop area to loosen the mass. If it does not empty and the area is still greatly enlarged, leave the bird confined with plenty of water for a few hours. If still not emptied, massage again. In extremely rare cases, the area over the crop must be cut and an incision made into the crop to empty it. With clean water, wash area of all feed particles and close by stitching opening in crop and skin with strong cotton thread. Spray with antibiotic, or dab on iodine. Keep the bird penned for one week so you can watch sutures and control the feed eaten. Feed lightly during the week. Young ducklings and goslings might only need to be held upside down, with gentle crop massage, to empty contents. Always keep water nearby so waterfowl can wash their feed down.

LEG SPRAINS

Occasionally waterfowl will sprain their legs and be found limping. It can be very hard to handle a duck or goose for any extended therapy, so I recommend treating with a homeopathic remedy called Arnica. Just mix a few of the tiny white tablets (3X strength is good) with a tablespoon of water and rub over the sprained area. Use all the entire mixture. The bird should be better almost immediately. It usually works the first time it is applied, even if the bird has been limping for many weeks. If not, repeat in another day.

LEUCOCYTOZOONOSIS

This is a disease of most domestic poultry. It occurs in ranged birds more than others, and in areas populated with black flies and biting midges. Parasitic microorganisms within the black flies and midges are responsible for the disease; the flies and midges transmit the disease to the birds. The organisms are host specific; that is, certain species only infect certain species of birds. Biting midges contain parasitic organism that infect only chickens, so they are not a threat to waterfowl, turkeys, or guinea fowl. The black flies are sometimes called

turkey gnats. The small humpbacked flies can be seen hovering over the heads of the birds. After they bite the bird, the parasite invades the tissues and blood cells. The disease is heralded a week later with fever, weakness, extreme anemia, lameness, lack of appetite, and loss of balance.

Prevention is best measure of control. Because black flies emerge in late spring and early summer it's best to keep birds off range at this time. This is usually in June and July. Buildings sometimes have to be screened from the insects in problem areas, although they usually attack only outdoor birds. The flies lay eggs on rocks and debris near streams of (usually) fast-running water. Treat infected birds with sulfadimethoxine or sulfaquinoxaline in the feed or water. Black flies are hard to control. Infested areas may prompt handlers to raise a different species of bird.

LICE

Geese usually have no lice and ducks might have a few on the head and neck. Waterfowl with access to swimming water will be quite free of any lice. If housed with chickens or raised by chickens, more lice will be found. Poultry lice are not of the same species which are found on humans. Poultry lice in the adult stage are wingless, flat-bodied, and about 1/8 inch long. They vary from gray to black or yellow and spend their entire breeding and life cycle on a bird.

Adult waterfowl can be lightly powdered with Sevin by parting the feathers and patting the powder down to the skin. Do not forget to powder under the wings. Hens that are to hatch waterfowl eggs should be powdered twice while setting because lice favor the young skin of newly hatched birds. It is not safe to powder young ducklings and goslings who are not feathered. Instead, apply sweet oil around the head, under throat and around navel area.

OPHTHALMIA (EYE INFECTION)

Occasionally waterfowl might develop a slight eye infection in one or both eyes, caused by bacteria. Waterfowl with access to clean swimming water and balanced rations do not usually get eye infections. The first sign can be pus in the corner of the eye.

Flush the affected eye twice daily with a boric acid solution, or use argyrol purchased in the 8-percent solution. Argyrol stains the feathers for awhile. Supplement feed with vitamin A for a faster recovery. Sanitize drinking water until infection clears up by placing 1 tablespoon of chlorine into 1 gallon of drinking water. Do not confuse with the ammonia burns of eyes in keratoconjunctivitis.

REPRODUCTIVE DISORDERS

These occasionally occur among ducks and geese, moreso with ducks. The conditions can range from an overly large goose and gander to internal malfunctions. Heavy ganders can have trouble mating, while a heavy goose can smother hatched goslings with her body. A handler can try limiting their ration a few months before breeding or artificially incubate these less-fertile eggs if a large hatch is not expected.

Ovarian disorders of ducks and female geese include a condition wherein the yolk enters the abdominal cavity as it's forced from the infundibulum in the oviduct. If this occurs too often, death will result. There is no remedy or cure; the bird should be disposed of. This is more likely to happen with ducks than geese, although it rarely occurs at all.

A prolapsed oviduct is most common in high-production, obese ducks. Part of the organs actually come out from the vent. This usually happens when small ducks begin laying early and lay large eggs. Another cause is too much fat in the pelvis and abdomen, which obstructs the egg's path. To save the bird, remove from flock and wash and sanitize the parts showing. Then grease fingers with antibiotic ointment or Vaseline, and carefully push the organs back into vent. Feed lightly in isolated quarters. Try to discourage laying so the strained muscles return to normal. If this were to occur in a mixed pen of hens and ducks, the chickens would harm the protruding organs by pecking at them, and the duck would probably have to be destroyed.

A similar condition called phallus prostration appears occasionally with drakes. It's a weakness in the muscles which prevents the penis from being retracted. The exposed part can become injured and infected from bacteria. The drake eventually dies after the part dries up and falls off. The cause is usually sexual over-indulgence. It's usually worse with drakes who cannot mate in water and with those who are placed with female ducks at an early age.

There is no specific treatment, but if a handler wants to try and salvage the drake he can try giving him access to deep, clean swimming water devoid of any other ducks and turtles. Let him stay alone on the water for a few weeks. The organ might go back to normal on its own. If it does, limit the mating for a while. If it doesn't, the drake must be destroyed.

SLIPPED AND TWISTED WINGS

These are two wing conditions that are usually correctable with time and patience. Slipped wings is the term used to describe wings in which the primary feathers fold out over the secondaries rather than under them when the wing is naturally folded towards the body. The condition can develop anytime. It can appear on only one wing. To correct the improper fold of the wing, wait until the primaries are shed during the molt. When all the primaries have just grown out again, pull them out. The new feathers that grow back should be in the normal position. A wide rubber band or tape fitted around the properly folded wing might help partially grown feathers to retain their position. Be sure feathers aren't restricted from further growing and do not bind the wing too tightly.

Twisted wings usually describes wings in which the primaries stick out at right angles to the bird's body when folded. Subsequently, the bird looks like an airplane with two legs. The cause of twisted wings can be an over-zealous handler who was growing the bird too fast and large. The strength available in the wings in relation to the size of the bird and its growth is not enough to support the heavy wings in their proper position. This condition is usually found more in ducks than geese, and in the very large types such as Muscovies.

A protein and amino acid imbalance in the diet,

or deficiencies of folic acid, niacin, panthothenic acid, or zinc can cause excessively long primaries and rough, uneven feathers. Occasionally the defect is genetic. It can be passed onto offspring.

To correct twisted wings, a handler must proceed as soon as the defect is noticeable. Cut a small plastic, stretch net onion bag or a nylon stocking to a length that will cover the horizontal width of the wing when folded. On a goose, this would be about 12 inches. Keep both ends open to form a sleeve. Fold the wing, and with the twisted primaries in proper position, slip the sleeve over the folded wing. Then, with a length of 1/2-inch elastic, go over and around the entire folded wing continually in order to hold all the feathers in place. Use enough elastic and don't wrap too tightly, or it will restrict circulation—especially if the bird is still growing. Keep on for at least one month before checking the progress. The bird might find that the unused wing is stiff. It will eventually limber up on its own, or a handler can exercise the wing daily to speed up the process.

STAGGERS

This is not a disease but a condition that occurs when ducklings and goslings consume dry feed without drinking water. It occurs more in ducklings. Waterfowl need water to help soften and wash the food down moreso than other poultry. If food is swollen and retained in the esophagus it can restrict breathing. Rather than choke, although some do, the inability to breath normally causes dizziness and the bird staggers when walking. Dry mash is the worst offender because it compacts when swallowed without water.

Always keep plenty of drinking water available for ducklings and goslings. Many handlers worry more over providing enough feed than they do water. This is a mistake. Water is always more important than the feed. It's not dangerous if feeders become empty for a few hours, but waterers should never become empty.

WORMS

These internal parasites do not usually infect ducks or geese. The copious amounts of water they drink helps flush out parasites and keeps them fairly worm-free. A lack of water and poor diets can wear waterfowl down enough so worms aren't readily expelled. Then a vermifuge (wormer) must be given.

Gizzard worms are hairlike worms that burrow under the lining of the gizzard, preventing normal functioning of the organ. This can prevent normal assimilation of feed, which weakens and starves bird. Use ivermectin, levamizole, or the over-the-counter drug Tramizole for treating. Waterfowl raised on bodies of water seldom have worms.

Refer to Chapter 7 for the following ailments and cures: ammonia burns, brooder pneumonia (aspergillosis), bumble foot, omphalitis (mushy chick disease), paratyphoid, rickets, spraddle legs, and staph infection.

Part 5

Further Management

Chapter 18

Procedures

SHIPPING

It's a good idea to be aware of the events that take place back at the hatchery before you receive your shipped birds. This can help you determine if your birds are stressed when they arrive. Stressed birds should be handled differently to avoid losses that can occur during the first week of life.

Many of the normal procedures at a hatchery can stress day-old poultry. These include untraying, sexing, desnooding of toms, toenail trimming, beak trimming, injections, and boxing. More post-hatching treatments are administered to turkey poults than any other type poultry.

Any gamebird (which does include guineas) is more highly strung and easily frightened. This is part of their survival instinct. Therefore, when you receive them, they will usually be trying to pile on top of one another in the corners of the shipping box. If they had a very rough trip, some might even be smothered.

Poultry are first hatched in hatching trays or hatch baskets (Fig. 18-1) in machines called hatchers. These machines are separate from the incubators. Hatchers are used for the final days of hatching only. Newly hatched poultry are placed into plastic or cardboard shipping boxes. The plastic boxes or trays are used for shipping in trucks to individual growers. The cardboard boxes are the type used to ship smaller lots of birds throughout the country. The procedure of removing the birds from the hatching trays to another box is called "taking off the hatch" (Fig. 18-2).

If poults are ordered to be beak-trimmed, this is usually done first and the poults are moved to the "poult-go-round." When toenail trimming is done, the poults are again handled and go into another poult-go-round. Sexing is next, along with desnooding the toms—which means handling the poults further. A small 1 1/2-inch tool is used to snip off the extremely tiny snood. Some hatcheries even use a kitchen gadget called a strawberry huller. The snood is so small and devoid of nerves at one day of age, that some handlers even use their thumb and forefinger nails to remove the snood.

Fig. 18-1. Note the pad inserts under these newly hatched poults to protect their legs. (Courtesy of Nicholas Turkey Breeding Farms)

Fig. 18-2. "Taking off the hatch" is when the poults are removed from the hatch baskets, counted, graded, and placed into boxes. (Courtesy of Cooper Hatchery, Inc.)

318

The last step before final boxing and shipment is another trip to a poult-go-round where the poults are given an injection containing vitamins, electrolytes, and an antibiotic (Fig. 18-3). Some hatcherymen say the injections don't noticeably strengthen the poults, but it's common practice—and an inexpensive one.

The birds are "hardened off " in their ventilated shipping boxes for a few hours, or sometimes overnight, before actual shipping so they can adjust to a 90-95-degree F. world. You must remember, the egg kept them in an even 100-degree F. world. The hardening off is similar to what gardeners do to their young started plants where they place them outdoors in a coldframe to protect them from winds and weather before actual planting. This gradual acclimation toughens them up so they are not shocked by the extremes of a totally different environment.

The prepunched ventilation holes in the shipping boxes are poked out according to the environmental temperatures the birds might encounter during shipment. For instance, 0-20 degrees F. might require only two holes in each of the four sections of the box to be punched open. Over 70 degrees F. might require all ventilation holes to be punched open.

Experienced hatcheries use common sense in determining the amount of ventilation required in combination with the amount of body heat from the birds that accumulates in the box. Because poults are larger than chicks, only 60-80 poults should be placed into a 100-chick-size box, because the body heat produced is tremendous. The hatcherymen consider the variances that can occur during a particular mode of transportation. For example, if the birds will be flown, the airplane compartment they ride in might be very cold. Birds shipped very long distances might encounter more exterior temperature changes and handling than a shorter distance would involve. They can further encounter unexpected weather conditions, shipping delays, and oc-

Fig. 18-3. A machine is used to give each poult an injection in the back of the neck. (Courtesy of Cooper Hatchery, Inc.)

casional rough handling. All these conditions can stress the birds.

It's important to notice the pad inserts in the bottom of shipping boxes. They are an important feature in safe shipping because they allow the birds steady footing to prevent spraddle legs, which would occur if day-old birds were simply placed on the smooth, slippery cardboard. It takes a few days for the cartilage in the legs of a newly hatched baby to harden enough in the top of the thighs to gain sure footing. Poultry are usually a few days old when received, so this weakness would not be too noticeable.

It takes three days for all birds to hatch from an egg setting. Do not assume all are only one day old because they are referred to as day-olds. This is just a term to refer to any poultry within a few days of age. A handler can determine the age of individual birds by looking for the egg tooth and watching their actions. The egg tooth is the whitish nail-like substance on the tip of the upper and lower mandible (beak or bill). The egg tooth usually sloughs off by the fourth day. Another indication is birds that seem to walk low to the ground. Even if birds are a few days old, they should be placed under or in a brooder that contains some type of litter or material that is rough for at least five days after receiving them. Because poults have taller legs than chicks, it takes a few days longer to gain steady footing. The original pad inserts from the boxes can be reused for this purpose if only a few birds are brooded.

I have seen keets so frightened from shipment that they have pushed and shoved enough to move the pad insert in the box up and over. This maneuvering of the pad caused the keets to remain on the slippery cardboard. If the pad has shed some of its material, the keets will have some footing. If not, you might have some spraddle-leg keets that you should dispose of. The majority of keets, however, come through shipment lively and in good shape.

Spotting stress in poults is not very difficult. The poults will be more quiet than usual, they won't be too perky, they'll sit around a lot with their heads drooping or drawn close to their bodies, and will have closed eyes (Fig. 18-4). All these symptoms

Fig. 18-4. These poults are chilled and are exhibiting stress. (Courtesy of L. Dwight Schwartz, D.V.M., Senior Pathologist, Michigan State University)

would be present at one time. A poult with only closed eyes is not an indication; all poults will do this. With keets, stress is tough to determine. They do not always peep when cold. If panting, they could be warm from piling on one another. It's best to treat keets like poultry that have been chilled and in transit a long time. Place a few filled waterers under their heat source, with a teaspoon of sugar in each quart jar of warm drinking water. This will provide warmth and energy. Take them from the shipping box individually and dip their beaks into the water until you see them swallow. Then place each keet under the heat with the other waterers.

Be sure the birds' new quarters are ready before their expected arrival. You never know when there might be a delay somewhere while shipping, or when it might be extremely important to get stressed birds heated right away and watered. Looking for signs of stress and being aware of what the birds have encountered before arriving can make all the difference in the birds' health.

EFFECTS OF CHILLING

Birds chilled during shipment or held in cold storage rooms will show obvious signs when you open the shipping container. Poults will be much quieter than normal. Poults are very noisy in the shipping container and for hours after they have been placed under the brooder. This is most noticeable when 20 or more poults are shipped. Another symptom of chilling is if the poults don't want to jump out of the shipping box at you when the lid is removed. Instead they sit huddled with their heads drawn in towards their bodies and their eyes closed most of the time. Do not confuse the "stand-offs" with chilled poults. Stand-offs are poults who stand up tall and rigid and push their backs into the corner of the box as if they were trying to avoid the whole commotion and experience. This is just another strange quirk some poults exhibit.

Keets that are shipped will not usually show visible signs of chilling as chicks do, except that their scared nature will cause keets to huddle in the boxes as if chilled. Severe conditions will ultimately show if there are many dead keets received. When keets die during shipment body heat is lost in the shipping containers, which will bring about more deaths. Scared keets will want to huddle under the heat, so this does not necessarily mean they were chilled either. However, treat keets as though they were chilled. Always place some feeders and waterers under the heat with them during the first few days. In this way, if they were chilled they will bounce back faster if allowed to stay under their heat. They will not be forced to stray from the heat in order to drink. Also, if they are chilled, many will not want to venture out looking for the water. This will lead to dehydration and mortality. Birds that have been stressed from chilling for long periods will not be as perky. They might develop diarrhea and not want to eat as much. All this can cause mortality, so measures to overcome chilling must be implemented.

When birds are chilled, do not worry about the feed. Getting them to drink water is much more important. If they won't drink, they won't eat either, and if they don't drink, they become dehydrated and soon perish. This is how chilling can kill birds. The beak should be dipped until they are noticeably swallowing, and then the bird should be placed

under the heat source with more waterers.

As chilled poults are placed under the heating element they might stand as tall as possible to get as close to the heat as they can. Chilled poults will not want to clamber to the nonheated areas to greet you when your voice is heard. Chilled and stressed poults should have the procedure of beak dipping repeated at least two more times spaced a few hours apart throughout the first day. As poults begin to feel comfortably warm they should gradually begin to drink on their own by nightfall or sooner. The following morning shove all poults out to the waterers in the open, unheated area and observe. They should appear more lively and most should go to the waterers on their own to drink. Poults not drinking can be picked out and have their beaks dipped at random throughout this second day. Chilled poults treated in this manner usually recover by this second morning without any losses. If you do not get the poults warmed and drinking by the second day, many will not survive.

If the heat goes off accidentally while being brooded later, the birds will display the same symptoms of chilling. Treat them the same way as day-olds. Unlike chicks, poults do not usually outlive prolonged chilling—as when brooding temperatures are too low. Chicks can develop respiratory problems, diarrhea, and long wing feathers. Poults are not as willing to live through this type of mismanagement.

Like other species, ducklings and goslings show they are cold by piling and huddling under the heat source. Because they are considered hardier and easier to raise than other species, some assume they also can take chilling. This is not so. Chilling for even a few hours can cause them to get stressed. When stressed, their resistance is lowered and they can become sick. A diarrhea condition usually results, along with pasted vents. When chilling causes stress, ducklings and goslings will not eat and drink properly. If this chilling goes on for days because of an incorrect brooder temperature, they may survive but they'll become unthrifty from not eating and drinking properly. Most of their time will be spent trying to hover under the heating element. This will set them way back; their growth will be retarded and they can become runts. Smothering can also result if they continue to pile and crowd for warmth, although this is not as common as with chicks and turkeys. Chilling can cause the feathers on the wings to grow abnormally long.

Pasted vents are usually an after-occurrence of chilling which can be noticed a couple days after the chilled birds are received. This is the term used for manure stuck to the vent. If not remedied, the manure hardens and obstructs the vent so defecation is impossible. The waste matter eventually backs up in the bird's system and kills him. The manure must be removed so the bird is not lost. Hold the bird's hind end under warm running water while gently working the mass loose with your fingers. A stubborn mass can be pinched together first to help break it apart. Remove all traces of manure so future droppings do not stick and cause the same problem. The down will also come away, leaving a very tender area on the delicate skin—but this helps prevent further pasting over the area. The wet vent area must then be thoroughly dried with a hand-held hair dryer. If slight bleeding occurs, spray the area with an antiseptic such as Blue Kote. Allow it to dry before placing the bird in with the others. There is no need to worry about cannibalism because of this small amount of blood when ducklings and goslings are brooded together. If desired, a very small amount of petroleum jelly can be put on to make it more comfortable for the bird. The pasting should not occur again after treatment if the chilling has been taken care of.

EFFECTS OF OVERHEATING

Although poults love their heat, too much can cause problems. Poults overheated prior to being received will be found standing up panting with wings drooped when the lid is first removed. These poults need water more than brooder heat to prevent dehydration. The respiration of poults in trying to rid the body of excessive temperatures uses up the natural body moisture. Overheating becomes a problem if birds do not have enough space to get away from overly heated areas. A sign of this overheating is darkened and shriveled shanks and feet, caused by dehydration.

Overheated poults still need their beaks dipped one by one into the drinking water to get them started. They will then push and shove one another to get at the thirst-quenching substance. This is why it's important to be sure waterers are not deep enough to allow birds to be shoved into them. A wet bird can become chilled if he is not quickly spotted and dried.

There is no need to place overheated birds under the heat source; they'll find their own way to it when their thirst is satisfied and they feel a bit cooler. Provide plenty of waterers filled with warm water. Cold water on a hot bird's insides can cause digestive upsets. Use a few extra waterers for a few days until water intake levels out. The birds will act thirsty for a few days, as if they cannot get enough water.

Prolonged overheating from brooding at too high a temperature will cause uneven growth, stunted growth, lack of vigor, slower-than-normal feathering, broken feathers, respiratory problems from dry air, panting, and crowding into brooder corners. This requires a longer, more costly brooding period because a bird must be feathered out to keep warm and be of sufficient size to discontinue brooding. Overheated birds do not eat enough and therefore do not receive enough heat and energy-producing fats to keep their body warmer. Keeping birds at the correct temperature weekly, along with supplying enough space to escape heat, will harden them off.

EFFECTS OF CROWDING

Birds will never become crowded if their future space requirements are considered and planned for in advance. Poults, especially, grow so fast it's sometimes difficult to realize how much brooder space they actually need. For each area birds will occupy, check that space requirements are adequate for the length of time the birds will remain there. If birds will remain in a brooding area for six weeks and then moved elsewhere for growing, be sure the birds can be readily moved at six weeks. Unexpected circumstances can occur when a handler might not be able to move the birds when planned. Allow one or two extra weeks of space as your insurance against crowding. Use the reference guides listed under space requirements in previous chapters.

As an example, an area of 100 square feet has been allotted for 50 day-old poults. This is sufficient space to carry them through the eight weeks until the handler plans to move them. If he is unable to do this, two weeks later, at 10 weeks of age, the 50 poults are still in the 100-square-foot area allotted for 50 eight-week olds, the poults will bump shoulders and become ragged-looking because feathers are being broken. At this point they need 150, not 100 square feet. The litter material needs almost constant replacing, which becomes a chore because there is no place to move poults over in the growing area when replacing the straw. If the handler is inclined to pass up this chore, he might find his poults attacked by an outbreak of coccidiosis because of the damp litter.

Crowding can cause many broken feathers and "barebacks." Beginning pinfeathers of young birds are easily broken or rubbed off, leaving stubs. Crowding can result in litter becoming damp faster; it has no chance to dry because of restricted ventilation. Many diseases are stimulated by the presence of damp litter. Because birds in crowded conditions get less exercise, they become bored and cannibalism might start. Less exercise also means birds do not need as much energy-producing food; they are then inclined to eat less, which can result in retarded growth.

Unintentional crowding can easily occur with battery-raised birds. Inexperienced handlers cannot foresee the problems; they only know the birds are not on damp litter and they are warm enough. They don't see the retarded growth or the bad feathering until it's too late.

Crowding will also make it almost impossible to inspect the areas properly for birds in trouble or those being pecked at. Dead or injured birds in crowded conditions can be missed during routine checking.

FEATHERING PROCEDURE

A handler should know what contributes to good feathering, why good feathering is important, and the order in which parts of the body feather. This will help a handler provide the right conditions for feathering and estimate when brooding is no longer needed.

Good feathering means the birds are feathered evenly over the entire body without excessive wing growth and no bare spots. Good feathering is not a matter-of-fact occurrence. The management a handler gives to his birds ultimately brings on good feathering. The resulting feather condition is a combination of good feed, humidity, ventilation, and the correct temperature.

At hatching time, a birds' body will consist of 75 percent moisture. Through the process of elimination, respiration, and growth, the body will gradually lose moisture daily. The moisture is replenished from the water the bird drinks, but not at a fast enough rate to overcome the effects of a dry atmosphere. Most starter rooms and brooders do not have a relative humidity of 75 percent. The very drying conditions under the heat of a brooder can cause the beginning pinfeathers to become dry and brittle. The dull-looking feathers are then easily broken off as the birds brush against each other.

Ventilation is needed to bring moisture to the level of the birds. If birds are being brooded near the floor, the air will be more stale there. In battery raising, the birds in the top compartments are always better feathered. The effect ventilation has on feathering can also be seen on the chicks, poults, and waterfowl raised by hens outdoors. They are always feathered out sooner because of the natural air movement. As the mother hen covers them for warmth, the respiration moisture from the chicks' breathing does not escape but is reabsorbed into the skin and feathers.

Guineas always seem to feather out a bit faster and in better condition than other poultry. Perhaps this is due to nature's eagerness to feather out wild species against the elements. Also, guineas are active, which creates more ventilation among the birds. Good feathering is a combination of ventilation, humidity, correct temperature, noncrowded conditions, a nutritionally balanced feed ration, and a good strain of birds. Both male and female keets of the dark varieties such as the Pearl and Royal Purple will have brown striped feathers up to about two months of age—of a color and pattern that resembles a ringneck pheasant. These brown, wild-looking feathers will be shed gradually up to two months of age, and will be replaced by the dark-pearled or solid-colored feathers seen on the adults. Light-colored guineas are not boldly striped like the dark brown keets of the dark colors.

Ventilation is restricted when birds are crowded. This is clearly seen when two separate brooders of birds are raised under all the same conditions except that one contains crowded birds. The crowded brooder will produce poorly feathered birds that must be brooded longer. These birds will be slightly to greatly undersized because they cannot eat, drink, and exercise as freely. When birds exercise, they burn up energy that must be replaced. This causes the birds to eat more.

If birds must be brooded near the floor, feathering can be enhanced by using a very small fan on low speed, pointed away from the birds. This will draw the stale, dry air out from under the brooders and bring fresher, more moist air to them without creating a draft.

Although droppings add to the moisture contained under brooders, the ammonia makes the air less healthy to breath. Strong ammonia can cause respiratory and eye problems. Only very dry conditions will prevent odor from being formed; a humid atmosphere will create odor. This might be offensive, but humidity is a necessity. Dry conditions can bring on lung and feathering problems. The bedding material must be changed often, but do not be discouraged if there's still an odor. It only means there is humidity in the air. The air can be misted with a hand sprayer if necessary.

The correct temperature will aid the feathering process. If temperatures are too high the available moisture will be dried up faster than it can be supplied through ventilation. A bird's body feathers out according to the temperature of the environment. Cooler temperatures produce faster body feathering and warmer temperatures slow up the process. Excessive heat will develop only abnormal wing growth. Furthermore, the warmer the tem-

perature the less the birds will eat. Cooler temperatures call for more energy-producing food so the birds eat more and in turn grow faster and produce a better growth of body feathers.

Commercial rations usually provide the correct nutrients to help produce nice feathers. A teaspoon of cod-liver oil added to each gallon of drinking water can be given to birds occasionally to help produce nice feathers. It won't promote faster feathering but the oil will help keep the feathers more pliable so there is less breakage.

It's important to judge whether bareback birds are simply poorly feathered or if the birds are developing a habit of feather pulling. Feather pulling brings the entire feather barb out of the skin pore. On dark-colored birds a small quantity of pigment oil will be seen in these pores. On white birds check that no part of the barb remains in the pores. If the pores are clearly without a piece of feather barb, feather pulling is occurring. If small portions of barbs remain in the pores, the feathers have been broken off because of dry conditions and/or poor feed and crowding. The first four weeks are the most important for good feathering because this is when most feather growth takes place. If these conditions have not been met, it will be hard to feather the birds later. Providing the correct feed and environment for good feathering means total brooding time will be shorter; this saves money.

The order in which feathers grow on the body is the same for all birds. The wing feathers grow first, with tail and breast feathers growing in next. Then the back will grow feathers. The neck (and mostly bald head of the turkey and guinea) grows feathers last. By six weeks of age all body feathers should be in. This is when brooding is usually discontinued. Although ducks and geese take 8 weeks to fully feather, their brooding period is shorter.

While this feathering process is taking place, the down is gradually lost. Battery brooder trays will display this lost down. The entire environment will contain minute particles of the shed down, droppings, and feed. This is called "chick dust." Every handler, including small children, should be aware that chick dust can adversely affect their health. It can cause a lung disease: bird fancier's, breeder's, handler's, or pigeon breeder's lung disease. Small traces of bird protein are constantly lost from the bowel of birds. They are then passed in the droppings which dry and turn to powder. These dried protein particles combine in the air with the shed down and feed dust that is inhaled by the handler. The most severe reactions are known to take place within the walls of the small air passage. A reaction will be induced in sensitive individuals.

Protect your lungs from chick dust by wearing a mask when changing bedding, dropping pans, and tending the birds. Disposable and filtered masks can be purchased where painter's supplies are sold, if unavailable at your local feed store. It's a law in most places that masks be rated as to the substance they are to filter. Choose one accordingly for the best protection. If a mask is not available it's better to use any substitute rather than nothing. In a pinch, use a cloth tied around your head to help protect your nose and mouth from these minute particles. It's better to be safe than sorry. If children help tend the poultry, they should be taught to use these masks and to stay clear of areas that become dusty—as when poultry buildings are being cleaned.

LIGHTING NEEDS

Some handlers do not understand the need for light while brooding birds, possibly because they compare birds naturally brooded under hens with the artificially brooded birds. Their reasoning tells them that these hen-raised birds do not use or need light to eat throughout the night so why should their brooder birds? The fact is that hen-raised birds are not subjected to the drying conditions the heating element of a brooder brings on. A humid condition exists among a brood of day-olds under a hen, which comes from the respiration process. It prevents the birds' body and system from drying out. These hen-raised birds can eat just as much as brooder birds, but it's done throughout the daylight hours. If they were observed for an entire day, they would be found eating constantly with only occasional naps under their mother. The extra energy used looking and scratching for feed can cause them to eat more.

Brooder-raised birds cannot be subjected to the drying conditions of the heating element for long. If they are, their bodies will dehydrate, which causes respiratory problems due to dried lung tissue. The birds will not feather properly. Some old-time brooders even contained moisture pans. Brooder-raised birds do not have a hen to teach them to constantly scratch for food. Their occasional scratching is only a slight reminiscence of instinct. Brooder birds do not burn up extra energy scratching about, so their feed requirements might not be as high as hen-raised birds.

The light for brooder birds, therefore, is supposed to stimulate their eating habits. Birds also need drinking water throughout the night so they do not dehydrate. The extra lighting provided during the night keeps birds from becoming confined under the heating element. The fact that birds cannot see in the dark is sometimes overlooked by handlers. Birds will not venture out into darkness to search for food or water.

With ducklings, lights also prevent nighttime stampeding. Strange noises or even the family cat can cause them to run in a frenzy in the dark. Some handlers leave the lights on until meat breed ducklings are butchered at eight weeks to prevent stampeding and keep the growth rate going to its peak.

The pilot light cannot be relied upon as lighting for eating and drinking purposes. A pilot light only remains lit while the heating element is operating. As soon as the desired temperature is reached, the thermostat commands the heating element to shut off, and the pilot bulb shuts off with it. Furthermore, if extra lighting is not provided, the birds will remain under the hover longer. Their body heat accumulates and the heating element does not need to come on as often. Then the pilot light does not come on as often either.

In one instance, a handler set up a single-battery stack brooder in her barn. Because the temperature would not hold at 95 degrees F. for her poults, she decided to cover the entire brooder with an old tarp. This conserved the heat and provided the necessary warmth to the poults, but it also cut off all sources of natural light. She wondered why poults were dropping like flies. She also noticed some having respiratory problems. The poults were unable to see their feed and water so they were not eating and drinking properly. They ventured out from under the heat only while the pilot light was on. Their respiratory problems were caused from a combination of the drying effects of the heating element and the dust particles from the old tarp.

When two continuously lit heat lamps are being used for brooding, extra light is not needed. If only one is being used, an extra light will be your insurance in case the heat lamp burns out. If no light is available birds will then crowd together for warmth; piling will suffocate them. The birds believe the light is what kept them warm and they actually become colder faster when the light is completely gone. This extra light can give the handler that extra few minutes to come across the burned out heat lamp before birds feel too cold. A safer option is to supply two heat lamps even if only one is needed.

Another safe lighting method some commercial turkey growers follow is using a timer to turn lights on and off every two hours. Some believe this stimulates the birds' appetites even more. With the lights on two hours, off two hours continuously throughout every 24 hours, the birds are not confined to the brooding area and receive 12 hours darkness and 12 hours of light. If the electricity accidentally is interrupted, causing the lights to go off, the birds simply believe it's bedtime again and do not become fearful.

Still another method used commercially is the constant lighting system: turning lights off for only one or two hours daily until market age. Birds accustomed to lights going off occasionally since day-old do not become worried when lights go out. They accept it as a natural occurrence. Older birds used to the timed lighting that was begun when they were day-olds can have the lighting removed later without fear of piling—the lights are simply left off one day when no longer needed.

Gas brooding can be considered a safer brooding system. If power is interrupted and lights go out, the infrared rays emitted while the burner is on will provide enough light for such emergencies.

The extra lighting does not need to be bright.

In fact, bright lights can bring on cannibalism. Even a small 7 1/2-watt pilot bulb can be used in a separate outlet to stay lit constantly for small amounts of birds. They need only to be able to spot their feed and water.

ENTERTAINMENT NEEDS

Inexperience can lead many handlers to believe young poultry only eat, drink, sleep, and defecate. Observing the birds will show they actually play as any baby does, only in a different way. Poults and keets chase each other, grab tidbits from each other's beaks, and jump to and from objects. In harmony, they stretch their wings and leap into the air. Even very small toms of one week will fan their wings down and strut their stuff like grown toms. This helps birds from becoming bored.

Sometimes handlers unintentionally prevent the birds from playing. There may be no waterers, feeders, or roosts which they can jump up on and down from—no place to test their wings. Battery-raised birds cannot easily grab bits of litter or paper to tease others with. Occasionally they might manage to grab a piece through the wire, and when they find they can reach it, they'll fight and pull at it like crazy until a piece is torn loose. They are not doing this to upset you. They are only amusing themselves.

More than other domestic poultry, energetic keets feel inclined to perch on top of things. They also enjoy eating greens. A handler should accommodate these needs. They will be getting what nature gives them in the wild. Contented keets will become tamer as they will learn to trust their handler. Wild guineas are not much fun to have around. This taming should begin at an early age. Although keets are not as cannibalistic as chicks, keeping keets occupied will ward off a tendency to peck on others. Providing small roosts will help keep the keets off the top of waterers, resulting in cleaner drinking water. Even small swings can be made and hung from the ceiling. These can be set in place as early as one week of age to accustom keets to their strange environment. Keets are wary of anything they haven't seen before, but this is why they're good "watch birds." Small roosts should also be placed through battery brooders.

A handler might not supply enough feeder and waterer space to keep birds busy. There might not be enough variety in texture and taste to sustain their interest in eating. When the only type of entertainment is each other, birds quickly become bored and will think of ways to amuse themselves. This can be in the form of cannibalism or dangling threads found on the edge of raveled brooder curtains. These loose threads become dangerous fun when the threads become tangled around necks, tongues, wings, feet, and legs. A thread wrapped tightly around these body parts for any length of time will cause considerable swelling; which makes removal of the thread by the handler almost impossible. Tiny nail scissors must carefully be placed under the thread for cutting loose. Sometimes the bird is cut in the process. Depending upon the extent of the swelling and injuries, the bird can become completely disabled and must be disposed of.

Keep curtains in good repair or replace them. Use the selvage, finished edges of yard goods for the lower portion of the exposed curtain, or double hem tightly and check for exposed threads. Small repairs of raveled edges can be made with rubberized and plastic products used to mend tents, shoes, and upholstery. Be sure the product is applied smoothly and allowed to cure and dry completely before replacing near birds.

There are many ways a handler can supply entertainment: Provide extra feeders and waterers and do not let these become empty. Vary the texture and type of feed to spark new interest. Changing from mash to crumbles, crumbles to mash, crumbles to pellets for older birds, pellets to grains, etc. A few handfuls of a different type and texture of feed can be sprinkled over the regular ration a few times weekly. (Large cracked grains or pellets should not be given to most birds until at least six weeks of age.) For small amounts of birds from day-old to six weeks, a few teaspoons of soaked baby cereal can be laid over the top of the regular feed. At two weeks of age, grass clippings can be given. Start with a small amount at first. Don't overdo it; too much greens can cause diarrhea. It's best to feed the greens in the feeder to show the birds it's

meant to be eaten. Of course the clippings won't stay in the feeder. The birds will soon take a liking to the greens. Be sure any vegetation used to vary the diet is free of poisonous sprays. If keets or poults are raised with chicks, all can receive the same treatment to keep them busy.

Offering fine grit or sand over the top of regular feed—beginning at one week of age—will further spur their interest. It will also aid in digestion and feed assimilation. Bits of uncolored paper can be given to poults and keets when they seem bored. (Color printed papers can be toxic to birds.) Give only a few pieces of torn paper and watch what happens. Insects would seem an ideal aid for boredom, but very young birds find lively insects too much a challenge. Try dead insects. They work better for inexperienced birds. From day-old, roosts should be placed in the growing area to keep poults and keets busy and to teach them to roost early. Poults can be a bit harder to teach to roost than chicks or keets, so start them early.

Providing entertainment for your birds should be considered a part of management. In turn, a handler will be rewarded with less losses and better health (and happiness) for the birds.

DISCONTINUING ARTIFICIAL HEAT

Do not be too quick in taking the brooder heat from young poultry, especially poults. Many birds can be lost after weeks of careful watching and brooding if this is not done correctly. Consider the following criteria before beginning the process:

How well-feathered are the birds? At six weeks of age, when all but the sparse neck feathers are in, a handler can begin thinking about discontinuing brooding. Do not attempt this unless all birds have all their body feathers. Feathers hold body heat in—down only accepts heat. You don't have to worry about the small amount of down on the neck.

How many birds are brooded together? The amount of birds brooded together will be a contributing factor to the amount of body heat released to sustain a warmer environment.

The size of the brooding area. Naturally, the smaller the total cubic footage from wall to wall and ceiling to floor, the more body heat will accumulate in the surroundings.

The temperature of the room or building they're housed in. This temperature will vary according to type and amount of insulation (if used), construction materials, and how much sheltered it is from the elements. Once the brooder heat is turned off, the temperature of the room becomes the temperature the birds must be able to withstand. The building must be no lower than 55 degrees F. (13 degrees C.) during the night.

How much the indoor temperature is affected by outdoor temperature changes. This also depends upon construction materials and how much the weather fluctuates. Insulated buildings will not show drastic fluctuations as much.

How good are poults and keets roosting? Provide roosts beginning at two weeks of age to assure that by six weeks of age most (if not all) will be sleeping on the roosts rather than under the brooder and on cold floors.

These conditions will vary on individual farms and ranches so a lot of common sense must be used when discontinuing brooding.

Keets are more sensitive to cooler temperatures than chicks. If brooded together, you might need to continue the heat just a bit longer to accommodate the keets. This will not harm the chicks as long as there is sufficient space for them to get away from the extra heat. Because keets are available later than most poultry, their brooding period is usually during the warmest part of the year. Unless you've decided to purchase them as late as September, most areas will have nightly temperatures that do not go much below 60 degrees F. during June and July. This is a good time to discontinue the heat for fully feathered keets. In colder areas it's not wise to start keets late because it necessitates longer and costlier brooding. It will be much tougher to harden the keets off for winter unless the interior of the building is kept warm either through body heat or artificial means.

If poults were started at 95 degrees F. when day-old, lowering the temperature 5 degrees weekly would bring the temperature under the brooder to 70 degrees F. by the beginning and end of five weeks of age. This beginning sixth week is when the poults are usually completely well-feathered up to their necks and can tolerate a 55-65-degree F. temperature. If they are not well feathered or are poorly feathered, reduce the heat by another 5 degrees and continue brooding through this sixth week and until the birds become well-feathered. If there are many "barebacks" caused by overheating or feather pulling, a longer brooding period might be required. Having only a few barebacks would not necessitate longer brooding as long as the rest of the brood is totally feathered.

When the birds are well feathered, check the inside of the building's temperature for a few nights to be sure the temperature is staying at 55 degrees F. or above. A brooder has a thermostat and can simply be lowered to keep the temperature under the hover at 55 degrees F. Be sure to do this when birds are not under hover because their body heat will affect the actual temperature. If the room's temperature is 55 degrees F. or above, the brooder will continue to stay off. Lamp brooders that do not have a thermostat should remain on until you're positive the nightly temperatures are staying at 55 degrees F. or above.

With either system of brooding, a small 7 1/2-watt bulb should stay lit throughout the night until *all* poults (and keets) are regularly roosting. Many birds believe the light thrown off from their brooder was their source of heat only because it's something they can see—they cannot see the heat radiated from the heating element. If the light is suddenly gone, birds that sleep on the floor will crowd together and pile on one another to try to keep warm, even if the room temperature is not cold.

At one time I was lamp brooding 100 five-week-old poults in a 3-foot-tall range shelter without many roosts. During the warmth of the day the lamps were kept off to help harden the poults off prior to the non-brooding period. At the beginning of dusk (which was 8:00 P.M.), the lamps were always turned back on. One day I had to leave home for a few hours and had asked a family member to turn the brooder lamps on at 8:00 P.M. It wasn't until 8:15 the family member remembered the lamps. By then it was too late. I returned home just in time to push and shove away all the piled poults from one another so the ones underneath could breath. Many were already dead. Some lay motionless except for an occasional breath. In all there were about 30 that died. In only a few minutes time about $60 were lost (poult, brooding, and feed costs)—not to mention labor.

If roosts have been made available early during brooding, many birds will break themselves from the brooder by six weeks of age if the room temperature is 55 degrees F. or over. This avoids piling when floor birds sense a need for heat (or the light) and helps lessen problems that can be encountered when discontinuing the heat. Be sure roosts are low enough for young birds to easily fly up to; a 1-foot height is good for poults and grown turkeys. Roosts for keets can be a bit taller. If poults are to be fully grown in the same pen area, provide extra-sturdy roosts. Or, have good sturdy roosts available for the birds when grown, but supply small closely spaced, portable roosts for the poults when young. Roosts, lights, and temperature go hand in hand when brooding is discontinued.

It takes about eight weeks for ducklings and goslings to become fully feathered. Unlike other species of domestic fowl, there is no need to wait until they are feathered up to their necks to discontinue their heat. As soon as they are accustomed to a 65-70-degree F. temperature, and the room is this temperature, the heat can be done away with. This is usually about five or six weeks of age, but can be sooner if the weather is very warm. Sometimes nightly temperatures might fall below 65 degrees F. In this case, you should provide some heat at night. It's good to keep the eating light on for another week or so, then the changes in their environment won't be so abrupt.

When you want to discontinue the heat, turn it off during the daytime so it's not as noticeable to them by the time night falls. Check to see if they seem comfortable as the outdoor temperature cools down. If they seem a bit chilled, use a small-watt heat bulb or keep the brooder on low. When they're comfortable, they will be sleeping together but not trying to huddle or shove into a corner.

VENTILATION NEEDS

This separate section on ventilation seemed to be a necessity since it is the most misunderstood of all shelter requirements. All housed poultry require ventilated quarters for comfort, health, and to protect the building from damaging moisture. Proper ventilation will force foul air, gasses, carbon dioxide, and excess vapor out of the building at the same time fresh air and oxygen is pulled into the building. Ventilation is natural air movement or mechanical air movement with the use of fans.

The type and amount of ventilation required depends upon a combination of factors: type of birds housed, amount of birds housed, size of building, insulation provided, desired temperature, relative humidity, outdoor temperature, and the amount and rate of air being moved.

Type Birds.—Poultry differ in the amount of moisture given off from their bodies and excrement. Larger birds will contribute more moisture into the atmosphere. The habits of the type bird housed will also affect the amount of moisture. Ducks and geese will cause damper conditions because of their vigorous drinking habits. If birds are allowed to bathe, this too, will create more moisture in the atmosphere and litter.

Bird Amount. The more birds housed, the more moisture created. Thus there is a need for more ventilation.

Building Size. The size of the building in relation to the amount of birds housed will be a number one factor in determining how much and what kind of ventilation is needed. The building size should also take into consideration the height of the ceiling—in other words, the total cubic feet of the entire area the birds are housed.

Insulation. Inside house temperatures will be much easier to maintain at a stable temperature when buildings are insulated. Insulation prevents a large fluctuation in the house temperature and prevents maintained temperature loss. This also means the built-up body heat from the birds in winter will not dissipate too quickly through the walls and ceilings. Cooler air brought into the building will be held much longer too. Insulation is sold with an R-value labeled on packages. Add the R values of materials which now make up the walls (and ceilings) to find the total (Table 18-1). Then refer to Fig. 18-5 to find heat loss (Q) in BTU's per hour. Purchase insulation to reduce this heat loss. A salesman can help figure your needs.

Insulation values in ceilings can easily be attained with fill-type insulation. Another method of insulating ceilings is termed the "straw loft." Loose or baled straw is simply placed over the top of the

ceiling. If the area is already used for straw storage, this method conveniently serves two purposes. Hay is not good to use because it can heat up to the point of starting a fire.

Desired Temperature. Adult poultry are most comfortable when they are housed in temperatures above 44 degrees F. (7 degrees C.). The temperature should not go above 86 degrees F. (30 degrees C.). Both egg production and feed con-

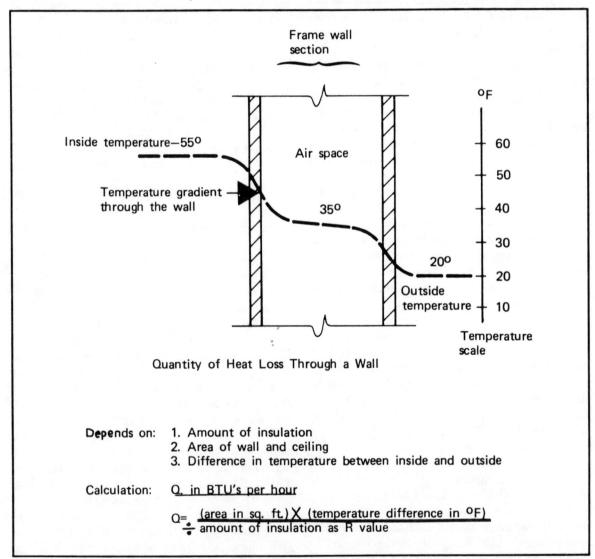

Fig. 18-5. Heat loss (Q) equals the exposed area multiplied by the temperature difference and divided by the present R value. (Courtesy of Michigan State University Cooperative Extension Service, from pub. no. 183, *Poultry Housing For Layers*)

Table 18-1. Insulation Values of Materials.

Material	Thickness	R (resistance) values per inch thick l/k	R (resistance) values thickness listed l/C
Building Materials			
Building board-			
Gypsum or plaster board	1/2 in.		0.45
Plywood (Douglas Fir)		1.25	
Plywood (Douglas Fir)	1/4 in.		0.31
Plywood (Douglas Fir)	3/8 in.		0.47
Plywood (Douglas Fir)	1/2 in.		0.62
Plywood or wood panels	3/4 in.		0.93
Fiber board sheathing	1/2 in.		1.32
Fiber board sheathing	25/32 in.		2.06
Hardboard-medium density		1.37	
Particleboard-medium density		1.06	
Wood subfloor	3/4 in.		0.94
Insulation			
Blanket or batt-			
Glass wool, mineral wool or			
fiber glass, *approximate	3-3 1/2 in.		11
	5 1/2-6 1/2 in.		19
	6-7 in.		22
	8 1/2-9 in.		30
	12 in.		38
Rigid-			
Glass fiber		4.00	
Expanded perlite		2.78	
Expanded rubber		4.55	
Expanded polystyrene extruded		4-5.00	
Cellular polyurethane			
(R-11 exp.,unfaced)		6.25	
Loose fill-			
Milled paper or wood pulp		3.13-3.70	
Sawdust or shavings		2.22	
Perlite, expanded		2.70	
Glass or mineral wool	3 3/4-5 in.		11
(*approximate)	6 1/2-8 3/4 in.		19
	7 1/2-10 in.		22
	10 1/4-13 3/4 in.		30
Vermiculite		2.13-2.27	
Masonry			
Concrete, solid		0.08	
Brick, common		0.20	
Brick, face		0.11	
Concrete blocks-			
Sand and gravel, 8" 12"			1.11
			1.28
Cinder, 8" 12"			1.72
			1.89
Lightweight, 8 12"			2.00
			2.27
with vermiculite, perlite			
or mineral filled cores, 8" 12			5.03
			5.82
Roofing			
Asphalt roll roofing			0.15
Asphalt shingles			0.44
Wood shingles			0.94
Siding			
Wood shingles, 16", 7 1/2" exp.			0.87
Wood, 8" drop	1 in.		0.79
Wood, 8" beveled	1/2 in.		0.81
Wood, 10" beveled	3/4 in.		1.05
Alum. or steel (residential)			
hollow backed			0.61
insulation backed			1.82
Alum. or steel			
(farm buildings) unbacked			0.00
Woods			
Hardwoods: maple, oak, etc.		0.91	
Softwoods: fir, pine, etc.		1.25	

*Insulation is produced by different densities; therefore, there is a wide variation in thickness for the same R-value among manufacturers. No effort should be made to relate any specific R-value to any specific thickness. See individual manufacturer's label.

(Reprinted by permission from ASHRAE Handbook: 1981 Fundamentals.)

sumption are affected by the temperature. Egg production does not vary much between 45 and 75 degrees F., but research has shown that for every drop of 1 degree, between these temperatures, there is an increase in feed consumption by about 1 1/2 percent. With a little figuring using the previous tables on feed consumption for the type poultry housed, you can see how much can be saved with a certain housing temperature; the amount may surprise you.

Relative Humidity. Air has a moisture-holding capacity. The warmer the air, the more moisture it will hold (Fig. 18-6). The relative humidity is thus the ratio produced when water vapor in the air is compared with the amount of water vapor the air can hold at a given temperature.

If the indoor temperature is lower when few poultry are housed, there will be less moisture contained in the cooler air. The cooler air does not hold much moisture so this excess collects as condensation on walls and ceilings (Fig 18-7). This causes very damp conditions. If an exchange of inside and outside air (ventilation) is attempted, the building's air will become even more cold. But if the air is not exchanged, the litter and interior of the building will become damp. If something can make the air in a

building warmer, such as housing more poultry together, more moisture can be trapped and contained in the latent (unusable) portion of the air. Then more inside air can be exchanged with fresh air to remove most of the moisture. If the fresh air coming in is cooler, it will naturally contain less moisture than the warmer air going out.

Of the total amount of heat produced by poultry, only part is available to heat the air. Most of the heat produced is through the respiratory system. The part which is used to heat the air is called the "sensible heat" or the usable heat. The rest is contained in the water vapor and is called "latent heat" or unusable heat, which should be removed to keep the building drier.

Outdoor Temperature. During ventilation it is the outdoor air that is drawn into the building. Depending upon the temperature of this air, it will contain a certain amount of moisture that will determine the amount of air exchange allowed in relation to all other factors. During very cold weather conditions, as the cooler outside air is drawn into the building, it is warmed and picks up and holds moisture. Although the outdoor air might be cooler, it could have a completely saturated relative humidity of 100 percent because it can hold only so much water vapor at a given temperature.

In warm weather, if moisture-saturated air is brought into a building more than 10 degrees cooler than the outside air, the excess moisture will deposit itself on walls, ceilings, and litter in the form of condensation.

Air Movement. All factors are combined in order to determine the amount and rate of outgoing air that must be exchanged with incoming air. The whole system can best be maintained with a thermostat that controls a fan set at a desired temperature. Use a hygrometer to measure the humidity.

Figure 18-8 shows how one pound of 20-degree F. outside air at 100 percent relative humidity enters the building through a vent. This air is then heated to the inside building temperature of 60 degrees F. (15 degrees C.) where it expands by 2.3 cubic feet and absorbs water vapor from the poultry and house to bring the relative humidity to 80

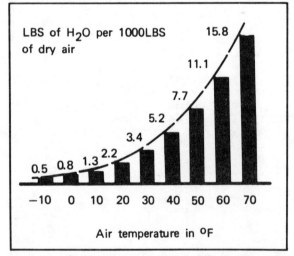

Fig. 18-6. Moisture-holding capacity of air showing how much more water vapor (H_2O) is contained in warmer air. (Courtesy of Michigan State University Cooperative Extension Service, from pub. no. 183, *Poultry Housing For Layers*)

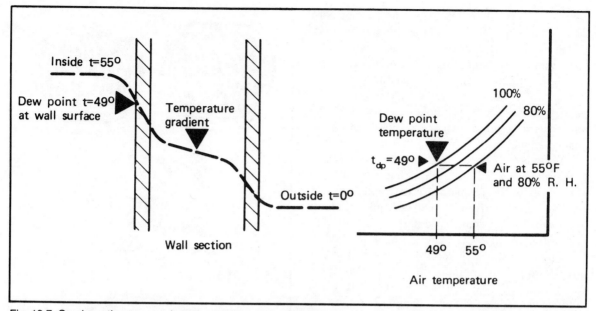

Fig. 18-7. Condensation occurs when air or objects are cooler than the dew point temperature (the temperature at which condensation occurs when air-water vapor mixture is cooled). (Courtesy of Michigan State University Cooperative Extension Service, from pub. no. 183, *Poultry Housing For Layers*)

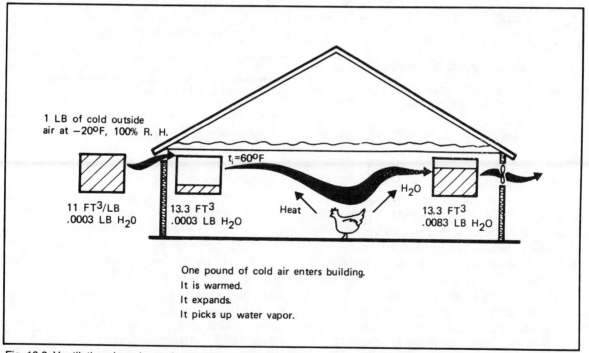

One pound of cold air enters building.
It is warmed.
It expands.
It picks up water vapor.

Fig. 18-8. Ventilation air exchange in a poultry house. (Courtesy of Michigan State University Cooperative Extension Service, from pub. no. 183, *Poultry Housing For Layers*)

percent. The ventilation air leaves the building with 28 times as much water vapor as when it entered.

Supplemental heat or a sufficient amount of birds should be used during cold weather to warm ventilation air to 60 degrees F. At the same time excess water vapor should be carried out of the poultry house. The vapor-holding capacity of the air should determine what the minimum of air exchange should be.

Various fans, vents, and cupolas can be used to ventilate (Fig. 18-9). A fan with a thermostat is simply set to the temperature that will keep the relative humidity from 50 to 80 percent. Windows and eaves can be considered part of the ventilating system. Vent boards can be made to slide or fold open and shut. All vents, cupolas, and manually operated fans are more difficult to control because they must be readjusted constantly when outdoor weather conditions change. Turbine fans can also be used. Most are dependent upon outside wind and will draw air from the building. These are installed on the roof. A sliding panel can be installed directly under them to help restrict air leaving. High-wind areas should install a wind-braced type turbine.

OBSERVING DROPPINGS

A bird's droppings can become a tool in detecting disease, especially the common coccidiosis and other intestinal disorders. By observing the appearance of the droppings daily, a handler can take care of the problem before it gets out of hand.

It's easy to check the droppings of battery brooded birds because all droppings are in the dropping trays. Their original form and texture are not disturbed by birds walking on top of them. Other brooding systems allow the droppings to be walked upon. Occasionally laying a folded paper under floor- and box-raised birds for a few minutes in order to observe droppings will help detect problems.

If intestinal disorders are present, there will be looseness, diarrhea, or very watery droppings. Pink or red coloring in the droppings can indicate blood as in enteritis, coccidiosis, or worm infestation. The result of irritating chemicals, acids, and medications can also be seen because the walls of the intestinal

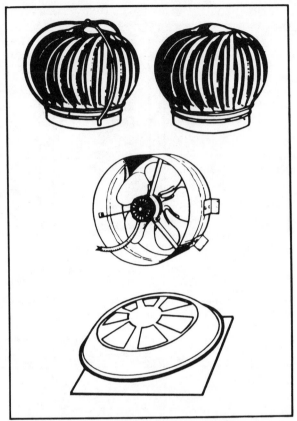

Fig. 18-9. Top—wind-braced and regular turbine; bottom—thermostatically controlled gable and roof power vents. (Courtesy of Leslie-Locke, Inc.)

tract can hemorrhage and cause blood to appear in the droppings. The intestinal wall is known to be thinner when antibiotics are fed to chicks. If these substances have not been fed, a handler can narrow down the diagnosis.

Normal droppings of poults and keets should be shapely yet crumble. Small, hard droppings indicate a lack of fiber in the feed or a highly concentrated ration. Feed should be changed. The droppings of guineas are normally much drier than other poultry. Young waterfowl have fairly wet droppings. Normal droppings during the first few days of life will appear watery and of a greenish-yellow color in all poultry. Any looseness other than this for up to two weeks of age will suggest a digestive upset from acids, medications, chemicals, chilling, too much cod-liver oil, or from bacteria on filthy equipment, dirty water, or dirty feed. Scrutinize the situation and make amendments accordingly.

Most outbreaks of coccidiosis are seen after two weeks of age. Looseness of the droppings with or without blood at this age will usually indicate an attack of coccidiosis. The normal coloration of droppings will be affected by the type feed being eaten. The color should be of no concern unless the droppings contain blood. Most other types of diseases or dietary deficiencies that would affect the droppings will usually not be seen in very young birds, therefore try to rule out the more common ailments first. Do not begin by looking for signs of less common diseases.

There is a characteristic sour odor that appears with loose droppings. A handler with experience will be able to tell something is not right simply by the odor emitted when first entering the room or building. Get to know this smell so you can do the same. If keets are not raised often, a handler might not detect the different smell of the loose droppings. The normal droppings of guineas have a wild smell that is quite different from other domestic poultry.

SANITATION

Because of the notion that certain poultry such as guineas, ducks, and geese are more disease-free than others, some handlers might become lax in keeping their quarters and equipment clean. Although these birds are hardy, they can get infections. Sanitation is very important in keeping them healthy. During brooding, daily sanitation measures include keeping the top of bedding material clean and dry. New litter can only be top-dressed for a few days before it builds up under brooders. Outbreaks of coccidiosis will require complete litter removal daily. This is all part of sanitation.

Waterers should always be disinfected daily. A busy handler can get by without a daily ritual of scrubbing utensils down with soap and water by using the following method: Rinse utensil of loose debris. A brush should be used on clinging dirt and manure and rinsed again with clear water. Use ordinary household bleach in your water as a final rinse. Mix a 5-gallon plastic bucket full of water with 2 1/2 cups of liquid bleach. Simply immerse

water jars, founts, and parts into this mixture without further rinsing. Drain well upside down on rags and refill waterers with fresh drinking water. Chlorine bleach contains sodium hypochlorite (5.25 percent by weight per 1 gallon of ordinary household bleach). The small amount of this acid left on the waterers helps to prevent coccidiosis and enteritis. The bleach solution can be reused for about one week if stored covered in a cool, dry place. Do not use metal buckets because they will eventually rust. You will be able to determine when the solution has lost its strength and therefore its disinfecting quality by sniffing the surface. If the chlorine smell is barely evident, the solution is no longer disinfecting.

Occasionally full-scale scrubbing for waterers, feeders, and equipment will be needed. This is also the case when equipment is to be reused between new broods of poultry. This cleaning job requires the use of a cleaning agent that will not interfere with the disinfecting action of the bleach. A soap containing sodium carbonate should be used. Most laundry soaps contain this compatible ingredient. For mixing this solution, add the soap to 2 1/2 gallons of water and 1 cup of liquid chlorine bleach. The purpose of disinfecting is to kill germs, while scrubbing is for the removal of germ-holding materials. To save labor, you can scrub only when needed—but be sure to disinfect daily.

Feeders are not usually washed and disinfected daily unless they are covered with manure. There can be more of a danger in washing feeders daily and not thoroughly drying them than in leaving them untouched. The seams in most feeders are not sealed and water can remain in these seams, even if feeders are towel-dried. After the dry feed is placed into the feeder, it acts as a sponge, drawing the water out of the seams. The feed can then mold near the bottom of the feeder where it cannot be seen. Mold can kill baby poultry, and large amounts of mold are toxic to large birds. If feeders must be washed and disinfected because they have become very dirty or there is a disease problem, completely air dry for a day—preferably in the sun. A handler should have extra feeders on hand to use while the others dry. The only other alternative is to purchase the one-piece molded feeders, but these hold very limited amounts of feed.

Other sanitation involves cleaning and disinfecting brooding houses or other poultry buildings. This is another time to warn against inhaling harmful poultry dust. Please: wear a good respirator when removing cobwebs, sweeping out buildings, and brushing down walls. If the dust gets too bad, get out and allow it to settle before entering again. Don't worry about getting every little cobweb; a good whitewash can take care of the things you missed.

The once-common practice of rigorously scrubbing all bare walls and floors with boiling hot lye water is almost obsolete. Many old-timers remember those days. They also remember the disastrous diseases that seemed to be waiting around every corner. Today's modern medicines and vaccines have done away with much of the fears that plagued poultry handlers years ago. Most small-scale raisers today do not go to these extremes to disinfect. Commercial raisers have too much to lose and economically cannot afford not to disinfect. Modern techniques and equipment have reduced some of the labor and time involved in performing these chores.

An old-time disinfectant still available today is cresol, which can be purchased at drug stores. This is mixed at the rate of 1 pint bottle of cresol to 2 gallons of water. The mixture should be sprayed over the interior walls and ceilings of a vacant building. It can be applied with a broom, but besides being a drippy mess, crevices cannot easily be reached. The building must be completely air-dried for a few days before birds are placed inside.

When disease has been a problem, a whitewash containing lye (sodium hydroxide) can be made (see following formula). Be aware of the precautions that should be taken when mixing and handling lye. Observe all label warnings to avoid being burned. Lye becomes a boiling hot, spattering mixture when added to water—always add it very slowly. Wear goggles or a face shield and keep away from skin, eyes, mucous membranes, and clothing.

Whitewash Formula. Mix 3 pounds of powdered agricultural lime with 4 gallons of cold water in a 5-gallon or larger non-aluminum container. Then very slowly add a 13-ounce can of lye to the surface of the water to avoid violent spattering. The cold water will actually boil from the lye addition. Allow the mixture to cool before painting on the vacant building walls. Painted and varnished surfaces are harmed by contact with the mixture, but metal and bare wood are not affected. When thoroughly dry, poultry can be placed into the building.

A less dangerous whitewash can be made using powdered milk. Naturally, it will not kill disease germs as the lye formula. It's main purpose is to brighten the interior of the building. Simply mix the following ingredients, strain, and spray or brush onto walls and ceilings: 4 gallons of water, a 4-pound box of powdered milk, and 50 pounds of powdered agricultural lime.

Sanitation also includes proper disposal of poultry remains. These should be buried, but preferably burned so they are not exposed to other animals and livestock who might eat them. This can be done in a burn barrel, although incinerators burn more thoroughly. These can be built or purchased. Figure 18-10 shows one manufactured type. Proper disposal means guarding against contamination of the air, water and soil. See "culling" in chapter 2 for disposal methods.

PROTECTION AGAINST PREDATORS AND PESTS

The amount of poultry lost to predators yearly is staggering. Most handlers will eventually be faced with predator problems. A handler can seem immune to the mortality and destruction caused by predators then have a culprit strike without warning. There are many reasons for this: Perhaps other prey has become scarce, or other predators increased. Nearby poultry raisers may have relinquished their flocks, making yours the only domestic flock for miles.

There are the obvious precautions in predator proofing your buildings and pens. A knowledge about what various predators accomplish and their tell-tale signs will help handlers to determine the best route of protection. Predators mainly cause

Fig. 18-10. Incinerator for farmers to provide quick, clean disposal to control disease and eliminate unsightly dead animals (with automatic turn-off, claimed to be almost odorless). (Courtesy of R & K Incinerator Company)

losses because a handler's poultry are made available to them. I hate to blame handlers, but the dirty, rotten so-and-so cannot be blamed when handlers let their birds roam outdoors to tempt a predator's taste buds. Rats that kill turkey poults cannot solely be blamed when the handler has placed the poults in a building full of holes and devoid of rat walls and traps. Turtles cannot be blamed for attacking waterfowl when a handler allows his ducks access to *their* ponds. An owl simply cannot help himself when he spots guineas roosting in a tree during his nightly hunting vigil. And a raccoon with his maneuverable paws knows just how to pry that loose door or cage door open to gain entrance and exit to your pigeons.

There is also the danger of other livestock hurting poultry either accidentally or purposely. Some cattle will deliberately trample poultry and some will play them to death with their constant butting. Hogs are carnivorous and can eat live poultry in almost one gulp.

Poultry that are locked up tightly are rarely bothered by predators. A busy handler does not always notice that broken stay in the poultry fence or that loose board or hinge. Periodic inspections should be made especially in the spring. Rain, snow, and ice take their toll on these building materials. What was a very strong fence in the fall can become weak enough in spots to be torn with your hands by early spring.

Following is a safe building checklist:

—A concrete wall foundation (ratwall) will help prevent burrowing animals, including rats, from easy entry. This foundation should be at least 4 inches thick and extend 36 inches below ground lever, or 24 inches into the ground with a 12-inch extension at the bottom extending outwards from the building. If new buildings are constructed, concrete foundations should extend at least 12 inches above ground level to discourage rats from gnawing.

—All openings should be boarded up or screened over, including eave vents. A least weasel can come through a 1-inch opening. Young rats will enter a 1/2-inch opening. Bottom edges of buildings should be checked and repaired if needed. Because a rat's upper teeth curve inward, they must find a small opening to begin their gnawing process. Where holes are found around materials that enter through masonry, such as pipes, shove hardware cloth or wire around the hole and pack with concrete. On wood sidings, cut and fit sheet-metal around openings.

—All edges of window sash and poultry entrances should be edged with sheet-metal or heavy hardware cloth. Door bottoms and sides should be covered over with sheet-metal up to 1-2 feet on sides.

—Buildings constructed with wooden floors should be raised at least 1 foot off the ground onto a foundation, piers, or blocks. The underside of the floor should be lined with sheet-metal. Although rats can chew through sheet-metal, cement, lead pipes, bricks, and solid oak, the purpose is to slow down their efforts—giving your barn cats a chance at them. Raising the building provides ventilation to prevent rotting floors (which are easier to gnaw through). It also gives the cats (and your dog) access to predators underneath.

—Buildings should have opaque or curtained windows to prevent predators (and thieves) from seeing the birds inside. Owls will try crashing through glass windows to get at domestic poultry.

—All doors and windows in a poultry house should be strong and tight with good hinges, latches, and bolt closures attached.

—Store all accessible feed in large, heavy metal containers with tight-fitting lids. Heavy wooden storage bins should be raised from the floor at least 1 foot so cats can get to rats trying to gnaw through. Bins should be lined with sheet-metal. Outdoor corn cribs should have a skirt of sheet-metal around the bottom. The height of this skirt will depend upon how deep snow might get around the bottom edge.

—All equipment, especially feeders, should be kept up off the floor. Not only will your equipment last longer, but cats will be able to hunt underneath.

—Do not intentionally allow nesting areas for rats outdoors. Keep anything that is stored, such as lumber, pipes, equipment, at least 2 feet off the ground.

—Do not provide roosts (or anything that can be used as a roost) in outdoor pens because it can encourage poultry to spend nights there.

A safe fencing checklist includes the following:

—Testing for weak stays and wires periodically should be done by pulling on fencing in opposite directions with hands. Test various staggered areas. If the fencing can readily be torn with your hands, it's weak. A large amount of weak areas indicate the entire fencing should be replaced. Cut out weak sections with wire cutters and replace with patches of new material slightly oversized. Use 17-gauge galvanized electric fence wire in a weaving pattern to hold the new section in place.

—Loose fence posts should be held stationary in the ground.

—A wire fence or netting, such as chicken wire, should cover the tops of all outdoor pens. This helps prevent predators from flying or climbing into pens.

—Gates should be sturdy and tight-fitting.

—Make it extremely hard for burrowing and digging animals to enter pens by constructing a barrier around the perimeter of pens. This can be done as follows: Pour a 2-foot-deep footing around edges of pens; dig a trench and fill it with rocks, bricks and broken concrete; bring an extra strip of fencing down the sides of pen a few inches and extend outward 2 feet over the ground, around the perimeter of pen. Then sink angle-iron or iron rods vertically 1 inch apart around the pen's perimeter.

—All indoor pens should contain access holes for cats so they can enter and exterminate rodents. Rodents will frequent pens that are safe from cats. Cut a hole about 5 inches square in the fencing about 18 inches from the floor. Attach four strands of 1/4-inch elastic vertically 1-inch apart without stretching. This will keep the poultry from escaping yet allow the cats to quickly squeeze through.

Rats can be the most troublesome and costly of all predators. They kill young poultry, rob eggs, spread disease and parasites, damage buildings and stored items, eat the poultry's feed, and make a mess wherever they go. A good cat will repay it's handler many times over in poultry and feed saved from rats.

Most cats must be trained for rat catching. Tom cats aren't as good ratters and mousers as females. A handler can start with full-grown cats or kittens. Begin with a few until you know which are the good ratters. A good ratter will also capture mean and nasty least weasels. If using strange adult cats, you must be sure they will not bother your poultry. Strange adult cats should not be trained in buildings housing young poultry. Place them only in buildings with grown birds until you know them well.

Begin training cats or kittens by feeding them inside the poultry house daily. Do not feed them anywhere else. If they're fed by your porch door, they'll hang around your house instead. This feeding is the main factor in getting the cats to accept the poultry house as their home. Kittens should be locked into the building as much as possible so they don't follow you back up to the house. Young kittens will not venture back to the poultry house on their own. Adult cats catch on much easier. Just be sure the adults can get into the building on their own. Construct a "catwalk" up one side of the building leading to an open eave vent. The bottom of the walk should be 4 feet from the ground to help prevent entry by predators. Our cats would enter the eave vent by first jumping on top of a 55-gallon feed drum next to the building, so a catwalk was not needed.

Kittens can and should be housed with baby poultry being brooded in a poultry house. Kittens brooded with poultry babies will not bother babies raised in the future. Watch carefully at first and scold them when they get too playful with the poultry. The kittens will sometimes sleep under the brooder hovers with the baby poultry. This is fine. It's a good sign they get along well together. After a few months of growing, the poultry will tower over the kittens, but they can take care of themselves.

Be sure provisions have been made to allow the cats access to every pen, isle, loft, and corner. Keep all feeders, waterers, nests, feed bins, and other equipment at least 6 inches up off the floor to allow the cats to get under these and hunt. The equipment can easily be hung from the ceiling or raised up onto bricks, blocks, or pieces of 4-×-6s. If this is not done, rodents will make nests and burrows under the equipment out of reach of the cats. Also, make provisions to feed the cats in an area where the poultry cannot eat their food.

Other devices to rid a poultry house of rodents include baits, traps and sonic devices. Baits must be placed out of the reach of children and all animals, including the poultry. Baits are not really safe to have around. Poultry and animals might eat dead rodents and feed containing the poisons. There is always a danger of children, livestock, and pets getting at the bait. Baits are not needed when good cats are given the opportunity to hunt. Baits may not work if the correct amount of poisoned bait is not consumed by each rat. For a rat to consume enough of the poisoned bait, it must smell good and look attractive to him. Unfortunately, this would be the same type feed attractive to poultry and pets.

Rodent baits work in a variety of ways with some being more effective or safer for farmstead use. Some poisons are available in concentrate form to be mixed with feed, and some are purchased as a pre-mixed bait. Some of the more common poisons are:

Antu. This single-dose poison is extremely toxic to other animals. It has a taste rats can distinguish, so they might not eat it often enough for it to be used effectively for long periods.

Norbormide. This is a single-dose poison available as a pre-mixed bait only. Rats are not fond of the mixture, although it is claimed to be *almost* nontoxic to other animals.

Red Squill. This is a single-dose poison. It has a strong taste and odor, but rats do not favor it. What they favor is the type feed it's mixed with. It can only be considered partially safe because other mammals usually vomit from consuming the poison, whereas rats can't vomit. Follow manufacturer's directions for mixing.

Zinc phosphide. This is a single-dose poison with a strong odor and taste. It attracts rats well although it is extremely hazardous to all types of animals. Follow manufacturer's directions for proper mixing.

Multiple dose poisons such as Diphacinone, Fumarin, Pival, and Warfarin work over extended periods of time by causing internal bleeding. Most are purchased as pre-mixed baits, but some are available as a concentrate to be mixed with feed. Animals, pets, and livestock (especially hogs) can be killed by the ingestion of these poisons or the dead rats. Chickens are said to be tolerant, but I would still keep all poisons from all poultry. Even-

tually, most poultry is consumed by humans and residues of poisons left in birds can be harmful.

Following is a simple bait mixture formula for a multiple-dose (anticoagulant) poison: 4 1/4 pounds poultry mash mixed with 1/4 pound powdered sugar, 1/4 pound peanut oil, and 1/4 pound anticoagulant poison (5-percent concentration).

Because no poisons are "safe," consider extra precautions in their use and placement in advance. One of the safest ways to place these baits is with the use of a bait box. Such a box, measuring 20 inches long, 6 inches wide, and 7 1/2 inches tall can be made with 1- × -8 wood stock. Construct a tight-fitting box that includes a bottom with a hinged top. By installing a clasp on the top, opposite the hinges, so the box can be kept locked. Cut a 3-inch entry hole in each end. For further safety, secure the box to the wall or floor area where it is set to help prevent it from becoming overturned. Fill a discarded ice cube tray with the bait and set it down into the middle of box, closing and locking the lid.

When there are no animals or children to get at baits, a quick, temporary bait station can be made with a cardboard box (Fig. 18-11). Place a weight on top so it cannot be easily overturned.

The best placement for the bait boxes is inside and outside along rat trails next to walls, entrance doors, feed storage areas, and near stacks of lumber, hay, or straw. Peanut butter and lard can be used to attract rodents to traps. Because poultry houses might have an abundance of scattered feed, cotton for nesting may be a better rodent bait. Simply attach to trap with a string. Place these rat traps in front of and across entrance trails and burrows rats might use.

Remember, poisonous baits should only be used when infestation is extreme. Use other methods first if the rodent problem isn't severe. Before using any pesticide, follow label instructions exactly, paying close attention to all warnings and cautions. Note any precautions about residues. Store containers where children and animals cannot get at them. Store away from foods, feed, seeds, etc. Dispose of properly. In cases of accidental consumption by humans, immediately induce vomiting and contact a physician.

Fig. 18-11. A quick, temporary bait station with a pan of poisoned feed inside for rat control.

Live traps of various types can be used, giving a handler a better sense of safety. I've found, however, most wild animals seem to avoid these traps while pets love to get into them. Other types of traps can be used with caution for various predators. Spring traps are sometimes better for rats than the common rat trap because rats will travel from one building to another to feed.

When larger predators are a problem, spring traps must usually be used. If animals such as raccoons have gained entrance to your poultry house, first attempt to make the building tighter. Then trap near another building. Many of these animals are fond of eggs; construct a nest in the vacant building to attract the animal. Set a number of large spring traps near a small entrance. Some handlers use at least four traps in one area. Secure traps with heavy wire to prevent trap loss. If the animal keeps getting out of set traps, it means the trap is not doing it's job. Some trappers recommend testing the trap by opening it. If it's extremely difficult to open, it's a good trap. Testing by pushing down in the center to see if it springs, is not considered a good method to test a trap. If the animal is getting out of traps, try using one of the newer types, such as

those put out by the Woodstream Company, which are called a "soft touch" trap. These have a rubber edging that helps prevent animals from slipping out. When hawks are a problem, a basket trap can be constructed (Fig. 18-12).

When poultry are bothered with predators, they should all be rounded up and confined until the predators are caught. Geese are not usually bothered by predators, although I had a problem with an aggressive, small (18-pound) raccoon once that killed a goose.

Many handlers wonder whether sonic devices really work. They can work well, but like anything, some are better than others. A good sonic device will keep insects as well as predators away from the poultry. Ours was installed by a salesman. The maximum effectiveness was said to depend upon the correct size of unit in relation to the square footage covered and to proper positioning of the unit for even wave distribution. Within three days, mites were visible on the interior walls and two rats were found dead in the isle facing the pens. The device did not affect the breeding and laying capabilities of the birds. It was installed with the provision that if it didn't do the job or affected the poultry, our

341

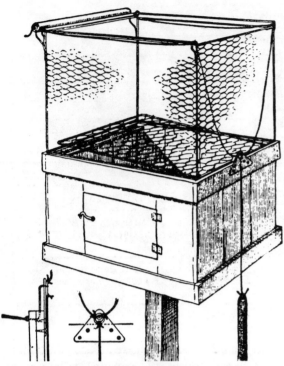

Fig. 18-12. A hawk goes after the bait (pigeon, chicken, etc.,) that is set into the box, steps onto the wire net floor in upper part of trap, and releases hanging weight that pulls the rolled curtain over top. (W.L. McAtee, courtesy of U.S. Fish and Wildlife Service).

money would be refunded. Because there is no way to determine beforehand whether the device will work, a handler should insist upon a written guarantee before purchase.

Table 18-2 gives a list of the predators that might be encountered. A combination of efforts will naturally work best.

RECORD KEEPING

Accurate record keeping is essential for all poultry raised. Without actual written records, you cannot truly know if the venture has been an economical success or merely an expensive hobby. There are too many small details and costs that can quickly be forgotten, causing you to mistakenly think you are doing well.

Written records will also help determine whether the correct feed, equipment, or type and amount of poultry was purchased. Constant replacements of equipment surely indicates waste; give consideration to purchasing better equipment, perhaps by simply choosing a different brand. Write down the reason equipment was replaced. Faulty construction or inappropriate materials can be detected this way. For instance, rusty seams indicate seams are not sealed; cracked plastic founts can mean a more resilient type of plastic fount should be used; rusted fount and feeder bottoms can indicate a poor galvanized metal.

Records kept on the poultry are management records. Keep these separate from equipment and feed purchase and sales records, although all can be compared against each other later. Breeding and egg collection records are best kept by notations on a calendar, so you can easily check on production and when egg laying commences and stops. Changes in feed and weather can be noted so you can see how growth, egg laying, fertility, and hatchability of eggs is affected. Note any deaths in the flock, along with any noticeable signs as to the cause of death. Also make notes as to the type and date any vaccinations, medications, and vitamins that were administered. Noting dates and symptoms of disease when they appear will help uncover the specific cause or disease more readily.

With adequate records, management practices can then be reviewed and revised if necessary. Record keeping eliminates guessing and overcomes forgetfulness most busy handlers are prone to. It will help in choosing breeds and hatcheries the following season. It will allow you to see and compare mortality rates, disease resistance, growth rate, ease of raising, managing, quality and price. All this can further help in figuring out poultry needed to fill the freezer. You can also decide if feed cost could have been reduced without skimping on the poultrys' nutritional needs (see Table 11-3). Perhaps it would have been worthwhile to purchase feed in half-ton lots. Maybe the more expensive and/or medicated feed was unnecessary—or, depending on the circumstances, more economical. But this you will not know unless you keep track of amount of feed consumed by a certain amount and type of bird.

Table 18-2. Predator Indication Guide.

Predator	Signs/Characteristics
Bobcat	Said to be minor problem with chickens on the West Coast. Usually attack ranged turkeys.
Cat (domestic)	Usually only 1 or 2 baby poultry devoured (usually by tomcats) with evidence of wings and legs left only. Will kill nightly. Trap near entries.
Coyote	Usually seen by handlers as they are not very shrewd in their attempts to gain entry into a poultry house. Fairly easy trapping.
Dog	Maimed, missing birds, wires and doors torn down. Will kill and maim many or just one. Usually takes bird home but may hide and eat, usually, the whole bird.
Fisher	Said to be a problem on the East Coast only. Will store extra food, returning later to eat it.
Fox	Will remove whole birds, day and night (usually night). Will travel 1/2 mile or more with the kill. Poultry legs found at fox den entries. Will not usually enter a poultry house—prefers ranged birds. Difficult to see and trap.
Hawk	Bothers ranged poultry. Hunts during the day. Swoops down and takes whole bird. Depending on how adept the hawk is, you might not hear bird squawk when attacked. Does not usually bother large turkeys or grown geese.
Mink	Usually remove smaller poultry only. Discharges an acrid musk that can be smelled hours later.
Muskrat	Prefers pond foods, but will attack poultry, eating insides out, leaving rest of carcass.
Owl	Great Horned Owl mainly. Usually takes head off only on grown guineas and ducks, very small poultry taken whole, at night, but will hunt daylight. Enters through 1 foot square openings in building. Will attempt flying through panes of glass upon spotting poultry. Will take roosting guineas from trees. Headless poultry carcasses found in area. Does not usually bother grown turkeys or adult geese, but will attack offspring in a flock of geese.
Opossum	Eats insides out on premises, likes eggs, picks away at bones. Mostly scavenges at night, occasionally daytime.
Raccoon	Takes small birds whole, adult guinea, grown ducks, large turkeys and geese—eaten where killed, eats breast only, usually takes head off too, but not always. Adept at squeezing through openings and using paws to remove birds from cages if cage door is flexible. Will come back nightly or every other night (even if freed from trapping). Loves eggs. Bits of coarse fur may be found attached to entry. Strong animals, need good traps—four spring-type jump traps set near entry.
Rats	Contusions and bites on legs, baby poultry dragged into rat tunnels usually with part of body (such as head and neck) down in tunnel, eaten around bone. Look for tunnels going under building walls and rat droppings near feed pans. Will sometimes eat with birds. Will travel from building to building only to feed. Eats eggs as quick as they're laid. Pulls and eats feathers off roosting birds, for protein.
Skunk	Eats insides out on premises, likes eggs, garbage, dead carcasses attract. Will take a broody's eggs out from under her. Sometimes faint skunk odor noticed around building, but not usually. Easy to trap.
Turtles	Usually attack waterfowl in open waters. Large ducks occasionally attacked showing contusions. Love ducklings and goslings most. First sign may only be missing waterfowl, or adult geese fighting them from offspring in water.
Weasel	Bites on neck found, will attack only a few or a lot, bluish coloration of skin about head and under wings. Sometimes run in family packs. Occasionally a faint skunk odor may be evident. Least Weasel will enter one-inch opening. Hard to trap.
Wolf	Usually birds the size of chickens are considered too small a game for them.

Sources

Air-O-Lator® Corporation
8100-04 PASEO
Kansas City, Missouri 64131
816-363-4242 (Missouri residents)
Watts Line: 1-800-821-3177

Pond aerators-deicers (motor-driven).

International A.I., Inc.
7909 South Fairfax
Bloomington, Indiana 47401
812-824-2473, 812-824-BIRD,
TLX 272204 TIS B

Artificial insemination equipment including straws.

Bio-Vet
3425 Des Cedres
St-Hyacinthe, Que.
Canada J2T 4E8
514-774-9914

Pigeon pharmaceuticals.

Brower Equipment Co.
P.O. Box 200
Houghton, Iowa 52631
319-469-4141
800-553-1791

Incubators, feeders, waterers, brooders, racks, nests and miscellaneous poultry equipment.

Chas. Siegel & Son
1011 E. Middle St.
South Elgin, Illinois 60177
312-697-4572

Complete line of pigeon supplies.

Clausing Company
7724 S. North Cape Road
Franklin, Wisconsin 53132
414-425-4034

Bands, vaccines, pharmaceuticals, vitamins, in-secticides, brooders, incubators, candlers, feed and water cups.

Cooper Hatchery, Inc.
Box 547
Oakwood, Ohio 45873
419-594-3325

Large-lot (1,280) sales of white poults.

Crow Poultry and Supply Co.
Windsor, Missouri 65360
816-647-2614

Incubators, brooders, feeders, waterers, bands, traps, pharmaceuticals, vaccines.

Ehrhart & Karl, Ltd.
Chicago, Illinois 60602
312-332-1046

Homeopathic remedies (such as Arnica), miscel-laneous items.

Empire Health Care Products, Inc.
50 W. 34th Street
Suite 11A8
New York, New York 10001
212-868-3460

Pigeon pharmaceuticals.

Foy's Pigeon Supplies
Box 27166
Golden Valley, Minnesota 55427
612-537-4242

Cones and tops, founts, dowel feeders, fount heaters, grit feeders, bath pans, nest training baskets, perches, nest bowls, pigeon traps, bobs, loft registers, bands, pharmaceuticals.

Hoffman's Hatchery, Inc.
Box 128-A
Gratz, Pennsylvania 17030
717-365-3694

Feeders, waterers, brooders, incubators, crates, and miscellaneous—plus day-old keets, duck-lings, goslings, and turkeys.

The J. W. Williamson Co.
Route 1
Box 340
Glassboro, New Jersey 08028
609-881-3267

Pigeon health grit.

Kester's Wild Game Food Nurseries, Inc.
P.O. Box V
Omro, Wisconsin 54963
414-685-2829

Pigeon feeds, vitamins, hard-to-find seeds.

Kuhl Corporation
Kuhl Road
P.O. Box 26
Flemington, New Jersey 08822-0026
201-782-5696

Feeders, waterers, brooders, incubators, egg equipment, butchering supplies, bands, and miscellaneous items.

Leslie Locke, Inc.
4501 Circle 75 Parkway
Suite 4300
Atlanta, Georgia 30339
404-953-6366

Turbines, vents, and fans.

Luytie's Pharmacal Co.
St. Louis, Missouri
1-800-325-8080

Homeopathic remedies (such as Arnica).

Lyon Electric Company, Inc.
P.O. Box 81303
San Diego, California 92138
619-297-9000

Brooders, cage tools, candlers, feeders, waterers, incubators, leg bands, beak trimming equipment, vitamins, and miscellaneous items.

New Delphos Manufacturing Co.
102 South Pierce Street
Delphos, Ohio 45833
419-692-8010

Feeders, scoops, founts, killing cones, wafers, pans, automatic waterers, range feeders, and other metal products for poultry.

Nasco West
P.O. Box 3837
Modesto, California 95352
209-529-6957

Shovels, scoops, mills, incubators, brooders, feeders, waterers, tattoo and butchering equipment, and miscellaneous items.

National Band and Tag Co.
Newport, Kentucky 41072
606-261-2035

Manufacturers of tags, bands, punches, and applicators.

National Wax Company
3650 Touhy Avenue
P.O. Box 549
Skokie, Illinois 60076
312-679-6300

Manufacturers of poultry wax for defeathering (Duxwax and Super Duxwax).

Omaha Vaccine Co.
P.O. Box 7228
3030 "L" Street
Omaha, Nebraska 68107
402-731-9600

Pharmaceuticals, tinctures, syringes, vitamins, and insecticides.

Perterson Sheet Metal
Box 373
South Haven, Minnesota 55383
612-274-8673

Pigeon founts, bath pans, cone tops, grills, pigeon holders, fount heaters, grit feeders, and other metal products.

R & K Incinerator Co.
Route 4
Decatur, Indiana 46733
219-565-3214
        and
Canada Farm Distributing Ltd.
Box 548
Tavistock, Ontario, Canada
NOB 2RD
515-655-2584

Manufacturers of incinerators for farm use.

Rocky Top General Store
P.O. Box 1006
Harriman, Tennessee 33748
615-472-7882

Incubators, brooders, feeders, waterers, pharmaceuticals, vaccines and miscellaneous items.

Shenandoah Manufacturing Co., Inc.
P.O. Box 839
Harrisonburg, Virginia 22801
703-434-3838

Brooders, hanging feeders, range feeders, and trough waterers.

Sidney Shoemaker
Box 331
Mt. Gilead, Ohio 43338
419-864-6666

Incubators, brooders, pharmaceuticals, vaccines, feeders, waterers, bands, butchering equipment, traps, cage supplies and miscellaneous items.

Stromberg's Chicks and Pets Ltd.
Pine River, Minnesota 56474
218-543-4223

Incubators, brooders, butchering equipment, poultry wax, feeders, waterers, founts, bands (including wide rubber-type goose and turkey neck bands), cages, candlers, vaccines, pharmaceuticals, mills, tattoo sets, pond aerators, pigeon supplies, livestock and miscellaneous items.

T. J. Scherer's Pigeon Supplies
2884-A Woodland Circle
Allison Park, Pennsylvania 15101
412-443-7477

Nest fronts, training baskets, other pigeon supplies. Wood products made at their own shop.

Veterinary and Poultry Supply, Inc.
P.O. Box 454
Goshen, Indiana 46526
210-534-2626

Pharmaceuticals, vaccines, syringes, insecticides, tinctures, feed additives and vitamins.

Wadler Manufacturing Co., Inc.
Rt. 2, Box 117
Galena, Kansas 66739
316-783-1355

Pond aerator-deicers (wind-driven).

Warner Corporation
North Manchester, Indiana 46962
219-982-2156

Range feeders, range waterers, metal and plastic founts, feeders, brooders and miscellaneous items.

Wildlife Laboratories, Inc.
P.O. Box 8938
Fort Collins, Colorado 80525
303-484-6267, 1-800-482-6267

Pigeon pharmaceuticals.

Index

Index

Edited by Cherie R. Blazer

Other Best Sellers From TAB

☐ **THE GARDENING IDEA BOOK—Editors of *Farmstead Magazine***

This exciting collection of articles shows how you can grow all kinds of delicious, healthful fruits and vegetables, easily and inexpensively. You can save hundreds of dollars on your year-round food bill, while eating better and more nutritionally than ever before! Here's expert advice that's guaranteed to make your garden more productive, easier to take care of, and less expensive! 208 pp., illustrated.
Paper $10.95   **Hard $15.95**
Book No. 2864

☐ **FARMSTEAD MAGAZINE'S GUIDE TO ANIMAL HUSBANDRY—Editors of *Farmstead Magazine***

Here's a gold mine of information for the homesteader raising a single cow or goat for their own use . . . or the small farmer using his animals as a source of income . . . the information you need is here. Just some of the other topics covered in this incredibly comprehensive sourcebook include: beekeeping, raising rabbits for fun and profit, how to buy and care for a horse, and the tricks of raising guinea birds, even advice on controlling insect pests that can annoy and even irreparably harm various farm animals. 168 pp., 20 illus.
Paper $9.95   **Hard $15.95**
Book No. 2764

☐ **111 YARD AND GARDEN PROJECTS —FROM BOXES AND BINS TO TABLES AND TOOLS—Percy W. Blandford**

Save $100's . . . even $1,000's . . . on more than 100 practical and exciting projects for your lawn and garden! Even build a patio, tool shed, or greenhouse at amazingly low cost!! Projects include: Potting and plant stands, storage shelves, climbing plant supports, benches, chairs, and tables, boxes and bins for everything from storing tools to composting leaves, planters, gardening tools, fences and gates, garden carts, trolleys, wheelbarrows, and more! 416 pp., 301 illus.
Paper $16.95   **Hard $25.95**
Book No. 2644

☐ **BUILDING OUTDOOR PLAYTHINGS FOR KIDS, WITH PROJECT PLANS—Bill Barnes**

Imagine the delight of your youngsters—children or grandchildren—when you build them their own special backyard play area! Best of all, discover how you can make exciting, custom-designed play equipment at a fraction of the cost of ordinary, ready-made swing sets or sandbox units! It's all here in this step-by-step guide to planning and building safe, sturdy outdoor play equipment! 240 pp., 213 illus.
Paper $12.95   **Hard $21.95**
Book No. 1971

☐ **BUILDING A LOG HOME FROM SCRATCH OR KIT—2nd Edition—Dan Ramsey**

This up-to-the-minute guide to log home building takes you from initial planning and design stages right through the final interior finishing of your new house. There's advice on selecting a construction site, choosing a home that's right for your needs and budget, estimating construction costs, obtaining financing, locating suppliers and contractors, and deciding whether to use a kit or build from scratch. 304 pp., illustrated.
Paper $14.95   **Hard $21.95**
Book No. 2858

☐ **HOME BUTCHERING AND MEAT PRESERVATION—Geeta and Sam Dardick**

Here's the perfect place to start on your way to enjoying more economical, convenient, nutritional, and delicious meat! It explains in step-by-step detail all the ins and outs, the pleasures and the pitfalls, of selecting, raising, caring for, breeding, slaughtering, butchering, preserving, and cooking poultry, rabbit, goats, sheep, venison, pigs, veal, and beef. 288 pp., 166 illus.
Paper $12.95   **Hard $24.95**
Book No. 2713

☐ **PLANNING AND BUILDING FENCES AND GATES—AAVIM**

This colorfully illustrated guide gives you all the expert, step-by-step guidelines and instructions you need to plan and build durable, cost-effective fences and gates. You will be able to design and construct just about any kind of fence you can think of—barbed wire, woven wire, cable wire, mesh wire, board fences, electric fences, gates, and much more! 192 pp., 356 illus., 8 1/2″ × 11″, 2-Color Throughout.
Paper $14.95   **Hard $22.95**
Book No. 2643

☐ **RAISING CHICKENS —Haynes**

Now veteran chicken handler and hatchery owner Cynthia Haynes puts you in touch with the realities, the rewards, and the potential hazards of raising your own chickens . . . and gives you the kind of practical, "voice of experience" advice and guidance that just isn't available from any other source. From choosing the chicken breed for your particular needs to finding a source for chicks or brood hens, you'll find it here! 272 pp., 264 illus., 7″ × 10″.
Paper $13.95   **Hard $21.95**
Book No. 1963

Other Best Sellers From TAB